ABORTION:
AN ANNOTATED INDEXED BIBLIOGRAPHY

BY

MAUREEN MULDOON

THE EDWIN MELLEN PRESS
NEW YORK AND TORONTO

Studies in Women and Religion, Volume Three

Copyright © 1980

The Edwin Mellen Press
New York and Toronto

Library of Congress Cataloging Number 79-91622

ISBN 0-88946-972-5

Studies in Women and Religion, ISBN 0-88946-549-5

Printed in the United States of America

GUIDE TO BIBLIOGRAPHY

The 3397 entries have been arranged in alphabetical order and have been assigned individual numbers. These numbers are used for referencing within the index.

The index contains 353 headings. Many entries are listed under more than one index heading.

The index has been placed at the beginning of this volume. Its general topics are as follows:

INDEX

III. MEDICAL AND SOCIAL ASPECTS
OF ABORTION

IV.   LEGAL ASPECTS OF ABORTION

V. ABORTION STUDIES IN THE STATES

VI. ABORTION STUDIES IN OTHER COUNTRIES

VII. COLLECTED ARTICLES AND SYMPOSIA PROCEEDINGS

America. 117 (December 9, 1967), 706-19. Replies: 118 (January 20, 1968), 80-83. The Abortion Question, Symposium: The Abortion Question: Life and Law in a Pluralistic Society. "The English Experience," by N. St. John-Stevas; "The Future in America," by R. Byrn; "Contemporary Protestant Thinking," by R. Drinan; "Aspects of the Moral Question," by R. McCormick.

American Journal of Public Health. 57 (November, 1967), 1906-47. Bibls. Tables. Chart. Map. "Abortion Law: The Approaches of Different Nations," by Ruth Roemer; "Abortion in Europe," by Christopher Tietze; "Abortion in American Hospitals," by Robert E. Hall; "A Survey Concerning Induced Abortions in New Orleans," by Carl L. Harter and Joseph D. Beasley.

American Journal of Public Health. (March, 1971). Nine articles dealing with abortion are presented.

Case Western Rewerve Law Review. 23 (Summer, 1972), 705. Symposium: Abortion and the Law. Preface. "The Evolving Law of Abortion," by B. J. George, Jr.; "The Genesis of Liberalized Abortion in

New York: A Personal Insight," by A. F. Guttmacher; "Abortion and the Rights of Minors," by H. F. Pilpel and R. J. Zuckerman; "Abortion Counselling: Shall Women be Permitted to Know?" by G. A. Messerman; "Abortion on Request: The Psychiatric Implications," by R. A. Schwarts; "Abortion Practices in the United States: A Medical Viewpoint," by K. R. Niswander.

Catholic Lawyer. 14 (Summer, 1968), 180-213. Symposium. "Demythologizing Abortion Reform," by R. Byrn; "The Morality of Abortion Laws," by R. Drinan; "New York Abortion Reform: A Critique," by W. Caron.

Christianity and Crisis. 32 (January 8, 1973). "Abortion." Entire issue is devoted to articles by John C. Bennett, Margaret Mead, Howard Moody, and Daniel Callahan.

Clinical Research. 23 (October, 1975). Symposium. "Toward a Definition of Fetal Life: Ethical and Legal Options and Their Implications for Biologists and Physicians."

Commonweal. 85 (March 17, 1967), 676-81. Abortion. Symposium. "A Biological View," by T. Hayes; "A Legal View," by R. Byrn.

Commonweal. 101 (February 14, 1975), 384-92. The Abortion Decision: Two Years Later. Symposium. "More Christian than Its Critics," by R. Decker; "Dred Scott Revisited," by W. Trinkaus.

Death Before Birth: Canada and the Abortion Question. Edited by E. J. Kremer and E. A. Synan. Toronto: Griffin House, 1974.

Dublin Review. 241 (Winter, 1967-68) 274-390. Symposium. "Abortion and the Law," by N. St. John-Stevas; "The Catholic Church and Abortion," by J. Noonan; "A Christian Approach to the Ethics of Abortion," by J. Gustafson; "The Right of the Foetus to Be Born," by R. Drinan; "Abortion: A Jewish View," by I. Klein.

Engage/Social Action. 2 (February, 1974), 6-62. Abortion. "The Right to Decide (Legal Aspects)," by S. R. Weddington; "The Sacredness of All Human Life (Religious and Moral Perspectives)," by E. C. Gardner; "Is the Answer Abortion? (Complexities of Counselling)," by R. E. Zimmerli; "A Misplaced Debate (Ethical Comments on Abortion Public Policy)," by A. R. Brockway; "Abortion Clinic," by M. J.

Zimmerli; "A Constitutional Amendment?" by L. Ranck and N. F. McConnell.

Hospital Progress. 55 (February, 1974), 52-68+. Strategies for Preserving Individual and Corporate Rights. Symposium. "Challenges to Individual and Corporate Rights," by E. Schulte; "Rationale and Implications of Sanctity of Life Commitment," by K. O'Rourke; "Strategy for Influencing Pro-Life Legislation," by R. Stratton; "Identity of the Catholic Health Facility," by A. Maida; "An Analysis of the 1st Amendment Rights of Catholic Health Facilities," by W. Regan.

The Human Life Review. 1 (Winter, 1975 and Spring, 1975). New York: The Human Life Foundation, 1975.

Human Rights. 1 (July, 1971), 23-53. Bibl. Abortion: Litigative and Legislative Processes: A Symposium. R. Lucas, R. D. Lamm. Commentators: L. Beebe, C. Poole, D. L. Handley.

Jurist. 33 (Spring, 1973), 113-237. Abortion Decisions: 1973, A Response. Symposium. "The Legal Impact of the *Roe* and *Doe* Decisions," by D. Granfield; "A Constitutional Lawyer Looks at the *Roe-Doe* Decisions," by A. Broderick; "Law and Theology: A Dialogue on the Abortion Decisions," by E. Gaffney; "The Nexus of Biology and the Abortion Issue," by R. Nardone; "Abortion: Law and Morality in Contemporary Catholic Theology," by C. Curran; "Church Law and Abortion," by J. Coriden; "Abortion as Indicative of Personal and Social Identity," by W. May; "Some Sociological and Psychological Reflections on the Abortion Decisions," by E. Ryle; "Abortion Decisions—Impact on Nursing Practice, Maternal and Child Care," by M. Liston.

Loyola Law Review. 16 (1969-1970), 275. Natural Law Institute 1970: Abortion. "Recent Statutes and the Crime of Abortion," by R. F. Brown; "Abortion: A Human Problem," by W. J. Kenealy; "Abortion: A Moral or Mdeical Problem?" by L. Salzman.

Lumiere. 21 (August-October, 1972), 6-107. Replies by Y. Milliasseau, A. Dumas, R. Bel, J. -J. Weber and D. Stein: 22 (January-March, 1973), 81-87. L'Avortement. Symposium. "Une Histoire d'Amour et de Mort," by M. Debout; "Liberte de l'Avortement et Liberation des Femmes," by H. Bonnet; "Legalite et Moralite Face a l'Avortement," by R. Boyer; "La Volonte de Procreer: Reflection Philosophique," by B. Quelquejeu; "Reflexions Theologiques Sur la Position de l'Eglise Catholique," by J. -M. Pohier.

The Morality of Abortion: Legal and Historical Perspectives. Edited by John Noonan, Jr. Cambridge: Harvard University Press, 1970. A variety of moral positions on abortion are provided, with articles by Paul Ramsey, James Gustafson, Bernard Haring, George Hunston Williams, John Finnis, David Louisell, and the editor.

Natural Law Forum. 12 (1967-1968), 85. 13 (1967-1968), 127. "Abortion and the Catholic Church: A Summary History," by J. T. Noonan, Jr.; "On Humanity and Abortion," by J. O'Connor; "Deciding Who is Human," by J. T. Noonan, Jr.

New York Law Forum. 17 no. 2 (1971), 335-436. "The Phoenix of Abortional Freedom: Is a Penumbral or Ninth-Amendment Right About to Arise From the Nineteenth-Century Legislative Ashes of a Fourteenth-Century Common-Law Liberty?" by Cyril C. Means, Jr. "Abortion and Public Policy—What Are the Issues?" by Emily C. Moore

Perkins Journal. 27 (Fall, 1973), 1-66. Aspects of the Abortion Question. "Pregnancy as a Personal and Social Crisis: A Panel Presentation," by A. R. Race, W. W. Entzminger and L. Patterson; "The Beginnings of Personhood: Medical Considerations," by A. E. Hellegers; "Legal Considerations," by H. J. Taubenfeld; "Philosophical Considerations," by H. T. Engelhardt; "Theological Considerations," by A. C. Outler; "The Social Context: The Woman's Right of Privacy," by S. R. Weddington; "Population and Human Welfare," by A. J. Dyck; "Professional Practices and Institutional Policies: A Discussion," by T. R. McCormick; "Personal Decisions and Social Policies in a Pluralist Society," by R. L. Shinn; "Abortion: A Selective Bibliography," Comp. by W. M. Longsworth and F. S. Carney.

The Rights and Wrongs of Abortion. Edited by Cohen, Marshall, et al. Princeton: Princeton University Press, 1974. These articles were originally published in *Philosophy and Public Affairs.* "A Defense of Abortion," by Judith Jarvis Thomson; "Rights and Deaths," by

Judith Jarvis Thomson; "Understanding the Abortion Argument," by Roger Wertheimer; "Abortion and Infanticide,"by Michael Tooley; "The Rights and Wrongs of Abortion," by John Finnis.

Rutgers Law Review. 22 (Spring, 1968), 415. Law, Morality, and Abortion: A Symposium. J. J. Francis, A. F. Guttmacher, A. A. Marchetti, T. J. O'Donnell, H. Rosen, R. E. Knowlton.

Sign. 46 (June, 1967), 34-35. Symposium. "The Debate on Legalized Abortion," by J. Kennedy, A. Hennessy, and A. McNally.

Sign. 52 (March, 1973), 26-27. Judicial Power and Public Conscience. Symposium. J. Kennedy, A. McNally, and M. Brennan.

Social Action. 37 (March, 1971), 3-39. Let's Look at Abortion. "On the Biological Basis of the Abortion Issue," by N. K, Mottet; "Facing an Agonizing Dilemma," by J. L. Kidd; "I Had an Abortion," (anonymous); "What About Abortion on Demand?" by R. M. Vaetch; "Toward a Position on Abortion."

Theological Studies. 31 (March, 1970), 3-176. "Fetal Development," by A. E. Hellegers; "Religious Residues and Presuppositions in the American Debate on Abortion," by G. H. Williams; "Immediate Animation and Delayed Hominization," by J. F. Donceel; "The Abortion Debate: An Epistemological Interpretation," by J. G. Milhaven; "The Wonder of Myself: Ethical-Theological Aspects of Direct Abortion," by J. T. Mangan; "The Jurisprudential Options on Abortion," by R. F. Drinan.

Triumph. 8 (March, 1973), 17-32. America's War on Life. Symposium: Where We Have Been, Where We Go From Here. "The Abortion Culture," by K. Mitzer. The Movement Coming Together. The Movement Staying Together. The Catholic Obligation.

Triumph. 10 (January, 1975), 11-16. Right to Life: Time for a New Strategy. Symposium. "Moral Credibility," by W. Carroll; "Grassroots Revolution," by R. Engel; "Conditional Allegiance," by W. Devlin; "The Best Chance," by P. Fisher; "Get Tough," by T. May; "Unacceptable Principle," by C. Rich; "Bear Witness," by M. Schwartz; "The Ethical Issue," by J. Willke.

U. S. News. 81 (September 27, 1976), 27-28. il. Ban All Abortions? Yes—"1 Million Lives are Destroyed Each Year," Interview with Archbishop Joseph L. Bernardin, President, National Conference of Catholic Bishops; No—"We Believe in a Woman's Right to Make Her Own Choice," Interview with Rabbi Richard S. Sternberger, Chairperson, the Religious Coalition for Abortion Rights.

[1]Aarons, Z. A. "Therapeutic Abortion and the Psychiatrist." *American Journal of Psychiatry*, 124 (December, 1967), 745-54.

[2]Abels, S. "The First Year of the Abortion Act." *Lancet*, 1 (May 24, 1969), 1051-52.

[3]Abercombie, C. F. "The Psychiatric Indication for the Termination of Pregnancy." *Proceedings of the Royal Society of Medicine*, 50 (May, 1957), 321.

[4]Abernethy, V. D. "The Abortion Constellation—Early History and Present Relationships." *Archives of General Psychiatry*, 29 (3) (1973), 346-50.

[5]"Aborted Discussion." *Ave Maria*, 103 (February 5, 1966), 17. [This is an editorial concerning the San Francisco Conference sponsored by the Society for Humane Abortion.]

[6]Abortion, Association for the Study of. *An Analysis of a Survey of Psychiatrists on Abortion*. Presented at the Annual Forum. New York, March 30, 1966.

[7]"Abortion." *Canadian Medical Association Journal*, 103 (December 5, 1970), 1314 passim.

[8]"Abortion." *Economist*, 243 (May 20, 1972), 55.

[9]"Abortion." *Journal of the American Medical Association*, 231(6) (February 10, 1975), 569-701.

[10]"Abortion." *Lancet*, 2 (July 29, 1967), 249.

[11]"Abortion." *Lancet*, 1 (February 15, 1969), 355-56.

[12]"Abortion." *Lancet*, 2(7980) (August 7, 1976), 296.

[13]"Abortion." *New Zealand Medical Journal*, 68 (December, 1968), 406-07.

[14]"Abortion." *New Zealand Medical Journal*, 81(531) (January 8, 1975), 31-32.

[15]"Abortion." *Notre Dame Law Review*, 43 (June, 1968), 686.

[16]"Abortion." *Nova Scotia Medical Bulletin*, 49 (April, 1970), 34.

[17]"Abortion." *Journal of Oklahoma State Medical Association*, 64 (July, 1971), 295-96.

[18]"Abortion Act." *British Journal of Hospitals and Medicine*, 2 (1969), 607-612.

[19]"The Abortion Act." *Royal Society of Health Journal*, 88 (May-June, 1968), 121-22. 1-32

[20]"The Abortion Act 1967." *Medico-Legal Journal*, 36:Suppl. 4 (1968), 55-56.

[21]"The Abortion Act (1967). Findings of an inquiry into the first year's working of the Act conducted by the Royal College of Obstetricians and Gynaecologists." *British Medical Journal*, 2 (May 30, 1970), 529-35.

[22]"The Abortion Act 1967—memorandum from Medical Defence Union." *British Medical Journal*, 1 (March 23, 1968), 759-62.

[23]"The Abortion Act of 1967; Society for the Protection of Unborn Children." *Tablet*, 227 (March 10, 1973), 287-89. [The society feels that under the British Abortion Act, abortions are available on demand. This article contains recommendations to overcome this situation.]

[24]*The Abortion Act 1967*. Symposium of Proceedings of the Medical Protection Society and Royal College of General Practitioners. London: Pitman Medical Publishing Company, Ltd., 1969.

[25]"The Abortion Act—Scotland 1968." *Health Bulletin* (Edinburgh), 27 (July, 1969), 60-74.

[26]"Abortion—actions by nineteen year-old unmarried female against the Arizona board of regents to determine the constitutionality of a state statute prohibiting nontherapeutic abortions at the university hospital." *Journal of Family Law*, 15 (1976-1977), 113-118.

[27]"Abortion Advocates Using False Statistics." *Our Sunday Visitor*, 63 (April 27, 1975), 3.

[28]"Abortion after *Roe (Roe v. Wade*, 93 Sup Ct 705) and *Doe (Doe v. Bolton*, 93 Sup Ct 739): a proposed statute." *Vanderbilt Law Review*, 26 (May, 1973), 823-35.

[29]"Abortion (Amendment) Bill." *British Medical Journal*, 2(5970) (June 7, 1975), 558-59.

[30]"Abortion (Amendment) Bill." *British Medical Journal*, 3(5975) (June 12, 1975), 99.

[31]"Abortion (Amendment) Bill." *British Medical Journal*, 2(5972) (June 21, 1975), 686-87.

[32]"Abortion (Amendment) Bill." *British Medical Journal*, 2(5973) (June 28, 1975), 748.

[33]"Abortion (Amendment) Bill." *British Medical Journal,* 3(5978) (July 19, 1975), 160.

[34]"Abortion Amendment Hearings Scheduled." *National Catholic Reporter,* 10 (February 8, 1974), 15.

[35]"Abortion and the Church." *America,* 128 (February 10, 1973), 110-11. [This editorial points out the situation after the ruling on *Roe v. Doe* by the U.S. Supreme Court. The need for a new kind of pastoral response becomes apparent. Women may be coerced into a decision. Care must be taken that her choice will be made in terms of moral values.]

[36]"Abortion and the Constitutional Question." *South Dakota Law Review,* 15 (Spring, 1970), 318.

[37]"Abortion and the Court." (Editorial) *Christianity Today,* 17 (February 16, 1973), 32-33.

[38]"Abortion and Dialogue." *Commonweal,* 85 (March 17, 1967), 667-68. [This editorial is concerned with explaining an evolving attitude toward abortion reform with all its nuances.]

[39]"Abortion and Divorce Reform." *America,* 116 (February 11, 1967), 200. [Catholics in New York could vote for reforming the divorce law and at the same time not vote to liberalize the "state's" abortion laws. The author sees broadening the divorce law, as mitigating the punishment without justifying the crime, while abortion is still killing.]

[40]"Abortion and the Doctor." *Annals of Internal Medicine,* 67 (November, 1967), 1111-13.

[41]"Abortion and the General Practitioner." *Medical Journal of Australia,* 2 (August 26, 1972), 513-14.

[42]"Abortion of the Law." *Tablet,* 225 (March 6, 1971), 218-19. [This article describes the purposes and the objectives of the Lane Commission. The task of the committee was to make an objective assessment. Safeguards against abuse can be recommended but the principles underlying the British Abortion Act are not open to inquiry.]

[43]*Abortion and the Law.* David T. Smith, ed. (Cleveland: Western Reserve University Press, 1967). [This collection of essays deals with the movement to reform current abortion laws, the medical abortion practices in the U.S., what signifies humane abortion laws, the psychiatric indications for abortion, the inviolability of the right to be born, Jewish views on abortion, the experience and medical aspects of law reform in Denmark and the German speaking countries of Europe.

[44]"Abortion and the Law: Anachronisms Racing Science." *Journal of the Mississippi Medical Association,* 11 (June, 1970), 335-36.

[45]"Abortion and the Law on Abortion; Document of the Permanent Council of the Italian Episcopal Conference." *L'Osservatore Romano* (English), no. 9 (361) (February 27, 1975), 4-5.

[46]"Abortion and the Law: A Proposal for Reform in Louisiana." *Tulane Law Review,* 43 (June, 1969), 834.

[47]"Abortion and the Lords." *New Statesman,* 74 (October 20, 1967), 489.

[48]"Abortion and Mental Health." *America,* 116 (February 18, 1967), 239. [This editorial deals with the problem of deciding who is able to pronounce a judgment on the "mental" health of the mother.]

[49]"Abortion and Money." *Lancet,* 2(7928) (August 16, 1975), 315.

[50]"Abortion and Moral Conscience." *Humanist,* 30 (January-February, 1970), 12-13.

[51]"Abortion and Pluralism." *Commonweal,* 85 (February 24, 1967), 582-83. Reply: (March 17, 1967), 667+. [This editorial discusses the morality of abortion, use of tactful Catholic pressure, and the humanity of the fetus.]

[52]"Abortion and the Pregnant Teenager." *Canadian Medical Association Journal,* 110 (February 2, 1974), 261-62.

[53]"Abortion and Pre-Natal Injury: A Legal and Philosophical Analysis." *Western Ontario Law Review,* 13 (1974), 97-123.

[54]"Abortion and the Sick Mind." *America,* 113 (July 10, 1965), 37. [This editorial presents a discussion of a legal case in New York. One party sues another for not procuring an abortion on the grounds of the birth of a deformed child.]

[55]"Abortion and Slavery Arguments Same, Ad Says." *National Catholic Reporter,* 8 (March 31, 1972), 4.

[56]*Abortion and Social Justice.* Thomas Hilgers and Dennis Horan, ed. (Mission, K. J. Sheed, Andrews and McMeel, 1973.)

[57] "Abortion and the States." *Lancet*, 2(7934) (September 20, 1975), 544.

[58] "Abortion and the Wisconsin Law." *Wisconsin Medical Journal* (January, 1968), 67-55.

[59] "Abortion Appeals Rejected." *National Catholic Reporter*, 9 (March 9, 1973), 3.

[60] "Abortions Abroad Arranged for 600." *National Catholic Reporter*, 6 (January 28, 1970), 7.

[61] "Abortions at Charity Prices." *Social Justice Review*, 66 (June, 1973), 87-88.

[62] "Abortion: Battle of Emotions." *Economist*, 222 (March 11, 1967), 914.

[63] Abortion. (Bibliography) *Catholic Library World*, 44 (October 9, 1972), 177.

[64] "Abortion Bills Signed, Defeated." *National Catholic Reporter*, 3 (May 3, 1967), 7.

[65] "Abortion Bothers Young Males." *National Catholic Reporter*, 11 (July 4, 1975), 4.

[66] "Abortion: Campaign to Upset Supreme Court Ruling." *Congressional Quarterly Service Report*, 31 (November 10, 1973), 2973-76.

[67] "Abortion Can be Costly." *America*, 116 (March 25, 1967), 411-12. [The author examines the latent personal involvement of the women in relation to abortion. Her desire for the baby can be determined by the relationship with the father of the child. The author feels that the woman should be informed that she may experience guilt feelings after the abortion.

[68] "Abortion Cases: A Return to Lochner, Or a New Substantive Due Process?" *Albany Law Review*, 37 (1973), 776.

[69] "Abortion: The Catholic Presentation." *America*, 124 (January 23, 1971), 62. [In this editorial, Clare Boothe Luce points out some of the major shortcomings in the Church's presentation of its teaching on abortion, referring to an article in the January 12, 1971 issue of the *National Review*.
Her first comment concerns the Catholic statements against abortion which decry the moral evil of feticide without trying to solve the social evil that causes it. Secondly, she remarks on the almost total failure of the Church to take the woman's side of the abortion question into consideration. Even though abortion is a moral and legal problem, the experience itself is "uniquely female." This attention to the "feminine" must be taken into account.]

[70] "Abortion Clinics." *Lancet*, 1 (1969), 355.

[71] "Abortion, Coercion and Anti-Catholicism." *America*, 126 (May 13, 1972), 502. [The author points out that the pro-abortion spokesmen impose their will on children (fetuses). This is in response to charges that Catholics are imposing their will on others.]

[72] "Abortion Conscience Clauses." *Columbia Journal of Law and Social Problems*, 11 (Summer, 1975), 571-628.

[73] "Abortion—Constitutional Law—Criminal Law—Statute Prohibiting Abortions Not 'Necessary to Preserve' Mother's Life Held Unconstitutional." *New York Law Forum*, 15 (Winter, 1969), 941.

[74] "Abortion—Constitutional Law—A Law Prohibiting All Abortions Except Those Performed 'For the Purpose of Saving the Life of the Mother,' Which Does Not Augment a Compelling State Interest, Unconstitutionally Infringes on the Mother's Ninth Amendment Right to Choose Whether to Bear Children." *Texas Law Review*, 49 (March, 1971), 537.

[75] "Abortion—Constitutional Law—A Law That Allows An Abortion Only When 'Necessary to Preserve' the Life of the Mother Violates a Qualified Constitutional Right to an Abortion and is Unconstitutionally Vague." *Texas Law Review*, 48 (May, 1970), 937.

[76] "Abortion Controversy: The Law's Response." *Chicago-Kent Law Review*, 48 (Fall-Winter, 1971), 191.

[77] "Abortion: Day of Prayer, Dec. 28th." *L'Osservatore Romano (English)*, no. 34 (125) (August 20, 1970), 7.

[78] "The Abortion Debate." (Editorial) *Commonweal*, 92 (April 24, 1970), 131-32. [There is no longer general public support for anti-abortion laws. The abortion discussion is set up in terms of slogans and examined premises which do not meet the problems that society is now encountering. Certain recommendations for the situation as it stands in 1970 are offered to the Church and other institutions.]

[79] "The Abortion Debate." *Medical Journal of Australia*, 2 (October 25, 1969), 833-34.

[80] "Abortion Debate and Tough Ecumenism." *America*, 116 (March 11, 1967), 336. [The author asks if it is possible

for people who are deeply divided on the morality and desirability of fundamental public policies to discuss their differences freely and honestly. His answer is yes. In order to chieve ecumenical objectives, the sincerity and honesty of those who do not totally agree with one point of view cannot be doubted.]

[81] "The Abortion Decision." *Commonweal,* 97 (February 16, 1973), 435-36. [This article discusses the "impotence" of the American Catholic Church. We are in danger of becoming an abortion culture where the rights of the strongest are protected. "Privacy" is not primarily the protection of the person but an isolation from the responsibilities of sexual love. Church "officials" who preach and act in inconsistent ways are criticized. It is suggested that the Church re-educate itself on the value of human life and take a more prophetic stance toward selfishness in our institutions. Responsible birth control should be supported. Women should be given real status in the community of the Church so that childbearing is not seen as a "joyburden."]

[82] "Abortion Decision: Right of Privacy Extended." *University of Miami Law Review,* 27 (Spring-Summer, 1973), 481-87.

[83] "Abortion Decisions: *Roe v. Wade* (93 Sup Ct 705), *Doe v. Bolton* (93 Sup Ct 739)." *Journal of Family Law,* 12 (1972-1973), 459.

[84] "Abortion Decision a Year Later." *America,* 130 (January 19, 1974), 22. [The author discusses the efforts to draft an amendment to overturn the Supreme Court decision. He suggests that even though it is the most direct legal route, it may be impossible to get it passed.
The legal aspect, though important, should not detract from the educational dilemma. The ethical questions must be considered, so as not to uncritically accept that which is now legally permissible.]

[85] "Abortion: Deterrence, Facilitation, Resistance." *America,* 128 (June 2, 1973), 506-07. [The author discusses the problems generated by the Supreme Court decision and the methods of resistance that can be employed. Three serious practical problems arise:
1. What should public policy be in the facilitation of abortions?
2. What should policy be in providing exemptions for individuals and institutions that are conscientiously opposed to abortions?
3. What should Catholic policy be in resisting abortion decisions?

[86] "Abortion: The Doctor's Dilemma." *Journal of the Medical Association of Alabama,* 36 (June, 1967), 1507-08.

[87] "Abortion: Due Process and the Doctor's Dilemma." *Journal of Family Law,* 9 (1970), 300.

[88] *Abortion: An Ethical Discussion.* (London: Church Information Office, 1965).

[89] "Abortion: The Father's Rights." *University of Cincinnati Law Review,* 42 (1973), 441-67.

[90] "Abortion—Fighting Group to Expand into Rural Areas." *National Catholic Reporter,* 10 (September 13, 1974), 3.

[91] "Abortion Fights On." *National Catholic Reporter,* 6 (October 9, 1970), 2.

[92] "Abortion: The Five-Year Revolution and Its Impact." *Ecology Law Quarterly,* 3 (Spring, 1973), 311-47.

[93] "Abortion: The Future Cases: Father's Rights." *University of San Francisco Law Review,* 8 (Winter, 1973), 472-92.

[94] "Abortion Goes Public. Hospitals Report 2,000 Abortions in First Week Under New N.Y. Law." *Modern Hospital,* 115 (August, 1970), 33-36.

[95] "Abortion: The High Court Has Ruled." *Family Planning Perspectives,* 5(1) (Winter, 1973), 1.

[96] *Abortion: A Human Choice.* Board of Christian Social Concerns of the United Methodist Church. Washington, D.C., May, 1971. [At the General Conference of the United Methodist Church in 1970, a proposal was made to remove the regulation of abortion from the criminal code, placing it instead under regulations similar to those guiding other medical practices. The three articles in this pamphlet present some of the reasoning that lay behind adoption of the position that abortion should be a decision between a woman and her physician. The authors write from the individual woman's, the ethical and theological, and the legal points of view.

[97] *Abortion in America: Medical, Psychiatric, Legal, Anthropological, and Religious Considerations.* Harold Rosen, ed. (Boston: Beacon Press, 1967). Revised and updated version of his 1954 work, *Therapeutic Abortion* (New York: Julian Press, Inc., 1954).

[98] *Abortion in Britain.* Proceedings of a Conference Held by the Family Planning Association at the University of

London Union on 22 April, 1966. (London: Pitman Medical Publishing Company Limited, 1966).

[99]*Abortion in a Changing World.* R. Hall, ed. 2 vols. (New York: Columbia University Press, 1970).

[100]"Abortion Incorporated." *Journal of the American Medical Association*, 214 (October 12, 1970), 362.

[101]"Abortion in Court." *Economist*, 234 (February 28, 1970), 48.

[102]"Abortion in New Zealand." *British Medical Journal*, 3 (1969), 62.

[103]*Abortion in Nineteenth Century America.* (Sex, Marriage and Society Ser.) (New York: Arno Press, 1974).

[104]*Abortion in the United States.* Mary S. Calderone, ed. (New York: Hoeber-Harper, 1958).

[105]"Abortion is Morally Wrong Says Italian Bishops' Council." *L'Osservatore Romano* (English), no. 9 (257) (March 1, 1973), 5.

[106]"Abortion Law." *British Medical Journal*, 2 (December 31, 1966), 1607-08.

[107]"Abortion Law." *New Statesman*, 80 (August 7, 1970), 138.

[108]"Abortion Law." *New Statesman*, 80 (December 11, 1970), 786.

[109]"Abortion Law—Friendship Medical Center, Ltd., v. Chicago Board of Health (505 F 2d 1141), Invalidating City Health Regulations Applicable to First Trimester Abortion Procedures." *Loyola University Law Journal* (Chicago), 6 (Summer, 1975), 718-37.

[110]"Abortion, the Law, and Defective Children." *Suffolk University Law Review*, 3 (Spring, 1969) 225-230.

[111]"Abortion Law Battle Rages." *National Catholic Reporter*, 3 (February 22, 1967), 5.

[112]"Abortion Law—California Abortion Law Voided." *Dickinson Law Review*, 74 (Summer, 1970), 772.

[113]"Abortion Law Enacted in Pennsylvania." *National Catholic Reporter*, 10 (September 20, 1974), 17.

[114]"Abortion Law in South Carolina." *South Carolina Law Review*, 24 (1972), 425.

[115]"Abortion Law in the USA." *British Medical Journal*, 1 (February 17, 1973), 428-29.

[116]"Abortion Law Reform." *British Medical Journal*, 2 (1966), 1650.

[117]"Abortion Law Reform at a Crossroads?" *Chicago-Kent Law Review*, 46 (Spring-Summer, 1969), 102.

[118]"Abortion Law (Reform) Bill Talked Out." *British Medical Journal*, 1 (1970), 508.

[119]"Abortion Law Reform Seen in New York." *National Catholic Reporter*, 5 (January 22, 1969), 3.

[120]"Abortion Laws." *Social Justice Review*, 63 (February, 1971), 374-76.

[121]"Abortion Laws: A Constitutional Right to Abortion." *North Carolina Law Review*, 49 (April, 1971), 487.

[122]"Abortion Laws Liberalized." *National Catholic Reporter*, 3 (June 28, 1967), 3.

[123]*Abortion Laws: A Survey of Current World Legislation.* (International Digest of Health Legislation Ser:, Vol. 21, No. 3). WHO (World Health Organization), 1970.

[124]"Abortion Laws, Under Challenge, Are Being Liberalized (United States)." *Congressional Quarterly Weekly Report*, 28 (July 24, 1970), 1913-16.

[125]"Abortion Law Still Binding." *National Catholic Reporter*, 7 (February 19, 1971), 16.

[126]"Abortion Law: Various Approaches." *American Journal of Public Health*, 57 (November, 1967), 1906-1947.

[127]*Abortion: Legal and Illegal.* Jerome Kummer, ed. (Santa Monica, California: J. M. Kummer, 1967).

[128]"Abortion: A Legal Cop Out." *New England Law Review*, 7 (Spring, 1972), 311.

[129]"Abortion Legislation and the Establishment Clause." *Catholic Lawyer*, 15 (Spring, 1969), 108-23. [In a brief, in support of the appellant in the *Belous* case, the following two issues are raised: 1) the contention that anti-abortion legislation offends the Establishment Clause and 2) the contention that society is powerless under the constitution to legislate any controls over abortion.]

[130]"Abortion Legislation: The Need for Reform." *Vanderbilt Law Review*, 20 (November, 1967), 1313.

[131]"Abortion Litigation." *Catholic Lawyer*, 15 (Spring, 1969), 106-07. [The article gives a description of the

132-
158

facts of the *Belous* case and the ex-
tract of the statute directly involved.]

[132]"Abortion: Medicaid's Unwanted
Child?" *Women's Rights Law Reporter,*
3 (September, 1975), 22-27.

[133]"Abortion: Noral Issues." *Medical Journal of Australia,* 1 (March
23, 1968), 499-500.

[134]"Abortion: Next Round." *Commonweal,* 98 (March 23, 1973), 51-52.

[135]"Abortion: Next Time." *National Catholic Reporter,* 3 (March 15,
1967), 8, 10.

[136]Abortion: New and Old Issues."
America, 122 (June 27, 1970), 666.
[The consequences of repeal of the
abortion law are elaborated. The AMA
generally has been favorable to the
repeal of the abortion laws; now they
must decide where their responsibility
lies.]

[137]"Abortion: New Studies." *Commonweal,* 93 (October 16, 1970), 76-
77.

[138]"Abortion. 1970 General Assembly of the Presbyterian Church in the
U.S." *Church and Society,* 61 (September-October, 1970), 8-11.

[139]"Abortion, 1973. Some Recent
World Events in Relation to Pregnancy
Termination." *Medical Journal of Australia,* 1 Suppl. (June 1, 1974), 27-
30.

[140]"Abortion on Demand in a Post-
Wade (*Roe v. Wade,* 93 Sup Ct 705).
Context: Must the State Pay the
Bills?" *Fordham Law Review,* 41 (May,
1973), 921.

[141]"Abortion on Request." *Tablet,*
221 (July 22, 1967), 790.

[142]"Abortion: On Whose Demand?"
America, 126 (April 1, 1972), 335.
[The Presidential Commission on Population Growth and the American Future
stated that unwanted fertility contri-
butes largely to the unacceptable
growth rate, therefore various means
of birth control should be encouraged,
including abortion on demand. The
deep commitment to individual freedom
and social justice is emphasized as
part of the American cultural tradition rather than the "protection of
life." It is asked if the Commission's purpose is to sponsor sophisti-
cated propaganda.]

[143]"Abortion or Contraception?"
British Medical Journal, 3 (July 31,
1971), 261-62.

[144]"Abortion, Oregon Style." *Oregon Law Review,* 49 (April, 1970), 302.

[145]"Abortion Picture in Britain."
America, 116 (April 1, 1967), 490-91.
[This comment describes the opposition
to a bill in Britain, that would, in
effect, allow abortion on demand. The
Society for the Protection of Unborn
Children and Sir John Peel are men-
tioned.]

[146]"Abortion Polemic: A Restate-
ment of Pros and Cons." *Revista Juri-
dica de la Universidad de Puerto Rico,*
42 (1973), 247-76.

[147]*The Abortion Problem.* Proceedings of the Conference held under the
auspices of the National Committee on
Maternal Health, Inc., at the New York
Academy of Medicine, June 19 and 20,
1942. H. C. Taylor, ed. (New York:
The Williams and Wilkins Co., 1944).

[148]"Abortion: Protect Yourself."
Wisconsin Medical Journal, 66 (January, 1967), 45.

[149]"Abortion: Public Attitudes are
Split Over Court Abortion Ruling."
Gallup Opinion Index (tables) (April,
1974), 22-24.

[150]"Abortion Recommendations Accepted." *British Medical Journal,*
4(5991) (November 1, 1975), 293-94.

[151]"Abortion Reform and the Courts:
Florida and Michigan Supreme Court Decisions." *America,* 125 (August 7,
1971), 52.

[152]"Abortion: Reform and the Law."
Journal of Criminal Law, 59 (March,
1968), 84.

[153]"Abortion Reform: History,
Status, and Prognosis." *Case Western
Reserve Law Review,* 21 (April, 1970),
521.

[154]"Abortion Reform in Michigan—
An Analysis of the Proposed Code's
Provisions." *Wayne Law Review,* 14
(Summer, 1968), 1006.

[155]"Abortion Regulation: Louisiana's Abortive Attempt." *Louisiana
Law Review,* 34 (Spring, 1974), 676-85.

[156]"Abortion—Repeal of Alaska
Law?" *Alaska Medicine,* 11 (September,
1969), 105-07.

[157]"Abortion: Rhetoric and Reality." *Christian Century,* 88 (July 21,
1971), 871.

[158]"Abortion: *Roe v. Wade* (93 Sup
Ct 705) and the Montana Dilemma." *Montana Law Review,* 35 (Winter, 1974),
103-18.

[159]"Abortions: Change of Heart." *Nature* (London), 227 (July 4, 1970), 11.

[160]"Abortion's Effect on Health Disputed." *National Catholic Reporter*, 10 (May 10, 1974), 5.

[161]"The Abortion Situation." *Canadian Medical Association Journal*, 104 (May 22, 1971), 941.

[162]"The Abortion Situation." *Canadian Medical Association Journal*, 105 (August 7, 1971), 241.

[163]"Abortion: Some Ethical and Legal Aspects." *Medical Journal of Australia*, 1 (March 2, 1968), 359-60.

[164]"Abortion: A Special Demand." *Journal of the American Medical Association*, 221 (July 24, 1972), 400.

[165]"Abortion Statement by New Jersey Bishop." *Catholic Mind*, 66 (June, 1968), 4-5.

[166]"Abortion Strategy." *National Catholic Reporter*, 3 (February 15, 1967), 3.

[167]"Abortion: Twenty-Four Weeks of Dependency." *Baylor Law Review*, 27 (Winter, 1975), 122-40.

[168]"Abortions Under the N.H.S." *British Medical Journal*, 4 (December 5, 1970), 617.

[169]"Abortion: The United States Supreme Court Decision." *Lancet*, 1 (February 10, 1973), 301-02.

[170]"Abortion and the Unwanted Child (United States): An Interview with Alan F. Guttmacher, M.D., and Harriet F. Pilpel." *Family Planning Perspectives*, 2 (March, 1970), 16-24.

[171]"Abortion Uproar Awaits Returning Airlift Nurse." *National Catholic Reporter*, 11 (April 25, 1975), 2.

[172]"Abortion Will Be an Issue at Protestant Conventions." *Our Sunday Visitor*, 65 (June 13, 1976), 2.

[173]"About Abortion." *Journal of the American Medical Association*, 215 (January 11, 1971), 286.

[174]Ackner, B. "The Law Relating to Abortion." *Proceedings of the Royal Society of Medicine*, 55 (1962), 376.

[175]"Action of Privy Council on Appeals from G.M.C." *British Medical Journal*, 1 (August 1, 1970), 292.

[175A] "Activities in Catholic Dioceses to Mark Anniversary of Court Ruling on Abortion." *L'Osservatore Romano* (English), no. 5 (305) (January 31, 1974), 12.

[176]Adamek, R. J. "Abortion, Personal Freedom, and Public Policy." *Family Coordinator* (April 4, 1974), 411-19.

[177]Adams, P. Scott. *Abortion and Our Canadian Laws*. Adams, 2d ed. (Toronto: P. Scott Adams, 1973).

[178]Addelson, Frances. "Induced Abortion. Source of Guilt or Growth." *American Journal of Ortho-Psychiatry*, 43 (5) (1973), 815-23.

[179]Addelson, Frances. "Therapeutic Abortion: A Social Work View." *American Journal of Obstetrics and Gynecology*, 111 (December 1, 1971), 984. [In an examination of social work performance at Beth Israel Hospital, Boston, the author recommends that social work be regarded as an integral approach to all obstetric-gynecologic care in facilities catering to therapeutic abortion thereby involving co-operation of the social workers.

[180]Addison, P. H. "Abortion Act 1967." *Lancet*, 2 (August 31, 1968), 503-07.

[181]Addison, P. H. "The Impact of the Abortion Act 1967 in Great Britain." *Medical-Legal Journal*, 38 (1970), 15-21.

[182]Adler, N. E. "Dimensions Underlying Emotional Responses of Women Following Therapeutic Abortion." *Proceedings of the 81st Annual Convention of the American Psychological Association*, Montreal, Canada, 8 (1973), 357-58.

[183]Adler, N. E. "Emotional Responses of Women Following Therapeutic Abortion." *American Journal of Orthopsychology*, 45 (April, 1975), 446-54.

[184]Adler, N. E. "Sample Attrition in Studies of Psychosocial Sequelae of Abortion. How Great a Problem." *Journal of Applied Social Psychology*, 6 (3) (1976), 240-59.

[185]"Administrative Commission Issues Pastoral Message On Abortion." *L'Osservatore Romano* (English), no.10 (258) (March 8, 1973), 9.

[186]"Advertising Abortion Service." *British Medical Journal*, 4 (supplement) (1969), 65.

[187]"After a Conviction—Second

188-
208 Thoughts About Abortions (Following the Manslaughter Conviction on Feb. 13, 1975, of a Boston Surgeon in the Death of a 20- to 24-Week Fetus)." *U.S. News,* 78 (March 3, 1975), 78.

[188]"After Lane." *Lancet,* 1 (April 20, 1974), 715-16.

[189]"Against the Act." *"Economist,* 254 (February 8, 1975), 24.

[190]Aitken-Swan, J. "Some Social Characteristics of Women Seeking Abortion." *Journal of Biosocial Science,* 3 (1971), 96-100.

[191]Akinla, Cladele. "Abortion in Africa." Paper presented at the International Conference on Abortion, Hot Springs, Virginia, November 17-20, 1968.

[192]Albe-Fessard, D., Bertolus, J. -R., Biraben, J. -N., Boue, A. and J., Chartier, M., Dumas, A., Garnier, J., Léridon, H., Ribes, B., Roqueplo, P., Simon, R., Thibault, C. and O. "Pour une Réforme de la Législation Française Relative à L'Avortement." *Etudes,* 338 (January, 1973), 55-84.

[193]Alhan, Lawrence E. "Constitutional Aspects of Present Criminal Abortion Law (seminar paper)." *Valparaiso University Law Review,* 3 (Fall, 1968), 102-21.

[194]Allen, D. V., Reichelt, P. A., Ager, J. W., Werley, H. H. "Relationships Among Knowledge, Attitudes, and Behavior of Nurses Concerning Abortion." *Proceedings of the 81st Annual Convention of the American Psychological Association,* Montreal, Canada, 8 (1973), 337-38.

[195]Allen, J. "The Abortionist Dictionary: Gilded Words for Guilty Deeds." *Liguorian,* 61 (May, 1973), 36-37.

[196]"Almost an Aggiornamento; and a Sad Regression." *America,* 117 (July 8, 1967), 27-28. [This article describes the change in the AMA policy on abortion. The delegates approved legislation for abortion for three purposes: 1) to safeguard the health or life of the mother, 2) to prevent the birth of a child with a physical or mental defect, and 3) to terminate pregnancies resulting from rape or incest. The author sees what is at stake here is the control of power over life and death.]

[197]"Alone, If Necessary." *Triumph,* 2 (April, 1967), 38.

[198]Alpern, H. D. "Contraception and Abortion Among Aleuts and Eskimos in Alaska: A Demographic Study." *Journal of Reproductive Medicine,* (November, 1971), 239-44.

[199]Alpern, W. M., *et al.* "Fatal Brain Damage Associated With Therapeutic Abortion Induced by Amniocentesis: Report of One Case." *Medicine, Science and the Law,* 7 (April, 1967), 70-72.

[200]Alsobrook, H. B., Jr. "Medicolegal Opinion. Re: On Demand Abortions in Public Hospitals." *Journal of Louisiana Medical Society,* 123 (January, 1971), 29-30.

[201]Alsopp, M. "Abortion, The Theological Argument." *Furrow,* 24 (April, 1973), 202-06. [Alsopp develops his position based upon several fundamental Christian insights, especially man's appreciation of himself and his orientation in life. He says that one cannot agree to an abortion in the case of rape because it would imply the contradiction of one's fundamental Christian action-orientation.]

[202]Altchek, A. "Abortion Alert." *Obstetrics and Gynecology,* 42 (September, 1973), 452-54.

[203]Amen, J. H. "Some Obstacles to Effective Legal Control of Criminal Abortions." In National Committee on Maternal Health, Inc., *The Abortion Problem.* Ed. H. C. Taylor (New York: The Williams and Wilkens Co., 1944).

[204]American Academy of Pediatrics. Committee on Youth. "Teen-Age Pregnancy and the Problem of Abortion." *Pediatrics,* 49 (February, 1972), 303-04.

[205]"American Bishops and Abortion." *Tablet,* 227 (March 17, 1973), 268-69. [This article describes the reaction of the Catholic Bishops to the U.S. Supreme Court decision. Liberal Protestants, the inconsistency of the Bishops in their response to the Vietnamese war and capital punishment, are reasons that were offered to explain how the Court could make such a decision.]

[206]American Friends Service Committee. *Who Shall Live? Man's Control Over Birth and Death* (New York: Hill and Wang, Inc., 1970).

[207]"AMA Policy on Therapeutic Abortion." *Journal of the American Medical Association,* 201 (August 14, 1967), 544.

[208]"Amniocentesis Requires Proper Care—Sonography Can Make it Safer." *Journal of the American Medical Association,* 235 (June 14, 1976), 2573-74.

[209]"Analysis of the Constitutionality of the Nebraska Abortion Statute." *Creighton Law Review,* 7 (Fall, 1973), 27-49.

[210]"Analysis of the Proposed Changes to the Ohio Abortion Statute." *University of Cincinnati Law Review,* 37 (Spring, 1968), 340.

[211]Anderson, David C. "Abortion and Life's Intrinsic Value." *Wall Street Journal,* 179 (April 7, 1972),8. [The practice of abortion in New York City under liberalized statutes is discussed.]

[212]Anderson, E. W. "The Psychiatric Indication for the Termination of Pregnancy." *Proceedings of the Royal Society of Medicine,* 50 (May, 1957), 321.

[213]Anderson, E. W. "Psychiatric Indications for the Termination of Pregnancy." *Journal of Psychosomatic Research,* 10(1) (1961), 127-34. Also in *World Medical Journal,* 13 (May-June, 1966), 81.

[214]Anderson, J. "Anti-Catholicism Trades Fantasy for Fact in the Media." *Our Sunday Visitor,* 63 (April 27, 1975), 1+.

[215]Anderson, J. "Are Women Becoming Endangered Species?" *Our Sunday Visitor,* 65 (October 24, 1976),1+.

[216]Anderson, J. "Beyond Abortion —Fetal Experimentation." *Our Sunday Visitor,* 63 (April 13, 1975)), 1+.

[217]Anderson, J. "INFANT Challenges Pro-Abortionists." *Our Sunday Visitor,* 62 (March 3, 1974), 10.

[218]Anderson, J. "Pat Goltz—Pro-Life Feminist." *Our Sunday Visitor,* 64 (May 18, 1975), 1+.

[219]Anderson, J. "The Real Abortion Story: A Conspiracy of Silence." *Our Sunday Visitor,* 63 (August 11, 1974), 1+.

[220]Anderson, J. "What You Can Do to Save Innocent Lives." *Our Sunday Visitor,* 62 (February 17, 1974), 1+.

[221]Anderson, J. "Women Exploited United." *Our Sunday Visitor,* 64 (September 21, 1975), 1+.

[222]Anderson, Stephen G. "Abortion and the Husband's Consent." *Journal of Family Law,* no. 2 (13) (1973-1974), 311-31. [The *Roe* and *Doe* decisions of the Supreme Court did not decide on the right of the father in regards to the abortion decision. The woman's right to control her own body may conflict with the father's right to a family. Consent requirements are considered but are viewed as being outweighed by the woman's basic right to privacy.]

[223]"Andolsek, Lydia. "Abortion in Yugoslavia." *Family Planning,* 14 (January, 1966).

[224]Andolsek, Lydia. "Current Status of Abortion and Family Planning in Yugoslavia." *Fourth Conference of International Planned Parenthood Federation,* paper 38 (1964).

[225]Andrews, J. "Theologians Add Little to Abortion Debate." *National Catholic Reporter,* 5 (December 4, 1968), 7.

[226]Andrews, J. "Jesuit Denies Abortion in Early Stages is Immoral." *National Catholic Reporter,* 5 (November 27, 1968), 6.

[227]"Anglican Synod Takes Stand Against Abortion on Demand." *Our Sunday Visitor,* 64 (August 10, 1975), 2.

[228]Annis, David. "Self-Consciousness and the Right to Life." *Southwestern Journal of Philosophy,* 6 (Summer, 1975), 123-28.

[229]"Anti-Abortion Campaign: Scotland." *L'Osservatore Romano* (English), no. 1 (301) (January 3, 1974), 3.

[230]"Anti-Abortionists Rally, Lobby for Amendment." *National Catholic Reporter,* 10 (February 1, 1974), 1-2.

[231]"Anti-Abortion Feeling: United States." *L'Osservatore Romano* (English), no. 10 (362) (March 6, 1975), 11.

[232]"Anti-Abortion Statement Turns Pro, Then Back." *National Catholic Reporter,* 12 (November 14, 1975), 6.

[233]"Anti-Abortion Resolution," *Congressional Quarterly Weekly Report,* 34 (March 27, 1976), 712.

[234]"The Anti-Life Movement at the Starting Gate." *Triumph,* 9 (February, 1974), 29-31.

[235]Anwyl, J. H. "The Role of Private Counselling for Problem Pregnancies." *Clinical Obstetrics and Gynecology,* 14 (December, 1971), 1225-29.

[236]Aoki, Hisao. *Selected Statistics Concerning Fertility Regulation in Japan.* (Tokyo: Institute of Population Programs—Ministry of Health and Welfare, 1967).

[237]"Appeal to All: Protect Human;

238-
261

Pastoral Letter of the German Episcopate." *L'Osservatore Romano* (English), no. 28 (276) (July 12, 1973),
9-12.

[238]"Approval for Abortion." *British Medical Journal*, 1 (April 19,
1969), 133-34.

[239]Aptekar, H. *Infanticide, Abortion and Contraception in Savage Society*. (New York: Godwin, 1931).

[240]"Archbishop Bernardin Calls
Ford Stand Disappointing." *Our Sunday
Visitor*, 64 (February 15, 1976), 1.

[241]"Archbishop Bernardin Open to
Meeting with Carter." *L'Osservatore
Romano* (English), no. 32 (436) (August
5, 1976), 6.

[242]"Are State Abortion Statutes
Reasonable?—The Recent Judicial Trend
Indicates the Contrary." *South Texas
Law Journal*, 11 (1970), 426.

[243]Aren, Per. "Legal Abortion in
Sweden." *Acta Obstetricia et Gynecologica Scandinavica*, 37 (suppl. 1)
(1958), 1-75.

[244]Aren, Per. and Amard, C. "The
Prognosis of Granted But Not Performed
Legal Abortion." *Svenska Lakartidnin-
gen*, 54(49) (1957), 3709-84.

[245]Aring, C. D. "Editorial: Abortion." *Journal of American Medical
Association*, 230(2) (October 14, 1974),
231.

[246]Arkes, Hadley. "Debating Abor-
tion: A Non-Catholic and a Scientist;
Amend the Constitution." *Wall Street
Journal*, 188 (October 26, 1976), 26.

[247]Arkle, J. "Termination of
Pregnancy on Psychiatric Grounds."
British Medical Journal, 1 (1957), 558.

[248]Armijo, Rolando. "Abortion in
Latin America." *Proceedings of the
Eighth International Conference of the
International Planned Parenthood Fed-
eration Santiago, Chile, April 1967*
(1967).

[249]Armijo, Rolando and Monreal,
Tequalda. "Abortion Problem in Chile."
*Journal of the American Medical Assoc-
iation*, 195(5) (1966), 405.

[250]Armijo, Rolando and Monreal,
Tequalda. "Epidemiology of Provoked
Abortion in Santiago, Chile." *The
Journal of Sex Research*, 1 (July,
1965).

[251]Armijo, Rolando and Requena, M.
"Epidemiological Aspects of Abortion
in Chile." *Public Health Reports*,
83(1) (1968), 41-48.

[252]Armstrong, James. "The Politics of Abortion." *Christian Century*,
93 (March 10, 1976), 215-16. [The author discusses how the abortion issue
has been politicized by the Roman
Catholic hierarchy in the 1976 presidential election.]

[253]Arney, W. R. and Trescher, W.
H. "Trends in Attitudes Toward Abor-
tion, 1972-1975." *Family Planning
Perspectives*, 8(3) (1976), 117-24.

[254]Arthur, H. R. "Contraception
or Abortion? Termination of Pregnancy." *Royal Society of Health Journal*,
92 (1972), 204-07.

[254]Ashford, T. "Countdown to an
Abortion." *America*, 136 (February 12,
1977), 128. [This is the story of a
college professor who offers to adopt
the child of one of his pregnant students.]

[255]Ashley-Montagu, M. A. *Life
Before Birth* (New York: New American
Library, 1965).

[256]Ashton, Jean. "Amniocentesis:
Safe But Still Ambiguous." *Hastings
Center Report*, 6 (February, 1976), 5-8.

[257]Ashworth, H. W. "Will She,
Won't She?" *Manchester Medical Gazette*, 49 (March, 1970), 7.

[258]Ashworth, H. W. "Requests for
Abortion in General Practice." *Journal of the Royal College of General
Practitioners*, 24(142) (May, 1974),
329-30, 335-39.

[259]Athanasiou, R., Oppel, W.,
Michelson, L., Unger, T., Yager, M.
"Psychiatric Sequelae to Term Birth
and Induced Early and Late Abortion.
A Longitudinal Study." *Family Plan-
ning Perspectives*, 5(4) (1973), 227-31.

[260]Atkinson, Gary M. "The Morality of Abortion." *International
Philosophical Quarterly*, 14 (Spring,
1974), 347-62. [The author points to
an indissoluble connection between
abortion, infanticide and involuntary
euthanasia as moral issues. The principles involved are such that acceptance of one entails the acceptance of
the other two. An analysis of the nature of morality is presented as well
as what constitutes a good reason in
morality. Arguments that justify
abortion or that explain the difference between abortion and infanticide
or involuntary euthanasia are shown to
be fallacious by failing to meet the
conditions requisite for good reason.]

[261]"The Attitude of the Roman

Catholic Church." Ed. Harold Rosen (Boston: Beacon Press). Reprinted from Good, F. L. and Kelly, O. F., *Marriage, Morals and Medical Ethics* (New York: P. J. Kenedy, 1951).

[262]"Attitudes to Abortion." *British Medical Journal*, 2 (April 13, 1974), 69-70.

[263]"Attitudes to Abortion." *British Medical Journal*, 2 (May 4, 1974), 276.

[264]"Attitudes to Abortions." *British Medical Journal*, 2 (June 1, 1974), 501.

[266]Aurele, J. "Respect for Human Life." *L'Osservatore Romano* (English), no. 19 (163) (May 13, 1971), 9.

[267]"L'Avortement, L'Attentat le Plus Grave Contre la Vie Humaine; Note de law Commission Episcopale Espagnole pour la Doctrine de la Foi." *La Documentation Catholique*, 71 (December 15, 1974), 1074-77.

[268]"L'Avortement et la Responsabilité du Chrétien; Declaration des Evêques Catholiques des Pays Nordiques, Goeteborg, Juillet 1971." *La Documentation Catholique*, 68 (December 5, 1971), 1076-84.

[269]"L'Avortement Provoqué; Déclaration des Evêques des Pays-Bas." *La Documentation Catholique*, 71 (November 3, 1974), 934-36.

[270]Awan, A. K. "Attempted Illegal Abortions in 156 Cases of Fetal Loss Occurring Among 1447 Married Women. Saddar Pregnancy Study (1963-1965)." *Journal of the American Medical Women's Association*, 24 (1969), 571-86.

[271]Axe, K. "Let's Lower Our Voices About Abortion." *U.S. Catholic*, 41 (June, 1976), 14-15. [The author admits being undecided about abortion and asks for more time to think.]

[272]Ayd, Frank J. "Liberal Abortion Laws." *America*, 120 (February 1, 1969), 130-32. [Frank Ayd offers his views of what will happen if abortion laws are liberalized. He begins by asserting that women do not have the right to destroy their unborn children. The same people who advocate liberalized abortion laws, also advocate sterilization and euthanasia. He says that abortion is more dangerous than pregnancy. Legislators who are considering liberal abortion laws must be made to realize that by defending the fetus' right to life, they are reaffirming the sanctity of life and at the same time will not be delegating anyone the right to decide who will live.]

[283]Ayd, Frank J. "Liberal Abortion Laws: An Appraisal." *Marriage and Family Living*, 51 (June, 1969), 40-43.

262-286

[274]Ayd, Frank J. "Liberal Abortion Laws: A Psychiatrist's View." In *The Reasons Against Abortion*. (A collection of testimonies before the Codes and Health Committees of the New York Legislature, February 3, 8, and 10, 1967, distributed by the New York State Catholic Welfare Committee) (mimeographed). Also in *American Ecclesiastical Review*, 158 (February, 1968), 73-91. [An argument is presented against liberalizing abortion laws for "psychiatric" reasons.]

[275]Bachi, R. "Induced Abortions in Israel." Paper delivered at the International Conference on Abortion, Hot Springs, Virginia, November 17-20, 1968.

[276]"Back Abortion Reform." *National Catholic Reporter*, 8 (April 7, 1972), 4.

[277]Bacon, H. M. "Psychiatric Aspects of Therapeutic Abortion." *Canada-S Mental Health*, 17(1) (1969), 18-21.

[278]Bacon, R. "How Liberalized Abortion Became Law in One State." *Ave Maria*, 106 (July 22, 1967), 16-18.

[279]Bagley, C. "On the Sociology and Social Ethics of Abortion." *Ethics in Science and Medicine*, 3(1) (1976), 21-32.

[280]Bailey, K. V. "Risks of Abortion." *British Medical Journal*, 2 (June 1, 1968), 557.

[281]Baird, D. "The Abortion Act 1967. (a). The Advantages and Disadvantages." *Royal Society Health Journal*, 90 (November-December, 1970), 291-95.

[282]Baird, D. "Abortion Games." *Lancet*, 2 (November 20, 1971), 1145.

[283]Baird, D. "Induced Abortion: Epidemiological Aspects." *Journal of Medicine and Ethics*, 1(3) (September, 1975), 122-26.

[284]Baird, D. "Legal Abortion—Experience at Aberdeen." In *Abortion in Britain* (London: Pitman Medical Publishing Company Ltd., 1966).

[285]Baird, D. "Sterilization and Therapeutic Abortion in Aberdeen." *British Journal of Psychiatry*, 13(500) (1967), 701-09.

[286]Baird, D. "Three Years of the

287-
309
Abortion Act: Gynecological Psychiatric Aftermaths." *Proceedings of the Royal Society of Medicine,* 65 (February, 1972), 160-62.

[287]Baird, William. "Abortion Activist Presents the Case for Supporting His Case. Steele, Joanne. Baird: What Got Him Started and What Keeps Him Going." *Majority Report,* 5 (April 3-17, 1976), 6-7.

[288]Bajema, Clifford E. *Abortion and the Meaning of Personhood* ([Direction Books], Grand Rapids: Baker Books, 1974).

[289]Baker, L. D. "Statistical Analysis of Applicants and of the Induced Abortion Workup. Grady Memorial Hospital—January-December, 1970." *Journal of the Medical Association of Georgia,* 60 (1971), 392-96.

[290]Balakrishnan, T. R., Ross, S., Allingham, J. D., Kantner, J. F. "Attitudes Toward Abortion of Married Women in Metropolitan Toronto." *Social Biology,* 19(1) (1972), 35-42.

[291]Balikci, A. "Female Infanticide on the Arctic Coast." *Man,* 2(4) (1967), 615-25.

[292]Ball, D. W. "An Abortion Clinic Ethnography." *Social Problems,* 1 (1967), 293-301. [This describes the social, psychological, economic and medical characteristics of a relatively costly abortion clinic on the California-Mexico border.]

[293]Ballard, W. "California Abortion Statistics for 1971." *California Medicine,* 116 (April, 1972), 55.

[294]Bannister, J. R. "Letter: Friends of Hippocrates." *Canadian Medical Association Journal,* 110 (June 22, 1974), 1337.

[295]Banwell, G. S. "Letter: Attitudes to Abortion." *British Medical Journal,* 2 (May 18, 1974), 383.

[296]"Baptists Say Bishops Are Threat to Liberty." *National Catholic Reporter,* 10 (March 22, 1974), 2.

[297]"Baptist Says Abortion Not a Catholic Issue." *National Catholic Reporter,* 10 (April 26, 1974), 5.

[298]Barber, C. J. "Abortion. A Survey of Attitudes and Research Materials." *Journal of Psychology and Theology,* 1(4) (1973), 66-76.

[299]Barcus, Nancy B. "Thinking Straight About Abortion." *Christianity Today,* 19 (January 17, 1975), 8-11.

[300]Bardis, Panos D. "Abortion Attitudes Among Catholic College Students." *Adolescence,* 10(39) (1975), 433-41.

[301]Bardis, Panos D. "Abortion Attitudes Among University Students in India." Paper delivered at 1974 annual meeting of the National Council on Family Relations. Available from author, Sociology Dept., Toledo Univ., Toledo, Ohio 43606. [Four hypotheses were tested by interviews with 150 students from two Calcutta colleges. These are: 1) university students tend to approve of abortion; 2) among these students, the approval is fairly uniform; 3) fairly conservative abortion attitudes are a result of the neutralizing effect of religiosity on education; 4) Indian students are almost as liberal as American Protestants and more liberal than American Catholic students. Statistical data supports all four hypotheses. In order for family planning to be effective, it must be combined with economic development.]

[302]Bardis, Panos D. "Abortion and Public Opinion. A Research Note." *Journal of Marriage and the Family,* 34(1) (1972), 111-12.

[303]Bardis, Panos D. "A Technique for the Measurement of Attitudes toward Abortion." *International Journal of Sociology of the Family,* 2(1) (1972), 98-104.

[304]Barell, U. and Engstrom, L. "Legal Abortions in Sweden." *World Medical Journal,* 13 (May-June, 1966), 72.

[305]Barglow, P. and Weinstein, S. "Therapeutic Abortion During Adolescence. Psychiatric Observations." *Journal of Youth and Adolescence,* 2(4) (1973), 331-342.

[306]Barnard, T. H. "An Analysis and Criticism of the Model Penal Code Provisions on the Law of Abortion." *Western Reserve Law Review,* 18 (Jan. 1967), 540.

[307]Barnes, A. C. "Fetal Indications for Therapeutic Abortion." *Annual Review of Medicine,* 22 (1971), 133-44.

[308]Barnes, J. "The Abortion Act—Gynecologist's View." *Medicine, Science and the Law,* 9 (January, 1969), 53.

[309]Barno, Alex. "Criminal Abortion, Deaths, Illegitimate Pregnancy Deaths, and Suicides in Pregnancy." *American Journal of Obstetrics and Gynecology,* 98 (1967). Also in *Minnesota Medicine,* 50 (January, 1967), 11-16.

[310]Barno, Alex. "Terminating Pregnancy After First-Trimester Rubella." *Postgraduate Medicine,* 46 (October, 1969), 177-79.

[311]Barr, John. "The Abortion Battle." *New Society* (March 9, 1967), 342-346.

[312]Barrett, F. M. and Fitz-Earle, M. "Student Opinion on Legalized Abortion at the University of Toronto." *Canadian Journal of Public Health,* 64(3) (1973), 294-99.

[313]Barrins, P. "Is it Right to Legalize Therapeutic Abortion?" *Social Justice Review,* 62 (March, 1970), 400-04.

[314]Barron, S. L. "New Trends in Therapeutic Abortion." *Lancet,* 2 (December 2, 1972), 1193.

[315]Barth, Karl. "The Protection of Life." *Church Dogmatics,* III/4 (Edinburgh: T & T Clark, 1961).

[316]Barsotti, D. "Must the Church Eliminate Morality?" *L'Osservatore Romano* (English), no. 14 (262) (April 5, 1973), 8.

[317]Bartlett, D. "Abortion." *Social Justice Review,* 66 (February, 1974), 357-60.

[318]Bateman, D. "Cases of Abortion Treated at the Lambeth Hospital 1960-67." *Journal of Obstetricians and Gynecologists of the British Commonwealth,* 75 (1968), 1169.

[319]Bates, Jerome E. and Zawadzki, Edward S. *Criminal Abortion: A Study in Medical Sociology* (Springfield, Illinois: Charles C. Thomas, 1964).

[320]"Battle for Unborn Life Will Go On as Bayh's Committee Vetoes Pro-Life Amendments." *Our Sunday Visitor,* 64 (September 28, 1975), 1.

[321]"Battle Underway on Funding of Abortions by Government." *Our Sunday Visitor,* 65 (August 8, 1976), 2.

[322]Barclay, W. R. "Editorial: Abortion." *Journal of American Medical Association,* 236(4) (July 26, 1976), 388.

[323]"A Baseline for Criminal Abortions?" *Lancet,* 2 (August 9, 1969), 309.

[324]Baude, Patrick L. "Constitutional Reflections on Abortion Reform." *Journal of Law Reform,* 4 (Fall, 1970), 1-10.

[325]Baudry, F. and Weiner, A. "The Pregnant Patient in Conflict About Abortion. A Challenge for the Obstetrician." *American Journal of Obstetrics and Gynecology,* 119(5) (1974), 705-11.

[326]Baum, G. "Abortion: An Ecumenical Dilemma." *Commonweal,* 99 (November 30, 1973), 231-35. [Baum draws three conclusions: 1) It is not possible to approve of the language and arguments adopted by Catholics in defending their traditional position which implies that those who defend abortion are immoral or lacking respect for life; 2) the Catholic position differs from many other Churches resulting from a difference in social and cultural background. Two models are presented. The traditional position, supported by the Church, is dominated by the concept of nature. The more liberal position is dominated by the concept of history. Baum concludes that the opposition of Catholics against abortion should place itself in man's historical responsibility for his sexual life. At Vatican II, the Church shifted from the first to the second model; 3) the task of the moral theologian is to offer a critique of society to examine how violence is fed by injustice.]

[327]Bauman, K. E., Koch, G. G., Udry, J. R., and Freeman, J. L. "The Relationship Between Legal Abortion and Marriage." *Social Biology,* 22(2) (1975), 117-24.

[328]Baunemann, H. "Letter: Therapeutic Abortion." *Canadian Medical Association Journal,* 112(1) (January 11, 1975), 27.

[329]Bausch, W. "The Absence of Sweat; Abortion on Demand." *U. S. Catholic,* 37 (April, 1972), 39-40. [The author states that abortion should not become the normal state of affairs and certainly should not become casual. At times, it may be the choice that is made, but it should only be considered reflectively for serious reasons, not simply on demand.]

[330]Bayer, Charles H. "Confessions of an Abortion Counsellor." *Christian Century,* 87 (May 20, 1970), 624-626. [This article is concerned with counseling in "problem pregnancies." The liberalization of abortion laws is supported.]

[331]Beard, R. W., Belsey, E. M., Lal, S., Lewis, S. C., and Greer, H. S. "King's Termination Study. II. Contraceptive Practice Before and After Outpatient Termination of Pregnancy." *British Medical Journal,* 1 (1974), 418-21.

[332]Beatty, Muriel J. "What It Is to Be Woman: Some Reflection." *CRUX,* 12(4) (1974-1975), 33-37.

[333]Beazley, Christine and Knight, Jill. *To Be or Not To Be? Pros and Cons of Abortion* (London: Conservative Political Centre, 1974).

[334]Beck, Mildred B., *et al.* "Abortion: A National Public and Mental Health Problem, Present and Proposed Research." *American Journal of Public Healty,* 59 (December, 1969), 2131-43.

[335]Beckwith, B. "Ellen McCormack: Campaigning for the Unborn." *St. Anthony's Messenger,* 83 (May, 1976), 30-36.

[336]Beeson, T. "Britain's Abortion Act: Inquiry Requested." *Christian Century,* 87 (August 19, 1970), 984.

[337]Behrstock, B., *et al.* "Obstetricians and Legal Abortions in San Francisco." *California Medicine,* 117 (September, 1972), 29-31.

[338]Beliveau, P. "La Reforme de L'Avortement d'une Reforme." *Revue du Barreau,* 35 (1975), 563-92.

[339]Benjamin, R. B. "Abortion or Compulsory Pregnancy?" *Minnesota Medicine,* 52 (March, 1969), 455-57.

[340]Bennet, John. *Abortion Law Reform* (South Yarra: Victoria, 1968).

[341]Bennet, Jonathan. "Whatever the Consequences." *Analysis,* 26 (1966), 83. [the principle of double effect and the application to abortion is presented. Various aspects of the action/consequence distinction is focused upon.]

[342]Bennett, John C. "Abortion Debate (in New York State)." *Christianity and Crisis,* 27 (March 20, 1967), 47-48. Replies (May 15, 1967), 113-15.

[343]Bennett, John C. "Avoid Oppressive Laws." *Christianity and Crisis,* 32 (January 8, 1973), 287-88.

[344]Bennett, O. "Some Additional Arguments Against Abortion." *Hospital Progress Report,* 73 (January, 1973), 50-53. [Two fundamental arguments against abortion are presented: 1) if a woman accepts the "right" to abort then she admits that the power of the legislator can enter what was previously God's law. Will the civil legislators invade the same area further? To whom can the woman appeal if not the Church?; 2) how violent can we get without destroying ourselves?]

[345]Berger, P. and C. "The Credibility Gap that Kills." *America,* 131 (August 10, 1974), 47-49. [The authors discuss the inconsistent stance of the official teaching of the Church with regards to abortion, war and capital punishment. They ask how an unconscious fetus can be saved but a conscious adult is sent to war or to the death chamber.]

[346]Berger, P. and C. "The Edelin Decision." *Commonweal,* 102 (April 25, 1975), 76-78. [Carol and Patrick Berger discuss the decision by a Boston Jury against Dr. K. Edelin. A fetus was born alive during an abortion and he took steps to prevent spontaneous respiration on the part of the unwanted fetus. The Bergers discuss the ambuguous terms which the jury had to consider: "When does human life begin," the terms "viability" and "humanity." Then they describe some concessions that have to be made by the pro-abortionists as well as the anti-abortionists. They conclude with a discussion of the difficulties of taking an absolute stand.]

[347]Bergin. "Somebody's Going to get Killed." *Hawaii Medical Journal,* 26 (November-December, 1966), 105-09.

[348]Berle, B. B. "An Analysis of Abortion Deaths in the District of Columbia for the Years 1938, 1939, and 1940." *American Journal of Obstetrics and Gynecology,* 43 (1942), 820.

[349]Bernardin, J., Abp. "Abortion: Questions and Answers from a Catholic Perspective; the Catholic Church's View." *L'Osservatore Romano* (English), no. 45 (449) (November 4, 1976), 9+.

[350]Bernardin, J., Abp. "Rencontres des Eveques Américains avec les Deux Candidats a la Présidence; le Candidat Démocrate Jimmy Carter, et le Candidat Républicain Gerald Ford." *La Documentation Catholique,* 73 (October 17, 1976), 859-63.

[351]Bernstein, A. H. "An Abortion Law Update." *Hospitals,* 50(11) (June 1, 1976), 90-92.

[352]Bernstein, I. C. "Psychiatric Indications for Therapeutic Abortion." *Minnesota Medicine,* 50 (January, 1967), 51-55.

[353]Bernstein, N. R., *et al.* "Group Therapy Following Abortion." *Journal of Nervous and Mental Disease,* 152 (May, 1971), 303-14.

[354]Berry, L. "Il Papa and the Pill." *Commonweal,* 90 (March 28, 1969), 44-46. [Birth control practices and the high instance of il-

legal abortion in Italy are examined.]

[355] "Best Law: No Law?" *America,* 117 (September 23, 1967), 292.

[356] Bevan, D. "Lifeline Pregnancy Care: Service Giving Social, Financial and Moral Help in Great Britain." *Clergy Review,* 61 (November, 1976), 441-43.

[357] Bhardwaj, K. S., and Mullick, S. "Attitudes of Indian Women Towards Abortion." *Indian Journal of Social Work,* 33(4) (1973), 317-22.

[358] Bianchi, E. "Compassion is Needed." *National Catholic Reporter,* 9 (June 8, 1973), 14.

[359] Bird, Lewis. *What You Should Know about Abortion.* Ed. William P. J. Petersen (London: Keats Publishers, n.d.)

[360] Bird, R. G. "Requests for Abortion." *British Medical Journal,* 1 (February 3, 1968), 311.

[361] *Birth Control and the Christian.* Spitzer, W. O., and Saylor, C. L., eds. (Wheaton, Illinois: Tyndale House, 1969).

[362] "Birthright Moves Ahead."*L'Osservatore Romano* (English), no. 30 (226) (July 27, 1972), 5.

[363] "Birthright's Goal: Stop 100,000 Abortions." *National Catholic Reporter,* 7 (September 10, 1971), 6.

[364] "Bishop Asks Catholics to Join Washington March for Life." *Our Sunday Visitor,* 64 (January 18, 1976), 3.

[365] "Bishop Bars Sacraments to Backers of Abortion." *National Catholic Reporter,* 11 (April 18, 1975), 1+.

[366] "Bishop Offers Diocesan Aid to Prevent Abortions." *National Catholic Reporter,* 9 (February 23, 1973), 5.

[367] "Bishops of Canada Propose Alternatives to Easier Abortions." *National Catholic Reporter,* 4 (February 14, 1968), 5.

[368] "The Bishops of Colombia for the Defence of Life." *L'Osservatore Romano* (English), no. 15 (419) (April 8, 1976), 8.

[369] "Bishops Draft Abortion Letter." *National Catholic Reporter,* 11 (January 24, 1975), 15.

[370] "Bishops—Illinois. A Statement on Abortion." *Catholic Mind,* 67 (May, 1969), 59-64.

[371] "Bishops Issue Rules on Abortion Laws." *National Catholic Reporter,* 9 (April 27, 1973), 19.

[372] "Bishops May Switch Plan on Abortion Amendments." *National Catholic Reporter,* 11 (October 3, 1975), 5.

[373] "Bishops' Move." *Economist,* 260 (September 11, 1976), 26.

[374] "Bishops of Pakistan on Abortion and Contraception: Joint Pastoral Letter." *L'Osservatore Romano* (English), no. 11 (363) (March 13, 1975), 9-10.

[375] "Bishops—Pennsylvania. In Defense of Human Life." *Catholic Mind,* 69 (January, 1971), 9-11. [This is a statement of the Bishops of Pennsylvania at the time of the 1970 election year, when abortion became an important political issue.]

[376] "The Bishops' Plan for Pro-Life Activities." *America,* 133 (December 27, 1975), 454-55. [This article describes the Bishops' effort to deal with the U.S. Court's decision on abortion. The full text of the Statement is found in *Origins* (N.C. Documentary Service) for December 4, 1975.
Efforts in three directions will be made: 1) to inform and educate the public on abortion issues; 2) to help women who have problem pregnancies or who have had abortions; 3) to secure anti-abortion laws from the departments of government.]

[377] "Bishops' Spokesman Says Next Step Must Be an Amendment." *Our Sunday Visitor,* 63 (March 2, 1975), 3.

[378] "Bishops—Texas. An Open Letter on the Abortion Problem." *Social Justice Review,* 64 (June, 1971), 86-93.

[379] "Black Activists Oppose Abortion." *National Catholic Reporter,* 11 (December 13, 1974), 20.

[380] Black, A. D. "Influence of Moral and Cultural Patterns on the Abortion Problem." National Committee on Maternal Health, Inc. *The Abortion Problem.* Ed. H. C. Taylor (New York: Williams and Wilkins Co., 1944).

[381] Black, E. F. E. "Abortion and Sterilization." *Manitoba Bar News,* 33 (1961), 33.

[382] Blackwood, R. "What are the Father's Rights in Abortions." *Journal of Legal Medicine,* 3(9) (1975), 28-36.

[383] Blaes, S. "Litigation: Preparation and Response." *Hospital Progress Report,* 54 (August, 1973), 70-72+.

[384]Blake, J. "Abortion and Public Opinion: the 1960-1970 Decade." *Science,* 171 (February 12, 1971), 540-49.

[385]Blasi, A. J., Macneil, P. J., and O'Neill, R. "The Relationship Between Abortion Attitudes and Catholic Religiosity." *Social Science,* 50(1) (1975), 34-39.

[386]"Blast and Counter-Blast." *Economist,* 249 (November 24, 1973), 31-32.

[387]Blice, P. "Curran: Theologians on Bishops' Side." *National Catholic Reporter,* 9 (March 2, 1973), 18.

[388]Bloch, S. K. "Occult Pregnancy. A Pilot Study." *Obstetrics and Gynecology,* 48(3) (September, 1976), 365-68.

[389]Bluett, D. "Termination of Pregnancy." *British Medical Journal,* 3 (September 16, 1972), 700.

[390]Bluford, Robert, Jr., and Petres, Robert E. *Unwanted Pregnancy* (New York: Harper and Row, 1973).

[391]Blum, V. "Politicizing the Catholic Community." *Hospital Progress Reports,* 56 (September, 1975), 84-88.

[392]Bogen, I. "Attitudes of Minnesota College Students Toward Abortion." *Pupil Personnel Services Journal,* 3(1) (1973), 17-23.

[393]Bogen, I. "Attitudes of Women Who Had Abortions." *The Journal of Sex Research,* 10(2) (1974), 97-109.

[394]Bognar, Z., and Czeizel, A. "Mortality and Morbidity Associated with Legal Abortions in Hungary, 1960-1973." *American Journal of Public Health,* 66 (June, 1976), 568-75.

[395]Bolognese, Ronald J., and Corson, Stephen L. *Interruption of Pregnancy* (New York: Williams and Wilkens Co., 1975).

[396]Bolt, J. "Abortion and Huntington's Chorea." *British Medical Journal,* 1 (March 30, 1968), 840.

[397]Bolter, S. "The Psychiatrist's Role in Therapeutic Abortion: The Unwitting Accomplice." *American Journal of Psychiatry,* 19 (October, 1962),312.

[398]Bok, S. "Ethical Problems of Abortion." *Hastings Centre Report,* 2 (no. 1) (1974), 33-52. [A central question is whether the life of the fetus should receive the same protection as other lives. Judith Thompson's approach to abortion as cessation of life-support is considered. Bok says that we must abandon the attempt to provide a criterion of personhood. This leads to mistreatment and killing. Other criteria, less dangerous and vague than those connected with humanity, are considered by asking what respect for life ought to protect. Reasons for protecting life are given. In looking at moral distinctions, four considerations are needed: 1) the time in pregnancy; 2) why the pregnancy is unwanted; 3) conflicts between mothers and fathers of the unborn; and 4) alternatives to abortion depending upon whether or not birth prevention is considered before or after conception.]

[399]Bompiani, A. "Medicine and Abortion: Interview by Vatican Radio." *L'Osservatore Romano* (English), no. 13 (261) (March 29, 1973), 4.

[400]Bompiani, A. "What Therapeutic Abortion?" *L'Osservatore Romano* (English), no. 15 (419) (April 8, 1976),9.

[401]Bong Hong, Sung. *Induced Abortion in Seoul, Korea* (Seoul: Dong-a Publishing Company, 1966).

[402]Borman, Nancy. "Harvey Karmen: Savior or Charlatan?" *Majority Report,* 3 (January, 1974), 6.

[403]Bosco, A. "Abortion Tangle in New York." *Marriage and Family Living,* 53 (July, 1971), 28-32+.

[404]Bosworth, N. L., et al. "Abortion Referral Agencies." *Journal of the Kentucky Medical Association,* 70 (October, 1972), 795-96.

[405]Boulas, Stanley H., Preucel, Robert H., and Moore, John H. "Therapeutic Abortion." *Obstetrics and Gynecology,* 19 (February, 1962), 222-227.

[406]Bouma, Donald H. "Abortion in a Changing Social Context." *Birth Control and the Christian.* Ed. W. O. Spitzer and C. L. Saylor (Wheaton, Illinois: Tyndale House, 1969).

[407]Bourne, J. P. "Influences on Health Professionals' Attitudes." *Hospitals,* 46 (July 16, 1972), 80-83.

[408]Bouscaren, A. T. *The Ethics of Ectopic Operations* (Milwaukee: The Bruce Publishing Company, 1944).

[409]Bowman, Elizabeth. "Move to Take up Abortion Amendment Fails." *Congressional Quarterly Weekly Report,* 34 (May 1, 1976), 1032.

[410]Bowman, Elizabeth. "Senate Rejects Anti-Abortion Amendment (key provisions. committee action. floor

action). *Congressional Quarterly Weekly Report,* 33 (April 19, 1975), 814-16.

[411]Bowman, Elizabeth. "Senate Votes Again to Reject Anti-Abortion Amendment by House." *Congressional Quarterly Weekly Report,* 34 (August 28, 1976), 2344-45.

[412]Bowman, Elizabeth, and Rankin, Bob. "Candidates on the Issues: Abortion." *Congressional Quarterly Weekly Report,* 34 (February 28, 1976), 463-66.

[413]Boyce, R. M., et al. "Therapeutic Abortion in A Canadian City." *Canadian Medical Association Journal,* 103 (September 12, 1970), 461-66.

[414]Boydell, C. L. "Public Attitudes Toward Legal Sanctions for Drug and Abortion Offences." *Canadian Journal of Criminology and Corrections,* 13 (1971), 209-32.

[415]Bozell, Leo Brent. "The Life Movement: Quo Vade?" *Triumph,* 9 (January, 1974), 23; (May, 1974), 15.

[416]Bozell, Leo Brent. "On Going to Jail." *Triumph,* 7 (January, 1972), 31; (February, 1972), 21; (March, 1972), 19. [Bozell discusses the possibility of Christians going to jail for their beliefs. He offers three means that might provoke the state.]

[417]Bozell, Leo Brent. "Stop the Death Merchants." *Triumph,* 7 (October, 1972), 19; (November, 1972), 31; (December, 1972), 18-19.

[418]Bozell, Patricia. "The Wages of Pluralism." *Triumph,* 6 (March, 1971), 18-20.

[419]Bracken, M. B. "Abortion Attitudes and Discrepant Behaviour. Some Theoretical Issues." *Health Education Journal,* 32(1) (1973), 4-9.

[420]Bracken, M. B., Grossman, G., Hachamovitch, M., Sussman, D., and Schreir, D. "Abortion Counseling. An Experimental Study of Three Techniques." *American Journal of Obstetrics and Gynecology,* 117(1) (1973), 10-20.

[421]Bracken, M. B., Hachamovitch, M., and Grossman, G. "The Decision to Abort and Psychological Sequelae." *The Journal of Nervous and Mental Disease,* 158(2) (1974), 154-62.

[422]Bracken, M. B., and Kasl, S. V. "First and Repeat Abortions. A Study of Decision Making and Delay." *Journal of Biosocial Science,* 7(4) (1975), 473-91.

[423]Bracken, M. B., and Kasl, S. V. "Psychosocial Correlates of Delayed Decisions to Abort." *Health Education Monographs,* 4(1) (1976), 6-44. 411-436

[424]Brady, David W., and Kemp, Kathleen. "The Supreme Court's Abortion Rulings and Social Change." *Social Science Quarterly,* 57 (December, 1976), 535-40. [The impact on the abortion policies of hospitals in Harris County (Houston) Texas is discussed.]

[425]Braestrup, A. "Teen-Age Pregnancies in Denmark, 1940-71." *Journal of Biosocial Science,* 6(4) (October, 1974), 741-45.

[426]Bragonier, J. R., et al. "The Experience of Two County Hospitals in Implementation of Therapeutic Abortion." *Clinical Obstetrics and Gynecology,* 14 (December, 1971), 1237-42.

[427]Bragonier, J. R., et al. "Preabortion Evaluation: Selection of Patients for Psychiatric Referral." *Clinical Obstetrics and Gynecology,* 14 (December, 1971), 1263-70.

[428]Branch, B. N., et al. "The Alternative Abortion." *Medical Annals of the District of Columbia,* 40 (November, 1971), 691-96.

[429]Brandmeyer, G. "Politics & Abortion." *Commonweal,* 103 (July 2, 1976), 432-33. [This article describes the election campaign of Ellen McCormack—the right to life advocate in the 1976 presidential election.]

[430]Brandt, R. B. "The Morality of Abortion." *The Monist,* 56 (October, 1972), 502-26.

[431]Branson, H. "Nurses Talk About Abortion." *American Journal of Nursing,* 72 (January, 1972), 106-09.

[432]Brashear, D. B. "Abortion Counseling." *The Family Coordinator,* 22(4) (1973), 429-35.

[433]Brautigan, Richard. *The Abortion* (London: Pan Books, Ltd., 1974).

[434]Bray, P. N. "Therapeutic Abortion: Incidence and Indications in Minnesota." *Minnesota Medicine,* 50 (January, 1967), 129-36.

[435]Breig, J. "Modest Proposal for Ending Poverty and War." *Worldview,* 17 (February, 1974), 46-47.

[436]Breig, J. "Religious Liberty and Abortion." *Ave Maria,* 103 (April 23, 1966), 20.

[437]Breig, J. "Telling it Like it is About Abortion." *Our Sunday Visitor*, 62 (August 26, 1973), 1+.

[438]Breitenecker, Leopold and Rudiger. "Abortion in the German-Speaking Countries of Europe." *Abortion and the Law*. Ed. David T. Smith (Cleveland: Western Reserve University Press, 1967).

[439]Brennan, John. "The Velvet Glove or the Iron Fist?" *Linacre Quarterly*, 40 (May, 1973), 128-32. [This article concerns the Ethical and Religious Directives for Catholic Health Facilities. These Directives from the Catholic bishops, approved in 1971, denounce contraception, sterilization, and abortion. The right of a hospital as an entity to follow its own religious beliefs is presented. "Pluralism" is taken to be an enemy.
An inevitable encounter between Catholic women and the bishops is pointed out. If sterilization is morally acceptable month by month by oral contraceptives for temporary reasons, then is it possible to sterilize permanently for permanent reasons? The bishops can encourage women to attend a Billings type ovulation-mucus-temperature class (the velvet glove), or excommunicate any woman or doctor who participates in sterilization (iron fist).]

[440]Brennan, W. "Abortion: Missouri HB 1470." *Social Justice Review*, 65 (July-August, 1972), 129-32.

[441]Brennan, W. "Should Your Tax Dollars Pay for Abortions and Fetal Research?" *Liguorian*, 63 (March, 1975), 8-12.

[442]Brennan, W. "The Vanishing Protectors." *Social Justice Review*, 66 (November, 1973), 239-44.

[443]Brennan, William C. "Abortion and the Techniques of Neutralization." *Journal of Health and Social Behaviour*, 15(4) (December, 1974), 358-65.

[444]Brenner, E. J. "The Beilenson Bill: Mercy or Murder?" *The Catholic Voice* (March 24, 1966).

[445]Brenner, P. H., et al. "Therapeutic Abortions. A Review of 567 Cases." *California Medicine*, 115 (July, 1971), 20-27.

[446]Breslin, John B. "Birthright-Alternative to Abortion." *America*, 125 (September 4, 1971), 116-19. [John Breslin describes the origin and organization of Birthright. The purpose of Birthright is to offer an opportunity for a woman to have her baby rather than an abortion. Each centre works with doctors, and welfare agencies. They do not associate themselves particularly with any one religious affiliation, the exception being New York where the program was launched by Cardinal Terrance Cooke.
Breslin notes that some people question the stand of the Roman Catholic Church against abortion when the bishops did not outrightly condemn the Vietnamese War.]

[447]Breslow, Lester. "Abortion: The Case for Repeal." Paper presented to the First National Conference on Abortion Laws, Chicago, February 15, 1969.

[448]Bretherton, R. C. "The Case for Abortion Law Reform." *Medical Journal of Australia*, 2 (October 25, 1969), 860-62.

[449]Brett, P., et al. "A Statement on Abortion in Victoria." *Medical Journal of Australia*, 2 (November 6, 1971), 982-83.

[450]Brewer, Colin. "Incidence of Post-Abortion Psychosis: A Prospective Study." *British Medical Journal*, 6059 (February 19, 1977), 476-77.

[451]Brewer, H. "Abortion and Syphilis." *Eugenics Review*, 57 (September, 1965), 153-54.

[452]Brian, Lord. "Medical Issues in Abortion Law Reform," *British Medical Journal*, I (March, 1966), 727.

[453]Bridwell, Margaret, and Tinnan, Louise W. "Abortion Referral in a Large College Health Service." *Journal of the American Medical Women's Association*, 27 (August, 1972), 420. [In July 1970, a full time gynecologist joined the staff of the Student Health Service of the University of Maryland at College Park. Since then, abortion referrals and follow-ups have been done. The average referral is ten a week. Abortion counseling, psychological guidance and post-abortion care can be done successfully within the confines of a student health service.]

[454]Briggs, E., et al. "Termination of Pregnancy in the Unmarried." *Scottish Medical Journal*, 17 (December, 1972), 399-400.

[455]British Medical Association Committee on Therapeutic Abortion. "Indications for Termination of Pregnancy." *British Medical Journal*, I (January 20, 1968), 33.

[456]"British Policy on Therapeutic Abortion." Report of the Royal Medi-

co-Psychological Association June 1966. *Journal of American Medical Association,* 199 (January 16, 1967), 199-200.

[457]Broderick, A. "A Constitutional Lawyer Looks at the *Roe-Doe* Decisions." *Jurist,* 33 (1973), 124-34. [The author sees his assignment as demonstrating that the Supreme Court decisions in the *Roe-Doe* case were without appropriate foundation in law and is "an improvident and extravagant exercise" of "raw judicial power." He examines how the Court explained itself, the medical evidence before the Court, and the distortions of history. Suggestions are offered as to the most probable course of action. Broderick believes that the opinion on an amendment is so diverse that it is very unlikely to come about. He is convinced that the internal defectiveness of the decision will produce the answer. The Supreme Court itself may reverse its decision. It seems necessary to the author to "limit the extent of the Supreme" Court's "finality." He suggests that it be possible for Congress to override, by majority of both Houses, a decision of the court which declared unconstitutional legislation of several states on 14th Amendment grounds.]

[458]Brodie, D. W. "New Biology and the Prenatal Child." *Journal of Family Law,* 9 (1970), 391.

[459]Brody, Baruch A. "Abortion and the Law." *Journal of Philosophy,* 68 (June 17, 1971), 357-68. [Brody offers new reasons advocating the distinction between the question of the morality of abortion and the question of legalizing abortion. However, he attempts to show that, given the moral claim about abortion, there is no reason to legalize abortions.]

[460]Brody, Baruch A. "Abortion and the Sanctity of Human Life." *American Philosophical Quarterly,* 10 (April, 1973), 133-40. [The author raises the following question: If the fetus is a human being, with all the rights that human beings are entitled to, are there any cases in which abortion would be morally permissible? Cases in which the mother's life is threatened are considered, and the author argues that, even in these cases, abortion is not morally permissible (with one exception).]

[461]Brody, Baruch A. *Abortion and the Sanctity of Human Life: A Philosophical View* (Boston: M.I.T. Press, 1976).

[462]Brody, Baruch A. "Thomson on Abortion." *Philosophy and Public Affairs,* 1 (no. 3) (Spring, 1972), 335-44. [Brody is responding to Judith Jarvis Thomson's article, "In Defense of Abortion" (*Philosophy and Public Affairs,* 1 [no. 1] [February, 1971], 47-66). Brody claims that Thomson has not taken sufficient account of the distinction between a duty to save X's life and a duty not to take life. This distinction is carefully considered and if it is true, as Thomson grants, that a fetus is a human being with human rights, then abortion is wrong even if performed to save a woman's life, except when both the mother and fetus would die without abortion.]

[463]Brody, H., *et al.* "Therapeutic Abortion: A Prospective Study." *American Journal of Obstetrics and Gynecology* I, 109 (February 1, 1971), 347-53.

[464]Broeman, P., *et al.* "Therapeutic Abortion Practices in Chicago Hospitals—Vagueness, Variation, and Violation of the Law." *Law and Social Order,* 1971 (1971), 757.

[465]Brooke, C. "Legalized Abortion: Reprint from The *Missoulian* January 31, 1971." *Catholic Mind,* 70 (May, 1972), 24-34. [Dr. Brooke begins his article with a description of the growth of the fetus through its various stages. He goes on to provide references to various court cases which demonstrate that the fetus does have legal rights. The law has recognized a fetus to be a child before it is born; the fetus is human and can be protected in the constitutional sense; and finally, the fetus is not just a piece of tissue but really human life.]

[466]Brooke, P. S. "Letter: Abortion." *New Zealand Medical Journal,* 79 (June 12, 1974), 1037.

[467]Brooke, E. "Political and Economic Factor." *Journal of Biosocial Science,* 1 (July, 1969), 297-305.

[468]Brown, H. "An Evangelical Looks at the Abortion Phenomenon." *America,* 135 (September 25, 1976), 161-64. [Harold Brown asserts that Protestantism, to the extent that it is biblical and not habitual, holds the doctrine that man is created in the image of God, and therefore, any destruction of innocent human life, including abortion, is unacceptable.

He reminds the Catholic readers that the abortion issue may make ecumenical issues more difficult, nevertheless, true ecumenism brings together, not just ecclesiastical bureaucracy, but, the people of God.

Also, he goes on to say that Protestants will not be moved by Catholics but by their own pastors and

469-
494

teachers, and their own biblical reasons.]

[469]Brown, J. "Abortion and Guffaws for Chastity." *New England Journal of Medicine,* 281 (July 31, 1969),
276.

[470]Brown, L. R., and Newland, K.
"Abortion Liberalization. A Worldwide
Trend." *The Futurist,* 10(3) (1976),
140-43.

[471]Brown, N., et al. *Abortion:
Women's Fight for the Right to Choose*
(New York: Pathfinder Press, Inc.,
May, 1977).

[472]Brown, N., et al. "The Preservation of Life." *Journal of the American Medical Association,* 211 (January
5, 1970), 76-82.

[473]Browne, F. W. S. "The Right of
Abortion." *Journal of Sex Education,*
5 (1952).

[474]Brungs, Robert. "Danger of
Abortion." *St. Louis Review* (January
16, 1970), 11.

[475]Brunner, E. K., and Newton, L.
"Abortions in Relation to Viable
Births in 10,809 Pregnancies." *American Journal of Obstetrics and Gynecology,* 38 (1939), 82.

[476]Bryant, M. David. "State Legislation on Abortion After *Roe v. Wade:*
Selected Constitutional Issues." *American Journal of Law and Medicine,* 2
(Summer, 1976), 101-32.

[477]Buckle, A. E., et al. "Implementation of the Abortion Act: Report
on a Year's Working of Abortion Clinics and Operating Sessions." *British
Medical Journal,* 3 (August 12, 1972),
381-84.

[478]"Buckley and Hatfield Lead
Fight for Anti-Abortion Measure in
Senate." *National Catholic Reporter,*
9 (June 8, 1973), 21.

[479]Buckley, J. "Catholic Alternatives Center Open to Counsel on Birth
Control." *National Catholic Reporter,*
13 (November 5, 1976), 6.

[480]Buckley, W. "The Abortion Decision: Condensed from a Washington
Star Syndicate Feature, 1973." *Catholic Digest,* 37 (May, 1973), 41-42.

[481]Bunson, M. "Dissent '76: Amendment Not Answer to Abortion." il. *National Catholic Reporter,* 12 (March
26, 1976), 5.

[482]Bunson, M. "The Fight for Life:
It's up to You: Some Practical Guide-

lines to Make your Voice Heard."
ports. *Our Sunday Visitor,* 64 (May 2,
1976), 1+.

[483]Bunson, M. "How Abortion
Spread to the Mideast and the Orient."
Our Sunday Visitor, 65 (June 27,
1976), 1+.

[484]Bunson, M. "Media Manipula-
tion Promotes World Abortion Craze."
Our Sunday Visitor, 65 (June 30,
1976), 1+.

[485]Bunson, M. "A New Set of Rules
for the Abortion Fight." *Our Sunday
Visitor,* 65 (August 17, 1975), 1+.

[486]Bunson, M. "They Exploded the
Abortion Myth." *Our Sunday Visitor,*
64 (January 18, 1976), 1+.

[487]Bunson, M. "U.S. Money Backs
International Abortion Cartel." *Our
Sunday Visitor,* 65 (June 13, 1976), 1+.

[488]Burch, Thomas K. "Induced
Abortion in Japan Under the Eugenic
Protection Law of 1948." *Eugenics
Quarterly,* 2 (September, 1955), 140-
51.

[489]Burch, Thomas K. "Patterns of
Induced Abortion and Their Socio-Moral
Implications in Postwar Japan." *So-
cial Compass,* 3 (1955), 178-188.

[490]Burge, E. S. "The Relationship of Threatened Abortion to Fetal
Abnormalities." *American Journal of
Obstetrics and Gynecology,* 61 (March,
1951), 603.

[491]"Burger Ruling Delays Court
Abortion Decision." *National Catholic Reporter,* 8 (July 21, 1972), 3.

[492]Burke, C. "Abortion: Law, Ethics and the Value of Life." *Manchester Medical Gazette,* 49 (July, 1970),
4-9.

[493]Burke, C. "The Abortion Movement: Reprint from Seido Foundation,
Catholic Position Paper Published in
Japan." *L'Osservatore Romano* (English), no. 19 (371) (May 9, 1975), 8-
11.

[494]Burke, W. "Abortion and the
Psychiatrist." *Homiletic and Pastoral Review,* 71 (December, 1970), 199-
207. [The purpose of the article is
to examine one professional group,
the psychiatrists criteria for recom-
mending therapeutic abortion. Burke
concludes that psychiatrists when
polled, favour the liberalization of
therapeutic abortion and yet he suggests that the clinical evidence
seems to point to the adverse psychological effects of this procedure.

Burke points out that there are really no psychiatric indications for therapeutic abortion. Psychiatrists have substituted socio-economic reasons in place of psychiatric ones as a justification for therapeutic abortion.]

[495]Burkman, R. T., et al. "University Abortion Programs: One Year Later." American Journal of Obstetrics and Gynecology, 119 (May 1, 1974), 131-36.

[496]Burnell, George M., et al. "Post-Abortion Therapy." American Journal of Psychiatry, 129 (August, 1972), 220-23.

[497]Burnhill, M. S. "Humane Abortion Services. A Revolution in Human Rights and the Delivery of a Medical Service." Mount Sinai Journal of Medicine, New York, 42(5) (1975), 431-38.

[498]Burns, W. A. "Rubella and Abortion Laws." Medico-Legal Bulletin, 208 (August, 1970), 1-7.

[499]Busby, David F. "Rape, Incest and Multiple Illegitimacy as Indications for Therapeutic Abortion." Birth Control and the Christian. Ed. W. O. Spitzer and C. L. Saylor (Wheaton, Illinois: Tyndale House, 1969).

[500]Buss, Martin. "The Beginning of Human Life as an Ethical Problem." Journal of Religion, 47 (July, 1967), 244-55. [This article traces the history of the abortion discussion. The arguments for and against abortion are offered. The author opts for more liberalized abortion laws as an indication of the Christian concern for personal relationships in faith, creative reason, and love.]

[501]Butler, C. W. "Psychiatric Indications for Therapeutic Abortion." Southern Medical Journal, 63 (June, 1970), 647-50.

[502]Butler, Patricia. "The Right to Abortion Under Medicaid." Clearinghouse Review, 7 (April, 1974), 713-20. [Even though the woman's right to have an abortion was established by the Supreme Court's decision, several states refuse to reimburse an abortion under Medicaid. The author discusses due process and equal protection rights of Medicaid recipients seeking abortions. The federal statutory requirements of states to provide abortions without limitation under Medicaid are also considered.]

[503]Butts, R. Y., and Sporakowski, M. J. "Unwed Pregnancy Decisions. Some Background Factors." The Journal of Sex Research, 10(2) (1974), 110-17.

[504]Buxton, C. L. "One Doctor's Opinion of Abortion Laws." American Journal of Nursing, 68 (May, 1968), 1026-28. 495-514

[506]Bygdeman, M., et al. "Early Abortion in the Human." Annals of the New York Academy of Science, 180 (April 30, 1971), 473-82.

[507]Byrn, Robert M. "Abortion Amendments: Policy in the Light of Precedent." St. Louis University Law Journal, 18 (Spring, 1974), 380-406.

[508]Byrn, Robert M. "Abortion: A Legal View." Commonweal, 85 (1967), 679-680.

[509]Byrn, Robert M. "Abortion-On-Demand: Whose Morality?" Notre Dame Lawyer, 46 (Fall, 1970), 5.

[510]Byrn, Robert M. "Abortion in Perspective." Duquesne University Law Review, 5 (Winter, 1966), 125.

[511]Byrn, Robert M. "The Abortion Question: A Nonsectarian Approach." Catholic Lawyer, 11 (Autumn, 1965), 316-22. [The author discusses the medical, eugenic, emotional and legal appeals for abortion. He views abortion as the deliberate destruction of innocent human life. The liberalization movement is based upon an ethic which is alien to jurisprudence and at odds with the general trend of law.]

[512]Byrn, Robert M. "American Tragedy: The Supreme Court on Abortion." Fordham Law Review, 41 (May, 1973), 807.

[513]Byrn, Robert M. "Confronting Objections to an Anti-Abortion Amendment." America, 134 (June 19, 1976), 529-34. [The author, a lawyer, examines four objections to a Federal amendment voiced by certain Catholics. These are: 1) we do not wish to impose our views on others; 2) restrictive abortion laws discriminate against the poor because the rich always find ways to evade the law; 3) the Church has not opposed other legalized killing, therefore, we will not give credence to its opposition to abortion; 4) a constitutional amendment is not the answer. The author, after considering Wade's legal basis, does find that they are unpersuasive.

[514]Byrn, Robert M. "Demythologizing Abortion Reform." Catholic Lawyer, 14 (Summer, 1968), 180-189. [The author attempts to dispel the following myths: the legal myth that the fetus is not a human being; the statistical myth that there are 1,000,000 illegal abortions in the U.S. annually;

515–
534
the theological myth that only Catholics oppose abortion; the clinical myth that induced abortion is clean and antiseptic; and the socio-familial myth that abortion is a technique of birth control.]

[515]Byrn, Robert M. "The Future in America." *America,* 117 (December 9, 1967), 710. [The author traces the rise of the movement for abortion-on-demand in America. He sees that the real issues against abortion are confused by non-issues.]

[516]Byrn, Robert M. "Goodbye to the Judeo-Christian Era in Law." *America,* 128 (June 3, 1973), 511-14. [Byrn states his thesis explicitly. The U. S. Supreme Court decision which pulled down Texas' restrictive abortion statute, ended the Judeo-Christian era in law. In its place, a quality-of-life ethic was adopted. Byrn sees it as going from Judeo-Christian to IK (story of people who do their own thing for their own advantage). He goes on to say that the Judeo-Christian ethic will not dominate the conscience of individuals unless there is a constitutional amendment to mandate the right to life for all innocent human beings.]

[517]Byrn, Robert M. "The New Jurisprudence." *Journal of the American Medical Association,* 236(4) (July 26, 1976), 359-60.

[518]Byrn, Robert M. "Up From Abortion." *Triumph,* 4 (November, 1969), 20-21.

[519]Byrn, Robert M. "*Wade* and *Bolton:* Fundamental Legal Errors and Dangerous Implications; Reprint from *Fordham Law Review,* 41 (1973)." *Catholic Lawyer,* 19 (Fall, 1973), 243-50. [The author presents the fundamental errors in general, the historical errors and the human life errors.
He sees the implications of the decision as compulsory abortion and involuntary euthanasia.]

[520]Byrne, Richard P. "Critical Look at Legalized Abortion." *Los Angeles Bar Bulletin,* 41 (May, 1966), 320.

[521]Byrne, Richard P. "What are the Rights of the Unborn Child?" *Marriage and Family Living,* 49 (February, 1967), 16-22.

[522]Caffarra, C. "The Moral Problem of Abortion; Reprint from *Medicina e Morale* (1, 1975)." *L'Osservatore Romano* (English), no. 44 (396) (October 30, 1975), 10-11.

[523]Calderone, Mary S. "Illegal Abortion as a Public Health Problem." *American Journal of Public Health,* 50 (July, 1960), 948.

[524]Caldwell, J. "A Voice in the Wilderness." *North Carolina Medical Journal,* 32 (November, 1971), 470-71.

[525]Calef, V. "The Hostility of Parents to Children. Some Notes on Infertility, Child Abuse, and Abortion." *International Journal of Psychoanalytic Psychotherapy,* , 1(1) (1972), 76-96.

[526]Calef, V. "The Unconscious Fantasy of Infanticide Manifested in Resistance." *Journal of the American Psychoanalytic Association,* 16 (October, 1968), 697-710.

[527]*California Committee on Therapeutic Abortion, Abortion and the Unwanted Child.* Ed. Carl Reiterman (New York: Springer Publishers, 1971).

[528]California: Population Study Commission. Report to the Governor ('67), 108 p., 2151 Berkeley Way, Berkeley, California 94704. [This includes recommendations regarding family planning services in the state and local community.]

[529]"California Therapeutic Abortion Act." *Hastings Law Journal,* 19 (November, 1967), 242.

[530]"California's 1967 Therapeutic Abortion Act: Abridging a Fundamental Right to Abortion." *Pacific Law Journal,* 2 (January, 1971), 186.

[531]Callahan, Daniel. *Abortion: Law, Choice and Morality* (New York: Macmillan Publishing Company, Inc., 1970). [This book examines many aspects of the abortion question such as the maternal and fetal indications and the legal and moral arguments. He makes recommendations for "implementing a moral policy."]

[532]Callahan, Danial. "Abortion: Thinking and Experiencing." *Christianity and Crisis,* 32 (January 8, 1973), 295-98.

[533]Callahan, Danial. "The New Setting of Abortion Decisions." *Ecumenists,* 8 (May-June, 1970), 65-68. [The author examines the Christian moral stand allowing the issue to be defined in civil rights terms. He proposes that the Church press for the moral dimension with increased social responsibility. Abortion should not be made an instrument of public policy.]

[534]Callahan, Danial. "Paging the Unbandaged." *America,* 123 (September

12, 1970), 143. [This is a reply to the critiques put forward by Eugene Diamond and Richard McCormick regarding *Abortion, Law, Choice and Morality* (New York: Macmillan Publishing Company, Inc., 1970).]

[535]Callahan, Danial. "The Sanctity of Life." *The Religious Situation* (Boston: Beacon Press, 1969). Also in *Updating Life and Death*. Ed. Donald Cutler (Boston: Beacon Press, 1969). [Two understandings of the "sanctity of life" are offered, the Christian view and the experiential approach. An impasse is reached between the two, resulting from a critique of each other. The "sanctity of life" is discussed as an abstract principle, continuing to point out the system of rules which emerge.]

[536]Camenisch, Paul F. "Abortion: For the Fetus's Own Sake?" *Hastings Centre Report*, 6 (April, 1976), 38-41.

[537]Cameron, P., and Tichenor, J. C. "The Swedish—Children Born to Women Denied Abortion—Study. A Radical Criticism." *Psychological Reports*, 39(2) (1976), 391-94.

[538]Campbell, J. "Abortion in Russia." *Eugenic Review*, 57 (September, 1965), 107-08.

[539]"The Canadian Medical Association Resolutions on Abortion," editorial. *Canadian Medical Association Journal*, 105 (September 4, 1971), 441.

[540]"CMA Policy on Abortion." *Canadian Medical Association Journal*, 111(9) (November 2, 1974), 900, 902, 905.

[541]Canavan, F. "The Church's Right to Speak on Public Issues." *Catholic Mind*, 65 (April, 1967), 13-16.

[542]Caplan, G. "Disturbances of Mother-Child Relations by Unsuccessful Attempts at Abortion." *Mental Hygiene*, 38 (1954), 67.

[543]Caprile, G. "Facts and Evils of Free Abortions." *L'Osservatore Romano* (English), no. 21 (425) (May 20, 1976), 5+. Reprinted from 127 *Civiltà Cattolica* (March 6, 1976), 463.

[544]Caprile, G. "Vote of Austrian Parliament on the Matter of Abortion." *L'Osservatore Romano* (English), no. 5 (305) (January 31, 1974), 9.

[545]"Cardinal Cooke Condemns State's Abortion Law." *L'Osservatore Romano* (English), no. 53 (144) (December 31, 1970), 11.

[546]Carlson, John. "Three Levels of Discussion About Abortion." *Catholic Mind*, 74 (November, 1976), 22-29. Also in *Dimension*, 8 (Spring, 1976), 37-45. [The author sets out to help people who wish to discuss abortion in a constructive way. He presents the abortion discussion at three levels. He explains what is the type of thought which can be conveyed: 1) factual level. These questions are not moral ones, but their answers may be relevant to arrive at a moral position. Example: at what point is fetal life to be regarded as human life?; 2) normative level: Norms for Action. This level is concerned about principles, how do we determine what is a good and bad action. Example: applying the most appropriate moral principle(s), what conclusion does one reach concerning the justifiability of abortion?; 3) Meta-Ethical Level: the Philosophical Context. The concerns of this level are a more reflective sort about the sphere of morality. One could ask if a moral claim could ever be considered "valid", or does some relativism characterize the moral sphere. Example: is the moral issue of abortion one on which everyone can be expected to agree?]

[547]Carlton, M. A., *et al.* "The Immediate Morbidity of Therapeutic Abortion." *Medical Journal of Australia*, 2 (December 5, 1970), 1071-74.

[548]Carmen, Arlene, and Moody, Howard. *Abortion Counselling and Social Change* (Valley Forge, Pa.: Judson Press, 1973).

[549]Carne, Stuart. "Abortion and the Health Services—The General Practitioner." *Abortion in Britain* (London: Pitman Medical Publishing Company, 1967).

[550]Carney, J. "The Right to Life: Pastoral Letter." *L'Osservatore Romano* (English), no. 32 (280) (August 9, 1973), 4+.

[551]Caron, Wilfred R. "New York Abortion Reform—A Critique." *Catholic Lawyer*, 14 (Summer, 1968), 199-213. [This discusses the report of the Committee on Public Affairs to the Queen's Chapter of the Catholic Lawyers Guild of the Diocese of Brooklyn, which looks at the New York Abortion Bill, not from the "Catholic" position, but as it merits as a legislative proposal.]

[552]Carr, A. "Abortion Used as Birth Control." *Homelitic and Pastoral Review*, 67 (March, 1967), 523-25.

[553]Carr, A. "Church's Doctrinal Decisions on Abortion." *Homelitic and Pastoral Review*, 67 (April, 1967),

554-
579

610-11. [The author replies to a question regarding the Church's doctrinal stand on abortion. The author cites the natural law argument, the Code of Canon Law, Pius XI's *Casti Conubi* and Pius XII's allocution in October 1952.]

[554]Carr, A. "Pressure to Change Abortion Laws." *Homelitic and Pastoral Review,* 67 (May, 1967), 702-04. [Commenting on the state of the abortion question, the author cites the section of the American Law Institute's Model Penal Code regarding justifiable and unjustifiable abortion, pressure of the mass media and the results of a survey of 151 dioceses by Fr. James T. McHugh NCC's Family Life Bureau.]

[555]Carrier, L. S. "Abortion and the Right to Life." *Social Theory and Practice,* 3 (Fall, 1975), 381-401.

[556]Carroll, C. "The Human Person: Experimental Laboratory or Privileged Sanctuary?" *Hospital Progress,* 52 (June, 1971), 34-41.

[557]Carruthers, G. "Letter: The Morgentaler Case." *Canadian Medical Association Journal,* 113(9) (November 8, 1975), 818.

[558]Carter, C. O. "Legal Abortion —Eugenic Aspects." *Abortion in Britain* (London: Pitman Medical Publishing Company, 1966).

[559]"Carter Opposed to Abortion but not for an Amendment." *Our Sunday Visitor,* 65 (August 29, 1976), 1.

[560]"Carter Says his Abortion Stand Same as Platform's." *Our Sunday Visitor,* 65 (August 1, 1976), 1.

[562]Cartwright, A., et al. "General Practitioners and Abortion. Evidence to the Committee on the Working of the Abortion Act." *Journal of the Royal College of General Practitioners,* 22 (August, 1972), Suppl. 1 (August, 1972), 1-24.

[563]Casady, M. "Abortion. No Lasting Emotional Scars." *Psychology Today,* 8(6) (1974), 148-49.

[564]"Case Developments: Abortion: Medicaid's Unwanted Child?" *Women's Rights Law Reporter,* 3 (September, 1975), 22-27.

[565]"Case Developments: Teachers: Discrimination Against Unwed Mothers." *"Women's Rights Law Reporter,* 3 (September, 1975), 28-33.

[566]"Case of Abortion." *Journal of Urban Law,* 52 (November, 1974), 277-338.

[567]"Case Study: The Unwanted Child: Caring for a Fetus Born Alive After an Abortion." *Hastings Center Report,* 6 (October, 1976), 10-14.

[568]Casey, R. "Bishops Condemn Abortion Decision." *National Catholic Reporter,* 9 (February 23, 1973), 1-2.

[569]Casey, R. "Bishops Encouraged by Ford Abortion Stand." *National Catholic Reporter,* 12 (September 17, 1976), 1-2.

[570]Casey, R. "Congress Faces Abortion Battle." *National Catholic Reporter,* 9 (August 3, 1973), 1+.

[571]Casey, R. "Edelin Says Jury in Boston Biased." *National Catholic Reporter,* 11 (February 28, 1975), 1+.

[572]Casey, R. "Five Doctors Indicted on Abortion Offenses." *National Catholic Reporter,* 10 (April 26, 1974), 1+.

[573]Casey, R. "High Court Rates Privacy Over Fetus." *National Catholic Reporter,* 9 (February 2, 1973), 1+.

[574]Casey, R. "St. Louis Action Tops in Fight Against Abortion." *National Catholic Reporter,* 12 (March 26, 1976), 1-2+.

[575]Casey, R. "Whistle-Stop: Abortion Out as Top National Issue." *National Catholic Reporter,* 12 (October 1, 1976), 3.

[576]Castelli, J. "Anti-Abortion, the Bishops and the Crusaders." *America,* 134 (May 22, 1976), 442-44. [Castelli's thesis states that the bishops are anti-abortion moderates. If this is the case, then he sees three things resulting: 1) passage of an amendment remains unlikely as long as such division continues; 2) the bishops are criticized for the actions and attitudes of others; 3) the bishops, in backing away from the image of abortion as a "Catholic issue," have helped raise the visibility of many whose handling of the issue is less responsible than their own.

[577]Castelli, J. "Catholic Left Torn on Abortion." *National Catholic Reporter,* 8 (July 21, 1972), 6.

[578]Castelli, J. "Catholic Member Offers Dissent on Fetal Rule." *Our Sunday Visitor,* 64 (June 8, 1975), 3.

[579]Castelli, J. "Family Planning Abortions Being Considered by HEW." *Our Sunday Visitor,* 64 (October 26, 1975), 1.

[580]Castelli, J. "Fight on Abortion Pushes Church on Rights Issues." *National Catholic Reporter,* 10 (January 25, 1974), 1+.

[581]Castelli, J. "Justice Byron White Gives Dissent on Abortion Cases." *Our Sunday Visitor,* 65 (July 18, 1976), 3.

[582]Castelli, J. "Pro-Lifers Will Challenge Democratic Abortion Plank." *Our Sunday Visitor,* 65 (July 11, 1976), 1.

[583]Castelli, J. "U.S. Catholic Conference Files Brief Asking Supreme Court Give Unborn Legal Protection." *Our Sunday Visitor,* 64 (January 25, 1976), 3.

[584]Castonguay, Paul R. "The 14th Amendment and Human Life." *America,* 126 (April 15, 1972), 400. [Any living thing ascribed to a species is a member of that species, therefore human life begins at conception.]

[585]Cates, W. Jr., and Rochat, R. W. "Illegal Abortions in the United States. 1972-1974." *Family Planning Perspectives,* 8(2) (1976), 86-90.

[586]"A Catholic Abortion." *Triumph,* 6 (April, 1971), 7-12.

[587]"Catholics and Abortion." *Commonweal,* 100 (May 31, 1974), 299-300. [This editorial suggests that it is necessary for Catholics to deal with the different views of others, such as the Jews of various theological outlooks and committed Christians of other denominations. It is a vain hope to procure a total legal ban on abortion. By working together, it may be possible to obtain legislation opposed to wholesale abortion and would permit abortion only for serious cases.]

[588]"Catholics Attack Abortion Decision." *National Catholic Reporter,* 9 (February 2, 1973), 3-4.

[589]"The Catholic Burden." *Triumph,* 8 (May, 1973), 45.

[590]"Catholic Doctors and Abortion Bills." *Social Justice Review,* 60 (November, 1967), 243.

[591]"Catholic Hospitals Won't Allow Abortions." *National Catholic Reporter,* 9 (February 2, 1973), 4.

[592]"The Catholic Interest." *Triumph,* 8 (November, 1973), 15.

[593]"The Catholic Interest." *Triumph,* 9 (January, 1974), 11.

[594]"Catholic League Charges Carter Endorsed Abortion." *Our Sunday Visitor,* 65 (September 19, 1976), 2.

[595]"Catholic League Supports Right of Doctors to Act in Harmony with their Consciences." ports. *Our Sunday Visitor,* 64 (August 3, 1975), 1.

[596]"Catholic Peace Fellowship Statement on Abortion." *Catholic Mind,* 73 (February, 1975), 7-8. [Protest against the Supreme Court decisions on *Roe v. Wade* and *Doe v. Bolton* is voiced.]

[597]"Cause of Action for 'Wrongful Life': A Suggested Analysis." *Minnesota Law Review,* 55 (November, 1970), 58.

[598]Cavadino, Paul. "Illegal Abortions and the Abortion Act of 1967." *British Journal of Criminology,* 16 (January, 1976), 63-67.

[599]Cavanagh, D. "Legalized Abortion: The Conscience Clause and Coercion." *Hospital Progress,* 52 (August, 1971), 86-90.

[600]Cavanagh, D. "Reader's Digest and the Debate Over Abortion." ports. *Our Sunday Visitor,* 63 (September 22, 1974), 1+.

[601]Cavanagh, D. "Reforming the Abortion Laws: A Doctor Looks at the Case." *America,* 122 (April 18, 1970), 406-11. Also in *Linacre Quarterly,* 37 (August, 1970), 155-65. [This article examines the Missouri abortion law reform from a medical-statistical standpoint.]

[602]Cerling, C. E., Jr. "Abortion and Contraception in Scripture." *Christian Scholar's Review,* 2 (no. 1) (1971), 42-58.

[603]Cernock, Anton. "Authorizations for Interruption of Pregnancy in Czechoslovakia: Study of Their Effects and Consequences." *Gynaecologia,* 160 (Prague, 1965), 293.

[604]Cernock, Anton. "Experiences in Czechoslovakia with the Effects and Consequences of Legalized Artificial Termination of Pregnancy." Unpublished paper delivered at United Nations World Population Conference, Belgrade, August 10-September 10, 1965.

[605]Cernock, Anton. "Social and Medical Aspects of Legal Abortion in Czechoslovakia." Paper presented to the Second Conference on Fertility and Contraception, State University of New York, Buffalo, October 31-November 1, 1966.

[606]"Certification of Rape Under

607–
630 Colorado Abortion Statute." *University of Colorado Law Review*, 42 (May, 1970), 121.

[607]Chamberlain, G. "The Abortion Debate is Revealing our Values." *New Catholic World*, 215 (September-October, 1972), 206–08. [The author sees the abortion issue as part of the expanse of "life" issues (i.e., capital punishment, Vietnam, etc.) He sees a shift from the "life" issues to the "quality of life" issue. He points to the necessity of spiritual growth in society wherein various services are provided for the mother and children. These problems offer the opportunity for genuine growth.]

[608]Chamberlain, G. "Contraception or Abortion?" *Royal Society Health Journal*, 92 (August, 1972), 191–94.

[609]Chamberlain, G., et al. "A Problem with Prematurity." *Journal of the American Medical Association*, 203 (January 22, 1968), 304.

[610]Chamblee, R. "Letter to a United States Senator." *Our Sunday Visitor*, 63 (June 23, 1974), 1+.

[611]Chand, Amir. "Abortion for Family Planning." *Journal of the Indian Medical Association*, 50 (April 16, 1968), 383–84.

[612]Chand, Amir. "Legalizing Abortion for Birth Control." *Journal of the Indian Medical Association*, 45 (July 15, 1965), 95. [This doctor, after examining the high rate of repeated abortion in Japan, concludes that India should not attempt to liberalize abortion laws for controlling the population.]

[613]Chandler, R. "New Look at Abortion (International Conference on Abortion, Washington, D.C., 1967)." *Christianity Today*, 11 (September 29, 1957), 28–30.

[614]Chandrasekhar, Sripati. *Abortion in a Crowded World: The Problem of Abortion with Special Reference to India*. John Danz Lecture Series (Seattle: University of Washington Press, 1974).

[615]Chandrasekhar, Sripati. "Should We Legalize Abortion in India." *Population Review*, 10(2) (1966), 17–22. [This includes a brief examination of the official attitudes toward abortion in Sweden, the Soviet Union, Denmark, East European communist countries, the United Kingdom and the United States.]

[616]"Changing Abortion Laws in the United States." *Journal of Family Law*, 7 (Fall, 1967), 496.

[617]"Chaplains Condemn Abortion." *Catholic Mind*, 69 (February, 1971), 4. [The executive committee of the National Association of Catholics issued a statement on July 24, 1970 reaffirming the Church's stand on abortion and pledging to help parents in a way consistent with the Christian perception of man's dignity.]

[618]Chappell, D., et al. "Public Attitudes to the Reform of the Law Relating to Abortion and Homosexuality." *Australian Law Journal*, 42 (August-September, 1968), 120, 175.

[619]Charles A., et al. "Abortions for Poor and Nonwhite Women: A Denial of Equal Protection?" *Hastings Law Journal*, 23 (November, 1971), 147.

[620]Chatowsky, A. P. "Some Thoughts on Therapeutic Abortion." *Rhode Island Medical Journal*, 54 (September, 1971), 462–66.

[621]Chatterjee, A. "Some Aspects of Implementation of Legal Abortion." *Journal of the Indian Medical Association*, 59 (October 16, 1972), 342–43.

[622]"Charge Rabbi with Abortion Conspiracy." *National Catholic Reporter*, 6 (January 21, 1970), 2.

[623]Charles, Alan. "California's New Therapeutic Abortion Act." *UCLA Law Review*, 15 (December, 1967), 1–31.

[624]Chaudhury, Rafiqul Huda. "Attitude of Some Elites Towards Introduction of Abortion as a Method of Family Planning in Bangladesh," bibl. tables. *Bangladesh Development Studies*, 3 (October, 1975), 479–94.

[625]Cheney, Clarence O. "Indication for Therapeutic Abortion from the Standpoint of the Neurologist and the Psychiatrist." *Journal of the American Medical Association*, 103 (December 22, 1934), 1914.

[626]Chesser, Eustace. "The Doctor's Dilemma." *New Statesman*, 55 (June 15, 1958), 722.

[627]Chesser, Eustace. "The Law of Abortion." *Medical World*, 72 (June 15, 1950).

[628]Chesser, Eustace. *Society and Abortion* (London: Abortion Law Reform Association, 1949).

[629]Cheung, K. W. "Abortion Decision—A Qualified Constitutional Right in the United States: Whither Canada?" *Canadian Bar Review*, 51 (December, 1973), 643–58.

[630]"Chicago Abortion Clinic Shut

Down After 3 Months for Law Violations." *National Catholic Reporter,* 10 (February 22, 1974), 4.

[631]"Child Support: Implications of Abortion on the Relative Parental Duties." *University of Florida Law Review,* 28 (Summer, 1976), 988-99.

[632]Chisholm, N. "Letter: Restriction of Medical Aid in Abortion." *British Medical Journal,* 1(5958) (March 15, 1975), 629.

[633]"Choose Life." *Social Justice Review,* 63 (July-August, 1970), 131-32.

[634]Chowdhury, N. N. "Therapeutic Abortion—Who May Have It?" *Journal of Indian Medical Association,* 54 (February 16, 1970), 163-64.

[635]Christakos, A. C. "Experience at Duke Medical Center after Modern Legislation for Therapeutic Abortion." *Southern Medical Journal,* 63 (June, 1970), 655-57.

[637]Christakos, A. C. "Fetal Indications for Therapeutic Abortions." *North Carolina Medical Journal,* 33 (February, 1972), 115-19.

[637]Christakos, A. C. "Genetics in Therapeutic Abortion." *Southern Medical Journal,* 64 (February, 1971), Suppl. 1 (February, 1971), 105-08.

[638]Christie, R. H. "Therapeutic Abortion." *Central Africa Journal of Medicine,* 19 (March, 1973), 54-58.

[639]"Church Leaders Believe Real Reason to Hope for a Pro-Life Constitutional Amendment." *Our Sunday Visitor,* 64 (June 8, 1975), 1.

[640]"Church Leaders See Pro-Life Setback as Only Temporary." *Our Sunday Visitor,* 64 (October 5, 1975), 1.

[641]Church of England, National Assembly Board. *Abortion: An Ethical Discussion* (London: Church Information Office, 1965).

[642]"Church to Make Anti-Abortion Drive." *National Catholic Reporter,* 9 (February 9, 1973), 1+.

[643]Cumbura, G. "Studies of Criminal Abortion Cases in Ontario." *Journal of Forensic Science,* 12 (April, 1967), 223-29.

[644]Cimmino, C. V. "Abortions." *Virginia Medical Monthly,* 96 (April, 1969), 236-37.

[645]"Cincinnati Paper Says Need for New Look at Abortion." *Our Sunday*

Visitor, 63 (April 13, 1975), 3.

[646]"Civil Conflicts." *Lancet,* 2 (August 12, 1972), 335.

[647]"Civil Rights Commission Against Rights of Unborn." *Our Sunday Visitor,* 63 (April 27, 1975), 1.

[648]"Claim Abortion can Eliminate Stress." *National Catholic Reporter,* 8 (December 17, 1971), 5.

[649]Claman, A. D., *et al.* "Impact on Hospital Practice of Liberalizing Abortions and Female Sterilizations." *Canadian Medical Association Journal,* 105 (July 10, 1971), 35-41. [Liberal attitudes towards abortion in Vancouver has resulted in a reduced number of children for adoption and an increase in psycho-social grounds for abortion.]

[650]Clare, R. M. "Letter: Abortion." *Canadian Medical Association Journal,* 109 (December 1, 1973), 1081-82.

[651]Clark, L. M. G. "Reply to Sumner on Abortion." *Canadian Journal of Philosophy,* 4 (September, 1974), 183-190. [This article offers a feminist perspective on the abortion problem. It is written in response to an article by L. W. Sumner, "Toward a Credible View of Abortion," in *Canadian Journal of Philosophy,* 4 (September, 1974), 163-81. Clark argues that Sumner's position is inadequate because it fails to deal with the issue as to whether or not women alone should have the ultimate authority to have an abortion. Reasons are offered as to why such authority should rest with women alone.]

[652]Clark, M., Forstner, I., Pond, D. G., and Tedgold, R. F. "Sequels of Unwanted Pregnancy." *Lancet,* 2 (August 31, 1968), 501.

[653]Clark, T. S. "Religion, Morality and Abortion: A Constitutional Appraisal." *Loyola University Law Review,* 2 (1969).

[654]Clarke, Alexander. "The Abortion Act Vindicated." *Humanist* (April, 1970).

[655]Clayton, R. A., and Tolone, W. L. "Religiosity and Attitudes Toward Induced Abortion: An Elaboration of the Relationship." *Social Analysis,* 34 (Spring, 1973), 26-39.

[656]Clement, O. "From France: the Orthodox Stand on Abortion." *Diakonia,* 9 (no. 1) (1974), 78-82.

[657]Clements, L. C. "Abortion:

the Right to Life—Or to End Life?" *Study Encounter*, 8 (no. 2) (September 23, 1972), 1-8.

658Clemmesen, Care. "State of Legal Abortion in Denmark." *American Journal of Psychiatry*. 112 (February, 1956), 662.

659"Clinical Indications for Terminating Pregnancy." *British Medical Journal*, 1 (January 20, 1968), 133-34.

660Clohesy, Stephanie. "Fetus Lobby Calls March of Dimes 'Anti-Life'." *Majority Report*, 5 (April 17-May 1, 1976), 1.

661Clouser, K. Danner. "Abortion, Classification and Competing Right." *Christian Century*, 87 (May 20, 1970), 626. [The author discusses the humanity of the fetus. He also comments on the beginning of human life.]

662Clyne, D. G. "Reasons for Abortion." *British Medical Journal*, 3 (September 26, 1970), 769-70.

663Clyne, M. B. "General Practitioners Forum. Habitual Abortion: A Psychosomatic Disorder." *Practitioner*, 199 (July, 1967), 83.

664"Coalition of 38 Agencies Opposes Buckley Amendment on Abortion." *National Catholic Reporter*, 10 (February 1, 1974), 6.

665Cobb, John C. "Abortion in Colorado, 1967-1969." Paper delivered to the American Association of Planned Parenthood Physicians, San Francisco, April 10, 1969.

666Cobliner, W. G., Schulman, H., and Romney, S. "The Termination of Adolescent Out of Wedlock Pregnancies and the Prospects for their Primary Prevention." *American Journal of Obstetrics and Gynecology*, 115(3) (1973), 432-44.

667Cocks, D. P., *et al.* "Letter: A State-Registered Abortionists?" *Lancet*, 2(7948) (December 27, 1975), 1308-09.

668Coffelt, C. F. "Role of Local Government in Therapeutic Abortions." *Clinical Obstetrics and Gynecology*, 14 (December, 1971), 1197-203.

669Coffey, P. G. "Therapeutic Abortion." *Canadian Medical Association Journal*, 103 (November 21, 1970), 1194.

670Coffey, P. G. "Letter: Therapeutic Abortion." *Canadian Medical Association Journal*, 112(3) (February 8, 1975), 283.

671Coffey, P. G. "Therapeutic Abortion." *Advocate, Vancouver Bar Association*, 31 (1973), 99-100.

672Coffey, P. G. "Therapeutic Abortion." *Laval Medicine*, 42 (June, 1971), 611-12.

673Coffey, Patrick J. "Toward a Sound Moral Policy on Abortion." *New Scholasticism*, 47 (Winter, 1973), 105-12. [This article advances the philosophical debate on the morality of abortion made by Daniel Callahan and German Grisez in their books. The author favors Grisez' position, with a modification. This modified position would advocate a moral policy on abortion which would be restrictive in practice but open in its perspective. Callahan's position is open both in practice and perspective.]

674Coffey, Patrick J. "When is Killing the Unborn a Homicidal Action?" *Linacre Quarterly*, 43 (May, 1976), 85-93. [Coffey discusses a study by Dr. James Diamond, *Theological Studies*, 36 (no. 2) (June, 1975), who argues that any killing of the unborn is considered homicidal if the killing takes place at or beyond implantation. He urges pro-life groups to support an amendment which would give the unborn protection against unjust homicides from the end of the first trimester onward. This should be understood as a political legislative action, not a morally justified one.]

675Cogan, N. M. "The Abortion Act 1967. (b). The Social Aspects." *Royal Society Health Journal*, 90 (November-December, 1970), 295-98.

676Cogan, N. M. "Account of the Environment: A Medical Social Worker Looks at the New Abortion Law." *British Medical Journal*, 2 (April 27, 1968), 235-36.

677Cohen, Armond E. "A Jewish View Toward Therapeutic Abortion and the Related Problems of Artificial Insemination and Contraception." *Abortion in America* (Boston: Beacon Press, 1967).

678Cohen, J. "Legal Abortions, Socioeconomic Status, and Measured Intelligence in the United States." *Social Biology*, 18(1) (1971), 55-63.

679Cohen, J. "Therapeutic Abortion." *Medical Journal of Australia*, 2 (August 17, 1968), 336-37.

680Cohen, M., *et al.* "Letter: The Canadian Abortion Law." *Canadian Medical Association Journal*, 114(7)

[681]Cohen, S. B. "Abortion for the Emotionally Disturbed?" *Journal of the Medical Association of Georgia,* 57 (November, 1968), 489-94.

[682]Cole, Martin. "Illegal Abortion—'Abortifacients' for Sale." *Abortion in Britain* (London: Pitman Medical Publishing Company, Ltd., 1966).

[683]Coles, P. N. "Letter: The Morgentaler Case." *Canadian Medical Association Journal,* 113(3) (August 9, 1975), 181.

[684]Coles, R. E., *et al.* "Letter: Effects of Legal Termination and Subsequent Pregnancy." *British Medical Journal,* 2(6026) (July 3, 1976), 45.

[685]Collins, L. D. "The Legal Aspects of Abortion." *Canadian Journal of Public Health,* 66(3) (1975), 234-36.

[686]Collins, R. "Abortion: An Ethical and Moral Appraisal." *Louvain Studies,* 3 (Spring, 1970), 17-30.

[687]Colombo, G., Card. "In Defence of Life and Love." homily. *L'Osservatore Romano* (English), 424 (no. 20) (May 13, 1976), 4-5.

[688]"Colorado First with Abortion Liberalization." *National Catholic Reporter,* 3 (April 19, 1967), 5.

[689]"Colorado Parish Survey Reveals Laity's Opinions." *National Catholic Reporter,* 8 (May 12, 1972), 7.

[690]"Colorado's New Abortion Law." *University of Law Review,* 40 (Winter, 1968), 297.

[691]Colpitts, R. V. "Trends in Therapeutic Abortion." *American Journal of Obstetrics and Gynecology,* 68 (October, 1954), 988-97. Also in *Birth Control and the Christian.* Ed. W. O. Spitzer and C. L. Saylor (Wheaton, Illinois: Tyndale House, 1969).

[692]Columbia University School of Social Work. *Counseling in Abortion Services: Physician-Nurse-Social Worker* (New York: University Book Service, 1974).

[693]"Comments Upon the Law Relating to Abortion and Sterilization." *Manitoba Bar News,* 33 (1961), 38.

[694]"Commission Backs Abortion." *National Catholic Reporter,* 8 (March 24, 1972), 5.

[695]Committee on Criminal Procedure of the California State Legislature on Assembly Bill 2614. *Therapeutic Abortion,* unofficial report, n.d.

[696]Compton, P. A., Goldstrom, L., and Goldstrom, J. M. "Religion and Legal Abortion in Northern Ireland." *Journal of Biosocial Science,* 6(4) (1974), 493-500.

[697]Coney, Sandra. "The Bobigny Trial." (French Abortion Trial, Michele Chevalier Plaintiff). *Broadsheet,* no. 35 (December, 1975), 25-29+.

[698]Coney, Sandra. "Counseling Makes All the Difference." (abortion). *Broadsheet: New Zealand's Feminist Magazine,* no. 31 (July, 1975), 25-27+.

[699]Conley, P., and McKenna, R. "The Supreme Court on Abortion: A Dissenting Opinion." *Catholic Lawyer,* 19 (Winter, 1973), 19-28. Also in *Review for the Religious,* 32 (May, 1973), 473-81. [The authors draw on the example of the Dred Scott decision's denial of the Negro's right to citizenship, to urge others to fight to protect the unborn.]

[700]"Conflicting Coverage Given Abortion Attitudes Survey." *Our Sunday Visitor,* 63 (March 23, 1975), 1.

[701]"Connecticut Asks New Look at Abortion." *National Catholic Reporter,* 9 (April 13, 1973), 2.

[702]Connell, E. B. "Abortion: Patterns, Technics, and Results." *Fertility and Sterility,* 24 (January, 1973), 78-91 (55 ref.)

[703]Connery, John. *Abortion: The Development of the Roman Catholic Perspective* (Chicago: Loyola University Press, 1977).

[704]Connery, John. "Callahan on Meaning of Abortion." *Linacre Quarterly,* 37 (November, 1970), 280.

[705]Connery, John. "The Right to Privacy." *Linacre Quarterly,* 40 (May, 1973), 138-43. [The right to privacy is examined, as it applies in the doctor-patient relationship. The author points out four exception-making criteria traditionally held by moral theologians. A doctor may reveal confidential information when necessary to: 1) keep a patient from doing serious harm to the community; 2) to an innocent third party; 3) to himself; or 4) to the doctor.]

[706]Cannon, A. F. "Abortion: Community Trends." Comment 2. *Medical Journal of Australia,* 2(8) (August 24, 1974), 293-95.

[707]Cannon, A. F. "Medical Abor-

tion in South Australia. The First
12 Months Under New Legislation."
Medical Journal of Australia, 2 (September 18, 1971), 608-14.

[708]Cannon, A. F. "Trends in Legalized Abortion in South Australia."
Medical Journal of Australia, 1 (February 3, 1973), 231-34.

[709]Connor, E. J., *et al.* "Therapeutic Abortion—Washington, D.C."
*Medical Annals of the District of Co-
lumbia,* 39 (March, 1970), 133-37.

[710]Connor, Michael J. "Moonlight-
ing Medics: Liberal Abortion Law
proves to be a Bonanza for New York
(N.Y.) doctors." doctors." *Wall
Steet Journal,* 177 (June 1, 1971), 1+.

[711]"Conscience Bill Survives Attack." *National Catholic Reporter,* 9
(June 8, 1973), 20.

[712]"Consent Provisions in Abortion
Statutes." *Florida State University
Law Review,* 1 (Fall, 1973), 645-62.

[713]"Constitutional Aspects of
Present Criminal Abortion Law." *Val-
paraiso University Law Review,* 3
(Fall, 1968), 102.

[714]"Constitutional Law—Abortions:
Abortion as a Ninth Amendment Right."
Washington Law Review, 46 (May, 1971),
565.

[715]"Constitutional Law—Abortion—
1850 California Statute Prohibiting
all Abortions not 'Necessary to Preserve (the Mother's) Life' is Unconstitutionally Vague and an Improper
Infringement on Women's Constitutional
Rights." *Notre Dame Lawyer,* 45 (Winter, 1970), 329.

[716]"Constitutional Law—Abortion—
Does a Woman Have a Constitutional
Right Under the Ninth Amendment to
Choose Whether to Bear a Child After
Conception." *Texas Tech Law Review,*
2 (Fall, 1970), 99.

[717]"Constitutional Law—Abortion—
Father's Rights." *Duquesne Law Review,*
13 (Spring, 1975), 599-610.

[718]"Constitutional Law—Abortion—
Lack of Compelling State Interests—
California's American Law Institute-
Type Therapeutic Abortion Statute Sub-
stantially Voided Because Interests in
the Woman's Health and in the Fetus
Dictate that Abortions Prior to Twenty
Weeks of Pregnancy may be Restricted
only for Medical Reasons." *University
of Cincinnati Law Review,* 41 (1972),
235.

[719]"Constitutional Law: Abortion,
Parental Consent, Minors' Rights to
Due Process, Equal Protection and
Privacy." *Akron Law Review,* 9 (Sum-
mer, 1975), 158-65.

[720]"Constitutional Law: Abortion,
Parental and Spousal Consent Require-
ments, Right to Privacy." *Akron Law
Review,* 10 (Fall, 1976), 367-82.

[721]"Constitutional Law—Abortion
—Parental and Spousal Consent Requirements Violate Right to Privacy
in Abortion Decision." *University of
Kansas Law Review,* 24 (Winter, 1976),
446-62.

[722]"Constitutional Law—Abortion
—Private Hospital may Refuse to Perform Abortion." *St. Louis University
Law Journal,* 18 (Spring, 1974), 440-
60.

[723]"Constitutional Law—Abortion
—Putative Father Has No Right to
Prevent Wife from Obtaining an Abor-
tion." *Memphis State University Law
Review,* 5 (Spring, 1975), 429-37.

[724]"Constitutional Law—Abortion
—Right of Privacy—State Statutes
Permitting Abortion Only for Life
Saving Procedure on Behalf of Mother
Without Regard for Other Interests
Violate Due Process Clause of the
Fourteenth Amendment." *Memphis State
University Law Review,* 3 (Spring,
1973), 359.

[725]"Constitutional Law—Abortion
—Standard Excepting Abortions Done
as 'Necessary for the Preservation of
the Mother's Life or Health' Held Unconstitutionally Vague." *Vanderbilt
Law Review,* 23 (May, 1970), 821.

[726]"Constitutional Law—Abortion
—State Statute Prohibiting Abortion
Except to Save Life of Mother Uncon-
stitutional." *Tulane Law Review,* 47
(June, 1973), 1159-67.

[727]"Constitutional Law—Abortion
—Statute Defining 'Justifiable Abor-
tional Act' Not Unconstitutional—
Constitution Does Not Confer or Re-
quire Legal Personality for Unborn—
Whether Law Should Accord Legal Per-
sonality is Policy Question to be
Determined by Legislature." *Notre
Dame Lawyer,* 48 (February, 1973), 715.

[728]"Constitutional Law—Abortion
Statute as Invasion of a Woman's
Right of Privacy." *St. Louis University Law Journal,* 15 (Summer, 1971),
642.

[729]"Constitutional Law—Abortion
—Statute Prohibiting Abortion of Un-
quickened Fetus Violates Mother's
Constitutional Right of Privacy."

Vanderbilt Law Review, 23 (November, 1970), 1346.

[730]"Constitutional Law—Abortion—Statutory Limitation on Reasons for Abortion is Violation of Fundamental Right to Privacy." *Mercer Law Review,* 22 (Winter, 1971), 461.

[731]"Constitutional Law—Blanket Parental Consent. Requirement for Minor's Abortion Decision is Unconstitutional." *Texas Tech Law Review,* 8 (Fall, 1976), 394-402.

[732]"Constitutional Law—Commercial Speech Doctrine—A Clarification of the Protection Afforded Advertising Under the First Amendment." *Brigham Young University Law Review,* 1975 (1975), 797-811.

[733]"Constitutional Law—Criminal Abortion—Statute Prohibiting Intentional Destruction of Unquickened Fetus Violates Mother's Right of Privacy." *Georgia Law Review,* 4 (Summer, 1970), 907.

[734]"Constitutional Law—Criminal Law—Requirement of Certainty in Legislation in a Criminal Abortion Statute." *Journal of Urban Law,* 47 (1969-1970), 901.

[735]"Constitutional Law—Denial of Equal Protection to Patient as also Constituting Denial of Equal Protection to Physician." *University of Toledo Law Review,* 7 (Fall, 1975), 213-29.

[736]"Constitutional Law—Denial of Medicaid Reimbursement for Elective Abortions—*City of New York v. Wyman.*" [(NY)—NE 2d—], *Albany Law Review,* 36 (1972), 794.

[737]"Constitutional Law—Due Process and Abortion." *Nebraska Law Review,* 51 (Winter, 1971), 340.

[738]"Constitutional Law: Elimination of Spousal and Parental Consent Requirements for Abortion." *Washburn Law Journal,* 16 (Winter, 1977), 462-68.

[739]"Constitutional Law—Expanding the Grounds for Abortion." *Wake Forest Law Review,* 7 (October, 1971), 651.

[740]"Constitutional Law—First Amendment—Freedom of Speech—Advertising Cannot be Denied First Amendment Protection, Absent a Showing by the State of a Legitimate Public Interest Justifying its Regulation." *University of Cincinnati Law Review,* 44 (1975), 852-59.

[741]"Constitutional Law—First Amendment—Newspaper Advertisement of Abortion Referral Service Entitled to First Amendment Protection." *University of Richmond Law Review,* 10 (Winter, 1976), 427-33.

[742]"Constitutional Law—First Amendment—United States Supreme Court Held that the First Amendment Protected an Abortion Advertisement which Conveyed Information of Potential Interest to an Audience, Despite its Appearance in the Form of a Paid Commercial Advertisement." *Indiana Law Review,* 8 (1975), 890-97.

[743]"Constitutional Law—Freedom of the Press—Prohibition of Abortion Referral Service Advertising Held Unconstitutional." *Cornell Law Review,* 61 (April, 1976), 640+.

[744]"Constitutional Law—'Liberalized' Abortion Statute Held Constitutional." *Fordham Law Review,* 41 (December, 1972), 439.

[745]"Constitutional Law—Minor's Right to Refuse Court-Ordered Abortion." *Suffolk University Law Review,* 7 (Summer, 1973), 1157-73.

[746]"Constitutional Law—Mother's Right to Abort is Greater than Unquickened Child's Right to Live." *Journal of Urban Law,* 48 (June, 1971), 969.

[747]"Constitutional Law—A New Constitutional Right to an Abortion." *North Carolina Law Review,* 51 (October, 1973), 1573-84.

[748]"Constitutional Law—New Jersey Abortion Statute Unconstitutionally Vague on its Face; Women Prior to Pregnancy have no Standing to Attack Statute, but Plaintiff-Physicians have Standing to Assert Deprivation of their Women Patients Right of Privacy." *Journal of Urban Law,* 50 (February, 1973), 505.

[749]"Constitutional Law—the Right of Privacy—Georgia's Abortion Law Declared Unconstitutional." *Georgia State Bar Journal,* 10 (August, 1973), 153-62.

[750]"Constitutional Law—Right to Privacy—Spousal Consent to Abortion: Foreshadowing the Fall of Parental Consent." *Suffolk University Law Review,* 9 (Spring, 1975), 841-72.

[751]"Constitutional Law—State Action—Private Hospitals Receiving Hill-Burton Funds do not Act Under Color of State Authority in Denying Access to their Facilities for Abortions." *Georgia Law Journal,* 62 (July, 1974), 1783-93.

[752]"Constitutional Law—State Ac-Actions—Denial of Abortion by Private Hospital Receiving Federal Financial Support Under the Hill-Burton Program does not Constitute State Action." *Fordham Urban Law Journal,* 2 (Spring, 1974), 611-19.

[753]"Constitutional Law—State Regulation of Abortion." *Wisconsin Law Review,* 1970 (1970),

[754]"Constitutional Law—Substantive Due Process—Abortion—Reasonable Statutory Record-keeping and Reporting Requirements Upheld." *Brigham Young University Law Review,* 1976 (1976), 977-99.

[755]"Constitutional Law—Void-For-Vagueness." *Suffolk University Law Review,* 4 (Spring, 1970), 920.

[756]"Constitutional Right of Privacy—Minor's Right to an Abortion—Statutory Requirement of Spousal Consent, or Parental Consent in the Case of an Unmarried, Minor Female, is an Unconstitutional Deprivation of a Woman's Right to Determine Whether to Undergo an Abortion." *Hofstra Law Review,* 4 (Winter, 1976), 531-47.

[757]"Constitutional Right to Life from the Moment of Conception." *Social Justice Review,* 64 (March, 1972), 408-18.

[758]"Constitutional Validity of the Tennessee Abortion Statute." *Memphis State University Law Review,* 4 (Spring, 1974), 593-600.

[759]"Consultants' Report on Abortion." *British Medical Journal,* 2 (May 30, 1970), 491-92.

[760]"Contraception and Abortion." *Christianity Today,* 13 (November 8, 1968), 13-19.

[761]Cook, Rebecca J. *Ten Years of Change in Abortion Law, 1967-76.* In tabular form; various countries. (London: International Planned Parenthood Federation, 1977).

[762]Cooke, T., Cardinal. "Abortion and the Value of Life." *L'Osservatore Romano* (English), no. 6 (202) (February 10, 1972), 7.

[763]Cooke, T., Cardinal. "Cardinal Terence Cooke Launches New Service: Birthright for Mothers." *L'Osservatore Romano* (English), no. 17 (161) (April 29, 1971), 4.

[764]Cooke, T., Cardinal. "Cardinal Terence Cooke on the Rights of the Unborn." *L'Osservatore Romano* (English), no. 41 (445) (October 7, 1976), 11-12.

[765]Cooke, T., Cardinal, and Bernardin, J., Abp. "Pastoral Plan for Pro-Life Activities; Statement." *L'Osservatore Romano* (English), no. 1 (405) (January 1, 1976), 3-4.

[766]Cooper, Boyd. *Sex Without Tears: A Guide for the Sexual Revolution.* Ed. Walter Schmidt (Hollywood, Calif.: Charles Publishing Company, n.d.)

[767]Cooper, J. A. "Therapeutic Abortion: A Survey with a Series from London Hospital." *British Journal of Clinical Practice,* 22 (February, 1968), 49-57.

[768]Cooper, L. S. "Rubella in Pregnancy." *Post Graduate Medicine,* 46 (December, 1969), 106-07.

[769]Cooper, Robert M. "Abortion: Privacy and Fantasy." *Encounter,* 37 (Spring, 1976), 181-88.

[770]Copeland, W. E., *et al.* "Therapeutic Abortion." *Journal of the American Medical Association,* 207 (January 27, 1969), 713-15.

[771]Corcoran, C. J. "Abortion—A Catholic View." *Illinois Medical Journal,* 135 (March, 1969), 300-02.

[772]Corenblum, B. "Locus of Control, Latitude of Acceptance and Attitudes Toward Abortion." *Psychological Reports,* 32(3)(1) (1973), 753-54.

[773]Corenblum, B., and Fischer, D. G. "Factor Analysis of Attitudes Toward Abortion." *Perceptual and Motor Skills,* 40(2) (1975), 587-91.

[774]Corkill, B. "Abortion Questionnaire and RCOG." *New Zealand Medical Journal,* 74 (December, 1971), 410-11.

[775]Cormier, R. "Three Against Abortion: None of Them Catholic." *St. Anthony's Messenger,* 84 (January, 1976), 18-22.

[776]Cornfy, R. T., and Horton, F. T., Jr. "Pathological Grief Following Spontaneous Abortion." *American Journal of Psychiatry,* 131(7) (1974), 825-27.

[777]Corsa, Leslie. "Abortion—A World View." *The Case for Legalized Abortion Now.* Ed. Alan F. Guttmacher (Berkeley: Diablo Press, 1967).

[778]Corson, S. L. "Voluntary Interruption of Pregnancy. Its Psychiatric and Contraceptive Correlates." *Journal of Reproductive Medicine,* 8 (1972), 151-54.

[779]Cory, L. "Court-Ordered Sterilization Performed at St. Vincent's Hospital, Billings." *Hospital Progress,* 53 (December, 1972), 22+.

[780]Cosgrove, S. A. "Lack of Relation Between Therapeutic and Criminal Abortion." *Quarterly Review of Surgery, Obstetrics and Gynecology,* 16 (October-December, 1959).

[781]Cosgrove, S. A., and Carter, P. A. "A Consideration of Therapeutic Abortion." *American Journal of Obstetrics and Gynecology,* 48 (1944), 893, 896.

[782]"The Cost of Life. A Symposium." *Proceedings of the Royal Society of Medicine,* 60 (1967), 1195.

[783]Cottam, J. "Abortion: A Changing Scene." *Lancet,* 2 (November 27, 1971), 1193-94.

[784]Cottrell, J. W. "Abortion and the Mosaic Law." *Christianity Today,* 17 (March 16, 1973), 6-9.

[785]Coulter, J. R. "A Statement on Abortion in Victoria." *Medical Journal of Australia,* 1 (January 1, 1972), 32-33.

[786]"Council Withholds Paper on Abortion, Avoids Feud." *National Catholic Reporter,* 9 (March 16, 1973), 3.

[787]"Court Abortion Decisions Draw Strong Criticisms." *Our Sunday Visitor,* 65 (July 18, 1976), 2.

[788]"Court Recognizes Rights of Unborn Child; Provides New Angle for Fighting Legalized Abortion." *St. Anthony's Messenger,* 75 (January, 1968), 11.

[789]"Court Rejects New Abortion Hearing." *National Catholic Reporter,* 9 (April 27, 1973), 2.

[790]Courtney, L. D. "Methods and Dangers of Termination of Pregnancy." *Proceedings of the Royal Society of Medicine,* 62 (August, 1969), 834.

[791]Crawford, J. "Abortion Act." *Lancet,* 2 (November 28, 1970), 1138.

[792]Crawford, J. "The Abortion Law and Legal Paradox." *Month,* 9 (March, 1976), 97-100.

[793]Credo. "Big Government in the Bedroom: Program of Life Prevention." *Social Justice Review,* 62 (March, 1970), 412-14.

[794]Creighton, P., ed. *Abortion: An Issue for Conscience* (Toronto: Anglican Church of Canada, 1974).

[795]*Crimes Without Victims: Deviant Behavior and Public Policy* (Hemel Hempstead: Prentice-Hall, Inc., 1965).

[796]A Criminal Approach to Abortion." *British Medical Journal,* 2 (5967) (May 17, 1975), 352-53.

[797]"Criminal Law—Abortion—Man, Being Without a Legal Beginning." *Kentucky Law Journal,* 58 (Summer, 1969-1970), 843.

[798]"Criminal Law—Abortion—The Need for Legislative Reform." *Kentucky Law Journal,* 57 (1968-1969), 555.

[799]"Criminal Law—Abortion—The New North Carolina Abortion Statute." *North Carolina Law Review,* 46 (April, 1968)', 585.

[800]"Criminal Law—Abortion Statute—Due Process—The Supreme Court of California Has Held that a Statute Prohibiting Abortions not 'Necessary to Preserve' the Mother's Life is so Vague and Uncertain as to be Violative to the Fourteenth Amendment's Due Process Clause." *Duquesne Law Review,* 8 (Summer, 1970), 439.

[801]"Criminal Law: A Call for Statutory Abortion Law Reform in Oklahoma." *Oklahoma Law Review,* 24 (May, 1971), 243.

[802]"Criminal Law—The Iowa Abortion Statute is not Unconstitutionally Vague and Does Not Deny Equal Protection." *Drake Law Review,* 20 (June, 1971), 666.

[803]"Criminal Law—Texas Abortion Statute—Criminality Exceptions Limited to Life-Saving Procedures on Mother's Behalf Without Regard to Stage of Pregnancy Violates Due Process Clause of Fourteenth Amendment Protecting Right to Privacy." *American Journal of Criminal Law,* 2 (Summer, 1973), 231-43.

[804]"Criminal Procedure—Search and Seizure—Electronic Eavesdropping—Abortion: Recording of Voluntary Conversation Between Police Agent and Defendant Admissible in Evidence." *Washington Law Review,* 45 (April, 1970), 411.

[805]Crist, T. "Abortion: Where Have We Been? Where Are We Going?" *North Carolina Medical Journal,* 32 (August, 1971), 347-51.

[806]Croghan, L. M. "Areas of Potential Psychological Vulnerability

807-
834

in the New Era of Liberalized Abortion." *Psychology*, 11(3) (1974), 35-44.

[807]Crosbie, S. "Abortion and Euthanasia." *Rocky Mountain Medical Journal*, 66 (November, 1969), 41-46.

[808]Crowley, R. M., and Laidlaw, R. W. "Psychiatric Opinion Regarding Abortion." *American Journal of Psychiatry*, 124 (1967), 559-62.

[809]Csapo, A. I., *et al.* "The Efficacy and Acceptability of Intravenously Administered Prostaglandin F2alpha as an Abortifacient." *American Journal of Obstetrics and Gynecology*, 111(1059) (December 15, 1971).

[810]Culiner, B. "Some Medical Aspects of Abortion." *Journal of Forensic Medicine*, 10 (1963).

[811]"Culmination of the Abortion Reform Movement—*Roe v. Wade* (93 Sup Ct 705) and *Doe v. Bolton* (93 Sup Ct 739)." *University of Richmond Law Review*, 8 (Fall, 1973), 75-87.

[812]Cushner, I. M. "The Therapeutic Abortion Committee." *Clinical Obstetrics and Gynecology*, 14 (December, 1971), 1248-54.

[813]Cushner, I. M. "Induced Abortion in Contemporary Medical Practice." *Journal of Religion and Health*, 7 (October, 1968), 324-32.

[814]Curran, Charles E. *A New Look at Christian Morality* (Notre Dame, Indiana: Fides Publishers, Inc., 1968).

[815]Curran, Charles E. *Absolutes in Moral Theology* (Washington, D.C.: Corpus Books, 1968).

[816]Curran, Frank J. "Religious Implications." *Abortion in America*. Ed. Harold Rosen (Boston: Beacon Press, 1967).

[817]Curran, R. "Babi Yar and Babies." *Linacre Quarterly*, 35 (n.d.) 240-42. [This contains a highly emotional account of the horrors perpetuated in Kiev during World War II. Abortion is equated to murder.]

[818]Curran, W. J. "Public Health and the Law. Illegal Therapeutic Abortions: The Modern Dilemma." *American Journal of Public Health*, 59 (August, 1969), 1434-35.

[819]Curran, W. J. "Legal Abortion: The Continuing Battle." *New England Journal of Medicine*, 290 (June 6, 1974), 1301-02.

[820]Curran, W. J. "Aftermath of the Abortion Decisions: Action in the Legislatures and in the Courts." *New England Journal of Medicine*, 289 (November 1, 1973), 955.

[821]Curran, W. J. "Abortion Law in the Supreme Court." *New England Journal of Medicine*, 285 (July 1, 1971), 30-31.

[822]Curran, W. J. "The Abortion Decisions: The Supreme Court as Moralist, Scientist, Historian and Legislator." *New England Journal of Medicine*, 288 (May 3, 1973), 950-51.

[823]"Current TMA Policy: Medical Guidelines for Abortion." *Texas Medicine*, 70 (July, 1974), 83-84.

[824]Curtin, L. "Nurses Who Work to Save Lives." *Our Sunday Visitor*, 64 (January 25, 1976), 16.

[825]Curtis, J. A. "Letter: Contraception and Abortion." *British Medical Journal*, 2 (April 27, 1974), 222-23.

[826]Curtis, W. "We Need a Right to Life Amendment." *U.S. Catholic*, 39 (June, 1974), 14-15.

[827]Daecon, A. L. "Sequels of Unwanted Pregnancy." *Lancet*, 2 (September 28, 1968), 730.

[828]Dafoe, C. "Colorado's Abortion Law: An Obstetrician's View." *Nebraska Medical Journal*, 55 (January, 1970), 3-4.

[829]Dahl, N. S. "Social and Psychological Aspects of Abortion. Selected Citations. 1965-1972." *Bibliography Series, Carolina Population Center*, 6 (1973), 1-6.

[830]Dailey, T. "The Catholic Position on Abortion." *Linacre Quarterly*, 34 (August 20, 1967), 218-20.

[831]Daily, E. F. "Family Planning Counseling." *British Medical Journal*, 3 (August 8, 1970), 345-46.

[832]Daily, E. F. "Prevention of Unwanted Pregnancies." *American Journal of Obstetrics and Gynecology*, 113 (August 15, 1972), 1148.

[833]Daily, E. F., Nicholas, N., Nelson, F. G., and Pakter, J. "Repeat Abortions in New York City. 1970-1972." *Family Planning Perspectives*, 5(2) (1973), 89-93.

[834]Daily, E. F., and Nicholas, N. "Use of Conception Control Methods Before Pregnancies Terminating in Birth or Requested Abortion in New

York City Municipal Hospitals." *Journal of Public Health*, 62(11) (1972), 1544-45.

[835]Daley, T. T. "Rights of the Unborn: A CAS Looks at Abortion." *Canadian Welfare, Canadian Welfare Council*, 48(3) (1972), 19-21.

[836]Daly, Mary. "Abortion and Sexual Caste." *Commonweal*, 95 (February 4, 1972), 415-19. Reply: Zahn, G. C. *Commonweal*, 95 (February 18, 1972), 470-01. [Daly avidly states that women are living in a sexual caste in a patriarchal society. This caste is enforced through sex-role segregation and patriarchal religion, which legitimates the caste.
Daly discusses a few "male authored" essays to point out how various assumptions and attitudes have not been considered but certain selected facts were concentrated on.
She sees the role of the "living healing and prophetic Church" as listening to what women are saying, supporting demands for the repeal of unjust laws, to point beyond abortion to more fundamental solutions—a social context in which abortion will not arise and finally work to the eradication of sex-role socialization and the sexual caste system.]

[837]Danon, A. H. Organizing an Abortion Service." *Nursing Outlook*, 21 (July, 1973), 460-64.

[838]Dannreuther, W. T. "Therapeutic Abortion in a General Hospital." *American Journal of Obstetrics and Gynecology*, 52 (1946), 54.

[839]Dant, J. Douglas. "Abortion and the Health Services—Concern for the Woman." *Abortion in Britain* (London: Pitman Medical Publishing Company Limited, 1966).

[840]Darby, P. "Legal Abortion?" *Medico-Legal Journal*, 34 (1966), 96.

[841]Darby, P. "The Frequency of Illegal Abortion." *Eugenic Review*, 56 (July, 1964), 121-22.

[842]Dardor, F. "L'Adoption, Une Alternative Méconnue à L'Avortement; France." *Etudes*, 338 (May, 1973), 701-14.

[843]"Dark Shadow at the Door." *Irish Medical Journal*, 68(6) (March 22, 1975), 150, 158.

[844]Darst, S. "He Runs for Their Lives." *Catholic Digest*, 38 (March, 1974), 45-47.

[845]Daube, D. "Sanctity of Life." *Proceedings of the Royal Society of Medicine*, 60, Suppl. (November, 1967) 1235-40.

[846]Dauber, B. "Abortion Counseling and Behavioral Change." *Family Planning Perspectives*, 4 (1972), 23-27.

[847]Dauber, B. "Profile of an Abortion Counselor." *Family Planning Perspectives*, 6(3) (1974), 185-87.

[848]David, H. P. "Abortion and Family Planning in the Soviet Union. Public Policies and Private Behaviour." *Journal of Biosocial Science*, 6(4) (1974), 417-26.

[849]"Abortion in Psychological Perspective." *American Journal of Orthopsychiatry*, 42(1) (1972), 61-68.

[850]David, H. P. "Abortion: Public Health Concerns and Needed Psychosocial Research." *American Journal of Public Health*, 61 (March, 1971), 510-16.

[851]David, H. P. "Abortion Trends in European Socialist Countries and in the United STates." *American Journal of Orthopsychiatry*, 43(3) (1973), 376-83.

[852]David, H. P. *Family Planning and Abortion in The Socialist Countries of Central and Eastern Europe: A Compendium of Observations and Readings* (Population Council, 1970).

[853]David, H. P., *et al.*, eds. *Abortion in Psychosocial Perspective: Trends in Transnational Research* (New York: Springer Publishing Co., 1978).

[854]David, H. P., and Wright, Nicholas H. "Abortion Legislation: The Romanian Experience." *Studies in Family Planning*, 2 (October, 1971), 205-10.

[855]Davies, D. Seaborne. "The Law of Abortion and Necessity." *The Modern Law Review*, 2 (Sept. 1938), 126-38.

[856]Davis, A. "2665 Cases of Abortion, A Clinical Survey," *British Medical Journal*, 2 (1950), 123.

[857]Davis. "ISMS Symposium on Medical Implications of Current Abortion Law in Illinois." *Illinois Medical Journal*, 131 (May, 1967), 683-85.

[858]Davis, G., *et al.* "Mid-Trimester Abortion." *Lancet*, 2 (November 11, 1972), 1026.

[859]Davis, K. "Population Policy. Will Current Program Succeed?" *Science*, 158(3802) (1967), 730-39.

[860]Day, R. L. "Is Reaction to the Population Problem Misplaced?" *Pediatrics,* 47 (May, 1971), 952-55.

[861]"Death of a Baby? Inquiry in Glasgow." *British Medical Journal,* 2 (June 14, 1969), 704-05.

[862]De Bary, Edward O. "One Pastor's Ministry to Those Who Experience Unwanted Pregnancies." *St. Luke's Journal of Theology,* 19 (March, 1976), 99-111.

[863]De Bary, Edward O. "Reply to Joseph Monti." *St. Luke's Journal of Theology,* 19 (June, 1976), 173-76.

[864]"Debate Continues." *Economist,* 254 (February 15, 1975), 31.

[865]"Declaration on Abortion. Congregation for the Doctrine of the Faith." *Catholic Mind,* 73 (April, 1975), 54-64. [The text of this declaration was made public on November 25, 1974. The document was prepared by the Vatican Congregation for the Doctrine of the Faith and approved by Pope Paul VI on June 28, 1974.]

[866]"Déclaration du Conseil Permanent de L'Episcopat Français sur L'Avortement." *La Documentation Catholique,* 70 (July 15, 1973), 676-79.

[867]"Déclaration du Conseil Permanent de L'Episcopat Français sur L'Avortement." *La Documentation Catholique,* 71 (April 7, 1974), 336-38.

[868]"Déclaration des Eveques du Québec." *La Documentation Catholique,* 70 (April 15, 1973), 382-84.

[869]"Déclaration des Eveques Belges sur L'Avortement." *La Documentation Catholique* (May, 1973), 432-38.

[870]"Déclaration des Eveques Suisses sur L'Avortement." *La Documentation Catholique,* 70 (April 15, 1973), 381.

[871]"Déclaration de 10,000 Medecins de France sur L'Avortement." *La Documentation Catholique,* 70 (July 1, 1973), 629.

[872]"The Declaration of Oslo." *South Africa Medical Journal,* 44 (November 14, 1970), 1281.

[873]"Declaration of Permanent Council of Italian Bishops' Conference: Abortion Issue." *L'Osservatore Romano* (English), no. 1 (405) (January 1, 1976), 9.

[874]"Déclaration du Secretariat de L'Episcopat Français sur L'Avortement: July 2, 1970." *La Documentation Catholique,* 67 (August 2-16, 1970), 729.

[875]De Costa. "ISMS Symposium on Medical Implications of Current Abortion Law in Illinois." *Illinois Medical Journal,* 131 (May, 1967), 667-69.

[876]Decker, D. G. "Medical Indications for Therapeutic Abortion: An Obstetrician's View." *Minnesota Medicine,* 50 (January, 1967), 29-32.

[877]De Danois, Vivian. *Abortion and the Moral Degeneration of the American Medical Profession* (A Science of Man Library Bk) (Albuquerque: American Classical College Press, 1975).

[878]Dedek, J. "Abortion: A Theological Judgment." *Chicago Studies,* 10 (Fall, 1971), 313-33. [Dedek begins his article with "The Making of a Human Baby?" Then he explores "What is Human Life?" The principles of the double effect and probabilism are discussed.]

[876]Deedy, J. "Catholics, Abortion and the Supreme Court." *Theology Today,* 30 (October, 1973), 279-86. [This article discusses why there is a "dissident Catholic opinion" concerning the official stand on abortion. Deedy states the reasons that there was not a confrontation with American law over the Supreme Court decision. On the one hand, there is the new freedom of the Catholic conscience, and on the other, the bishops' near-total dissipation of their moral authority. Dissident Catholic opinion responds to the rigid official position and the unwillingness to entertain any theological or medical possibilities beyond what is presently permissible.
Deedy urges the leadership to re-educate itself on the value of all human life, to speak against selfishness in our institutions, support birth control, take women seriously, and make it acceptable financially and socially to have a child outside of marriage.]

[877]"Deformed Infants' Suits for Failure to Recommend Abortions." *Journal of the Kansas Medical Society,* 73 (February, 1972), 80.

[878]De George, R. "Legal Enforcement, Moral Pluralism and Abortion." In: McLean G. "Philosophy and Civil Law." *American Catholic Philosophi-*

cal Association Proceedings, 49 (1975), 171-80.

[879]Degnan, D. "Law, Morals and Abortion." *Commonweal,* 100 (May 31, 1974), 305-08. [The article deals with the relationship between law and morals in regard to abortion.

Degnan sees two ways to deal with the Supreme Court's decision of *Roe v. Wade:* 1) a constitutional amendment returning to the states the power to prohibit abortions; 2) finding a common position among as many Americans as possible, which allows for some abortions but would restrict them in the middle and later months of pregnancy.]

[880]Dehler, D. "Abortion and the Law." *Chitty's Law Journal,* 16 (1968), 13.

[881]Dejanikus, Tacie. "Abortion Counselors Fired." *Off Our Backs,* 6 (March, 1976), 14-16.

[882]Delgado, R. "Parental Preferences and Selective Abortion: A Commentary on *Roe v. Wade* (93 Sup Ct 705), *Doe v. Bolton* (93 Sup Ct 789) and the Shape of Things to Come." *Washington University Law Quarterly,* 1974 (1974), 203-26.

[883]Delhave, P. "Press Conference Summary on Procured Abortion; Rome, November 25, 1974." *L'Osservatore Romano* (English), no. 49 (349) (December 5, 1974), 8.

[884]Dellapenna, J. W. "Nor Piety Nor Wit: The Supreme Court on Abortion." *Columbia Human Rights Law Review,* 6 (Fall-Winter, 1974-1975), 379-413.

[885]"Demand for Abortion." *British Medical Journal,* 1 (January 25, 1969), 199-200.

[886]De Marco, Donald. "Abortion: Legal and Philosophical Considerations." *American Ecclesiastical Review,* 168 (April, 1974), 251-67. [The author begins by asking if popularity justifies law and if democracy renders leadership. To answer such questions, an understanding of the presuppositions of democracy and authoritarianism is necessary. De Marco sees the democratic solution to the abortion problem by people exercising "intellectual vision" to embrace the world of real values. De Marco presents six philosophies which he sees as representing a one-sided and fragmented approach to reality. These are Atomism, Cartesianism, Existentialism, Empiricism, Mathematical-Physics and Sociologism.

In conclusion, these Western varieties of thought must be examined at their point of origination. Reflection is needed to come to terms with Western materialism.

[887]De Marco, Donald. *Abortion in Perspective* (Cincinnati: Hiltz and Hayes, 1974).

[888]De Marco, Donald. "Abortion: Denial of Freedom to Care." *Our Sunday Visitor,* 62 (July 1, 1973), 1+.

[889]De Marco. "The Merchants of Calumny." *Linacre Quarterly,* 40 (November, 1973), 271-82. [The author sets the abortion issue in a literary context. The fetus is compared to Shylock, a Jew in Shakespeare's *Merchant of Venice,* Act III, Scene 1. The personhood of the fetus and the physical development of the fetus are discussed.]

[890]De Marco, Donald. "Parallels in Treachery." *Sisters Today,* 45 (October, 1973), 82-89.

[891]De Marco, Donald. "The Philosophical Roots in Western Culture for the Pro-Abortion Stand." *Linacre Quarterly,* 41 (May, 1974), 87-99. [Five major philosophical roots are set forth: 1) Atomism separates the individual from the community and treats him as absolute; 2) Cartesianism separates the ego from the other and man from nature, rendering their inter-relationships unaccountable; 3) Existentialism (Sartrean) separates existence from essence and makes freedom absolute; 4) Empiricism separates the material from the spiritual and makes matter absolute; 5) Sociologism separates the intrinsic from the extrinsic and treats the extrinsic as absolute.

Dr. Marco's evaluation and criticism of each school provides new discussion grounds for those who defend the pro-life movement.]

[892]De Marco, Donald. "The Right to Be Born." *Sisters Today,* 44 (April, 1973), 490-95.

[893]De Marco, Donald. "Society as an Art Form." *Triumph,* 9 (February, 1974), 21.

[894]De Marco, Donald. "Two Essays on Abortion." *Review for Religious,* 32 (September, 1973), 1064-69.

[895]"Democratic Murder." *Triumph,* 3 (February, 1968), 9.

[896]"Democrats for Life Formed to

897-
917
Work for an Amendment." *Our Sunday Visitor,* 65 (August 1, 1976),
2.

[897]"Democrats Take Stand
gainst Pro-Lifers." *Our Sunday
Visitor,* 65 (June 27, 1976), 1.

[898]De Muth, J. "Court Strikes
Anti-Abortion Law in Illinois."
National Catholic Reporter, 7 (Feb-
ruary 12, 1971), 16.

[899]Denes, Magda. *In Necessity
and Sorrow: Life and Death in an
Abortion Hospital* (New York: Pen-
guin Books, 1977).

[900]Dennis, K. J. *Abortion,
Babies and Contraception: A.B.C. of
Eugenics* (Southampton: University
of Southampton, 1975).

[901]Dennis, K. J. "Indications
for Therapeutic Abortion in Aberdeen, 1966-67." *Journal of Biosocial Science,* 3 (January, 1971),
101-05.

[902]Deobhakta, V. G. "Therapeutic Abortion in the Maori." *New
Zealand Medical Journal,* 75 (March,
1972), 174.

[903]Derrick, C. "The Rules of
the Game." *Triumph,* 6 (March,
1971), 14-17.

[904]Destro, N. "Psychiatric Indications for the Termination of
Pregnancy." *Medical Journal of
Australia,* 1 (February 6, 1971),
350-51.

[905]Destro, Robert A. "Abortion
and the Constitution: The Need for
a Life-Protective Amendment." *California Law Review,* 63 (September,
1975), 1250-351.

[906]Devereux, George. *A Study
of Abortion in Primitive Societies*
(New York: Julian Press, 1955).

[907]Devereux, George. *A Study
of Abortion in Primitive Societies,*
revised edition (New York: International Universities Press, Inc.,
1976).

[908]Devine, G. "Church Authori-
ties Must do Much More." *National
Catholic Reporter,* 9 (April 20,
1973), 13.

[909]Devlin, W. "America:
There's a Nigger in the Woodpile."
Triumph, 8 (May, 1973), 27.

[910]Devlin, W. "Which Amendment?" *Triumph,* 9 (January, 1974),
12-16+.

[911]Deyak, T. A., and Smith, V. K.
"Economic Value of Statute Reform:
The Case of Liberalized Abortion,"
bibl. *Journal of Political Economy,*
84 (February, 1976), 83-99.

[912]Diamond. "ISMS Symposium on
Medical Implications of Current Abortion Law in Illinois." *Illinois Medical Journal,* 131 (May, 1967), 677-80.

[913]Diamond, E. "Contraception and
Abortifacients." *Linacre Quarterly,*
38 (May, 1971), 122-26.

[914]Diamond, E. "Do the Medical
Schools Discriminate Against Anti-
Abortion Applicants." *Linacre Quarterly,* 43 (February, 1976), 29-35. [This
article contains the questions and a
discussion of the results of a survey
on the admission practices of all
American medical schools by questionnaire. It was administered by the ad-
hoc Committee on Medical School Discrimination.
   Also, included is a letter sent to
all Regional Medical officiaries. This
letter concerns the elimination of
appointments and promotion of obstetricians, anesthesiologists and psychiatrists opposed to abortion by
reason of conscience.]

[915]Diamond, E. "The Humanity of
the Unborn Child." *Catholic Lawyer,*
17 (Spring, 1971), 174-80. [Diamond's
position is to speak for the fetus and
be his advocate. He traces the typical pregnancy as it relates to the
question of abortion, describing the
reactions of fetuses to the various
methods of abortion. Each reason when
abortion might be considered is discussed as to its feasibility. These
include abortions performed either to
preserve the health of the mother, because of possible congenital defects,
or because of an unwanted child.]

[916]Diamond, E. "The Physician
and the Rights of the Unborn: Bibliography." *Linacre Quarterly,* 34 (May,
1967), 174-81.

[917]Diamond, E. "'Quality' vs.
'Sanctity of Life' in the Nursery."
America, 135 (December 4, 1976), 396-
98. [Eugene Diamond exposes a new
problem—what to do with the "viable
newborn infant"? The traditional regard for the "sanctity of life" is now
challenged by the "quality of life
ethic."
   "If we are to reclaim protection
for the unborn child, we cannot con-
cede the logical extension of the
abortion mentality into the nursery.
The sanctity of life ethic that now

spreads its tattered mantle of protection over newborn defective infants must be upheld. It is really protecting all of us."]

[918]Diamond, E. "Right to Life vs. Upjohn." *Linacre Quarterly,* 41 (August, 1974), 147-48. [This editorial discusses the research of the Upjohn Company which produces Prostaglandin F_2 Alpha. This drug has been approved by the Food and Drug Administration for the induction of abortion in the second trimester. The policy of the corporation, even though it states that it "takes not position", actually has announced that the company will divert part of its research into finding the most effective and convenient means of killing.]

[919]Diamond, E. "Who Speaks for the Fetus?" *Linacre Quarterly,* 36 (February, 1969), 58-62. [The author states that "any life is of infinite value and that this value is not significantly diminished by physical or mental defect or the circumstances of that life's beginning."]

[920]Diamond, J. "Abortion, Animation, and Biological Hominization." *Theological Studies,* 36 (June, 1975), 305-24.

[921]Diamond, J. "Humanizing the Abortion Debate." *America,* 121 (July 9, 1969), 36-39.

[922]Diamond, J. "A Physician Reports." *America,* 123 (July 11, 1970). [This is a review of Daniel Callahan's *Abortion: Law, Choice, and Morality* (New York: Macmillan Publishing Co., 1970).

[923]Diamond, J. "Pro-Life Amendments and Due Process." *America,* 130 (January 19, 1974), 27-29. [It is possible for the state to deprive constitutional persons of their lives by the due process. So it is implied that a non-discriminatory, right-to-life amendment must also permit the state to take unborn life, if due process is seen as the implementation of the Fifth and Fourteenth Amendments.]

[924]Diamond, J. "Suicide American Style: The Danger of Birth Rate Decline." *Liguorian,* 60 (April, 1972), 45-49.

[925]Diamond, J. "The Troubled Anti-Abortion Camp." *America,* 131 (August 10, 1974), 52-53. [Rigoristic Catholic supporters threaten the Human Life Amendment because it

falls short of natural-law moral theology. The controversy centers around "fertilization" and "contraception".
The author states that the amendment "may fall short of purism", but it is better than no amendment at all; compromise is necessary.]

[926]Diamond, M., *et al.* "Abortion in Hawaii." *Family Planning Perspectives,* 5 (Winter, 1973), 54-60. [Hawaii was the first state in March 1970 to make induced abortion legally available.]

[927]Diamond, M., Steinhoff, P. G., Palmore, J. A., and Smith, R. G. "Sexuality, Birth Control and Abortion. A Decision-Making Sequence." *Journal of Biosocial Science,* 5(3) (1973), 347-61.

[928]Dickens, B. *Abortion and the Law* (London: MacGibbon and Kee, 1966).

[929]Dickens, B. M. "The 'Conscience Clause' and the Law on Abortion." *Nursing Times,* 70 (June 20, 1974), 968-69.

[930]Dickens, B. M. "Morgentaler (*Morgentaler v. Regina* [1975] 53 D L R [3d] 161) Case: Criminal Process and Abortion Law." *Osgoode Hall Law Journal,* 14 (October, 1976), 229-74.

[931]Dickens, H. O., Mudd, E. H., Garcia, C. R., Tomar, K., and Wright, D. "One Hundred Pregnant Adolescents, Treatment Approaches in a University Hospital." *American Journal of Public Health,* 63(9) (1973), 794-800.

[932]Diddle, A. "Rights Affecting Human Reproduction." *Obstetrics and Gynecology,* 41 (May, 1973), 789-94.

[933]"Difficult Delivery of New Abortion Laws." *New England Journal of Medicine,* 280 (May 29, 1969), 1240-41.

[934]Diggory, Peter. "Abortion Analysis." *Lancet,* 2 (August 22, 1970), 413-14.

[935]Diggory, Peter. "Some Experiences with the New British Abortion Law." Paper delivered at the International Conference on Abortion, Hot Springs, Virginia, November 17-20, 1968.

[936]Diggory, Peter. "Some Experiences of Therapeutic Abortion." *Lancet,* 1 (April 26, 1969), 873-75.

[937]Diggory, Peter, and Simms, Madeleine. "Two Years After the

938-
961

Abortion Act." *New Scientist* (November 5, 1970).

[938]Diggory, Peter, *et al.* "Preliminary Assessment of the 1967 Abortion Act in Practice." *Lancet,* 1 (February 7, 1970), 287-91.

[939]DiGiacomo, James, ed. *Abortion: A Question of Values.* Conscience and Concern Ser: No. 1. (Minneapolis, Minnesota: Winston Press, 1975).

[940]Dillon, V. "ISMS Symposium on Medical Implications of Current Abortion Law in Illinois." *Illinois Medical Journal,* 131 (May, 1967), 669-74.

[941]Dillon, V. "Abortion: The Moment of Truth." *U. S. Catholic,* 38 (September, 1973), 37-38. [Dillon sees two problems in educating people about abortion: 1) reverence for human life must not be limited to the unborn but to all human life; 2) teaching efforts must reach beyond "judgmental proclamations" such as, "Abortion is murder!", to philosophical concepts of personhood and the "ethics of expediency".]

[942]Dillon, V. "Birthright." *Sign,* 50 (July, 1971), 27-29.

[943]Diner, M. C. "Survey of Ottawa Area General Practitioners and Obstetrician-Gynecologists on Abortion." *Canadian Journal of Public Health,* 65(5) (September-October, 1974), 351-58.

[944]"D.C. Abortion Law is Upheld." *National Catholic Reporter,* 7 (April 30, 1971), 3-4.

[945]District of Columbia Government Commission on the Status of Women. Annual Report (Washington, D.C., 1967). [The Commission states its objectives: to elevate the status of women in education, employment, family relationships and correctional areas.]

[946]Dittrich, J. P. "On Abortion, a Dissent." *Alaska Medicine,* 11 (December, 1969), 119-23.

[947]"Divorce Wasn't the End of it." *Economist,* 252 (August 31, 1974), 34.

[948]Dixit, Ramesh, and Shri Rajesh Mathew. "Motives Related to the Desire for Children: A Psychological Study of Parenthood." *Journal of Family Welfare,* 122 (March, 1976), 40-43.

[949]Dixon, G., *et al.* "Letter: Effects of Legal Termination on Subsequent Pregnancy." *British Medical Journal,* 2(6030) (July 31, 1976), 299.

[950]Djerassi, D. "Some Observations on Current Fertility Control in China," il. *China Quarterly,* no. 57 (January, 1974), 40-62.

[951]Dobbin, M. "The Two Separate Issues in the Abortion Debate." *Medical Journal of Australia,* 1 (June 9, 1973), 1165-66.

[952]Dobson, J. R., *et al.* "Therapeutic Abortion." *New Zealand Medical Journal,* 74 (October, 1971), 274.

[953]"Doctor Claims Hundreds of Fetuses Die Needlessly." *National Catholic Reporter,* 7 (March 15, 1971), 3.

[954]"Dr. Daly Says Law Prohibiting Abortion Should be Repealed." *National Catholic Reporter,* 7 (April 2, 1971), 8.

[955]"Doctor's Dilemma." *Canadian Medical Association Journal,* 101 (August 9, 1969), 176.

[956]"Doctor Predicts Abortion Without Death in Future." *Our Sunday Visitor,* 64 (March 7, 1976), 1.

[957]"Doctor, What Does the Aborted Baby Feel While It's Dying?" *Triumph,* 7 (March, 1972), 20-23+.

[958]"Doctors Against More Abortions." *National Catholic Reporter,* 6 (December 17, 1969), 6.

[959]"Documentation: Missouri House Bill No. 1211." *Jurist,* 35 (Winter, 1975), 110-14.

[960]*Doe v. Doe* [(Mass) 314 N E 2d 128]: The Wife's Right to an Abortion Over Her Husband's Objections." *New England Law Review,* 11 (Fall, 1975), 205-24.

[961]Doherty, D. "The Morality of Abortion." *American Ecclesiastical Review,* 169 (June, 1975), 37-47. [The author suggests two approaches to the investigation of the moral force of the official condemnation of abortion—first, by a more general teaching on the making of a moral judgment, secondly, through the overall context of the respect to he shown to human life.
An examination of conscience is offered for those who claim to be pro-life. In conclusion, the author

sees that conscience is the only forum where the abortion dilemma can be resolved.]

[962]Dolan, W. V. "Letter: Abortion vs. Manslaughter." *Archives of Surgery,* 111(1) (January, 1976), 93.

[963]Dollen, Charles J. *Abortion in Context: A Select Bibliography* (Metuchen, N.J.: Scarecrow Press, Inc., 1970).

[964]Donald, I. "Abortion and the Obstetrician." *Lancet,* 1 (June 12, 1971), 1233.

[965]Donahue, J. M. "Therapeutic Abortion: A Psychiatric View." *Journal of the Indiana State Medical Association,* 64 (August, 1971), 833-34.

[966]Donceel, J. "Abortion: Mediate vs. Immediate Animation." *Continuum,* 5 (Spring, 1967), 167-71. [The author poses both sides of the animation question but opts for the evolutionary theory of St. Thomas who described three stages of soul: vegetative, animal and human. He then can argue that the potential to be human is not fundamentally human.]

[967]Donceel, J. "Immediate Animation and Delayed Hominization." *Theological Studies,* 31 (March, 1970), 76. [The author gives an account of Aristotelian-Thomistic views on delayed animation and substitutes the term by "delayed hominization". He reviews the definition of the substantial form of man by the Council of Vienne.]

[968]Donceel, J. "Why is Abortion Wrong?" *America,* 133 (August 16, 1975), 65-67. [Father Donceel offers the history of the question concerning the hominization of the fetus, or when does the fetus become human.

He concludes that Catholic doctrine is not certain about the moment of hominization. What can be said is that every abortion may be a homicide, therefore, abortion is always immoral. In case of doubt, one cannot perform an action which might kill a person.]

[969]Donovan, D. M. "Psychotherapy in Abortion." *Current Psychiatric Therapies,* 15 (1975), 77-83.

[970]Donovan, H. M. "Therapeutic Abortion and Acculturation." *Nursing Forum,* 10 (1971), 378-81.

[971]Douglas, C. P. "Twin Survival in Therapeutic Abortion." *British Medical Journal,* 3 (September 26, 1970), 769.

[972]Dourlen-Rollier, A. M. "Legal Problems Related to Abortion and Menstrual Regulation." *Columbia Human Rights Law Review,* 7(1) (1975), 120-35.

[973]Dowrick, F. "Christian Values in the Legislative Process in Britain in the Sixties." *American Journal of Jurisprudence,* 16 (1971), 156-83.

[974]Doyle, J. "Action in the Wake of Death Monday." *Social Justice Review,* 66 (July-August, 1973), 133-35.

[975]Doyle, J. "Taxes—Where the Dollars Go—Abortions Yes, Private Schools No." *Liguorian,* 63 (September, 1975), 7-11.

[976]Doyle, J., Dranke, W. Jr., L'Ecuyer, J., and Byme, P. "Fight for Life: Missouri, March 8, 1972, Missouri House Bill 1470; Statements to the Committee on Civil and Criminal Procedures." *Social Justice Review,* 65 (June, 1972), 89-94.

[977]Dozier, C. "The Right to Life vs. the Right to Privacy." *Our Sunday Visitor,* 61 (April 8, 1973), 1+.

[978]"Draft Letter on Abortion Sent Bishops." *National Catholic Reporter,* 12 (January 9, 1976), 14.

[979]Draper, P. "Reviewing the Abortion Act." *British Medical Journal,* 3 (August 8, 1970), 344.

[980]Drinan, R. F., SJ. "The Abortion Decision." *Commonweal,* 97 (February 16, 1973), 438-40. [Drinnan comments on the Supreme Court's method of balancing the privacy of the woman and pregnancy.]

He points out that there are some good results. The Court is harsh on non-physicians or delicensed physicians practicing abortion. The Court indicated that the state does have the power to protect the right to life of a viable fetus. Also, in the opinion of the Supreme Court, the medical profession is now the sole regulator of what standards should be followed by a physician in terminating a pregnancy in the first trimester.

It must be noted that the Supreme Court's decision virtually gave exclusive jurisdiction over who will live and who will die during the first three months from conception. Drinan urges those who cannot agree with abortion under the present Court decision to speak out.]

[981]Drinan, R. F., SJ. "Abortions on Medicaid." *Commonweal,* 102 (May 9, 1975), 102-03. [This article presents the attempt of Republican Dewey Bartlett to propose an amendment which would refuse to condition use of the statutory benefit of Medicaid for abortion.

The Catholics in the Senate were divided on the issue.

One note of importance is that there are six federal decisions which state that if the Federal government provides financial aid for maternity care, then it must also provide for abortions.]

[982]Drinan, R. F., SJ. "Catholic Moral Teaching and Abortion Laws in America." *Catholic Theological Society Association Proceedings,* 23 (1968), 118-30.

[983]Drinan, Robert F., SJ. "Contemporary Protestant Thinking." *America,* 117 (December 9, 1967), 713. [The views of various Protestant Conferences (Lambeth of 1958 and National Council of Churches of Christ, 1961) are discussed as well as Barth, Bonhoeffer and Ramsey, on abortion.]

[984]Drinan, Robert F., SJ. "The Inviolability of the Right to Be Born," in *Abortion and the Law.* Ed. David T. Smith (Cleveland: Western Reserve University Press, 1967).

[985]Drinan, Robert F., SJ. "The Jurispurdential Options on Abortion." *Theological Studies,* 31 (March, 1970), 149.

[986]Drinan, Robert F., SJ. "Morality of Abortion Laws." *Catholic Lawyer,* 14 (Summer, 1968), 190-198. [The principles which Catholics should articulate about the appropriate law regulating abortion in a pluralistic society are discussed, as well as the procedure or strategy which Catholics should follow in this area.]

[987]Drinan, Robert F., SJ. "Review of D. Granfield, *The Abortion Decision*." *America,* 120 (May 31, 1969), 653.

[988]Drinan, Robert F., SJ. "The Right of the Fetus to Be Born." *Dublin Review,* 514 (Winter, 1967-1968), 365. [The author concludes that any attempt to legislate that some fetuses may die, pose a problem of establishing and justifying norms to judge which they would be.]

[989]Drinan, Robert F., SJ. "Should There be Laws Against Abortion?" *U. S. Catholic,* 35 (April, 1970), 15-17.

[990]Drinan, Robert F., SJ. "The State of the Abortion Question." *Commonweal,* 92 (April 17, 1970), 108-09. [The question posed by Drinan is: "Is it better to allow the state to establish by law a limited number of reasons which would justify an abortion or would it be better if the law were silent about abortion and thus left the matter to the good conscience of parents and physicians?"

In an address to the Catholic Theological Society of America in 1968, he made the following recommendation: "It is submitted that episcopal statements going beyond the morality of abortion and entering into the question of jurisprudence or the best legal arrangement are inappropriate intrusions in a pluralistic society by an ecclesiastical official who wrongly assumes that he can pronounce a moral and uniform position for his church on a legal-political question.]

[991]Drinan, Robert F., SJ. "Strategy on Abortion." *America,* 116 (February 4, 1967), 177-79. [Drinan presents the results of the survey by the National Opinion Research Centre. A strong majority of American people thought that legal abortion should be possible if the mother's health is in danger, while a slim majority feels that abortion should be available for victims of rape or for a defective child. There was a large majority who felt that legal abortion should be allowed for unwanted pregnancy by a poor family or for those who simply do not want another child.

Several proposals were offered to meet some of the objectives advanced by the abortion advocates, in cases of rape, provisions for the care of a defective child, and abortion for "therapeutic" reasons to save the life of the mother.]

[992]"Drive to Legalize Abortion in Italy Starts Uneasily." *National Catholic Reporter,* 11 (May 23, 1975), 20.

[993]Droegemueller, W., *et al.* "The First Year of Experience in Colorado with the New Abortion Law." *American Journal of Obstetrics and Gynecology,* 103 (March 1, 1969), 694-702.

[994]Droegemueller, W., *et al.* "The Second Year's Experience with Colorado's Abortion Law." *American Journal of Obstetrics and Gynecology,* 109 (March 15, 1971), 957-58.

[995]Droegemueller, W., *et al.* "Is

Therapeutic Abortion Preventable?" *Obstetrics and Gynecology,* 35 (May, 1970), 758-59.

[996]"Le Droit de Naitre; Document du Conseil Permanent de la Conférence Episcopale Italienne sur L'Avortement." *La Documentation Catholique,* 69 (April 2, 1972), 312-14.

[997]Drunn, H. P. "Therapeutic Abortion in New Zealand." *New Zealand Medical Journal,* 68 (1968), 253-58.

[998]Dubec, P. "Abortion Isn't a Catholic Issue But an Issue for All, Protestant Pro-Life Leaders Say." *Our Sunday Visitor,* 64 (December 21, 1975), 1.

[999]Du Bois, R. "Julie Who Walks in the Sunlight." *Liguorian,* 63 (July, 1975), 26-29.

[1000]Dudgeon, J. A. "Maternal Rubella and Its Effect on the Fetus." *Archives of Diseases of Childhood,* 42 (April, 1967), 110-125.

[1001]Duffy, Edward A. "United States. Maternal and Child Health Service. The Effect of Changes in the STate Abortion Laws." *Public Health Service,* no. 2165 (February, 1971).

[1002]Duffy, M. A. "Law on Abortion." *Pennsylvania Bar Association Quarterly,* 43 (January, 1972), 212.

[1003]Duffy, Paul J. *The Politics of Abortion* (Homebush, Australia: Alba House, 1971).

[1004]Duin, V. N. "New York's Abortion Reform Law: Unanswered Questions." *Albany Law Review,* 37 (1972), 22.

[1005]Dukette, Rita, and Stevenson, Nicholas. "The Legal Rights of Unmarried Fathers: The Impact of Recent Court Decisions." *The Social Service Review,* 47 (March, 1973), 1-15. [In 1972, in the case of *Stanley* vs. *the State of Illinois,* the U.S. Supreme Court ruled that the unwed father is entitled to the same rights as a married father in matters concerning guardinaship of the child. The *Rothstein* vs. *Lutheran Social Services of Wisconsin and Upper Michigan* decision includes the rights over the release for adoption of illegitimate children also. The author discusses possible effects

of these decisions on the adoption process.]

[1006]Dunbar, Flanders. "A Psychosomatic Approach to Abortion and the Abortion Habit." *Abortion in America* (Boston: Beacon Press, 1967).

[1007]Duncan, Jack A., and Moffett, Catherine F. "Abortion Counseling and the School Counselor." *The School Counselor,* 21 (January, 1974), 188-94.

[1008]Dunea, G. "Letter From... Chicago. Confrontations." *British Medical Journal,* 3(5976) (July 19, 1975), 151-53.

[1009]Dunn, H. L. "Frequency of Abortion. Its Effects on Maternal Mortality Rates." *The Abortion Problem.* Ed. H. C. Taylor (New York: Williams and Wilkins Co., 1944).

[1010]Dunn, H. P. *What's Wrong with Abortion?* (Dublin: Irish Messenger Office, 1972).

[1011]Dunn, H. P. "Abortion Law." *New Zealand Medical Journal,* 75 (April, 1972), 229-30.

[1012]Dunn, H. P. "Letter: Abortion." *New Zealand Medical Journal,* 80(527) (November 13, 1974), 410.

[1013]Dunn, H. P. "Therapeutic Abortion in New Zealand." *New Zealand Medical Journal,* 68 (October, 1968), 253-58.

[1014]Dunn, L. J. "Availability of Abortion, Sterilization, and Other Medical Treatment for Minor Patients." *UMKC Law Review,* 44 (Fall, 1975), 1-22.

[1015]Dunwoody, I. "Abortion on Social Grounds." *Lancet,* 1 (1968), 857.

[1016]Dupré, L. K. "New Approach to the Abortion Problem." *Theological Studies,* 34 (September, 1973), 481-88.

[1017]Durbin, T. "The Catholic Hospital Faces Abortion." *American Ecclesiastical Review,* 163 (October, 1970), 244-54. [Despite government grants, the Catholic hospital has the right to manage its own internal policies. The author views the imposition of abortion upon the Catholic hospital as a violation of the First Amendment.]

[1018]Dutta, R. "Abortion and Fertility Control (A Brief World Review)." *Journal of the Indian Medical Associa-*

tion, 64(11) (June 1, 1975), 315-
20.

[1019]Dwyer, Karen. "You'd
Think Fetuses Could Vote." *Majority Report,* 5 (March 6-20, 1976),
1.

[1020]Dyck, Arthur J. "Perplex-
ities for the Would-Be Liberal in
Abortion." Paper presented to the
National Canadian Conference on
Abortion, Toronto, Canada, May,
1972. [The rights of the fetus
and the mother are discussed. The
author points out that liberal
abortion laws do not provide population control but a lessening of
the use of contraceptives. Survival and progress depend upon
viewing children as a community
responsibility.]

[1021]Dyck, A., and Williams, G.
"The Right to Life: The Harvard
Statement." *Catholic Digest,* 36
(March, 1972), 29-32.

[1022]Dytrich, Z. "Psychological Aspects of Abortion in Czechoslovakia." *Journal of Psychiatric Nursing and Mental Health
Services,* 8(3) (1970), 30-33.

[1023]Dytrych, Z., Matejcek, Z.,
Schuller, V., David, H. P., and
Friedman, H. L. "Children Born to
Women Denied Abortion." *Family
Planning Perspectives,* 7(5) (1975),
165-71.

[1024]Eames, J. R., *et al.* "A
General-Practitioner Survey of the
Abortion Act 1967." *Practitioner,*
207 (August, 1971), 227-30.

[1025]Early, T. "NCC Abortion
Statement: A Few Questions."
Christianity and Crisis, 33 (Octo-
ber 1, 1973), 188-92. [This is
the statement on abortion by the
National Council of Churches (NCC).
The paper speaks of the "need" for
abortions in certain situations.]

[1026]Easterling, W. E., Jr.,
et al. "Abortion: The First Five
Years at North Carolina Memorial
Hospital." *Texas Medicine,* 69
(April, 1973), 61-67.

[1027]Eastman, N. J. "Induced
Abortion and Contraception: A Consideration of Ethical Philosophy
in Obstetrics." *Obstetrics and
Gynecology Survey,* 22 (February,
1967), 3-11.

[1028]Eastman, N. J. "Liberalization of Attitudes Toward Abortion." *Current Medical Digest*
(June, 1959).

[1029]"Easy Abortion Loses in Two
States." *National Catholic Reporter,*
9 (November 24, 1972), 4.

[1030]Ebaugh, F. G., and Heuser, K.
D. "Psychiatric Aspects of Therapeutic Abortion." *Postgraduate Medicine,*
2 (November, 1947), 325-332.

[1031]Edelstein, R., Herman, E.,
and Herman, M. "Moral Consistency
and the Abortion Issue." *Commonweal,*
100 (March 22, 1974), 59-61. [The
authors analyzed the voting patterns
by members of the Pennsylvania House
on the abortion bills and bills which
were related to the preservation and
enhancement of life after birth. They
concluded that the Catholics were
ready to support anti-abortion proposals but not those that would for-
bid capital punishment or protest the
Vietnam War. The Catholic legislators voting pattern seemed incompati-
ble with any real adherence to a
general principle of "right-to-life."]

[1032]"'*Edelin*' Case: Victims of
Ambiguity." *America,* 132 (March 1,
1975), 141. [The fundamental ambiguity in the Supreme Court's 1973 abortion decisions are brought to the
fore. The central issue in the Edelin case asks if a fetus survives the
abortion procedure does the birth
confer legal personality and require
the doctor to employ ordinary measures to preserve infant life.]

[1033]"Edelin Spent $10,000 to Sur-
vey Prospective Jurors." *Our Sunday
Visitor,* 63 (March 16, 1975), 2.

[1034]"Edelin Supported." *New England Journal of Medicine,* 292(13)
(March 27, 1975), 705.

[1035]Edwards, J. H. "Uses of
Amniocentesis." *Lancet,* 1 (March 21,
1970), 609-09.

[1036]"Effects of Abortion Act:
Some Observations." *Nursing Times,*
64 (July 12, 1968), 931-32.

[1037]Effenberger, D. "Paper Says
Aborted Babies Left to Die: University of Minnesota Hospitals." *National Catholic Reporter,* 10 (March 15,
1974), 3.

[1038]Effenberger, D. "Wanderer
Forum Backs Amendment." *National
Catholic Reporter,* 9 (July 20, 1973),
17.

[1039]Egdell, R. "Experience with
Therapeutic Abortion Clinic. Methods
and Complications." *Delaware Medical*

Journal, 44 (August, 1972), 207-12.

[1040]Ehrenberg, C. J. "Unwanted Pregnancies." *Minnesota Medicine,* 50 (January, 1967), 61-63.

[1041]Ehrensing, Rudolph. "When is it Really Abortion?" *National Catholic Reporter* (May 25,]966), 3. [The humanity of the fetus is discussed. The author is attempting to justify the IUD as a method of birth control.]

[1042]Ehrhardt, H. E. "Ending Life of Unborn or Moribund-Dommon Problems of Abortion and Euthanasia." *Politische Studien,* 26 (June, 1975), 225-44.

[1043]Eibel, P. "Abortion and the Law." *Canadian Medical Association Journal,* 98 (May 25, 1968), 1017.

[1044]Eichhorst, C. J. "Abortion—No! (Reply to C. F. Parvey)." *Dialog,* 12 (Winter, 1973), 62-65.

[1045]Eichhorst, C. J. "Sickness Unto Death." *Dialog,* 13 (Summer, 1974), 169-71.

[1046]Eickhoff, L. F. "Letter: Abotion and Promiscuity." *British Medical Journal,* 3(5975) (July 12, 1975), 99-100.

[1047]"86 Per Cent of M.D.'s Favor Abortion Changes." *National Catholic Reporter,* 3 (May 10, 1967), 7.

[1048]Eisenberg, John A., and Bourne, Paula. *The Right to Live and Die* (Toronto: Ontario Institute for Studies in Education, 1973).

[1049]Ekblad, Martin. "Relation of the Legal-Abortion Clientele to the Illegal-Abortion Clientele and the Risk of Suicides." *Acta Psychiatrica Scandinavia,* suppl. 99 (1955), 93-98.

[1050]Ekblad, Martin. "The Sociopsychiatric Indications for Legal Termination of Pregnancy in Sweden." *Fourth International Conference on Planned Parenthood* (1953).

[1051]Elford, R. W. "Therapeutic Abortion." *Canadian Medical Association Journal,* 105 (September 18, 1971), 638-39.

[1052]Eliasberg, Wladimir G. "Psychiatry in Pre-Natal Care and the Problem of Abortion." *Medical Woman's Journal,* 58 (January-February, 1951).

[1053]Eliasberg, Wladimir G. "The Pre-Natal Psychotic Patient." *Abortion in America.* Ed. Harold Rosen (Boston: Beacon Press, 1967).

[1054]"Eliminate the Causes of Abortion; Says Bp. Martensen of Copenhagen." *Tablet,* 221 (February 18, 1967), 192.

[1055]Eliot, J. "What Will Abortion Regulations be if Law is Reformed? Here are Clues." *Michigan Medicine,* 71 (November, 1972), 959-62.

[1056]Eliot, John, *et al.* "Therapeutic Abortions in Teaching Hospitals in the United States and Canada." Paper delivered at the International Conference on Abortion, Hot Springs, Virginia, November 17-20, 1968.

[1057]Eller, Vernard. "Let's Get Honest About Abortion: A Reply to Joseph Fletcher." *Christian Century,* 92 (January 1-8, 1975), 16-18. Also, *Brethren Life & Thought,* 20 (Spring, 1975), 115-18. [This article is written in response to Joseph Fletcher's article of November 27, in *Christian Century,* "Abortion and the True Believer." Eller examines two interpretations adduced by the proponents of abortion to demonstrate the inconsistency of their argument that the fetus is not a person, but he says that even if the pro-abortion interpretation stands, the real nature of the ethical situation is not affected. Then, the second argument concerns the woman's right to freedom of control over her own body. Eller sees the issue as "control over their own body" (the father's and mother's). He sees freedom as implying responsibility.]

[1058]Ellis, J. M. "Poor Legislative Response to *Walsingham vs. State* [(Fla) 250 S 2d 857)." *Florida Bar Journal,* 47 (January, 1973), 18.

[1059]Ely, John Hart. "The Wages of Crying Wolf: A Comment on *Roe vs. Wade.*" *Yale Law Journal,* 82 (April, 1973), 920-49. [This article discusses the way in which the *Roe* decision was not made on the basis of constitutional law, but was a decision based on the court's own value preferences.

[1060]"An Emergency Operation." *Lancet,* 2 (n.d.), 495.

[1061]Emerson, M. S. "Personal Factors." *Journal of Biosocial*

Sciences, 1 (July, 1969), 300-314.

[1062]Endres, Richard J. "Abortion in Perspective." *American Journal of Obstetrics and Gynecology,* 111 (October 1, 1971). [Abortion in the USSR from 1920 to the present is discussed.]

[1063]Engel, R. "From Womb into Tomb." *Liguorian,* 59 (December, 1971), 22-24.

[1064]Engelhardt, H. Tristram Jr. "On the Bounds of Freedom: From the Treatment of Fetuses to Euthanasia." *Connecticut Medicine,* 40(1) (January, 1976), 51-54, 57.

[1065]Engelhardt, H. Tristram Jr. "The Ontology of Abortion." *Ethics,* 84 (April, 1974), 217-34. [Reply: Newton, L. *Ethics,* 85 (July, 1975), 332-36.] [The abortion question is seen as being centered on the humanity of the fetus. The author argues that a distinction should be made between human biological life and human personal life. Two senses of person are given. First, a person can be a self-conscious, moral agent. Or, the person denotes instances of human life which play active social roles. Fetuses do not fit into either category. Therefore, no one is wronged in abortion, since our obligations are solely to persons.]

[1066]"English Nurses Reject Legalized Abortion." *L'Osservatore Romano* (English), no. 34 (125) (August 20, 1970), 7.

[1067]Epstein, R. A. "Substantive Due Process by any Other Name: The Abortion Cases." *Supreme Court Review,* 1973 (1973), 159-85.

[1068]Erickson, Milton H. "The Psychological Significance of Vasectomy." *Abortion in America.* Ed. Harold Rosen (Boston: Beacon Press, 1967).

[1069]Erickson, N. S. "Women and the Supreme Court: Anatomy is Destiny." *Brooklyn Law Review,* 41 (Fall, 1974), 209-82.

[1070]Ernst, Morris. "There is a Desperate Need of Medical Wisdom to Deal With the Problem of 'Abortion'." *New Medical Materia* (July, 1962).

[1071]"La Escalada Del Aborto." *Christus,* 36 (February, 1971), 29.

[1072]"Ethics and Abortion." *British Medical Journal,* 2 (April 20, 1968), 173.

[1073]"Ethics of Selective Abortion." *British Medical Journal,* 4 (5946) (December 21, 1974), 676.

[1074]Etzioni, Amitai. "The Fetus: Whose Property?" *Commonweal,* 98 (September 21, 1973), 493. [Etzioni discusses the implications of a Federal Court ruling in Miami, Florida, that a woman does not need the consent of her husband to obtain a legal abortion. It is based on the Supreme Court's decision that no authority should interfere with a woman's right to handle the matter. Many new issues result from this issue. The author sees this ruling as disregarding the marital contract. The fetus is not viewed as the creation of the couple but solely as the property of the mother.

Etzioni suggests that, by requiring the couple's consent, the father would reaffirm his parental role and solidify the marriage bond. For couples who could not agree arbitrators may be employed. Obtaining the husband's consent is seen as helping to uphold the family.]

[1075]Etzioni, Amitai. "Husband's Rights in Abortion." *Trial,* 12 (November, 1976), 56-58.

[1076]Etzioni, Amitai. "Issues of Public Policy in the USA Raised by Amniocentesis." *Journal of Medical Ethics,* 2 (March, 1976), 8-11.

[1077]"Europe is Moving Both Ways (Abortion Law in France, Italy and West Germany)." Il. *Economist,* 254 (March 1, 1975), 52-53.

[1078]Evans, D. "Right of Action for Injury to, or Death of a Woman Who Consented to Abortion." *Journal of the Medical Association of the State of Alabama,* 40 (November, 1970, 334 passim.

[1079]Evans, D., *et al.* "Post-Abortion Attitudes." *North Carolina Medical Journal,* 34 (April, 1973), 271-73.

[1080]Evans, J. Claude. "Abortion Law Reform is Inevitable." *Christian Century,* 88 (May 5, 1971), 54.

[1081]Evans, J. Claude. "The Abortion Decision: A Balancing of Rights." *Christian Century,* 40 (February 14, 1973), 195-97. [Evans views the U. S. Supreme Court's decision on abortion as a balancing of individual vs. social rights, with the individual rights gradually giving ground to social rights as the woman's term progresses. The decision is left to those most involved (woman and doctor). Moral counseling should be available, but not mandatory.]

[1082]Everingham, D. "Letter: Psychological Factors in Contraceptive Failure and Abortion Request." *Medical Journal of Australia*, 2(15) (October, 1975), 617-18.

[1083]"Evidence of the Royal College of General Practitioners to the Select Committee of Parliament on the Abortion (Amendment) Bill." *Journal of the Royal College of General Practitioners*, 25(159) (October, 1975), 774-76.

[1084]Ewing, J. A., and Rouse, B. A. "Therapeutic Abortion and a Prior Psychiatric History." *American Journal of Psychiatry*, 130(1) (1973), 37-40. [The results of this study showed that the women with a history of prior psychiatric illness, as well as those without such a history, did not show a significant difference in their emotional symptoms after an abortion was performed to prevent psychiatric crisis reaction.]

[1085]Ewing, J. A., Liptzin, M. B., Rouse, B. A., Spencer, R. F., and Werman, D. S. "Therapeutic Abortion on Psychiatric Grounds. A Follow-Up Study." *The North Carolina Medical Journal*, 34(4) (1973), 265-70.

[1086]Fabre, H. "Contraception Versus Abortion." *Eugenics Review*, 5 (1965), 21-25.

[1087]Facer, W. A. P., Simpson, D. W., and Murphy, B. D. "Abortion in New Zealand." *Journal of Biosocial Science*, 5(2) (1973), 151-58.

[1088]"Facing a Grand Jury." *American Journal of Nursing*, 76 (March, 1976), 398-400.

[1089]Facione, P. "The Abortion Non-Debate." *Cross Currents*, 23 (Fall, 1973), 349-53. [The author sees the abortion debate as over because it has gone through all of the steps necessary to the completion of a philosophical debate. Attention has shifted from theoretical matters of whether and in what cases to the practical issue. Most people approach the problem, not philosophically, but at the gut level.]

[1090]Facione, P. "Callahan on Abortion." *American Ecclesiastical Review*, 167 (May, 1973), 291-301. [The author briefly describes Daniel Callahan's book, *Abortion: Law, Choice and Morality* (New York: MacMillan, 1970). Facione points out Callahan's discussion on four levels—scientific, moral, legal and philosophical. Each level is taken individually and certain theoretical difficulties are pointed out. The virtue and vice of Callahan's position is his flexibility.

In conclusion, Facione sees Callahan as offering clear explanations on the relationship between law and morality, value and desires and, data and its scientific and philosophical interpretation. The author would take a position close to that of Callahan.]

[1091]Fackre, G. J. "Ethics of Abortion in Theological Perspective." *Andover Newton Quarterly*, 13 (January, 1973), 222-26.

[1092]"Facts About Abortions." *British Medical Journal*, 2 (May, 1973), 438.

[1093]Fagar, C. "Abortion Positions: So Where's the Radical?" *National Catholic Reporter*, 9 (March 2, 1973), 12.

[1094]Fager, C. "Clinic Head Quits After 60,000 Abortions." *National Catholic Reporter*, 11 (December 20, 1974), 3+.

[1095]Fahr, S. M. "Therapeutic Abortion—the Law." *Journal of the Iowa Medical Society*, 59 (March, 1969), 197-200.

[1096]"Failure of Advise: A Basis for Malpractice under the Revised Oregon Abortion Act." *Willamette Law Journal*, 6 (June, 1970), 349.

[1097]Fairchild, E., *et al.* "Should Family Planning Clinics Perform Abortions?" *Family Planning Perspectives*, 3 (April, 1971), 15-17.

[1098]Fairweather, Eugene, and Gentles, Ian. *The Right to Birth* (Toronto: Anglican Book Center, 1976).

[1099]Fallaci, Oriana. *Letter to a Child Never Born* (London: Arlington Books Publishing, Ltd., 1976).

[1100]Family Planning Association. *Abortion in Britain: Conference Proceedings* (Pitman Medical Publishing Company, Ltd., 1966).

[1101]*Family Planning and Popula-*

1102-1128

lation Programs. Edited by Bernard Berelson, *et al*. (Chicago: University of Chicago Press, 1966.)

[1102]Farmer, C. "Mechanism of Selection and Decision-Making in Therapeutic Abortion." *Journal of Biosocial Science,* 3 (January, 1971), 121-27.

[1103]Farr, Louise. "I Was a Spy at a Right-to-Life Convention." *MS,* 4 (February, 1976), 77-78+.

[1104]"Father's Rights in the Abortion Decision." *Texas Tech Law Review,* 6 (Spring, 1975), 1075-94.

[1105]Faust, Beatrice. "Abortion Legislation and Policy." *Forum on Abortion.* Kingston A.C. I., Australian Frontiers, 1969.

[1106]Fazziola, P. "The Mystery of the Unborn." *Bible Today,* no. 78 (April, 1975), 388-90.

[1107]"Federal Judge Rules Juveniles May Not Be Denied Abortions." *National Catholic Reporter,* 9 (February 23, 1973), 5.

[1108]Feinberg, Joel. *Problems of Abortion* (Belmont, Calif.: Wadsworth Publishers Co., Basic Problems in Philosophy series, 1973).

[1109]Feldman, David M. *Birth Control in Jewish Law* (New York: University Press, 1968).

[1110]Feldt, E. von. "Clear Answer to a Political Dilemma: the Church's Teaching on Abortion." *Columbia,* 55 (February, 1975), 4.

[1112]Felton, G., *et al*. "Administrative Guidelines for an Abortion Service." *American Journal of Nursing,* 72 (January, 1972), 108-09.

[1113]"Feminists Say Male Chauvinists Promote Abortion." *National Catholic Reporter,* 10 (June 21, 1974), 21.

[1114]Fernandes, A., Archbishop. "Memorandum on The Medical Termination of Pregnancy Bill 1971; Presented to Shrimati Indira Gandhi, Prime Minister of India." *L'Osservatore Romano* (English), no. 39 (183) (September 30, 1971), 4.

[1115]"Fetal Experimentation: Moral, Legal, and Medical Implications." *Stanford Law Review,* 26 (May, 1974), 1191-207.

[1116]"Feticide: Mens Rea With Partial Immunity?" *Washburn Law Journal,* 10 (Spring, 1971), 403.

[1117]"Fetus as a Legal Entity—Facing Reality." *San Diego Law Review,* 8 (1971), 126.

[1118]Ferris, P. *The Nameless: Abortion in Britain Today* (London: Hutchison Publishing Group, 1966).

[1119]Ficarra, B. J. "The Abortion Issue." *New York State Journal of Medicine,* 72 (October 1, 1972), 2460-63.

[1120]Field, Mark G. "The Re-Legalization of Abortion in Soviet Russia." *New England Journal of Medicine,* 255 (August 30, 1956), 421.

[1121]Fields, G. L., *et al*. "A Review of Therapeutic Abortions at a Southern University Hospital." *Woman Physician,* 26 (August, 1971), 414-16.

[1122]Figa-Talamanca, I. "Estimating the Incidence of Induced Abortion in Italy." *Genus,* 32 1-2 (1976), 91-108.

[1123]"Fight New Abortion Law, Bishops Plead." *National Catholic Reporter,* (July 10, 1970), 19.

[1124]Filteau, J. "Concern Grows Over Abortion Conscience Bills." *National Catholic Reporter,* 9 (April 13, 1973), 3-4.

[1125]Fingerer, M. E. "Psychological Sequelae of Abortion. Anxiety and Depression." *Journal of Community Psychology,* 1(2) (1973), 221-25.

[1126]Fink, J. "Key Weapon in Fight for Life: Bishops Outline a Workable Plan Against Abortion." *Our Sunday Visitor,* 64 (January 25, 1976), 1+.

[1127]Finlay, D. "The Fight for Life Can Be Won: Good News from Britain for Pro-Life." *Our Sunday Visitor,* 65 (December 5, 1976), 1+.

[1128]Finn, J. "A Physician Looks at the Abortion Problem." *Dimension,* 5 (Spring, 1973), 14-24. [Dr. Finn discusses many aspects of the abortion question. He describes the factors that have brought about a conservative-radical shift in medical circles. He discusses each claim of the pro-abortionists in an attempt to dismiss them. Also, the rights of the fetus are discussed.]

[1129]Finner, Stephen L., and Hamache, Jerome D. "The Relation Between Religious Commitment and Attitudes Toward Induced Abortion." *Sociological Analysis,* 30 (Spring, 1969).

[1130]Finnis, J. "Abortion and Legal Rationality." *Adelaide Law Review,* 3 (August, 1970), 431.

[1131]Finnis, J. "The Rights and Wrongs of Abortion: A Reply to Judith Thomson." *Philosophy and Public Affairs,* 2 (Winter, 1973), 117-45. [The author views it as unnecessary to speak of people's rights when debating the moral character of types of action such as "abortion". The pursuit of basic premoral values and the unpermissibility of choosing directly against them is a better strategy. Finnis explains this strategy. He suggests why fetuses from conception should be given the same consideration as other human beings.]

[1132]Finnis, J., et al. *The Rights and Wrongs of Abortion.* (Philosophy and Public Affairs Reader Ser.) (Princeton, N.J.: Princeton University Press, 1974).

[1133]Finkbine, Sherri. "The Lesser of Two Evils." *The Case for Legalized Abortion Now.* Ed. Alan Guttmacher (Berkeley: Diablo Press, 1967).

[1134]Finlay, S. E. "Illegal Abortion—Abortion in British Universities." *Abortion in Britain* (London: Pitman Medical Publishing Company, Ltd., 1966).

[1135]Finley, S. C. "Genetics, Abortion and Sterilization." *Birth Control and the Christian.* Ed. W. O. Spitzer and C. L. Saylor (Wheaton, Ill.: Tyndale House, 1969).

[1136]"First Notifications." *Economist,* 229 (November 2, 1968), 50.

[1137]"The First Year of the Abortion Act." *Lancet,* 1 (April 26, 1969), 867-68.

[1138]Fischer, E. H., and Caudle, J. "Outsiders—Reactions to Abortion. Personal Beliefs and Situational Influences." *Proceedings of the 81st Annual Convention of the American Psychological Association, Montreal, Canada,* 8 (1973), 339-340.

[1139]Fischman, Susan H. "De-livery or Abortion in Inner-City Adolescents." *American Journal of Orthopsychiatry,* 47 (January, 1977), 1.

[1140]Fisher, R. "Criminal Abortion." *Journal of Criminal Law, Criminology and Police Science,* 42 (July-August, 1951). Also, *Abortion in America.* Ed. Harold Rosen (Boston: Beacon Press, 1967).

[1141]Fisher, R., et al. "Abortion: Responsibilities and Relationships." *Duke Divinity Review,* 35 (Spring, 1970), 96-111.

[1142]Fitzgerald, J. "Abortion on Demand." *Linacre Quarterly,* 37 (August, 1970), 184-89. [The author discusses the convenience in abortion as a failure of society to be more humane and more earnest in its attempt to develop techniques for saving life rather than destroying it.

[1143]Fitzgerald, J. "The American Catholic: Contraception and Abortion." *Linacre Quarterly,* 38 (November, 1971), 264-67.

[1144]Fitzgerald, J. "The Beginning: The End." *New York State Journal of Medicine,* 72 (October 1, 1972), 2458-59.

[1145]Fitzgerald, J. "Ramifications of Permissive Abortion." *Linacre Quarterly,* 38 (May, 1971), 102-05.

[1146]Fitzgerald, J. "Thanatopsis." *Linacre Quarterly,* 37 (November, 1970), 254-58.

[1147]Fleck, J. C. "Canada Debates Abortion, Homosexuality." *Christian Century,* 86 (March 12, 1969), 354-58. [The views of Catholics, Protestants, and the medical profession on the Omnibus Bill, 1969, are offered.]

[1148]Fleck, S. "Some Psychiatric Aspects of Abortion." *Journal of Nervous and Mental Diseases,* 151 (July, 1970), 42-50 (42 ref.).

[1149]Fleming, Alice. *Contraception, Abortion, Pregnancy* (Nashville: Nelson, Thomas, Inc., 1974).

[1150]Fletcher, J. C. "The Brink: the Parent-Child Bond in the Genetic Revolution." *Theological Studies,* 33 (September, 1972), 457-85.

[1151]Fletcher, J. C. "Moral Problems in Genetic Counseling," biblo. *Pastoral Psychology,* 23 (April, 1972), 47-60. [This article presents a study which is designed to develop hypotheses about the structure of

1152-
1173   moral problems in one genetics counseling. unit. Seven hypotheses are formulated. These include 1) consideration of abortion is the major moral problem of parents in genetic counseling; 2) parents are inclined to favor abortion in case of a positive diagnosis, and they have reached this position prior to counseling.]

[1152]Fletcher, Joseph F. Abortion and the True Believer: Private Opinions Should not be Imposed by Law." *Christian Century* (November 27, 1974), 1126-27. [Fletcher describes the Catholic Church as holding the substance theory. The fetus is not known personally but the person is actually there, unverifiably. He asserts that this theory should not be forced by law on those who do not find it reasonable.]

[1153]Fletcher, Joseph F. "The Ethics of Abortion." *Clinical Obstetrics and Gynecology*, 14 (December, 1971), 1124-29.

[1154]Fletcher, Joseph F. "Four Indicators of Humanhood: The Enquiry Matures." *Hastings Center Report*, 4 (December, 1974), 4-7. [In order to determine human values and "right to life" questions, a view of humanness is needed. The author offers four essential human criterion: self-awareness, capacity for relationship, feeling "happy" (euphoria?) and neocortical function.

[1155]Fletcher, Joseph F. *Morals and Medicine* (Princeton, New Jersey: Princeton University Press, 1954).

[1156]Flood, P. "The Abortion Act 1967: Some Moral Implications." *Clergy Review*, 53 (January, 1968), 42-48.

[1157]"Florida Abortion Law—Reform or Regression in 1972." *University of Florida Law Review*, 24 (Winter, 1972), 346.

[1158]Flowers, C. E., Jr. "Improving the Quality of Life." *Alaska Journal of Medical Sciences*, 7 (July, 1970), 297-99.

[1159]Flowers, C. E., Jr. "Tubal Ligation and Abortion in the State of Alabama." *Journal of the Medical Association of Alabama*, 39 (April, 1970), 945-47.

[1160]Floyd, Mary K. *Abortion Bibliography for 1975* (New York: Whitson Publishers, 1976).

[1161]Floyd, Mary K. *Abortion Bibliography for 1974* (New York: Whitson Publishers, 1975).

[1162]Floyd, Mary K. *Abortion Bibliography for 1973* (New York: Whitson Publishers, 1974).

[1163]Floyd, Mary K. *Abortion Bibliography for 1972* (New York: Whitson Publishers, 1973).

[1164]Floyd, Mary K. *Abortion Bibliography for 1971* (New York: Whitson Publishers, 1972).

[1165]Floyd, Mary K. *Abortion Bibliography for 1970* (New York: Whitson Publishers, 1970).

[1166]Fogarty, J. "Religious Groups Plan Abortion Rights Drive." *National Catholic Reporter*, 12 (February 6, 1976), 6.

[1167]Foley, J. "Abortion: Law of Nation or Law of God." *Dimenson*, 5 (Spring, 1973), 35. [Fr. Foley is commenting on the United States Supreme Court decision. He asserts that no Catholic hospital, no Catholic doctor and no Catholic woman may participate in an abortion.]

[1168]Fonseca, J. D. "Induced Abortion: Nursing Attitudes and Action." *American Journal of Nursing*, 68 (May, 1968), 1022-27.

[1169]Foot, Philippa. "The Problem of Abortion and the Doctrine of the Double Effect." *Moral Problems*. Ed. by James Rachels (New York: Harper and Row, 1967). Reprint from *Oxford Review*, 5 (1967), 5-15.

[1170]Forbes, John A. "Rubella: Historical Aspects." *American Journal of Diseases of Children*, 118 (July, 1969), 5.

[1171]Force, R. "Legal Problems of Abortion Law Reform." *Administrative Law Review. American Bar Association*, 19 (July, 1967), 364.

[1172]"For Defence of Life in the Mother's Womb." *L'Osservatore Romano* (English), no. 8 (204) (Fenruary 24, 1972), 9-10.

[1173]Ford, Charles V., Castelnuovo-Tedesco, Pietro, and Long, Kahlila D. "Abortion: Is it a Therapeutic Procedure in Psychiatry?" *Journal of the American Medical Association*, 218 (November 22, 1971), 1173-78.

[1174]Ford, Charles V., Castelnuovo-Tedesco, and Long, K. D. "Women Who Seek Therapeutic Abortion. A Comparison with Women Who Complete Their Pregnancies." *American Journal of Psychiatry*, 129(5) (1972), 546-53.

[1175]Ford, Charles V., *et al.* "Therapeutic Abortion. Who Needs a Psychiatrist?" *Obstetrics and Gynecology*, 38 (August, 1971), 206-13.

[1176]Ford, J. H. "Mass-Produced, Assembly-Line Abortion. A Prime Example of Unethical, Unscientific Medicine." *California Medicine*, 117 (November, 1972), 80-84.

[1177]Ford, K. "Abortion and Family Building Models. Fertility Limitation in Hungary." *Demography*, 13(4) (1976), 495-506.

[1178]Forer, L. G. "Case for Abortion on Demand." *Pennsylvania Bar Association Quarterly*, 43 (January, 1972), 203.

[1179]"Former NAL Member Hits Abortion Statement." *National Catholic Reporter*, 9 (February 16, 1973), 3.

[1180]Forssman, H., and Thuwe, I. "One Hundred Twenty Abortions Refused." *Acta Psychiatrica Scandinavica*, 42 (1966), 71-88. [This is a study of what happens to children who were born after abortions were refused to their mothers. The authors conclude that these children do not present a danger to society but they have a greater social and psychological handicaps to overcome.]

[1181]Fort, A. T. "Abortion and Sterilization. An Insight into Obstetrician Gynecologists— Attitudes and Practices." *Social Biology*, 18(1) (1971), 192-94.

[1182]Fortier, L. "La Droit a La Vie: Droit Etre Laisse a Chacum. *Canadian Bar Journal*, 3(4) (1972), 23-26.

[1183]*Forum on Abortion* (Kingston A.C.I.: Australian Frontier, 1969).

[1184]Fost, N. "Our Curious Attitude Toward the Fetus." *Hastings Center Report*, 4(1) (February, 1974), 4-5.

[1185]Foster, C. "Thousands March in National Capital in Protest Against Legalized Abortion." *Our Sunday Visitor*, 64 (February 8, 1976), 1.

[1186]Foster, J. T. "Abortion— Three States Have New Laws and More are Coming." *Modern Hospital*, 109 (August, 1967), 90-94.

[1187]"4 Cardinals to Testify for Unborn in Senate." *National Catholic Reporter*, 10 (February 22, 1974), 4.

[1198]"4 Cardinals Testify at Senate Abortion Hearings." *National Catholic Reporter*, 10 (March 15, 1974), 20.

[1189]"Four Panelists Disagree on Morality of Abortion." *National Catholic Reporter*, 10 (March 8, 1974), 7.

[1190]Fox, L. P. "Abortion Deaths in California." *American Journal of Obstetrics and Gynecology*, 98 (July 1, 1967), 645-53.

[1191]Fox, R. "Can God Forgive Abortion?" *Our Sunday Visitor*, 63 (April 6, 1975), 1+.

[1192]Fox, R. "Abortion: A Question of Right or Wrong? *American Bar Association Journal*, 57 (July, 1971), 667.

[1193]Fox, R. "The Law on Abortion." *Lancet*, 1 (March 5, 1966), 542.

[1194]"France: We've had One (Defiance of the French Penal Code)." *Economist*, 239 (April 10, 1971), 34.

[1195]Francis, D. "The Plot to Kill My Son." *Catholic Digest*, 31 (April, 1967), 20-22.

[1196]Francis, John J. "Law, Morality and Abortion." *Rutgers Law Review*, 22 (Spring, 1968), 415.

[1197]Francis, T. "Unwanted Child Wanted." *National Catholic Reporter*, 11 (January 24, 1975), 14.

[1198]Francome, Colin. "How Many Illegal Abortions?" *British Journal of Criminology*, 16 (October, 1976), 389-92.

[1199]Frankfort, Ellen. "More on Mini-Abortion: Pregnancies and Profits." *Village Voice* (December 7, 1972), 25+.

[1200]Franklin, J. "Doctor Views Abortion," (interview). *Church and Society*, 60 (March-April, 1970), 40-49.

[1201]Fraser, G. R. "Selective Abortion, Gametic Selection, and the X Chromosome." *American Journal of Human Genetics,* 24 (July, 1972), 359-70.

[1202]Frech, F. "How I Handle Abortion Hecklers." *Liguorian,* 62 (April, 1974), 23-27.

[1203]Frech, F. "Salty Tears, Salty Death; the Saline Mode of Abortion: A Comparison." *Liguorian,* 64 (October, 1976), 29-31.

[1204]Frederiksen, H. "Demographic Effects of Abortion." *Public Health Reports,* 83 (1968), 999-1010.

[1205]Frederiksen, H., *et al.* "Effects of Legalizing Abortion." *Lancet,* 2 (July 20, 1968), 167-68.

[1206]"Freedom of Choice Concerning Abortion (Pronouncement, United Church of Christ, 8th General Synod)." *Social Action,* 38 (September, 1971, 9-12.

[1207]"Freedom of the Press, the Commercial Speech Doctrine Applied to Abortion Advertisement." *Emory Law Journal,* 24 (August, 1975), 1165-90.

[1208]Freehof, Soloman B. *Recent Reform Responsa* (Cincinnati: Hebrew Union College Press, 1963).

[1209]Freeland, W. D. "Inter-Faith Debate on Easing Abortion Laws." *Christianity Today,* 11 (April 28, 1967), 43.

[1210]Freeman, E. W. "Abortion. Beyond Rhetoric to Access." *Social Work,* 21(6) (1976), 483-87.

[1211]Freeman, Lucy. *The Abortionist* (Garden City, New York: Doubleday, 1962).

[1212]Freedman, S. "Jewish Religious Tradition and the Issue of Abortion." *Dimension,* 5 (Summer, 1973), 90-93. [Rabbi Freedman presents the Jewish perspective on abortion as presented in the *Halakah,* or law. He states that while in utero, the embryo is considered a living creature. It is against Jewish law to destroy it. Even if the fetus is the product of rape or incest, or might be defective, it still has the right to life. The only condition that would allow for an abortion is when the fetus threatens the physical life of the mother.]

[1213]"French Episcopate, Firm and Clear Against Revision of Abortion Law." *L'Osservatore Romano* (English), no. 33 (281) (August 16, 1973), 3+.

[1214]Freund, L. "Surveys in Induced and Spontaneous Abortion in the Copenhagen Area." *Acta Psychiatrica Scandinavica,* 40, suppl. (1964), 180.

[1215]Friedenberg, E. Z. "Evolution of Canadian Justice: The Morgentaler Case." *Canadian Forum,* 55 (June, 1975), 28-30.

[1216]Friedman, Cornelia Morrison. "Making Abortion Consultation Therapeutic." *American Journal of Psychiatry,* 130 (November, 1973), 1257-61. [Since the U.S. Supreme Court decision on abortion, the psychiatric community no longer needs to justify a client's decision; the focus of care can be a more complete counseling of women who are ambivalent about having an abortion.]

[1217]Friedman, Cornelia Morrison, Greenspan, R., and Mittleman, F. "The Decision-Making Process and the Outcome of Therapeutic Abortion." *The American Journal of Psychiatry,* 131(12) (1974), 1332-37.

[1218]Friedman, E. A. "Therapeutic Abortion." *Obstetrics.* Ed. J. P. Greenhill (Philadelphia: Saunders Publishing, 1965).

[1219]Friedman, H. J. "The Vagarity of Psychiatric Indications for Therapeutic Abortions." *American Journal of Psychotherapy,* 26 (April, 1962), 585.

[1220]Fuchs, F. "Amniocentesis and Abortion: Methods and Risks." *Birth Defects: Original Article Series,* 7 (April, 1971), 18-19.

[1221]Fujikura, T., *et al.* "A Simplified Anatomic Classification of Abortions." *American Journal of Obstetrics and Gynecology,* 95 (August 1, 1966), 902-05.

[1222]Fultz, G. S. "Therapeutic Abortions." *Southern Medical Journal,* 47 (January, 1954).

[1223]Furler, I. K. "On Legal Abortion." *Medical Journal of Australia,* 1 (February 27, 1971), 489-96.

[1224]Furlow, B. "Abortion Issue Factor in Congressional Race." *National Catholic Reporter,* 10 (March 15, 1974), 2.

[1225]"Furor Over Abortion—Hotter than Ever: What are the Rights of an Unborn Child? The Question is Stirring Debate—and a Nation-Wide Drive by Anti-Abortion Forces to Overturn a Historic Court Ruling." *U.S. News and World Report,* 76 (March 4, 1974), 43-44.

[1226]Furstenberg, F. F., Jr. "Attitudes Toward Abortion Among Young Blacks." *Studies in Family Planning,* 3 (1972), 66-69.

[1227]"Further Comment on *People vs. Belous.*" *Catholic Lawyer,* 16 (Winter, 1970), 92-97.

[1228]Furusawa, Yoshio, and Koya, Tomohiko. "The Influence of Artificial Abortion on Delivery." *Harmful Effects of Induced Abortion* (Tokyo: Family Planning Federation of Japan, 1966).

[1229]Gabrielson, I. W., *et al.* "Adolescent Attitudes Toward Abortion: Effects on Contraceptive Practice." *American Journal of Public Health,* 61 (April, 1971), 730-38.

[1230]Gaffney, Edward McGlynn. "Law and Theology: A Dialogue on the Abortion Decisions." *Jurist,* 33 (1973), 134-49. [Gaffney outlines his paper examining four elements: 1) a preliminary consideration of the notion of dialogue; 2) a methodological consideration of the Court's use of history; 3) a comment on the anthropological presuppositions of its holdings; and 4) a practical conclusion on the value of freedom of conscience after the two abortion cases.]

[1231]Gager, V. "In Defense of the Unborn." *Marriage and Family Living,* 55 (June, 1973), 38-45.

[1232]Gail, Norman. "Births, Abortions and the Progress of Chile." *Fieldstaff Reports: West Coast South America Series,* 19 (no. 2) (May, 1972).

[1233]Gallagher, J. P. "Therapeutic Abortion." *Medical Journal of Australia,* 1 (June 8, 1968), 1017.

[1234]Gammeltoft, M., and Somers, R. L. "Abortion Views and Practices Among Danish Family Physicians." *Journal of Biosocial Science,* 8(3) (1976), 287-92.

[1235]Gampell, Ralph J. "Legal Status of Therapeutic Abortion and Sterilization in the U.S." *Clinical Obstetrics and Gynecology,* 7 (March, 1964), 22-36.

[1236]Gannon, F. "Is the Pro-Life Movement Dying at the Grass-Roots?" *Our Sunday Visitor,* 65 (August 9, 1976), 1+.

[1237]Gardner, R. F. R. *Abortion* (Moonachie, N.J.:Pyramid Publishing, 1974).

[1238]Gardner, R. F. R. *Abortion: The Personal Dilemma* (Old Tappan, N.J.: Revell, Flemming H. Co., 1974).

[1239]Gardner, R. F. R. "Christian Choices in a Liberal Abortion Climate." *Christianity Today,* 14 (May 22, 1970), 6-8.

[1240]Gardner, R. F. R. *What About Abortion?* (Exeter: Paternoster Press, 1972).

[1241]Garner, J. "Pastoral Letter on Abortion; July 26, 1972." *L'Osservatore Romano* (English), 244 (no. 48) (November 30, 1972), 3.

[1242]Gartlan, J. V. "Abortion Controversy. Remarks. L. B. Cummings: Statement. J. L. Nellis; Remarks. A. L. Scanlan; Remarks. J. V. Gartlan, Jr." *District of Columbia Bar Journal,* 39 (January-April, 1972), 17.

[1243]Gastonguay, P. "Abortion: Assault on Human Life." *Liguorian,* 60 (December, 1972), 27-30.

[1244]Gaylor, Anne N. *Abortion is a Blessing* (New York: Psychological Dimensions, Inc., n.d.)

[1245]Gayton, W. F., Fogg, M. E., Tavormina, J., Bishop, J. S., Citrin, M. F., and Basset, J. S. "Comparison of the MMPI and Mini Mult with Women Who Request an Abortion." *Journal of Clinical Psychology,* 32 (3) (1976), 648-50.

[1246]Gaziano, E., *et al.* "Infectious Complications Following Legal Abortion." *Minnesota Medicine,* 56 (April, 1973), 269-72.

[1247]Gebhard, A. "Abortion Dilemma." *Church and Society,* 60 (March-April, 1970), 36-39.

[1248]Gebhard, Paul H., *et al.* *Pregnancy, Birth and Abortion* (Indiana University Institute for Sex Research Ser.) Reprint of 1958 edition. (Westport, Ct.: Greenwood

Press, Inc., 1976.

[1249]Gedan, S. "Abortion Counseling with Adolescents." *American Journal of Nursing*, 74 (10) (1974), 1856-58.

[1250]Geekie, D. A. "Abortion: A Review of CMA Policy and Positions." *Canadian Medical Association Journal*, 111(5) (September 7, 1974), 474-77. [This article reviews the position of the CMA. The resolution of the CMA General Council in 1966 is given, which describes when termination of pregnancy is lawful. The abortion must be performed by a qualified licensed medical practitioner, approved by a hospital committee, performed in an active treatment hospital, with the written consent of patient, and spouse where the pregnancy would endanger the physical or mental health of the mother. In 1967, the Council included as a basis for legal abortion the substantial risk that the child may be born with grave mental or physical disability. In 1971, recognition was given to the justification that there may be certain non-medical grounds for abortion. But, abortion on demand is rejected. Various recommendations concerning contraceptives and family planning advice are as presented to the federal government. The CMA views the solution to the controversy is responsible family planning. Excerpts from the Criminal Code, relating to abortion, are included.]

[1251]Geijerstam, Gunnar K. "Abortion in Scandinavia." Paper presented at the International Conference on Abortion, Hot Springs, Virginia, November 17-20, 1968.

[1252]Geijerstam, Gunner K. *An Annotated Bibliography of Induced Abortion* (Ann Arbor, Mich.: Centre for Population Planning, University of Michigan, 1969).

[1253]Gendel, E. S. "Abortion, the Patient, the Physician and the Law. The First Year's Experience." *Journal of the Kansas Medical Society*, 73 (January, 1972), 18-19.

[1254]Gendel, E. S., et al. "Education About Abortion." *American Journal of Public Health*, 61 (March, 1971), 520-29. [The need for increased adult education on abortion is stressed. This would include contraception, facilities,

procedure, diagnosis, counseling and associations involved in abortion.]

[1255]"General Practitioner and the Abortion Act." *Journal of the Royal College of General Practitioners*, 22 (August, 1972), 543-46.

[1256]"General Practitioners and Abortion." *Journal of the Royal College of General Practitioners*, 24 (142) (May, 1974, 298, 303.

[1257]Genne, William H. "Abortions." *Concerns for Christian Citizens*, 5 (January, 1965).

[1258]George, B. J., Jr. "Current Abortion Laws." *Illinois Medical Journal*, 131 (May, 1967), 696-700.

[1259]George, B. J., Jr. "Current Abortion Laws: Proposals and Movements for Reform." *Western Reserve Law Review*, 17 (1965), 86. Also in *Abortion and the Law*. Ed. David T. Smith (Cleveland: Western Reserve University Press, 1967).

[1260]"Georgia, Texas File Appeals." *National Catholic Reporter*, 9 (February 23, 1973), 3.

[1261]Gerber, R. J. "Abortion: Parameters for Decision." *International Philosophical Quarterly*, 11 (December, 1971), 561-84. Also in *Ethics*, 82 (January, 1972), 137-54. Reply, Gerber, D., 83 (October, 1972), 80-83. [Studies by Noonan, Callahan and Grisez are presented. They illustrate the conflict between the metaphysical and sociological views of human value. The humanity of the fetus is examined in terms of structure and function. Structurally, predication of humanity to the fetus would be supported by the evidence of genetics. Functionally, it could be argued that the fetus is only potentially human, considering the inability of the fetus to perform rational, emotional or volitional operations. Gerber asks whether such potentiality is otherwise protected at later stages of life and if protection should be offered (for example, to criminals, the aged, the sick, etc.)].

[1262]Gerber, D. "Abortion: The Uptake Argument." *Ethics*, 83 (October, 1972), 80-83. [R. J. Gerber in *Ethics*, 82 (1971), 154, argued that the psychological theory lessens resistance to such objectionable activities as infanticide and euthanasia. It is this theory which serves as the rationale for liberalizing abortion legislation. D. Gerber asserts that: 1) it is not obvious that euthanasia and infanticide are always objectionable; 2) some factors important for the liberalized abortion laws do not apply to infanticide and euthanasia; 3) it is unlikely that the courts will interpret liberalized abortion laws to sanction euthanasia and infanticide; 4) it is unlikely that broad permissions to kill will result from the relaxed abortion laws.]

[1263]Gerber, R. "Abortion: Two Opposing Legal Philosophies." *American Journal of Jurisprudence,* 15 (1970), 1-24.

[1264]Gerber, R. "When is the Human Soul Infused?" *Laval Theologique et Philisophique,* 22 (1966), 234.

[1265]Gerson, Lloyd. "Abortion and the Right to Life." *CRUX* 12 (no. 4) (1974-1975), 25-29.

[1266]Gerstein, H., *et al.* "Abortion, Abstract Norms, and Social Control: The Decision of the West German Federal Constitutional Court." *Emery Law Journal,* 25 (Fall, 1976), 849-78.

[1267]Gest, J. "Comment on Fr. Drinan's Article on Abortion Laws." *Catholic Lawyer,* 14 (Fall, 1968), 326-28.

[1268]Gest, J. "Proposed Abortion Laws Slaughter of the Innocents." *Linacre Quarterly,* 36 (February, 1969), 47-52. [In describing the move towards liberal abortion laws, the author discusses the moral law of "thou shalt not kill," immediate and mediate animation, the ALI provisions for justifiable abortion and the incumbency of concessions in liberalization of abortion.]

[1269]Giannella, Donald A. "The Difficult Quest for a Truly Humane Abortion Law." *Villanova Law Review,* 13 (Winter, 1968), 297.

[1270]Gibbard, B. "Letter: Therapeutic Abortion." *Canadian Medical Association Journal,* 112 (1) (January 11, 1975), 25, 27.

[1271]Gibbs, R. F. "Editorial: *Commonwealth vs. Edelin.*" *Journal of Legal Medicine,* 3(3) (March, 1975), 6.

[1272]Gibbs, R. F. "Therapeutic Abortion and the Minor." *Journal of Legal Medicine,* 1(1) (March-April, 1973), 36-42.

[1273]Gibeau, D. "NAL Applauds Court for Abortion Ruling." *National Catholic Reporter,* 9 (February 9, 1973), 3.

[1274]Gilbert, E. "Abortion: Legal But Still Wrong." *Liguorian,* 61 (October, 1973), 2-4.

[1275]Gilbert, E. "Letters to John and Mary Ann, Preamble to an Exodus." *Triumph,* 6 (October, 1971), 24-26.

[1276]Gilbert, E. "Why We Need a Human Life Amendment." *Liguorian,* 62 (November, 1974), 17-20.

[1277]Gillespie, A., *et al.* "Ideal Means of Fertility Control." *Lancet,* 1 (April 4, 1970), 717.

[1278]Gillett, P. G., Kinch, R. A. H., Wolfe, L. S., and Paci-Asciak, C. "Therapeutic Abortion with the Use of Prostaglandin F_2 Alpha." *American Journal of Obstetrics and Gynecology,* 112 (February 1, 1972), 330.

[1279]Gillis, A. "Follow-Up After Abortion." *British Medical Journal,* 1 (February, 1969), 22.

[1280]Gillis, A. "Follow-Up After Abortion." *British Medical Journal,* 4 (November, 1969), 368.

[1281]Gilmore, J. O. "Mississippi State Medical Association Statement on Abortion." *Journal of the Mississippi State Medical Association,* 15 (January, 1974), 21-23.

[1282]Gilsenan, T. "Catholic Hospitals Told Protect Right to Life." *National Catholic Reporter,* 11 (June 20, 1975), 4.

[1283]Girardeau, J. L. "The Abortion Law." *Journal of the Medical Association of Georgia,* 56 (August, 1967), 340.

[1284]Gitlow, H. S. "A Methodology for Determining the Optimal Design of a Free Standing Abortion Clinic." *Management Science,* 22(2) (1976), 1289-98.

[1285]Gittlesohn, S. M. "Family Limitation Based on Family Composition." *American Journal of Human Genetics,* 12 (1960), 425-33.

[1286]Glass, Bentley. "Debating Abortion: A Non-Catholic and a

1263-
1286

1287–
1297

Scientist: It's an Individual Choice." *Wall Street Journal*, 188 (October 26, 1976), 26.

[1287]Glass, David. "Attitudes to Abortion—Attitudes in Continental Europe." *Abortion in Britain* (London: Pitman Medical Publishing Company Ltd., 1966).

[1288]Glass, L., *et al.* "Effects of Legalized Abortion on Neo-Natal Morality and Obstetrical Morbidity at Harlem Hospital Center." *American Journal of Public Health*, 64 (July, 1974), 717-18.

[1289]Glasser, M. L., and Pasnau, R. O. "The Unwanted Pregnancy in Adolescence." *Journal of Family Practice*, 2(2) (1975), 91-94.

[1290]"*Gleitman vs. Cosgrove* [(NJ) 227 A 2d 689]: A Study of Legal Method." *Maine Law Review*, 20 (1968), 143.

[1291]Glenister, T. "Abortion and Christian Compassion." *Tablet*, 226 (June 3, 1972), 518. [The author discusses a book by R. F. R. Gardner. *Abortion: The Personal Dilemma* (Exeter, Paternoster Press, 1972). [Glenister asks the important question, "Ought there be a specifically Christian ethic in medicine?" Thrist's demand is basically that we should fulfill our potential norms which should be accepted by a Christian, namely, those that help man to be fully human. The distinction lies not between those who wish to achieve the full potential of their humanity and those who are not interested.]

[1292]Glenister, T. "Perspectives of Abortion: Abortion and the Unborn Child I, II, III." *Tablet*, 225 (March 27, 1971) , 300+; (April 3, 1971), 326-27; (April 10, 1971), 350-51. [Dr. Glenister describes the growth of the embryo to the fetus. He sees that this is an essential part of any assessment of the status of the unborn child.]

[1293]Glenister, T. "The Rights of the Unborn." *Tablet*, 227 (June 16, 1973), 557-59. Reply: 227 (June 30, 1973), 603. [The author comments on "Dossier sur L'Avortement" published in January 1973, in *Etudes*, A French Jesuit Monthly. Certain recommendations have been made after a detailed examination of the situation in France. The document considers the dangers which a change to more liberalized law might engender, and the humanity of the embryo is explored. The embryo is explored. The embryo is considered human throughout pregnancy; it is humanized by being recognized by humanity. Abortion is socially justifiable if it presents itself as a lesser evil, as the refusal to provoke a dehumanization or to create an inhuman situation.
The work of Bernard Haring, *Medical Ethics* (edited by Gabrielle L. Jean, St. Paul Publications, 1970), is discussed. Haring considers the principle of totality which sees man in his highest capacity to reciprocate love and to exercise responsibility. His writings on abortion are written in this spirit. The author suggests that the Church's teaching could be more precise about the certainties and where there is doubt, allow some latitude.]

[1294]Glenn, H. P. "Constitutional Validity of Abortion Legislation: A Comparative Note." *McGill Law Journal*, 21 (Winter, 1975), 673-84.

[1295]Glenn, G. "Abortion and Inalienable Rights in Classical Liberalism." *American Journal of Jurisprudence*, 20 (1975), 62-80.

[1296]Gluckman, L. "Maori Attitudes Toward Abortion." *Linacre Quarterly*, 40 (February, 1973), 44-48. [The New Zealand Polynesian (Maori) tradition held that the fetus, from the time of diagnosis of pregnancy, has an advanced spirit or soul and because of this, must not be destroyed. Paradoxically, the Maori practiced infanticide. They believed that the intant's spirit had a minimal experience of life and had less objection to being destroyed.
Gluckman strongly suggests that even in the introduction of European ideas, it is better not to terminate pregnancies on Maori women.]

[1297]Glynn, E. "Misplace Allegiance." *America*, 128 (March 3, 1973), 177. [This article notes the statement from the Administrative Committee of the National Conference of Catholic Bishops issued on February 13, 1973. The statement rejected the recent Supreme Court decision, regarding abortion as immoral. This endorses civil disobedience. Whenever there is a conflict of human law and God's law, we are to follow God's law.]

[1298]Gold, Edwin M. "Abortion
—1970." *American Journal of
Public Health,* 61 (March, 1971),
487-88. [The article describes
the change of attitudes towards
abortion during the 1960s and
raises questions about the future.]

[1299]Gold, Edwin M., *et al.*
"Therepeutic Abortions in New
York City: A Twenty Year Review."
New York Department of Health,
Bureau of Records and Statistics,
October 14, 1963.

[1300]Gold, S. "Observation on
Abortion." *World Medical Journal,* 13 (1966), 76.

[1301]Gold, S. "Psychiatric
Indications for the Termination
of Pregnancy." *Medical Journal
of Australia,* 1 (February 27,
1971), 499-500.

[1302]Gold, S. "Therapeutic
Abortion." *American Journal of
Public Health,* 55 (July, 1965),
506.

[1303]Gold, S. "Therapeutic
Abortion in New York City: A
Twenty Year Review." *American
Journal of Public Health,* 55
(July, 1965), 964.

[1304]Golden, E. "Suffer the
Little to Come: Interview by J.
Breig." *U. S. Catholic,* 39 (June
31, 1974), 25-31. [Edward Golden
is the first president of the newly formed National Right to Life
Committee. He answers questions
on various aspects of the pro-life
movement in the U.S.
   The efforts of the committee
are directed at procuring an
amendment.]

[1305]Goldenberg, D. "The
Rights to Abortion: Expansion of
the Privacy Through the Fourteenth
Amendment." *Catholic Lawyer,* 19
(Winter, 1973), 36-57. [The author offers the legal history of
the abortion controversy as well
as the history of the right to
privacy. He discusses the ramifications of the abortion decision.
   In conclusion, the decision
seems to be legally erroneous in
two areas: 1) the court strayed
from established principles of
constitutional law in its application of the compelling interest
test "to the realm substantive due
process"; 2) when an alleged fundamental liberty is being sup-
pressed, then the rational basis

test is of little value.

[1306]Golditch, I. M., *et al.*
"Therapeutic Abortion Without In-
patient Hospitalization. An Early
Experience with 325 Cases." *California Medicine,* 116 (March, 1972),
1-3.

[1307]Goldman, M. J. "Abortion:
Jewish Law and the Law of the Land."
Illinois Medical Journal, 135 (Janu-
ary, 1969), 93-95.

[1308]Goldscheider, C. "Trends in
Jewish Fertility." *Sociology and
Social Research,* 50 (1966), 173-186.

[1309]Goldsmith, A., Goldberg, R.,
Eyzaquirre, H., and Lizana, L. "Immediate Post-Abortal Intrauterine
Contraceptive Device Insertion: A
Double-Bline Study." *American Journal of Obstetrics and Gynecology,*
112 (April 1, 1972), 957. [This
article examines the feasibility of
inserting an IUD right after an
abortion. It concludes that conditions are favorable, both psychologically and physiologically.]

[1310]Goldsmith, S. "Early Abor-
tion in a Family Planning Clinic."
Family Planning Perspectives, 6(2)
(Spring, 1974), 119-22.

[1311]Goldstein, P., *et al.* "Trends
in Therapeutic Abortion in San Francisco." *American Journal of Public
Health,* 62 (May, 1972), 695-99.

[1312]Gombay, André. "The Trials
of Dr. Morgantaler." *CRUX,* 12 (no.
4) (1974-1975), 30-32.

[1313]Gonzalez-Quiroga, A. "Attitudes Toward Family Planning in
Turrialba, Costa Rica." *Milbank Memorial Fund Quarterly,* 46(3, part 2)
(1968), 237-55.

[1314]Good, F. L., and Kelly, O. F.
Marriage, Morals and Medical Ethics
(New York: P. J. Kenedy and Sons,
1951).

[1315]Goodhart, C. B. "Abortion
Act." *British Medical Journal,* 2
(June 17, 1972), 714.

[1316]Goodhart, C. B. "Abortion
Act in Action." *(London),* 227 (August 15, 1970), 757-58.

[1317]Goodhart, C. B. "Abortion
Capital." *Lancet,* 1 (February 14,
1970), 367.

[1318]Goodhart, C. B. "Abortion
Regulations." *British Medical Jour-*

nal, 2 (May 4, 1968), 298.

[1319]Goodhart, C. B. "The Biologist's Dilemma." *Nature* (London), 229 (January 15, 1971), 213.

[1320]Goodhart, C. B. "Criminal Abortion in the U.S.A." *Eugenic Review,* 57 (June, 1965), 98.

[1321]Goodhart, C. B. "Estimation of Illegal Abortions." *Journal of Biosocial Science,* 1 (July, 1969), 235-45.

[1322]Goodhart, C. B. "The Frequency of Illegal Abortions." *Eugenic Review,* 55 (1964), 197.

[1323]Goodhart, C. B. "On the Incidence of Illegal Abortion (Great Britain)." *Population Studies,* 27(2) (1973), 207-33.

[1324]Goodhart, C. B. "Therapeutic Abortion." *Lancet,* 1 (April 13, 1968), 624-25.

[1325]Goodhart, C. B. "U.S. Supreme Court on Abortion." *Lancet,* 1 (February 24, 1973), 429.

[1326]Goodhart, C. B., *et al.* "U.S. Supreme Court on Abortion." *Lancet,* 1 (March 24, 1973), 663.

[1327]Goodlin, R. "Risks of Legal Abortion." *Lancet,* 1 (January 8, 1972), 97.

[1328]Goodman, Janice, Schoenbrod, Rhonda Copelon, and Stearns, Nancy. "*Doe* and *Roe*: Where do We Go From Here?" *Women's Rights Law Reporter,* 1 (Spring, 1973), 20-38.

[1329]Goodnight, Linda, and Rutledge, Judy. "Abortion: Twenty-Four Weeks of Dependency." *Baylor Law Review,* 27 (Winter, 1975), 122-40.

[1330]Goraya, R., *et al.* "A Pilot Study of Demographic and Psychosocial Factors in Medical Termination of Pregnancy." *Journal of the Indian Medical Association,* 64(11) (June 1, 1975), 309-15.

[1331]Gordon, David A. "The Unborn Plaintiff." *Michigan Law Review,* 63 (Feb. 1965) 579.

[1332]Gordon, H. "Contraception or Abortion? (b) Is Abortion a Form of Contraception?" *Royal Society of Health Journal,* 92 (August, 1972), 194-97.

[1333]Gordon, H. "Genetical, Social and Medical Aspects of Abortion." *South African Medical Journal,* 42 (n.d.), 721-30.

[1334]Gough, C. L. "Abortion." *Modern Churchman,* 10 (April, 1967), 231-35.

[1335]Gould, D. "Abortion: An Act of Mercy." *New Statesman,* 87 (April 12, 1974), 510.

[1336]Gould, D. "Abortion in Perspective." *New Statesman,* 78 (July 11, 1969), 42-43.

[1337]Gould, D. "Abortion Story." *New Statesman,* 82 (October 8, 1971), 465.

[1338]Gould, D. "Abortion Touts." *New Statesman,* 83 (February 11, 1972), 165-66.

[1339]Gould, D. "No Going Back." *New Statesman,* 89 (January 31, 1975), 132.

[1340]Gould, D. "None but the Brave." *New Statesman,* 89 (June 13, 1975), 774.

[1341]Gould, D. "Snags of Legal Abortion." *New Statesman,* 75 (April 26, 1968), 543-44.

[1342]Gould, D. "Unborn Baby Campaign." *New Statesman,* 86 (November 16, 1973), 728.

[1343]Gould, D. "Women's Lib Pill." *New Statesman,* 84 (October 20, 1972), 542.

[1344]Grabbe, George. *Abortion: An Eastern Orthodox Statement.* Original title: *Eastern Orthodox Statement on Abortion* (Willits, Cal.: Eastern Orthodox Books, n.d.).

[1345]Granfield, David. *Abortion Decision* (New York: Doubleday, 1971).

[1346]Granfield, David. "The Present Status of the Abortion Controversy." *American Ecclesiastical Review,* 162 (March, 1970), 195.

[1347]Granfield, David. "The Legal Impact of the Roe and Doe Decisions." *Jurist,* 33 (1973), 113-22. [The author examines the judicial statement. The legal base is the Fourteenth Amendment; two compelling points are taken as the end of the first trimester and the beginning of viability, the three stages of pregnancy and the four procedural prohibitions. The court ruled that the four requirements which the Georgia legislation imposed as a means to regulate abortion were unconstitutional. These included: 1) that the woman must be a resident of the state; 2) that the hospital be accredited by the Joint Committee on the Accreditation of Hospitals (JCAH); 3) that the physician required the approval of a hospital committe to perform an abortion; and 4) that the physician's judgment be supported by two other physicians.

The practical implications are considered. The problematic areas are discussed. These are: 1) the rights of the father and parents; 2) the rights of the hospital, physicians and employees; 3) the rights of the pregnant woman; and 4) the rights of the viable fetus.]

[1348]Gray, D. E. "The Freedom and the Responsibility." *Journal of the Kansas Medical Society,* 73 (January, 1972), 32-34.

[1349]Green, L. W., and Krotki, K. J. "Class and Parity Biases in Family Planning Programs. The Case of Karachi." *Eugenics Quarterly,* 15(4) (1968), 235-51.

[1350]Green, R. M. "Abortion and Promise-Keeping." *Christianity and Crisis,* 27 (May 15, 1967), 109-13. Reply: Ramsey, P. 27 (August 7, 1967), 195-96. 2nd reply: Sprague, R. L. (October 2, 1967), 220-22. [The author suggests that the moral category of promise-keeping is more helpful than that of the rights of and duties toward the fetus. The author explains that whenever a woman willingly engages in coitus, she, in so doing, makes an implicit promise that, in the event of conception, she will carry the child to term. This promise would exist even in the case of the woman who responsibly uses contraception. But Green does allow for abortion in certain health and eugenic situations.]

[1351]Green, R. M. "Conferred Rights and the Fetus." Bibliography with reply by J. F. Childress. *Journal of Religious Ethics,* 2 (Spring, 1974), 55-83. [The author attempts to determine the moral status of the fetus directly by means of a rational theory of rights. Green argues that agents with a rational and moral capacity are entitled to full human rights, while those that lack moral and rational capacity must have these capacities conferred by rational, moral agents. The author concludes that agents would probably not choose to confer substantial rights on the fetus thereby restricting their liberty.

[1352]Greenberg, Blu. "Abortion: A Challenge to Halakhah." *Judaism,* 25 (Spring, 1976), 201-08.

[1353]Greenglass, Esther R. "Therapeutic Abortion, Fertility Plans, and Psychological Sequelae." *American Journal of Orthopsychiatry,* 47 (January, 1977), 1. [Women who had therapeutic abortions and planned to have children exhibited more neurotic symptoms following abortion than did those who planned not to have children. Greenglass suggested that the ambivalence of women who have abortions while still planning for future children is of clinical importance, even though the extent of the disturbances was not abnormal.]

[1354]Greenglass, Esther R. *After Abortion* (Canadian Social Problems series) (Don Mills, Ont.: Longman Canada, 1976).

[1355]Greenhill, J. P. *Obstetrics.* From the original text of Joseph B. DeLee, 13th ed. (Philadelphia: Saunders, 1965).

[1356]Greenhill, J. P. "World Trends of Therapeutic Abortion and Sterilization." *Clinical Obstetrics and Gynecology,* 7 (March, 1964), 37.

[1357]Greenhouse, S. "Facts About Abortion for the Teenager." *The School Counselor,* 22(5) (1975), 334-37.

[1358]Greer, S., Lal, S., Lewis, S. C., Belsey, E. M., and Beard, R. W. "Psychological Consequences of Therapeutic Abortion." *British Journal of Psychiatry,* 138 (1976), 74-79.

[1359]Gregson, R. A., *et al.* "Opinions on Abortion from Medical Practitioners." *New Zealand Medical Journal,* 73 (May, 1971), 267-73.

[1360]Greinacher, N. "Tubingen Theologian Condemned by Bishop: Interview by Konkret (periodical)." *L'Osservatore Romano* (English), 218 (no. 22) (June 1, 1972), 4.

[1361]Grinder, R. E., and
Schmitt, S. S. "Coeds and Contraceptive Information." *Journal
of Marriage and the Family,* 28
(1966), 471-79.

[1362]Grisez, G. "Abortion and
Catholic Faith: International Col-
loquium on Sexology, Louvain, May
10, 1968." *American Ecclesiastical Review,* 159 (August, 1968),
96-115.

[1363]Grisez, G. *Abortion:
Myths, the Realities, and the Arguments* (New York: Corpus Books,
1970). [The abortion question is
viewed from the medical, sociological, religious, legal and ethical perspectives. The author attempts to place the facts concerning abortion into an historical
and theoretical framework. He
critically assesses the reasons
for rejecting the "traditional
moral condemnation of Abortion"
and the arguments against the legal policy based on that rejection.
He thinks that the unborn should
eb allowed to make their own
choice about life.]

[1364]Grisez, G. "Legal Personality and Abortion Law." Paper
presented to the National Canadian
Conference on Abortion, Toronto,
Canada, May, 1972. [In formu-
lating the status of the unborn
child, the author offers 5 theses:
1) in the past the law has regarded the unborn as persons to
some extent, but has not been consistent in so regarding them; 2)
inconsistency on the part of the
law, in regard to what it regards
as a person is intolerable; 3) the
unborn ought to be regarded consistently as persons from conception; 4) the unborn ought not to
be regarded consistently as non-
persons; 5) the issue of the legal
personhood of the unborn is not of
social utility, nor is it a problem of finding a solution acceptable to most. The issue is one of
fundamental justice.]

[1365]Grob, P. R. "The Aetiol-
ogy of Abortion is a Rural Community." *Journal of the Royal
College of General Practitioners,*
22 (August, 1972), 499-507.

[1366]Grogone, E. R. "Abortion
on Demand." *Lancet,* 1 (January 1,
1972), 45-46.

[1367]Grones, F. "They Fight
for Life—By Telephone." il. *Columbia,* 55 (July, 1975), 6-15.

[1168]Group for the Advancement of
Psychiatry (GAP). *The Right to
Abortion: A Psychiatric View,* vol.
7 (New York: Scribner's, 1970).

[1369]Grunebaum, H. U., Abernathy,
V. D., Rofman, E. S., and Weiss, J.
L. "The Family Planning Attitudes,
Practices and Motivations of Mental
Patients." *American Journal of Psy-
chiatry,* 128(6) (1971), 740-44.

[1370]Gudgeon, D. "Sterilization
on Abortion." *Lancet,* 1 (June 12,
1971), 1240.

[1371]Guharaj, A. "Attitude Survey
of Married Women Regarding Family
Planning at Urban Health Center,
Alambagh, Lucknow." *Indian Journal
of Public Health,* 12 (1968), 165-71.

[1372]*A Guide to the Abortion Act
1967* (London: Abortion Law Reform
Association, 1968).

[1373]"Guidelines for Action about
the New York Abortion Law." *Social
Justice Review,* 63 (December, 1970),
266-73.

[1374]"Guidelines for the Perform-
ance of Abortions as Adopted by the
Minnesota State Medical Association,
May, 1973." *Minnesota Medicine,* 56
(December, 1973), 1079-83.

[1375]Guindon, A. "Chronique: La
Conference Nationale Canadienne sur
L'Avortement (May 23-25, 1972)."
Eglise et Theologia, 3 (October,
1972), 391-407.

[1376]Gullattee, A. C. "Psychiatric Aspects of Abortion." *Journal
of the National Medical Association,*
64 (1972), 308-11.

[1377]Gupta, P. S. "Family Planning for the Home, Working Wives and
Mothers." *Social Welfare,* 19(7)
(1972), 8-10.

[1378]Gustafson, James. M. "A
Christian Approach to the Ethics of
Abortion." *Dublin Review,* 514 (Win-
ter, 1967-68), 346.

[1379]Gustafson, James M. "A
Protestant Ethical Approach." *The
Morality of Abortion.* Ed. J. Noonan
(Cambridge, Mass.: Harvard University
Press, 1970). [The author views
Catholics and Protestants as divided,
not only on the substantial moral
judgment, but also on the question of
method in regard to abortion. He offers what he sees as the salient aspects of the traditional Catholic
argument.] Then he goes on to con-

sider the way in which a Christian moralist should relate to the pregnant woman—interpret the situation, include his perspective, reflect on principles, and finally, decide and follow up his responsibilities to the mother. He concludes with a comparison of the two approaches.]

[1380]Gustafson, James M., Pleasants, Julian R., and Beecker, Henry K. "Comment on the 'Sanctity of Life'." *The Religious Situation* (Boston: Beacon Press, 1969).

[1381]Guttmacher, Alan F. "Abortion Laws Make Hypocrites of Us All." *New Medical Materia,* 4 (1962).

[1382]Guttmacher, Alan F. "Abortion—Yesterday, Today, and Tomorrow." *The Case for Legalized Abortion Now* (Berkeley: The Diablo Press, 1967).

[1383]Guttmacher, Alan F., ed. *The Case for Legalized Abortion Now* (Berkeley: The Diablo Press, 1967).

[1384]Guttmacher, Alan F. "Induced Abortion." *New York State Journal of Medicine,* 63 (August 15, 1963), 2334.

[1385]Guttmacher, Alan F. "Law of Criminal Abortion." *Indiana Law Journal,* 32 (Winter, 1957), 193.

[1386]Guttmacher, Alan F. "Legal and Moral Status of Therapeutic Abortion." *Progress in Gynecology,* 4 (1963), 279.

[1387]Guttmacher, Alan F. "The Shrinking Non-Psychiatric Indications for Therapeutic Abortion." *Abortion in America.* Ed. H. Rosen (Boston: Beacon Press, 1967).

[1388]Guttmacher, Alan F. "Techniques of Therapeutic Abortion." *Clinical Obstetrics and Gynecology,* (March, 1964), 7.

[1389]Guttmacher, Alan F. "Therapeutic Abortion: The Doctor's Dilemma." *Journal of Mt. Sinai Hospital,* 21 (May-June, 1954), 111.

[1390]Guttmacher, Alan F. "Therapeutic Abortion in a Large General Hospital." *Surgical Clinics of North America,* 37 (April, 1957), 459.

[1391]Guttmacher, Alan F. "The Population Problem." *Obstetrics and Gynecology,* 16 (July, 1960), 127.

[1392]Guttmacher, Alan F., *et al.* "Abortion and the Unwanted Child." *Family Planning Perspectives,* 2 (March, 1970), 16-24.

[1393]Guttmacher, M. S. "The Legal Status of Therapeutic Abortions." *Abortion in America.* Ed. Harold Rosen (Boston: Beacon Press, 1967).

[1394]Guzzetti, G. "Dangerous Developments on the Subject of Therapeutic Abortion: Italy's Decisions after the Seveso Contamination." *L'Osservatore Romano* (English), 443 (no. 39) (September 23, 1976), 11.

[1395]Gwynne, J. "Abortion—A Matter of Life and Death." *New Zealand Medical Journal,* 76 (November, 1972), 355-57.

[1396]Habinont, P. O., *et al.* "Abortion in Western and Southern Europe." Paper presented at the International Conference on Abortion, in Hot Springs, Virginia, November 17-20, 1968.

[1397]Hachey, R. "Decision in the Hodgson Case." *Social Justice Review,* 63 (November, 1970), 228-34.

[1398]Hagan, Michael R. "*Roe vs. Ward:* The Rhetoric of Fetal Life." *Central States Speech Journal,* 27 (August, 1976), 192-99.

[1399]Haidane, F. P. "Sequels of Unwanted Pregnancy." *Lancet,* 2 (September 21, 1968), 678-79.

[1400]Haire, Norman. "Abortion in Australia." *Journal of Sex Education,* 2 (February-March, 1959).

[1401]Hakanson, E. Y. "An Obstetrician's View of Therapeutic Abortion." *Minnesota Medicine,* 50 (January, 1967), 23-28.

[1402]Halevi, H. S., and Brzezinski, A. "Incidence of Abortion among Jewish Women in Israel." *American Journal of Public Health,* 48 (May, 1958), 615.

[1403]Halimi, Giselle. *The Right to Choose* (Lawrence, Ma.: University of Queensland Press, 1977).

[1404]"Half Favor Easier Abortion, Poll Says." *National Catholic Reporter,* 8 (March 17, 1972), 24.

[1405]Hall, Francoise M. "Male

1406-
1427   Use of Contraception and Attitudes Toward Abortion, Santiago, Chile, 1968 (responses in a survey)," tables. *Milbank Memorial Fund Quarterly,* 48 (April, 1970), 145-66.

[1406]Hall, I. B., *et al.* "The Attitude of the Protestant Churches." *Abortion in America.* Ed. Harold Rosen (Boston: Beacon Press, 1967).

[1407]Hall, Robert E., ed. *Abortion in a Changing World.* 2 volumes. (Irvington-on-Hudson: Columbia University Press, 1970).

[1408]Hall, Robert E. "Abortion in American Hospitals." *American Journal of Public Health,* 57 (November, 1967), 1933-36.

[1409]Hall, Robert E. "Abortion Laws: A Call for Reform." *De Paul Law Review,* 18 (Summer, 1969), 584.

[1410]Hall, Robert E. "Abortion: Physician and Hospital Attitudes." *American Journal of Public Health,* 61 (March, 1971), 517-19.

[1411]Hall, Robert E. "Commentary." *Abortion and the Law.* Ed. David T. Smith (Cleveland: Western Reserve University Press, 1967).

[1412]Hall, Robert E. *A Doctor's Guide to Having an Abortion* (Scarborough, Ontario: The New American Library of Canada Ltd., 1971).

[1413]Hall, Robert E. "The Future of Therapeutic Abortions in the United States." *Clinical Obstetrics and Gynecology,* 14 (December, 1971), 1149-53.

[1414]Hall, Robert E. "Induced Abortion in New York City." *American Journal of Obstetrics and Gynecology,* 110 (July 1, 1971), 601.

[1415]Hall, Robert E. "The Medico-Legal Aspects of Abortion." *Obstetrics and Gynecology Annual,* 1 (1972), 339-50.

[1416]Hall, Robert E. "The Supreme Court Decision on Abortion." *American Journal of Obstetrics and Gynecology,* 116 (May 1, 1973), 1-8.

[1417]Hall, Robert E. "Thalidomide and Our Abortion Laws." *Columbia University Forum,* 6 (Winter, 1963).

[1418]Hall, Robert E. "Therapeutic Abortion, Sterilization, and Contraception." *Journal of Obstetrics and Gynecology,* 91 (February, 1965), 518-532.

[1419]Hall, Robert E. "The Truth about Abortion in New York." *Columbia Forum,* 13 (Winter, 1970), 18-22.

[1420]Hallett, G. "The Plain Meaning of Abortion." *America,* 124 (June 19, 1971), 632-33. [Hallett asserts that there is no doubt that the fetus is a human fetus. Referring to the work of Wittgenstein, he says that our indecision about using the expression "human being" for the fetus comes from indeterminacy of the concept "human being" and not from lack of information. The question of ensoulment is seen as a linguistic move, not directly related to the problem of abortion.
Hallett goes on to discuss how life at different stages is valued. He notes that the death of a young child is mourned but not that of a fetus. It is suggested that the most important single factor is the termination of human existence rather than concentrating attention upon line drawing.]

[1421]Halley, M. M. "Abortion." *Journal of the Kansas Medical Society,* 69 (November, 1968), 530-33.

[1422]Halley, M. M. "Law-Medicine Comment: A Model Abortion Statute." *Journal of the Kansas Medical Society,* 69 (December, 1968), 599-603

[1423]Halliday, R. "Letter: Therapeutic Abortion." *Canadian Medical Association Journal,* 113(4) (August 23, 1975), 276-78.

[1424]Hamer, J. "Declaration on Abortion: A Religion, Not Political Act: Interview of J. Hamer, Secretary of S. Congregation for the Doctrine of the Faith." *L'Osservatore Romano* (English), 354 (no. 2) (January 9, 1975), 8.

[1425]Hamill, F., and Ingram, I. M. "Psychiatric and Social Factors in the Abortion Decision." *British Medical Journal,* 1 (1974), 229-32.

[1426]Hamill, R. H. "Abortion: A Campus Chaplain's Reply to His Colleagues." *Christian Century,* 28 (August 11, 1971), 957.

[1427]Hamilton, Virginia C. "Medical Status and Psychologic Attitude of Patients Following Abortion." *American Journal of Obstetrics and Gynecology,* 41 (Feb. 1941), 285-288.

[1428]Hamilton, Virginia C. "Some Sociologic and Psychologic Observations on Abortion." *American Journal of Obstetrics and Gynecology*, 39 (1940), 61.

[1429]Hanily, E. "The Courage to Speak." *Catholic Digest*, 37 (April, 1973), 22-24. Cond. from a speech to the John Carroll Society.

[1430]Hannaford, J. M. "Abortion: Crime or Privilege?" *Mayo Clinic Proceedings*, 45 (July, 1970), 510-16.

[1431]Hardin, Garett. "Abortion —or Compulsory Pregnancy." *Journal of Marriage and the Family*, 30 (May, 1968), 246-51.

[1432]Hardin, Garett. "Abortion and Human Dignity." Public lecture delivered at the University of California in Berkeley. Also: *The Case for Legalized Abortion Now.* Ed. Alan Guttmacher (Berkeley: Diablo Press, 1967).

[1433]Hardin, Garett. "Blueprints, DNA and Abortion: A Scientific Analysis." *Medical Opinion and Review*, 3 (February, 1967).

[1434]Hardin, Garett. *Mandatory Motherhood: The True Meaning of the "Right to Life"* (Boston: Beacon Press, 1974).

[1435]Hardin, Garett. "Semantic Aspects of Abortion." *ETC, A Review of General Semantics*, 24 (September, 1967).

[1436]Hardy, E., and Herud, K. "Effectiveness of a Contraceptive Education Program for Post-Abortion Patients in Chile." *Studies in Family Planning*, 6(7) (1975), 188-92.

[1437]Hare, R. M. "Abortion and the Golden Rule." *Philosophy and Public Affairs*, 4 (Spring, 1975), 201-22.

[1438]Haring, Bernard. "New Dimensions of Responsible Parenthood." *Theological Studies*, 37 (March, 1976), 120-32.

[1439]Harlap, S., and Davies, A. M. "Characteristics of Pregnant Women Who Report Previous Induced Abortions." *Bulletin of the World Health Organization*, 52(2) (1975), 149-54.

[1440]*Harmful Effects of Induced Abortion* (Tokyo: Family Planning Federation of Japan, 1966).

[1441]Harmsen, H. *The Medical Evil of Abortion* (Bombay: The Family Planning Association of India, 1952).

[1442]Harper, M. W., Marcom, B. R., and Wall, V. D. "Abortion. Do Attitudes of Nursing Personnel Affect the Patient's Perception of Care?" *Nursing Research*, 21(4) (1972), 327-31.

[1443]Harrington, Paul V. "Abortion." *Linacre Quarterly*, 32 (November, 1965), 339. [The legalization of abortion is viewed as an attempt at the legalization of murder. The fetus is denied, not only its right to life, but also happiness.]

[1444]Harrington, Paul V. "Abortion—Part II." *Linacre Quarterly*, 33 (February, 1966), 81. [The author states that it is in the legislative assemblies that abortion laws will be determined. Various conferences are discussed. These include: the World Population Conference in Belgrade, August-September, 1965; the White House Conference on Health, November, 1965; and the American Medical Association in Philadelphia, November, 1965.]

[1445]Harrington, Paul V. "Abortion—Part III." *Linacre Quarterly*, 33 (May, 1966), 153. [The author points out that medical professionals are increasingly advocating the liberalization of abortion laws. He recommends a renewed acceptance of the principle of the sanctity of life.]

[1446]Harrington, Paul V. "Abortion—Part IV." *Linacre Quarterly*, 33-34 (February, 1967), 67. [Great Britain's and New York's abortion bills are discussed.] He concludes that solutions to social problems should be found in social services rather than in liberalized abortion laws.]

[1447]Harrington, Paul V. "Abortion—Part V." *Linacre Quarterly*, 33-34 (May, 1967), 158. [Reasons are offered against performing therapeutic abortion on grounds of the mental and physical health of the mother and in cases of rape.]

[1448]Harrington, Paul V. "Abortion—Part VI." *Linacre Quarterly*, 33-34 (August, 1967), 250. [Fetal indications are discussed, focusing on the thalidomide tragedy and rubella. Reasons against abortion are given.]

[1449]Harrington, Paul V.
"Abortion—Part VII." *Linacre
Quarterly,* 33-34 (November, 1967),
311. [The "population explosion"
is the subject of this article.]

[1450]Harrington, Paul V.
"Abortion—Part VIII." *Linacre
Quarterly,* 35 (February, 1968),
43. [This is a summary of Roger
J. Huser's doctoral dissertation,
*The Crime of Abortion in Canon
Law* (Washington, D.C.: The Catho-
lic University Press, 1942).

[1451]Harrington, Paul V.
"Abortion—Part IX." *Linacre
Quarterly,* 35 (May, 1968), 126.
[The Code of Canon Law of 1918 is
reviewed as well as papal state-
ments until 1967.]

[1452]Harrington, Paul V.
"Abortion—Part X: A Legal View."
Linacre Quarterly, 35 (August,
1968), 190. [The status of the fetus is explored in light of English and American law.]

[1453]Harrington, Paul V.
"Abortion—Part XI: A Legal View
Continued." *Linacre Quarterly,*
35 (November, 1968), 265.

[1454]Harrington, Paul V.
"Abortion—Part XII." *Linacre
Quarterly,* 36 (May, 1969), 139.

[1455]Harrington, Paul V.
"Abortion—Part XIII." *Linacre
Quarterly,* 36 (August, 1969), 174.

[1456]Harrington, Paul V.
"Abortion—Part XIV." *Linacre
Quarterly,* 36 (November, 1969),
242. [The legislative changes in
the United States are discussed.
Three states are mentioned: Colorado, California and Maryland.]

[1457]Harrington, Paul V.
"Abortion—Part XV." *Linacre
Quarterly,* 37 (May, 1970), 117.
[The status of the fetus is dis-
cussed with regards to the biolog-
ical and legal aspects.]

[1458]Harrington, Paul V.
"Abortion—Part XVI." *Linacre
Quarterly,* 37 (November, 1970),
270. [The "sanctity of life" is
discussed as opposed to the "quality of life."]

[1459]Harrington, Paul V.
"Abortion: Japan." *Linacre Quarterly,* 36 (May, 1969), 139-43.

[1460]Harrington, Paul V. "Is
Abortion a Crime?" *Family Digest,*

23 (January, 1968), 7-13.

[1461]Harrington, Paul V. "Human
Life and Abortion." *Catholic Lawyer,*
17 (Winter, 1971), 11-44. [Harring-
ton asserts that Catholics should
speak against liberal abortions,
even for those who do not hold the
same views, for two reasons: 1) he
disputes the assumption that voluntary abortion will never become mandatory abortion; 2) the norm for
right conduct is that which is ob-
jectively good and virtuous. A history of the Church's position and
legislation in Great Britain and the
United States, as well as medical
attitudes, are presented as in favor of the anti-abortion stance.]

[1462]Harrington, Timothy J. "Legalization of Abortion." *Homiletic
and Pastoral Review,* 69 (June, 1967),
635.

[1463]Harris, D., *et al.* "Legal
Abortion 1970-1971—the New York
City Experience." *American Journal
of Public Health,* 63 (May, 1973),
409-18.

[1464]Harris, Harry. *Pre-Natal
Diagnosis & Selective Abortion* (Cam-
bridge, Mass.: Harvard University
Press, 1975).

[1465]Harris, T. E. "A Functional
Study of Existing Abortion Laws."
Columbia Law Review, 35 (Jaunary,
1935), 87-97.

[1466]Harrison, C. P. "Abortion
and the Law." *Canadian Medical Association Journal,* 98 (May 18, 1968),
973.

[1467]Harrison, C. P. "Effects of
Legalizing Abortions." *Lancet,* 1
(April 27, 1968), 917-18.

[1468]Harrison, C. P. "Teenage
Pregnancy—Is Abortion the Answer?"
*Pediatric Clinicians of North Ameri-
ca,* 16 (1969), 363-369.

[1469]Harrison, C. P. "Therapeutic Abortion." *Canadian Medical
Association Journal,* 102 (May 30,
1970), 1209-11.

[1470]Harrison III, Frank R.
"What Kind of Beings Can Have Rights?"
Philosophy Forum, (Dekalb) 12 (Sep-
tember, 1972), 113-28.

[1471]Harrison, S. M. "Supreme
Court and Abortional Reform: Means
to an End." *New York Law Forum,* 19
(Winter, 1974), 685-701.

1472Hart, H. L. "Abortion Law Reform: The English Experience." *Melbourne University Law Review,* 8 (May, 1972), 388.

1473Hart, T. M. "Legalized Abortion in Japan." *California Medicine,* 107 (October, 1967), 334-37.

1474Harter, C. L., *et al.* "A Survey Concerning Induced Abortions in New Orleans." *American Journal of Public Health,* 57 (November, 1967), 1937-47.

1475Harting, Donald. "Abortion Techniques and Services: A Review and Critique." *American Journal of Public Health,* 61 (October, 1971), 2085-105.

1476"Has Legal Abortion Contributed to U.S. 'birth dearth'?" *Family Planning Perspective,* 4 (April, 1972), 7-8.

1477Hassard, H., *et al.* "Abortion in California. State Supreme Court Decision Under Former Law Sheds Some Light on Conduct Under Amended Act." *California Medicine,* 111 (December, 1969), 491-92.

1478Hassing, Arne. "Bishop of Borg Says No." *Christian Century,* 92 (October 29, 1975), 972-73. [Bishop Lonning resigned as a bishop of the Church of Norway (Lutheran State Church) in protest when the Storting passed legislation to liberalize the abortion law. The debate moved to Church-State relations. The Bishop's resignation is seen as a move which will hasten Norway's separation of Church from State.]

1479Hatcher, S. L. M. "The Adolescent Experience of Pregnancy and Abortion. A Developmental Analysis." *Journal of Youth and Adolescence,* 2(1) (1973), 53-102.

1480Hauerwas, S. "Abortion: the Agent's Perspective." *American Ecclesiastical Review,* 167 (February, 1973), 102-20. [The author analyzes and questions the assumption that the "New Ethics" knows what is meant by the term "abortion." Our language understands "abortion" to be a morally doubtful practice.
He asks: 1) When does life begin? 2) When can life be taken legitimately? His response is that the fetus should be regarded as human life and the range of exceptions for taking such life is very narrow. A third question should be asked: 3) What does the agent understand to be happening? A reference is made to Gustafson's case in "The Protestant Ethical Approach." *The Morality of Abortion* (Cambridge: Harvard Press, 1970), 101-22. He attempts to point out that an abortion decision is not simply a satisfied feeling in handling the issue but rather to understand what an abortion is, in terms of the kind of life implied by the decision.

1481Hauerwas, S. "Abortion and Normative Ethics." *Cross Current,* 21 (Fall, 1971), 399-414. [The author critically contrasts Danial Callahan's book, *Abortion: Law, Choice and Morality,* with Germain Grisez's, *Abortion, the Myths, the Realities and the Arguments.* Hauerwas hopes to show the limitations of each and suggests that there are aspects of this problem where, as yet, we have no adequate ethical stance.]

1482"Haunting Shadows from the Rubble of *Roe's (Roe v. Wade.* 93 Sup Ct 705) Right of Privacy." *Suffolk University Law Review,* 9 (Fall, 1974), 145-84.

1483Hausknecht, R. U. "Free Standing Abortion Clinics: A New Phenomenon." *Bulletin of the New York Academy of Medicine,* 49 (November, 1973), 985-91.

1484Hausknecht, R. U. "The Termination of Pregnancy in Adolescent Women." *Pediatric Clinics of North America,* 19 (August, 1972), 803-10.

1485Hay, D. "Whither Therapeutic Abortion?" *Manchester Medical Gazette,* 50 (October, 1970), 7-1.

1486Hayasaka, Y., Today, H., Zimmerman, A., Ueno, T., and Ishizaki, M. "Japan's 22-Year Experience with a Liberal Abortion Law." *Linacre Quarterly,* 38 (February, 1971), 33-44.

1487Hayashi, Motoyuki, and Momose, Kazuo. "Statistical Observations on Artificial Abortion and Secondary Sterility." *Harmful Effects of Induced Abortion* (Tokyo: Family Planning Federation of Japan, 1966).

1488Hayes, A. C. "Letter: Therapeutic Abortion." *Canadian Medical Association Journal,* 112(10) (May 17, 1975), 1166.

[1489]Hayes, Thomas L. "Abortion: A Biological View." *Commonweal*, 85 (1967), 676.

[1490]"Health Legislation. Abortion: A Survey of Current Legislation." *World Health Organization Chronicle*, 25 (July, 1971), 328-33.

[1491]"Health of the Nation." *British Medical Journal*, 4 (October 25, 1969), 183-84.

[1492]Heath, D. S. "Psychiatry and Abortion." *Canadian Psychiatric Association Journal*, 16 (February, 1971), 55-63 (32 ref.).

[1493]Hedderson, J., Hodgson, L. G., Bogan, M., and Crowley, T. "Determinants of Abortion Attitudes in the United States in 1972." *The Cornell Journal of Social Relations*, 9(2) (1974), 261-76.

[1494]Heer, D. M. "Abortion, Contraception and Population Policy in the Soviet Union." *Soviet Studies*, 17 (1965), 76-83.

[1495]Hefferman, R. J., and Lynch, W. A. "What is the Status of Therapeutic Abortion in Modern Obstetrics?" *American Journal of Obstetrics and Gynecology*, 66 (1953), 335.

[1496]Heiman, M. "New Abortion Laws and Help for Nurses." *American Journal of Psychiatry*, 129 (September, 1972), 360.

[1497]Heimer, David D. "Abortion Attitudes Among Catholic University Students: A Comparative Research Note." *Sociological Analysis*, 37 (no. 3) (1976), 255-60.

[1498]Heine, C. "Abortion." *Canadian Medical Association Journal*, 102 (May 30, 1970), 1121.

[1499]Heine, C. "Therapeutic Abortion." *Canadian Medical Association Journal*, 104 (March 6, 1971), 421.

[1500]Heineman, R. K. "The Evolution of an Abortion Counseling Service in an Adoption Agency." *Child Welfare*, 52(4) (1973), 253-60. [This program was initiated to meet the counseling needs of the rising numbers of women who are seeking legal abortion in New York City.]

[1501]"Held up by Abortions." *British Medical Journal*, 3 (1969), 367.

[1502]Hellegers, Andre. "Abortion, the Law and the Common Good," tabs. *Catholic Mind*, 65 (December, 1967), 28-39.

[1503]Hellegers, Andre. "Amazing Historical and Biological Errors in Abortion Decision—Dr. Hellegers." *Hospital Progress*, 54 (May, 1973), 16-17. Reprint from *Washington Star News*, excerpt from interview by T. Ascik.

[1504]Hellegers, Andre E. "A Doctor Looks at Abortion." Unpublished lecture by Edward Douglas White, Georgetown University Law Center, March, 16, 1966.

[1505]Hellegers, Andre E. "Fetal Development." *Theological Studies*, 31 (March, 1970), 3. [Fetal development is described. The author concludes that science cannot predict when human life begins (in the philosophical sense).]

[1506]Hellegers, Andre E. "Law and the Common Good." *Commonweal*, 86 (1967), 418.

[1507]Hellegers, Andre E. "A Look at Abortion: Reply." *National Catholic Reporter*, 3 (March 1, 1967), 4.

[1508]Hellegers, Andre E. "Population, Rhythm, Contraception and Abortion Policy Questions." *Linacre Quarterly*, 40 (May, 1973), 91-96. [The author points out that the world is presently undergoing an unprecedented rate of population growth, the U.S. may go back to the growth rates of the 1950s, and if a family size of two children were reached it would be in spite of *Humanae Vitae*. Also, early marriage and reproduction drastically increase population growth.
Several recommendations are offered: 1) The Catholic Church should lobby for more expenditures in reproductive biology research; 2) also, that demographic research be supported; 3) advocate a later age for marriage; 4) major research centers on problems of population, reproduction and the family be established at Catholic universities; 5) Catholics should join with those other sectors of the population who consider abortion less than desirable; 6) the Supreme Court decision must be viewed as an opportunity to

reflect on deficiencies and now take the lead.]

[1509]Hellegers, Andre E. *"Wade and Bolton:* Medical Critique." *Catholic Lawyer,* 19 (Fall, 1973), 251-58. [Hellegers reviews what is happening in various Federal Government Committees, NIH and in other areas such as this where one can foresee various problems.]

[1510]Heller, A. "The Colorado Story. Denver General Hospital Experience with the Change in the Law of Therapeutic Abortion." *American Journal of Psychiatry,* 125 (1968), 809-16.

[1511]Heller, A. "Therapeutic Abortion Trends in the United States." *Current Psychiatric Therapy,* 12 (1972), 171-84.

[1512]Heller, R. N. "Pre-Natal Diagnosis and the Prevention of Birth Defects." *Maryland State Medical Journal,* 20 (May, 1971), 59-62.

[1513]Hellman, L. M. "Family Planning Comes of Age." *American Journal of Obstetrics and Gynecology,* 109 (January 15, 1971), 214-24.

[1514]Hemingway, L., *et al.* "A Statement on Abortion in Victoria." *Medical Journal of Australia,* 1 (March 18, 1972), 608.

[1515]Hemphill, R. E. "The Abortion Bill." *Lancet,* 1 (February 11, 1967), 324-26.

[1516]Hendershot, G. E., and Grimy, J. W. "Abortion Attitudes Among Nurses and Social Workers." *American Journal of Public Health,* 64(5) (1974), 438-41.

[1517]Henker, F. O. "Abortion and Sterilization from Psychiatric and Medico-Legal Viewpoints." *Arkansas Medical Society Journal,* 57 (February, 1961), 368-73.

[1518]Henker, F. O. "Abortion Applicants in Arkansas." *Journal of the Arkansas Medical Society,* 69 (March, 1973), 293-95.

[1519]Henle, R. "Georgetown University Statement on Abortion." *Catholic Mind,* 71 (September, 1973), 9-10. [Fr. Henle is the president of Georgetown University, Washington, D.C. Because this university specializes in fetal physiology, Henle states that those who work here are greatly aware of the biological fact regarding the beginning of biological human life. The statement asserts that all human life will be protected and the obstetrician is taught that he is responsible medically and morally for the health and welfare of two patients, the mother and the child.]

[1520]*"Henrie vs. Derryberry* (358 F Supp 719) and the current status of the Oklahoma Abortion Laws." 10 (1974), 273-80.

[1521]Henthoff, M. "Abortion." *Jubilee,* 14 (April, 1967), 4-5.

[1522]Hepworth, Philip H. *Family Planning and Abortion Services and Family Life Education Programs* (Ottawa: Canadian Council on Social Development, 1975).

[1523]Herak-Szabo, J. "Legal and Illegal Abortion in the People's Republic of Croatia." *Third Conference of the Region for Europe, Near East and Africa of the International Planned Parenthood Federation,* 1962.

[1524]Herbenick, R. M. "Remarks on Abortion, Abandonment, and Adoption Opportunities." *Philosophy and Public Affairs,* 5(1) (1975), 98 passim.

[1525]Herbert, P. "Is Legalized Abortion the Solution to Criminal Abortion?" *University of Colorado Law Review,* 37 (Winter, 1965), 283.

[1526]Hern, Warren M. "The Politics of Abortion (United States)." il. *Progressive,* 36 (November, 1972), 26-29.

[1527]Herndon, J. E. "Religious Aspects and Theology in Therapeutic Abortion." *Southern Medical Journal,* 63 (June, 1970), 651-54.

[1528]Hershey, N. "Abortion and Sterilization. Status of the Law in Mid-1970." *American Journal of Nursing,* 70 (September, 1970), 1926-27.

[1529]Hershey, N. "A Society's Views Change, Law Changes." *American Journal of Nursing,* 67 (November, 1967), 2310-12.

[1530]Hertel, B., Hendershot, G. E., and Grimm, J. W. "Religion and Attitudes Toward Abortion. A Study of Nurses and Social Workers." *Journal for the Scientific Study of*

Religion, 13(1) (1974), 23-34.

[1531]Hertz, D. G. "Rejection of Motherhood, a Psychosomatic Appraisal of Habitual Abortion." *Psychosomatics,* 14(4) (1973), 241-44.

[1532]Hess, Glenda Adams. "Biological Personhood." *Christian Century,* 88 (December 8, 1971), 1450.

[1533]Heuskin, Lucie. "Rapport de Synthese (Abortion)." *Revue de L'Institut de Sociologie,* no. 3 (1971), 457-59.

[1534]Hewetson, John. "Birth Control, Sexual Morality and Abortion." *Twentieth Century Magazine,* (Winter, 1962-1963).

[1535]Heymann, P. B., *et al.* "Forest and the Trees: *Roe v. Wade* (93 Sup Ct. 705) and its Critics." *Boston University Law Review,* 53 (July, 1973), 765-84.

[1536]Hickok, D., *et al.* "Attitudes Toward Abortion Law Reform at the University of Michigan Medical Center." *Michigan Medicine,* 71 (April, 1972), 327-29.

[1537]Higgins, J. "Is Abortion Only a Catholic Issue?" *Liguorian,* 64 (May, 1976), 24-28.

[1538]"High Court Again Gives Approval for Abortion in Three New Decisions." *Our Sunday Visitor,* 65 (July 11, 1976), 1.

[1539]"High Court Forbids Parental-Spouse Veto Over Abortions." *Family Planning Perspectives,* 8 (July-August, 1976), 177-78. [The U.S. Supreme Court on July 1, 1976 declared unconstitutional state laws that require a married woman to get her husband's consent or a minor to have her parents' or guardian's permission to obtain a first-trimester abortion.]

[1540]"High Court Hears Cases on Abortion." *National Catholic Reporter,* 8 (October 20, 1972), 18.

[1541]Hilgers, Thomas, and Horan, Dennis J., eds. *Abortion and Social Justice* (Mission, Ks.: Sheed Andrews & McMeel, 1973.

[1542]"Hill-Burton Hospitals after *Roe* and *Doe:* Can Federally Funded Hospitals Refuse to Perform Abortions?" *New York University Review of Law and Social Change,*

4 (Winter, 1974), 83-91. [Under the Hill-Burton Act, many hospitals, both private and public, have received federal and state funds. Can a private hospital which receives these funds refuse to perform abortions? The Courts have held both ways concerning the issue. The author discusses three different interpretations of Section 401 of the Health Programs Extension Act of 1973. He concludes that private hospitals cannot refuse to perform abortions under the theory of state action.]

[1543]Hill, E. J. "Termination of Pregnancy." *New Zealand Medical Journal,* 74 (December, 1971), 412.

[1544]Hill, E. L., *et al.* "Black Physicians' Experience with Abortion Requests and Opinion about Abortion Law Change in Michigan." *Journal of the National Medical Association,* 64 (January, 1972), 52-58.

[1545]Hill, H. "Educational Factors: Personal and Community Factors on Fertility Control." *Journal of Biosocial Science,* 1 (July, 1969), 321-25.

[1546]Hill, J. G. "Birth Control Usage Among Abortion Patients." *Journal of the Kansas Medical Society,* 73 (June, 1972), 295-301 passim.

[1547]Hindell, Keith, and Simms, Madeleine. *Abortion Law Reformed* (London: Peter Owen Ltd., 1971).

[1548]Hindell, Keith, and Simms, Madeleine. "How the Abortion Lobby Worked." *Political Quarterly,* 39 (July, 1968), 268-82.

[1549]Hinsberg, T. F. "Church: An Agent of Social Change." *Journal of Applied Behaviour Science,* 10 (no. 3) (1974), 432-37.

[1550]Hipkiss, R. A. "Abortion Language and Logic." *A Review of General Semantics,* 33 (June, 1976), 207-12.

[1551]Hirschler, Imre. "Abortion in Hungary." Paper presented at the International Conference on Abortion, Hot Springs, Virginia, November 17-20, 1968.

[1552]Hirsh, H. L. "Impact of the Supreme Court Decisions on the Performance of Abortions in the United States." *Forensic Science,* 3 (June, 1974), 209-23.

[1553]Hirsh, H. L. "Legal Guidelines for the Performance of Abortions." *American Journal of Obstetrics and Gynecology,*]22(6) (July 15, 1975), 679-82.

[1554]Hodge, K. E. "Therapeutic Abortion and Ultrasound." *Canadian Medical Association Journal,* 105 (November 20, 1971), 1021.

[1555]Hodgson, J. E. "Community Abortion Services. The Role of Organized Medicine." *Minnesota Medicine,* 56 (March, 1973), 239-42.

[1556]Hodgson, J. E. "Teenage Mothers." *Minnesota Medicine,* 55 (January, 1972), 49.

[1557]Hodgson, J. E. "You May Be Right. Therapeutic Abortion in Medical Perspective." *Minnesota Medicine,* 53 (July, 1970), 755 passim.

[1558]Hoffman, Robert. "The Moral Right to Abortion." *Michigan Quarterly Review,* 8 (October, 1969), 273-77.

[1559]Hoffman, W. "Some News Just Isn't Fit to Print." *Triumph,* 6 (December, 1971), 19-23.

[1560]Hoffmeyer, Henrik. "Medical Aspects of the Danish Legislation on Abortion." *Abortion and the Law.* Ed. David T. Smith (Cleveland: Western Reserve University Press, 1967).

[1561]Hoffmeyer, H., Norgaard, M., and Skalts, V. "Abortion, Sterilization and Contraception." *Journal of Sex Research,* 3 (1967), 1-24.

[1562]Hoggett, A. J. C. "Abortion Act 1967." *Criminal Law Review* (English), 1968 (May, 1968), 247.

[1563]Hoheisel, P. "Abortion— A Complex Issue Today Calling for More Discussion." *Michigan Medicine,* 66 (July, 1967), 900-02.

[1564]Holman, E. J. "United States Supreme Court and Abortion. 1." *Journal of the American Medical Association,* 225 (July 9, 1973), 215-16.

[1565]Holman, E. J. "United States Supreme Court and Abortion. 3." *Journal of the American Medical Association,* 225 (July 23, 1973), 447-48.

[1566]Holton, R. "Feminists for Life Fight Abortion." *National Catholic Reporter,* 10 (September 6, 1974), 4.

[1567]Holtzman, L. "Medical-Legal Considerations of Abortion in New York State Under the New Abortion Law." *Clinical Obstetrics and Gynecology,* 14 (March, 1971), 36-47. Also: *Modern Treatment,* 8 (February, 1971), 38-49.

[1568]"Homo Sapienism: Critique of *Roe v. Wade* (93 Sup Ct 705) and Abortion." *Albany Law Review,* 39 (1975), 856-93.

[1569]Hook, K. "Refused Abortion. A Follow-Up Study of 249 Women Whose Applications Were Refused by the National Board of Health in Sweden. *Acta Paediatrica Scandinavica,* 39 (suppl.) (1963), 168.

[1570]Horan, Dennis. "Abortion and the Conscience Clause: Current Status." *Catholic Lawyer,* 20 (Fall, 1974), 289-302. [Horan speaks of a "sane solution" to the abortion problem. 1) Educate people about the nature of unborn life, and why it should be protected by law; 2) support political efforts to obtain a constitutional amendment; 3) support alternatives to abortion; 4) create a national Legal Defense Fund, the purpose of which will be to reverse the *Roe* and *Doe* decisions. He goes on to examine what could be achieved in the courts.]

[1571]Horan, Dennis. "Viability, Values, and the Vast Cosmos." *Catholic Lawyer,* 22 (Winter, 1976), 1-37. [The primary intent of this article is to illuminate the importance of the concept of viability through a discussion of cases which have arisen since the Supreme Court decision. The opinions of the West German Federal Constitutional Court are presented. Then, four state supreme court decisions in the United States concerning the viability and the legal personhood of the unborn child are examined. The case of *Commonwealth vs. Edelin* and life and death in the special care nursery are discussed.]

[1572]Hordon, A. *Legal Abortion: The English Experience* (Oxford: Pergamon Press, 1971).

[1573]Horobin, G. W., ed. *Experience with Abortion* (Cambridge: Cambridge University Press, 1973).

[1574]Horobin, G. W. "Therapeutic

1575–
1600

Abortion in North-East Scotland: Introduction." *Journal of Biosocial Science,* 3 (January, 1971), 87–88.

[1575]Horty, J. F. "Court Declares California Abortion Law Invalid, Reverses Doctor's Conviction." *Modern Hospital,* 113 (December, 1969), 50–52.

[1576]"Hospital Abortion Committee as an Administrative Body of the State." *Journal of Family Law,* 10 (1970), 32.

[1577]"Hospital Asked to Boycott Maker of Abortion Drug." *National Catholic Reporter,* 10 (March 15, 1974), 5.

[1578]"Hospital Ruling Favors Abortions." *National Catholic Reporter,* 10 (March 8, 1974), 14.

[1579]"Hospitals—A Current Analysis of the Right to Abortions and Sterilizations in the Fourth Circuit: State Action and the Church Amendment." *North Carolina Law Review,* 54 (September, 1976), 1307.

[1580]Hotchkiss, W. S. "Editorial: Abortion Without Medical Indication." *Virginia Medical Monthly,* 97 (December, 1970), 747–48.

[1581]Houghton, Vera. "Abortion Law." *Eugenics Review,* 57 (September, 1965), 105–07.

[1582]Houghton, Vera. "Medical Termination of Pregnancy Bill." *Eugenics Review,* 53 (July, 1961), 93.

[1583]"House of Lords Okays Abortion Bill." *National Catholic Reporter,* 4 (November 1, 1967), 5.

[1584]"House Unit Hears Prelates, Legal Experts Argue For, Against Abortion Amendment." *National Catholic Reporter,* 12 (April 2, 1976), 32.

[1585]Howell, E. M. "A Study of Reported Therapeutic Abortions in North Carolina." *American Journal of Public Health,* 65(5) (1975), 480–83.

[1586]Howells, R. *What Price Abortion?* (Llandysal, Dyfed: Gomer Press, 1973).

[1587]Hoyt, R. "Abortion Issue Clouded by Differing Approaches: International Conference on Abortion." *National Catholic Reporter,*

3 (September 13, 1967), 1+.

[1588]Hoyt, R. "Afterthoughts on a Conference: Sponsored by Harvard Divinity School and Kennedy Foundation." *National Catholic Reporter,* 3 (September 20, 1967), 10.

[1589]Haunt, E. "The 'Humanae Vitae' Centre and the Legislation on Abortion." *L'Osservatore Romano* (English), 122 (no. 31) (July 30, 1970), 5.

[1590]Hudson, I. D. "Abortion— An Excuse for a Policy." *Public Health,* 87 (September, 1973), 239–44. Also: *Community Health* (Bristol), 5 (November–December, 1973), 143–48.

[1591]Huff, J. W. "The New Georgia Abortion Law." *Journal of the Medical Association of Georgia,* 62 (June, 1973), 241–42.

[1592]Huges, G. E. F. "England's Great Leap Backward—The Abortion Act, 1967." *Australia Law Journal,* 43 (January, 1969), 12.

[1593]Huges, J. H. "Fertility Control: Health and Educational Factors for the 1970's. Contraception or Abortion." *Journal of Biosocial Science,* 2 (April, 1970), 161–6.

[1594]Hughes, G. "Who is a Victim?" *Dalhousie Law Journal,* 1 (October, 1974), 425–40.

[1595]Huldt, L. "Outcome of Pregnancy when Legal Abortion is Readily Available." *Lancet,* 1 (March 2, 1968), 467–68.

[1596]*Human Fertility and Population Problems.* Ed. Roy O. Greep (Cambridge, Mass.: Schenkman, 1963).

[1597]"Human Life is Sacred: Pastoral Letter of the Archbishops and Bishops of Ireland." *L'Osservatore Romano* (English), 373 (no. 21) (May 22, 1975), 6–8+; 376 (no. 24) (June 12, 1975), 6–8; 377 (no. 25) (June 19, 1975), 6–9.

[1598]Humber, James M. "The Case Against Abortion." *Thomist,* 39 (January, 1975), 65–84.

[1599]Hume, K. "Letter: Abortion: Community Trends." *Medical Journal of Australia,* 2(14) (October 5, 1974), 542.

[1600]"Hungary Works Against Abortions." *National Catholic Reporter,* 4 (February 14, 1968), 5.

[1601]Hunt, W. "Theologian Challenges Drinan on Abortion Laws." *National Catholic Reporter*, 4 (June 19, 1968), 6.

[1602]Hunter, M. E. "Applications for Abortion at a Community Hospital." *Canadian Medical Association Journal*, 111(10) (November 16, 1974), 1088-89, 1092.

[1603]Huntingford, P. J. "Abortion—A Matter for Controversy." *British Journal of Hospitals and Medicine*, 2 (1969), 555.

[1604]Huntingford, P. J. "Abortion or Contraception?" *Royal Society of Health Journal*, 91 (November-December, 1971), 292-94.

[1605]Huntingford, P. J. "Letter: Disclosure on Abortion." *Lancet*, 1(7956) (February 21, 1976), 434-35.

[1606]Huntingford, P. J. "Letter: Working of the Abortion Act." *British Medical Journal*, 2(5965) (May 3, 1975), 278.

[1607]Huntston, G. "The No. 2 Moral Issue of Today." *America*, 116 (March 25, 1967), 452-53.

[1608]Hurley, M. "Letter on Abortion Morality." *Social Justice Review*, 64 (November, 1971), 241-42.

[1609]Huser, Roger John. *The Crime of Abortion in Canon Law* (Washington, D.C.: The Catholic University Press, 1942).

[1610]Hyatt, Jim. "Legalized Abortions: Colorado's Cautious Use of Liberalized Statute may Spur Similar Laws; Doctors Turn Down Requests of Many Women; 28 Other States Now Mull Changes; But Controversy Still Exists." *Wall Street Journal*, 170 (August 18, 1967), 1.

[1611]Hyde, G. "Abortion and the Birth Rate in the U.S.S.R." *Journal of Biosocial Science*, 2 (July, 1970), 283-92.

[1614]Hyer, M. "Chaos Greets New N.Y. Abortion Law." *National Catholic Reporter*, 6 (July 24, 1970), 20.

[1613]Hyer, M. "Yano Explains Vote on Abortion." *National Catholic Reporter*, 7 (December 11, 1970), 14-15.

[1614]Iffy, L. "Letter: Abortion Laws in Hungary." *Obstetrics and Gynecology*, 45(1) (January, 1975), 115-16.

[1615]"Illinois Abortion Report Scored as Anti-Catholic." *National Catholic Reporter*, 10 (February 15, 1974), 14.

[1616]"Illinois Catholic Conference on Abortion." *Social Justice Review*, 63 (March, 1971), 414.

[1617]"Illinois Leaders Oppose Abortion Law Repeal." *Social Justice Review*, 62 (May, 1969), 61-62.

[1618]"The Implications of Abortion." *Tablet*, 229 (January 18, 1975), 51. [This editorial voices support for the Church's traditional position on abortion. Then, it is explained how abortion law reform has become the endorsement of the "thin end of the wedge" argument. Better services should be offered to pregnant women.]

[1619]"Implications of the Abortion Act (of 1967: Great Britain), by a Welfare Officer." *Municipal and Public Services Journal*, 77 (March 14, 1969), 652.

[1620]"Implications of the Abortion Decisions: Post *Roe* (Roe v. Wade, 93 Sup Ct 705) and *Doe* (Doe v. Bolton, 93 Sup Ct 739) Litigation and Legislation." *Columbia Law Review*, 74 (March, 1974), 237-68.

[1621]"Implications of Abortion Law Reform." *Nursing Times*, 62 (November 11, 1966), 1478-80.

[1622]"In Center of Latest Dispute on Abortion: Nixon, Rockefellers." *U.S. News and World Report*, 72 (May 22, 1972), 50.

[1623]"In Defense of Liberty: A Look at the Abortion Decisions." *Georgetown Law Journal*, 61 (July, 1973), 1559-75.

[1624]"In Defense of the Right to Live: The Constitutionality of Therapeutic Abortion." *Georgia Law Review*, 1 (Summer, 1967), 693.

[1625]"In Defense of Unborn Human Life: Pastoral Letter." *L'Osservatore Romano* (English), 162 (no. 18) (May 6, 1971), 162.

[1626]"In Defense of Unborn Human Life." *Social Justice Review*, 64 (May, 1971), 54-55.

1627-
1653

[1627]"Indications for Termination of Pregnancy. Report of B.M.A. Committee on Therapeutic Abortion." *British Medical Journal,* 1 (January 20, 1968), 171-75.

[1628]"Induced Maude Abortion Charged." *National Catholic Reporter,* 10 (November 9, 1973), 12.

[1629]Ingelfinger, F. J. "Editorial: The Edelin Trial Fiasco." *New England Journal of Medicine,* 292(13) (March 27, 1975), 697.

[1630]Ingelman-Sundberg, Axel, and Huldt, Lars. "Twenty-Five Years of Legal Abortion in the Stockholm Region." *Fifth World Congress of Gynecology and Obstetrics.* Ed. C. Woods and W. R. W. Williams (Sydney, Australia, September, 1967).

[1631]Ingerslev, M. "The Danish Abortion Laws." *Medicine, Science and the Law,* 7 (April, 1967), 77-82.

[1632]Ingham, C., and Simms, M. "Study of Applicants for Abortion at the Royal Northern Hospital, London." *Journal of Biosocial Science,* 4(3) (1972), 351-69.

[1633]Ingraham, H. S. "New York State Department Health Report on Abortions," tabs. *Social Justice Review,* 63 (February, 1971), 377-84.

[1634]Ingraham, H. S., *et al.* "Abortion in New York State Since July 1970." *Modern Treatment,* 8 (February, 1971), 7-26. Also: *Clinical Obstetrics and Gynecology,* 14 (March, 1971, 5-24.

[1635]Ingram, I. M. "Abortion Games: An Inquiry into the Working of the Act." *Lancet,* 2 (October 30, 1971), 969-70.

[1636]Ingram, J. M. "Changing Aspects of Abortion Law." *American Journal of Obstetrics and Gynecology,* 105 (September 1, 1969), 35-45.

[1639]Ingram, J. M., *et al.* "Interruption of Pregnancy for Psychiatric Indication—A Suggested Method of Control." *Obstetrics and Gynecology,* 29 (February, 1967), 251-55.

[1638]International Planned Parenthood Federation Conference. *Induced Abortion: A Hazard to Public Health.* Proceedings (Beirut, 1971).

[1639]Introcaso, D. A. "Letter: Abortion." *Obstetrics and Gynecology,* 45(2) (February, 1975), 234-35.

[1640]"Investigation into Baby Deaths Acknowledged." *National Catholic Reporter,* 10 (March 22, 1974), 3.

[1641]Isaacs, N. F. "Abortion and the Just Society." *Thémis,* 5 (1970), 27.

[1642]"Is Abortion Catholic Issue? *Christianity Today* Says No." *Our Sunday Visitor,* 64 (January 25, 1976), 3.

[1643]"Isolating the Male Bias Against Reform of Abortion Legislation." *Santa Clara Lawyer,* 10 (Spring, 1970), 301.

[1644]Israel, S. L. "The Liberation of Women from Unwanted Pregnancy." *Clinical Obstetrics and Gynecology,* 14 (December, 1971), 1113-23.

[1645]Israel, S. L. "Therapeutic Abortion." *Postgraduate Medicine,* 33 (June, 1963), 619.

[1646]"Issue They Wanted to Avoid." *Economist,* 255 (January 25, 1975), 33.

[1647]"Italian Abortion Law Faces Opposition." *National Catholic Reporter,* 9 (February 9, 1973), 5.

[1648]"Italian Catholic Jurists on Question of Abortion." *L'Osservatore Romano* (English), 418 (no. 14) (April 1, 1976), 4.

[1649]"It's Alright, Ma (I'm Only Bleeding) (Views on abortion), by Washington D.C., Women's Liberation." *Motive,* 30 (March, 1970), 33-38.

[1650]"It's a New Game." *Triumph,* 6 (March, 1971), 46.

[1651]Jackson, E. W., *et al.* "Therapeutic Abortions in California." *California Medicine,* 115 (July, 1971), 28-33.

[1652]Jacobs, D., Garcia, C. R., Rickels, K., and Preucel, R. W. "A Prospective Study on the Psychological Effects of Therapeutic Abortion." *Comprehensive Psychiatry,* 15(5) (1974), 423-34.

[1653]Jacobsson, L., Roman, O.,

von Schoultz, B. "Attitudes to Legal Abortion in Hospital Staff." *Acta Psychiatrica Scandinavica* (suppl.), 255 (1974), 299-307.

[1654]Jacobsson, L., and Solheim, F. "Women's Experience of Abortion Procedure." *Social Psychiatry,* 10(4) (1975), 155-60.

[1655]Jacobsson, L., Schoultz, B. V., and Solheim, F. "Repeat Aborters, First Aborters, A Social Psychiatric Comparison." *Social Psychiatry,* 11 (2) (1976), 75-86.

[1656]Jacobsson, L., et al. "Psychological Feminity and Legal Abortion." *Acta Psychiatric Scandinavica* (suppl.), 255 (1974), 291-98.

[1657]Jacobsson, L., et al. "A Psychiatric Comparison of 399 Women Requesting Abortion and 118 Pregnant Women Intending to Deliver." *Acta Psychiatric Scandinavica* (suppl.), 255 (1974), 279-90.

[1658]Jacques, R. "Abortion and Psychological Trauma." *Medical Arts and Sciences,* 27(3) (1973), 52-59.

[1659]Jain, Sagar C., and Gooch, Laurel F. "Georgia Abortion Act 1968: A Study in Legislative Process." School of Public Health, University of North Carolina, 1972.

[1660]Jaggar, Alison. "Abortion and a Woman's Right to Decide." *Philosophical Forum* (Boston), 5 (Fall-Winter, 1973), 347-60.

[1661]Jakobovits, Immanual. "Jewish Views on Abortion." *Abortion and the Law.* Ed. David T. Smith (Cleveland: Western Reserve University Press, 1967).

[1662]James, G. B., et al. "Abortion and the Law (Symposium)." *Western Reserve Law Review,* 17 (December, 1965), 369.

[1663]James, William H. "The Incidence of Illegal Abortion." *Population Studies,* 25 (July, 1971), 327-39.

[1664]James, William H. "Legal Abortion and Social Class." *Lancet,* 2 (September 26, 1970), 658.

[1665]Jann, P. "Questions about Abortion." *Liguorian,* 59 (October, 1971), 14-19.

[1666]Jansson, Bengt. "Mental Disorders After Abortion." *Acta Psychiatrica Scandinavica,* 41 (1965), 87-110.

[1667]"Japan's Abortion Law Threatened." *World,* 1 (December 5, 1972), 50.

[1668]Jasinski, D. R. "Minors, ObGyn Practice and the Law." *Hawaii Medical Journal,* 31 (March-April, 1972), 116.

[1669]Jarvinen, P. A. "Legal Abortions in Finland." *Annales Chirurgiae et Gynaecologiae Fenniae,* 60 (1971), 65-66.

[1670]Javert, C. T. *Spontaneous and Habitual Abortion* (New York: McGraw-Hill, 1957.)

[1671]Jeffcoate, T. N. A. "Indications for Therapeutic Abortion." *British Medical Journal,* 1 (February 27, 1960), 581.

[1672]Jekel, J. F., Klerman, L. V., and Bancroft, D. R. E. "Factors Associated with Rapid Subsequent Pregnancies Among School Age Mothers." *American Journal of Public Health,* 63 (9) (1973), 769-73.

[1673]Jendins, Richard L. "The Significance of Maternal Rejection of Pregnancy for Future Development of the Child." *Abortion in America: Medical, Psychiatric, Legal, Anthropological and Religious Considerations.* Ed. Harold Rosen (Boston: Beacon Press, 1967).

[1674]Jenkins, Alice. *Law for the Rich* (London: Victor Gollancz Ltd., 1961).

[1675]Jermann, T. "Five Popular Myths about Abortion." *Our Sunday Visitor,* 62 (May 27, 1973), 1+.

[1676]Jessee, R. W., et al. "Abortion—the Hidden Epidemic." *Virginia Medical Monthly,* 95 (August, 1968), 447-56.

[1677]"Jesuit Warns Against Abortion." *Tablet,* 221 (July 29, 1967), 834.

[1678]Jewett, J. F. "Committee on Maternal Welfare. Paralytic Ileus." *New England Journal of Medicine,* 290 (February 7, 1974), 340-41.

[1679]Jewitt, P. K. "Relation of the Soul to the Fetus." *Christianity Today,* 13 (November 8, 1968), 6-9. Also: *Birth Control and the*

1680-
1705

Christian. Ed. W. O. Spitzer and C. L. Sayler (Wheaton, Illinois: Tyndale House, 1969).

[1680]John, A. H., *et al.* "Effects of Legal Abortion on Gynecology." *British Medical Journal,* 3 (July 8, 1972), 99-102.

[1681]John, P. D. "The Impact of the Abortion Act." *British Journal of Psychiatry,* 122 (January, 1973), 115-16.

[1682]Johnson, H. "Abortion." *Social Justice Review,* 66 (December, 1973), 255+.

[1683]Johnson, H. "Is Embryonic or Fetal Life Human Life?" *Social Justice Review,* 60 (March, 1968), 420-21.

[1684]Johnson, J. "Termination of Pregnancy on Psychiatric Grounds." *Manchester Medical Gazette,* 49 (July, 1970), 10.

[1685]Johnson, Thomas L. "Abortion: A Metaphysical Approach. *Freeman,* 22 (August, 1972), 498-505.

[1686]Joling, R. J. "Abortion—The Breath of Life." *Medical Trial Technique Quarterly,* 21(2) (Fall, 1974), 199-232 (85 ref.).

[1687]Jones, A. P., *et al.* "Abortion Act in Somerset." *British Medical Journal,* 3 (July 14, 1973), 90-92.

[1688]Jones, J. M. "Relations of Personality Factors and Student Nurses—Attitudes Toward Abortion." *Psychological Reports,* 35(2) (1974), 927-31.

[1689]Josey, A. "Abortion: An End to the Taboo." *Far Eastern Economic Review,* 86 (November 22, 1974), 28+.

[1690]Joyce, M. "The Abortion Tragedy." *Marriage and Family Living,* 51 (December, 1969), 22-26+.

[1691]Joyce, Robert E., and Rosera, Mary. *Let Us Be Born: The Inhumanity of Abortion* (Chicago: Franciscan Herald Press, 1970).

[1692]Joyston-Bechal, M. P. "The Problem of Pregnancy Termination on Psychiatric Grounds." *Journal of the College of General Practitioners,* 12 (November, 1966), 304-12.

[1693]Jubb, E. D., *et al.* History, Opinions, and What's New in the U.S." *Canadian Bar Journal* (N.S.), 4(3) (1973), 8-12.

[1694]"Judge Backs Defender of Fetus." *National Catholic Reporter,* 8 (January 14, 1972), 4.

[1695]"Judges OK Abortion for Rape Victim." *National Catholic Reporter,* 6 (April 17, 1970), 8.

[1696]Jurukovski, N. J. "Social Aspects of Legal Abortion in Yugoslavia." *Godisen Zbornik na Medicinskiot Fakultent vo Skopje,* 20 (1974), 159-64.

[1697]"Jury Clears Hospital Staff in Abortions: University of Minnesota Hospitals." *National Catholic Reporter,* 10 (June 21, 1974), 3.

[1698]Kahan, R. S., *et al.* "The Effect of Legalized Abortion on Morbidity Resulting from Criminal Abortion." *American Journal of Obstetrics and Gynecology,* 121(1) (January 1, 1975), 114-16.

[1699]Kahn, J. B., *et al.* "The Impact of Recent Changes in Therapeutic Abortion Laws." *Clinical Obstetrics and Gynecology,* 14 (December, 1971), 1130-48.

[1700]Kahn, J. B., *et al.* "Surveillance of Abortions in Hospitals in the United States, 1970." *H.S. M.H.A. Health Report,* 86 (May, 1971), 423-30.

[1701]Kaij, L., *et al.* "Psychiatric Aspects of Spontaneous Abortion. II. The Importance of Bereavement, Attachment and Neurosis in Early Life." *Journal of Psychosomatic Research,* 13 (March, 1969), 53-59.

[1702]Kalland, Lloyd A. "Views and Position of the Christian Church —An Historical Review." *Birth Control and the Christian.* Ed. W. O. Spitzer and C. L. Sayler (Wheaton, Illinois: Tyndale House, 1969).

[1703]Kallop, D. F. "Preoperative Instructions for the Patient Undergoing Elective Abortion." *Clinical Obstetrics and Gynecology,* 14 (March, 1971), 60-66.

[1704]Kaltreider, D. F. "Changing Attitudes Toward Abortion, Sterilization and Contraception." *Texas Medicine,* 62 (1966), 40-45.

[1705]Kaltreider, N. B. "Emotional

Patterns Related to Delay in Decision to Seek Legal Abortion. A Pilot Study." *California Medicine,* 118(5) (1973), 23-27.

[1706]Kaltreider, N. B. "Psychological Factors in Mid-Trimester Abortion." *Psychiatry in Medicine,* 4(2) (1973), 129-34.

[1707]Kane, F. J., Jr., and Lachenbruch, P. A. "Adolescent Pregnancy. A Study of Aborters and Non-Aborters." *American Journal of Orthopsychiatry,* 43(5) (1973), 796-803.

[1708]Kane, F. J., Jr., Feldman, M., Jain, S., and Lipton, M. A. "Emotional Reactions in Abortion Services Personnel." *Archives of General Psychiatry,* 28(3) (1973), 409-11.

[1709]Kane, F. J., Jr., Lachenbruch, P. A., Lipton, M. A., and Baram, D. "Motivational Factors in Abortion Patients." *American Journal of Psychiatry,* 130(3) (1973), 290-93.

[1710]Kane, F. J., Jr. "Therapeutic Abortion—Quo Vadimus." *Psychosomatics,* 9 (July-August, 1968), 202-07.

[1711]Kantzer, Kenneth. "The Origin of the Soul as Related to the Abortion Question." *Birth Control and the Christian.* Ed. W. O. Spitzer and C. L. Sayler (Wheaton, Ill.: Tyndale Press, 1969). [The traditional views on the origins of the soul are reviewed (traducianism and creationism). The author states that from "conception" the fetus is of immeasurable value because of its potential humanity. To destroy the fetus is an evil which can only be willed by man in obedience to God as a lesser evil in order that other immeasurable values would not be destroyed.]

[1712]Kapotsy, Bela. "The Demographic Effects of Legal Abortion in Eastern Europe." *European Demographic Information Bulletin,* 3 (November 4, 1972), 193-207.

[1713]Kapotsy, Bela. "The Demographic Effects of Legal Abortion on the Hungarian Labor Force." *European Demographic Information Bulletin,* 4 (November 3, 1973), 136-43.

[1714]Kar, S. B. "Opinion Towards Induced Abortion Among Urban Women in Delhi, India." *Social Science and Medicine,* 6(6) (1972), 731-36.

[1715]Karim, R. "The Case Against Public Funding for Abortion." *Our Sunday Visitor,* 62 (April 28, 1974), 1+.

[1716]Karim, S. M. "Prostaglandins in Fertility Control." *Lancet,* 1 (May 23, 1970), 115.

[1717]Karim, S. M., and Gilshie, G. M. "Use of Prostaglandin E_2 for Therapeutic Abortion." *British Medical Journal,* 3 (July 25, 1970), 198.

[1718]Katafiasz, K. "It's Time to Speak Out for All Life." *St. Anthony's Messenger,* 81 (October, 1973), 26-27.

[1719]Kaufman, Sherwin A. "The Medical Risks of Abortion: A Doctor's View." *New York* (July 24, 1972), 37. In New York handbook: "Abortions in New York, What you Need to Know." *New York* (July 24, 1972), 31-38. [In early pregnancy, abortion under proper circumstances is a simple and safe procedure. Statistically, early abortion is much safer than childbirth.]

[1720]Kaur, S. "Attitudes Towards Induced Abortion." *International Social Science Journal,* 26 (2) (1974), 265-83.

[1721]Kavanaugh, J. "Rallying Romans to Fight Abortion." *National Catholic Reporter* (suppl.) 7 (September 10, 1971), 9.

[1722]Kay, D. W. K., and Schapira, Kurt. "Psychiatric Sequelae of Termination of Pregnancy." *British Medical Journal,* 1 (February 4, 1967).

[1723]Kaye, R. E. "Procedures for Abortions at The New York Lying-In Hospital." *Clinical Obstetrics and Gynecology,* 14 (March, 1971), 153-65.

[1724]Keast, A. C. "Therapeutic Abortion." *South African Medical Journal,* 45 (August 14, 1971), 888-91.

[1725]Keast, Laury. *The Abortion Controversy* (Charlottesville, N.Y.: Story House Corp. [Som Har Press], 1973).

[1726]Keemer, E. B., Jr. "Looking Back at Luenbach: 296 Non-

1727-
1751
Hospital Abortions." (Luenbach,
J. H.) *Journal of the National
Medical Association,* 62 (July,
1970), 291-93.

[1727]Keemer, E. B., Jr. "Update on Abortion in Michigan."
*Journal of the National Medical
Association,* 64 (November, 1972),
518-19.

[1728]Kellenberg, W., and National Conference of Catholic Bishops.
"Two Statements on Abortion."
Catholic Mind, 68 (September,
1970), 1-3.

[1729]Keller, A., Pabagoderod-
riquez, A., and Correu, S. "The
Mexican Experiences with Post-
Partum/Post-Abortion Programs,
1970-1972." *Studies in Family
Planning,* 5(6) (1974), 195-200.

[1730]Kellett, J. "Letter: Psychological Sequelae of Therapeutic
Abortion." *British Medical Journal,*
2(6026) (July 3, 1976), 45.

[1731]Kellogg, D. A. "A Psychiatric Syndrome in Women Evaluated
for an Unwanted Pregnancy." *Maryland State Medical Journal,* 20
(October, 1971), 75-78.

[1732]Kelly, Gerald. *Medico-
Moral Problems* (St. Louis, Mo.:
Catholic Hospital Association,
1954).

[1733]Kelly, M. "Birthright—Alternative to Abortion," il. *American Journal of Nursing,* 75 (January, 1975), 76-77.

[1734]Kemp, J. "The Abortion
Act 1967. (c). Implications for
Family." *Royal Society of Health
Journal,* 90 (November-December,
1970), 299-301.

[1735]Kennedy, A. M. "Abortion."
*Canadian Medical Association Jour-
nal,* 104 (January 9, 1971), 70.

[1736]Kennedy, J., *et al.* Society Today and the Value of Life:
Symposium." *Sign,* 49 (May, 1970),
30-31.

[1737]Kennedy, R. B. "Abortion:
Issue of the Shadows, Dilemma of
Antiquity." *Journal of the Mississippi Medical Association,* 8 (November, 1967), 661-65.

[1738]"KMA Resolution on Abortion." *Journal of the Kentucky
Medical Association,* 72 (January,
1974), 36.

[1739]Kenyon, F. E. "Psychiatric Referrals Since the Abortion
Act 1967." *Postgraduate Medical
Journal,* 45 (November, 1969), 718-
21.

[1740]Kenyon, F. E. "Termination of Pregnancy on Psychiatric
Grounds. A Comparative Study of
61 Cases." *British Journal of
Medical Psychology,* 42 (1969),
243-54.

[1741]Kerenyi, I. D., Glascock,
E. L., and Horowitz, M. L. "Reasons for Delayed Abortion. Results
of Four Hundred Interviews." *American Journal of Obstetrics and
Gynecology,* 117(3) (1973), 299-311.

[1742]Kerslake, Dorothea. "Abor-
tion and the Health Services—
Vacuum Aspiration." *Abortion in
Britain* (London: Pitman Medical
Publishing Company Ltd., 1966).

[1743]Kerslake, Dorothea, and
Casey, Donn. "Abortion Induced by
Means of the Uterine Aspirator."
Obstetrics and Gynecology, 30
(July, 1967), 35-45.

[1744]Kerslake, K. "Letter: Why
Admit Abortion Patients?" *Lancet,*
2(7888) (November 2, 1974), 1078.

[1745]Kessler, K., and Weiss, T.
"Ward Staff Problems With Abortions." *The International Journal
of Psychiatry in Medicine,* 5(2)
(1974), 97-104.

[1746]Kestelman, P. "New Trends
in Legal Abortion." *Lancet,* 2
(December 16, 1972), 1307-08.

[1747]Kestelman, P. "Registrar
General's Supplement on Abortion."
Lancet, 2 (September 12, 1970),
566-67.

[1748]Ketzchmar, R., and Norris,
B. "Psychiatric Implications of
Therapeutic Abortion." *American
Journal of Obstetrics and Gynecol-
ogy,* 98 (1967), 368-373.

[1749]Kibel, H. D. "Staff Reactions to Abortion. A Psychiatrist's View." *Obstetrics and
Gynecology,* 39 (January, 1972),
128-33.

[1750]"Kidney Disease and Pregnancy." *British Medical Journal,*
2 (April 13, 1968), 69-70.

[1751]Kiesewetter, William B.
"Christian Ethics, the Physician
and Abortion." *Birth Control and*

The Christian. Ed. W. O. Spitzer and C. L. Sayler (Wheaton, Illinois: Tyndale House, 1969). [Does the Protestant Christian physician include this religious dimension in making an ethical decision? Is this decision different from that of a physician who does not participate in a religious tradition?]

[1752]Kilby-Kelberg, S., and Wakin, E. "A Nurse's Biography of an Abortion." *U. S. Catholic,* 38 (February, 1973), 19-21.

[1753]"Killing Babies is Legal." *Triumph,* 2 (July, 1967), 41.

[1754]Kilroy, E. G. "Is Abortion on Demand Good Medicine?" *Ohio State Medical Journal,* 67 (January, 1971), 39-46.

[1755]Kimball, C. P. "Some Observations Regarding Unwanted Pregnancies and Therapeutic Abortions." *Obstetrics and Gynecology,* 35 (February, 1970), 293-96.

[1756]Kimble, W. K. "Abortion on Request: Is it Really 'Liberal'?" *Texas Southern University Law Review,* 1 (1971), 173.

[1757]Kimmel, A. "British Abortion Law May Bring Pressures, Catholic Medics Fear." *National Catholic Reporter,* 4 (March 13, 1968), 9.

[1758]Kimura, M. "Induced Abortions in Japan in 1953-1954." *Milbank Memorial Fund Quarterly,* 37 (April, 1959), 154.

[1759]Kimura, M. "A Review of Induced Abortion Surveys in Japan." *International Population Conference,* New York, 1961.

[1760]Kindregan, Charles P. *Abortion, The Law, and Defective Children: A Legal-Medical Study* (Washington, D.C.: Corpus Books, 1969). Also: *Suffolk University Law Review,* 3 (Spring, 1969), 225.

[1761]Kindregan, Charles P. "Eugenic Abortion." *Suffolk University Law Review,* 6 (Spring, 1972), 405.

[1762]Kindregan, Charles P. *Quality of Life: Reflections on the Moral Values of American Law* (New York: MacMillan Publishing Company Inc., 1969).

[1763]King, L. "GOP and God." *Commonweal,* 93 (October 9, 1970), 37-38. Also: *National Catholic Reporter,* 6 (May 29, 1970), 19.

[1764]Kinoshita, K., *et al.* "The Induction of Abortion by Prostaglandin F_2 Alpha." *American Journal of Obstetrics and Gynecology,* 111 (November 15, 1971), 855.

[1765]Kinsella, V. J. "Therapeutic Abortion." *Medical Journal of Australia,* 1 (June 29, 1968), 1148-49.

[1766]Kinsolving, Lester. "What About Therapeutic Abortion?" *The Christian Century,* 81 (May 13, 1964), 632.

[1767]Kinton, J. F., and Kinton, E. R. *Abortion: Social Attitudes and Practices* (Aurora, Illinois: Social Science and Sociological Resources, 1973).

[1768]Kinzer, Nora Scott. "Priests, Machos and Babies: Latin American Women and the Manichaean Heresy." *Journal of Marriage and the Family,* 35 (May, 1973), 300-12.

[1769]Kirsch, E. J. "Letter: On Abortion and the Right to Life." *American Journal of Public Health,* 66(9) (September, 1976), 906.

[1770]Kirchner, Corinne, and Colombotos, John. "The Abortion Issue: Religious and Political Correlates of Physician's Attitudes." Paper presented at the American Sociological Association, August, 1973, 24 pp.

[1771]Kirk, J. "Four Questions About Sex in Our Society." *Medical Times,* 102(11) (November, 1974), 68-80.

[1772]Kirkwood, B. J., and Facer, W. A. P. "Public Opinion and Legal Abortion in New Zealand." *New Zealand Medical Journal,* 83(556) (1976), 43-47.

[1772]Kleegman, Sophia J. "The Influence of Moral and Cultural Factors on the Abortion Problem." *The Abortion Problem.* Ed. H. C. Taylor (New York: The Williams and Wilkins Co., 1944).

[1774]Kleegman, Sophia J. "Planned Parenthood: Its Influence on Public Health and Family Welfare." *Abortion in America* (Boston: Beacon Press, 1967).

[1775]Klein, Isaac. "Abortion—A Jewish View." *Dublin Review,* 514 (Winter, 1967-1968), 382.

[1776]Klein, Isaac. *Responsa*

(New York: The Rabbinical Assembly.

[1777]Klein, L. R. "Abortion as Homicide (with reply by C. F. Parvey)." *Dialog,* 12 (Spring, 1973), 142-47.

[1778]Kleinman, Ronald L. *Induced Abortion* (International Publishers Service, 1972). Distributed by London Central Books Ltd.

[1779]Klinger, Andras. "Abortion Programs." *Family Planning and Population Programs.* Bernard Berelson, *et al.* (Chicago: University of Chicago Press, 1960).

[1780]Klinger, A. "Consequences of the Legalization of Induced Abortion in Eastern Europe." *Therapeutische Umschau,* 27 (October, 1970), 681-92.

[1781]Klinger, A. "Demographic Effects of Abortion Legislation in Some European Socialist Countries." *Proceedings of the World Population Conference, Belgrade, 1965,* 2 (New York: United Nations, 1967).

[1782]Kloboria, V. "Legal Abortion in Czechoslovakia." *Journal of the American Medical Association,* 196(4) (1966), 371.

[1783]Klotz, J. A. *The Christian View of Abortion.* Contemporary Theology Series (Cambridge: Concordia Publishing House Ltd., 1973).

[1784]Kluge, Eike, and Henner, W. *The Practice of Death* (New Haven: Yale University Press, 1975). [This book includes arguments for and against the voluntary termination of life, in cases of abortion, suicide, euthanasia and infanticide.]

[1785]Knauer, Peter. "The Hermeneutic Function of the Principle of the Double Effect." *Natural Law Forum,* 12 (1967). (Now called *American Journal of Jurisprudence*).

[1786]Knapp, R. D., Jr. "Similarly I Will Not—Cause Abortion." *Journal of the Louisiana State Medical Society,* 122 (October, 1970), 297-301.

[1787]Knight, J. "The Right to Be Born." *Tablet,* 221 (March 18, 1967), 285-86.

[1788]Knowles, John H. "The Health System and the Supreme Court Decision: An Affirmative Response." *Family Planning Perspec-*

tives, 5(2) (Spring, 1973), 113-16.

[1789]Knowles, John H. "Public Policy on Abortion." *Society,* 11 (July-August, 1974), 15-18.

[1790]Knutson, Andie L. "The Definition and Value of a New Human Life." *Social Science and Medicine,* 1 (1967), 7.

[1791]Knutson, Andie L. "When Does a Human Life Begin? Viewpoints of Public Health Professionals." *American Journal of Public Health,* 37 (December, 1967), 2163.

[1792]Kobayashi, T. "Social Problems of Abortion." *Fifth World Congress of Obstetrics and Gynecology.* Ed. C. Wood and W. R. W. Williams (Sydney, Australia: September, 1967).

[1793]Koeniger, P. J. "The Physician and Abortion Law." *Alaska Medicine,* 10 (September, 1968), 119-20 passim.

[1794]Koguchi, Yasuaki. "The Prevalence of Induced Abortion in Present-Day Japan." *Report of the Proceedings, The Fifth International Conference on Planned Parenthood,* 1951.

[1795]Kohl, Marvin. "Abortion and the Argument from Innocence." *Inquiry,* 14 (Summer, 1971), 147-51. [The author rejects as unsound the argument that abortion is immoral because it is the killing of an innocent human being. At times, morality demands the killing of the innocent. He argues that a human fetus is not a human being, given the structure of English and the differences between unborn and born progeny.]

[1796]Kohl, Marvin. *The Morality of Killing: Euthanasia, Abortion and Transplants* (Atlantic Highlands, N.J.: Humanities Press Inc., 1979).

[1797]Kok, C. W. "Letter: Unwanted Pregnancy and Abortion." *Canadian Medical Association Journal,* 112(4) (February 22, 1975), 419-20.

[1798]Kildstad, Per. "Therapeutic Abortion: A Clinical Study Based Upon 968 Cases from a Norwegian Hospital, 1940-1953." *Acta Obstetrica et Gynecologica Scandinavica,* 36 (suppl.) (1957), 6.

[1799]Kondo, K., *et al.* "Abortion Programme in Duchenne Muscular Dystrophy in Japan." *Lancet*, 1 (March 10, 1973), 543.

[1800]Kopelman, J. J., *et al.* "Abortions by Resident Physicians in a Municipal Hospital Center." *American Journal of Obstetrics and Gynecology*, 111 (November 1, 1971), 666-71.

[1801]Kosling, M. G. "Abortions: Where Do We Stand in Louisiana?" *Journal of the Louisiana State Medical Society*,]26(12) (December, 1974), 429-32.

[1802]Koslowsky, M., Pratt, G. L., and Wintrob, R. M. "The Application of Guttman Scale Analysis to Physicians—Attitudes Regarding Abortion." *Journal of Applied Psychology*, 61(3) (1976), 301-04.

[1803]Koya, Yoshio. *Harmful Effects of Induced Abortion* (Family Planning Federation of Japan, 1966).

[1804]Koya, Yoshio. "A Study of Induced Abortion in Japan." *Milbank Memorial Fund Quarterly*, 32 (July, 1954), 282-93.

[1805]Koya, Yoshio, *et al.* "Preliminary Report of a Survey of Health and Demographic Aspects of Induced Abortion in Japan." *Archives of the Population Association of Japan*, 2 (1953).

[1806]Kramer, H. "Abortion, Who Should Decide?" *Liguorian*, 56 (January, 1968), 33-36.

[1807]Kramer, M. J. "Legal Abortion Among New York City Residents. An Analysis According to Socioeconomic and Demographic Characteristics." *Family Planning Perspectives*, 7(3) (1975), 128-37.

[1808]Krass, A. "The Abortion Problems Seen in Criminal Courts." *The Abortion Porblem*. Ed. H. C. Taylor (New York: The Williams and Wilkins Co., 1944).

[1809]Krause, H. D. "The Non-Marital Child." *Family Law Quarterly*, 1 (June, 1967), 1-20.

[1810]Krause, J. "Is Abortion Absolutely Prohibited?" *Continuum*, 6 (Fall, 1968), 436-40.

[1811]Krayenhoff, J. J. "Letter: Therapeutic Abortion." *Canadian Medical Association Journal*, 112

(12) (June 21, 1975), 1388.

[1812]Krayenhoff, J. J. "Letter: Therapeutic Abortion." *Canadian Medical Association Journal*, 112 (1) (January 11, 1975), 25.

[1813]Kremer, Elmar J., and Synan, A. *Death Before Birth* (Toronto: Griffin House, 1974).

[1814]Kremer, Elmar J. "The Humanity of the Fetus." Paper presented to the National Canadian Conference on Abortion, Toronto, Canada, May, 1972.

[1815]Kress, R. "The Anti-Feminism of Abortion." *Marriage and Family Living*, 58 (February, 1976), 2-5.

[1816]Kretzschmar, R. M., *et al.* "Psychiatric Implications of Therapeutic Abortion." *American Journal of Obstetrics and Gynecology*, 98 (June 1, 1967), 368-73.

[1817]Krol, J. "L'Episcopat des Etats-Unis et la Décision de la Cour Supreme sur L'Avortement." *La Documentation Catholique*, 70 (March 18, 1973), 271-73.

[1818]Krotoski, W. A., *et al.* "Intra-Uterine Devices: Contraceptive or Abortifacient." *Science*, 157 (September 22, 1967), 1465.

[1819]Kubo, Hidebumi, and Ogimo, Heroshi. "Current Aspects and Post-Operative Follow-Up Study." *Harmful Effects of Induced Abortion* (Tokyo: Family Planning Federation of Japan, 1966).

[1820]Kucharsky, D. E. "New-Style N.C.C., Stalling on Abortion, Eyeing the Jews." *Christianity Today*, 17 (March 30, 1973), 44-45.

[1821]Kuck, M. "Abortion in Czechoslovakia." *Proceedings of the Royal Society of Medicine*, 62 (August, 1969), 831-32.

[1822]Kuhn, H. B. "Prospect of Carbon-Copy Humans." *Christianity Today*, 15 (April 9, 1971), 11-14.

[1823]Kummer, Jerome M., ed. *Abortion, Legal and Illegal: A Dialogue Between Attorneys & Psychiatrists*. 2nd ed. (Kummer, Jerome, M., MD, PO Dwr 763, Santa Monica, Cal., 90406), 1969.

[1824]Kummer, Jerome M. "Coun-

seling Women who are Considering
Abortion," (bibliography). *Journal of Pastoral Care,* 25 (December,
1971), 233-40.

[1825]Kummer, Jerome M. "Don't
Shy Away from Therapeutic Abortion." *Medical Economics,* 37
(April 11, 1960), 165.

[1826]Kummer, J. M. "New Trends
in Therapeutic Abortion in California. Complete Legalization is
Imminent." *Obstetrics and Gynecology,* 34 (December, 1969), 883-
87.

[1827]Kummer, Jerome M. "Post-Abortion Psychiatric Illness—A
Myth?" *American Journal of Psychiatry,* 119 (April, 1963), 980.

[1828]Kummer, Jerome M. "Psychiatric Contra-Indications to
Pregnancy." *California Medicine,*
79 (July, 1953), 31-35.

[1829]Kummer, Jerome M. "A Psychiatrist Views Our Abortion
Enigma." *The Case for Legalized
Abortion Now.* Ed. Alan Guttmacher
(Berkeley, Diablo Press, 19).

[1830]Kummer, Jerome M., and
Leavy, Z. "Criminal Abortion—A
Consideration of Ways to Reduce
Incidence." *California Medicine,*
95 (September, 1961), 170.

[1831]Kummer, Jerome M., and
Leavy, Z. "Therapeutic Abortion
Law Confusion." *Journal of American Medical Association,* 195 (January 10, 1966), 96.

[1832]Kutner, Luis. "Due Process of Abortion." *Minnesota Law
Review,* 53 (November, 1968), 1.
[The present status of the law,
its enforcement, its constitutionality and recent reform measures
are discussed.]

[1833]Kwa, S. B., *et al.* "The
Abortion Act, 1969—A Review of
the First Year's Experience."
Singapore Medical Journal, (October, 1971), 250-55.

[1834]Labby, Daniel H. *Life or
Death: Ethics and Options* (Seattle:
University of Washington Press,
1968.

[1835]Lachance, P. "Canadian
Newspaper on Abortion Document."
L'Osservatore Romano (English),
360 (no. 8) (February 20, 1975), 5.

[1836]Lackey, H. S., Jr. and

Barry, J. R. "A Measure of Attitudes Toward Abortion." *Journal
of Community Psychology,* 1(1)
(1973), 31-33.

[1837]Lacoursiere, R. "The Mental Health of the Prospective
Father: A New Indication for Therapeutic Abortion?" *Bulletin of
the Menninger Clinic,* 36 (November,
1972), 645-50.

[1838]Lader, Lawrence. *Abortion*
(Boston: Beacon Press, 1966).

[1839]Lader, Lawrence. *Abortion
Two: Making the Revolution* (Boston:
Beacon Press, 1974).

[1840]"Laissez-Nous Vivre."
L'Express, 1170 (December, 1973),
24-27. [This new program was proposed for possible adoption by the
French government, concerning revision of the abortion law: 1)
Mothers of three or more children
could receive financial assistance;
2) minors would have access to the
pill without parental permission;
3) abortions would be allowed before the 10th week of pregnancy;
and 4) abortion would be allowed
after the 12th week of pregnancy
only if the life of the woman is
in danger.]

[1841]Lakey, G. A. "'Winds of
Change' The Problem of Abortion."
Medico-Legal Bulletin, 179 (March,
1968), 1-7.

[1842]Lambert, J. "Survey of
3,000 Unwanted Pregnancies."
British Medical Journal, 4 (1971),
156-60.

[1843]Lambert, Thomas F. "The
Legal Rights of the Fetus." *Birth
Control and the Christian.* Ed.
W. O. Spitzer and C. L. Saylor
(Wheaton, Illinois: Tyndale House,
1969).

[1844]Lamm, R. D. "Therapeutic
Abortion: The Role of State Government. I." *Clinical Obstetrics and
Gynecology,* 14 (December, 1971),
1204-07.

[1845]Lamm, R. D., *et al.* "Abortion and Euthanasia: A Reply."
Rocky Mountain Medical Journal, 68
(February, 1971), 40-42.

[1846]Lamm, R. D., *et al.* "The
Legislative Process in Changing
Therapeutic Abortion Laws. The
Colorado Experience." *American
Journal of Orthopsychiatry,* 39
(July, 1969), 684-90.

[1847]Land, P. W. "What About Me?" *Canadian Bar Journal* (N.S.), 4(1) (1973), 27-29.

[1848]"Landmark Abortion Decisions: Justifiable Termination or Miscarriage of Justice?—Proposals for Legislative Response." *Pacific Law Journal,* 4 (July, 1973), 821-60.

[1849]Lane, G. "Abortion Statements in Canada: Catholic Clarity, Protestant Ambivalence." *Christian Century,* 88 (November 3, 1971), 1303.

[1850]Lane, T. "Population and the Crisis of Culture." *Homiletic & Pastoral Review,* 75 (n.d.), 61-65. [This article describes how the culture of materialism, which we now live in, is at war with the very nature of man. "Only when society returns to a culture philosophically in harmony with man's role as a creature of God can it achieve that unity of mind and spirit for which men yearn."]

[1851]"Lane's Verdict." *Nursing Times,* 70 (April 11, 1974), 527.

[1852]"The Lane Report." *Lancet,* 1 (April, 1974), 672.

[1853]Lang, L. P. "Outpatient Termination of Pregnancy." *Medical Journal of Australia,* 1 (April 20, 1974), 611-13.

[1854]Langmyhr, G. "The Role of Planned Parenthood—World Population in Abortion." *Clinical Obstetrics and Gynecology,* 14 (December, 1971), 1190-96.

[1855]Langston, Henry J. "Abortion and the Law." *Southern Medicine and Surgery* (July, 1942).

[1856]Lanham, J. T., Kohl, S. G., and Redell, J. H. "Changes in Pregnancy Outcome After Liberalization of the New York State Abortion Law." *American Journal of Obstetrics and Gynecology,* 118(4) (1974), 485-92.

[1857]Lanman, J. T., *et al.* "The Effects of a Liberalized Abortion Law on Pregnancy Outcome." *Birth Defects: Risks and Consequences.* Ed. S. Kelly, *et al.* (New York: Academic Press, 1976), pp. 135-37.

[1858]Lappe, Marc. "Abortion Research." *The Hastings Center Report,* 5(3) (1975), 21-22.

[1859]"Large Majority of Public Supports Liberalization of Abortion Laws," tables. *Gallup Opinion Index* (September, 1972), 13-15.

[1860]Larson, S. L., *et al.* "Chromosomes and Abortions." *Mayo Clinic Proceedings,* 45 (January, 1970), 60-72 (65ref.).

[1861]Lask, B. "Short Term Psychiatric Sequelae to Therapeutic Termination of Pregnancy." *The British Journal of Psychiatry,* 126 (1975), 173-77.

[1862]Lauth, E. "Liberal Abortion Laws: The Antithesis of the Practice of Medicine." *Linacre Quarterly,* 34 (November, 1967), 367-73. Also: *Journal of the Florida Medical Association,* 54 (September, 1967), 916-20.

[1863]Lauth, E. "Liberal Abortion Laws and the Practice of Medicine." *Catholic Mind,* 66 (March, 1968), 20-27.

[1864]Lavalette, H. de. "Objectifs de Morale Chretienne." *Etudes,* 338 (April, 1973), 499-509.

[1865]Lavelle, J. "Is Abortion Good Medicine?" *Linacre Quarterly,* 35 (February, 1968), 16-23. [The author concludes that therapeutic abortion is rarely indicated.]

[1866]Lavole, J. "Legal Abortion." *Canadian Medical Association Journal,* 106 (April 22, 1972), 855 passim.

[1867]"Law and the Life Sciences: Abortion and the Supreme Court: Round Two." *Hastings Center Report,* 6 (October, 1976), 15+.

[1868]"Law and the Unborn Child: The Legal and Logical Inconsistencies." *Notre Dame Law Review,* 46 (Winter, 1971), 349.

[1869]"The Law on Abortion and the Defence of Life: A Declaration of the Belgian Bishops." *L'Osservatore Romano* (English), 272 (no. 24) (June 14, 1973), 9.

[1870]"Law to Protect the Unborn: New Orleans, Louisiana." *L'Osservatore Romano* (English), 278 (no. 30) (July 26, 1973), 3.

[1871]Lawrence, M. "Business as Usual." *Triumph,* 7 (June, 1972), 15.

[1872]Lawrence, M. "The Impossible Dream." *Triumph,* 10 (March, 1975), 9-11.

1873-
1891

[1873]Lawrence, M. "The Pro-Life Movement at the Crossroads." *Triumph*, 8 (June, 1973), 11-15.

[1874]Lawrence, M. "The Trial: Action for Life Anti-Abortion Demonstration." *Triumph*, 5 (October, 1970), 11-14.

[1875]Lawrence, M. "The Vindication of Milan Vuitch." *Triumph*, 6 (July, 1971), 8-11.

[1876]Lawrence, W. J. "Anxiety Adjustment and Other Personality Factors in Teenage Patients Before and After Abortion." *Proceedings of the 81st Annual Convention of the American Psychological Association, Montreal, Canada*, 8 (1973), 413-14.

[1877]Leavy, Zad. "Criminal Abortion: Facing the Facts." *Los Angeles Bar Bulletin*, 34 (October, 1959), 355.

[1878]Leavy, Zad. "Criminal Abortion. A Failure of Law." *American Bar Association Journal*, 50 (January, 1964), 52.

[1879]Leavy, Zad. "Criminal Abortion—Human Hardship and Unyielding Laws." *South California Law Review*, 35 (Winter, 1962), 123.

[1380]Leavy, Zad. "Current Developments in the Law of Abortion: 1969—A Landmark Year." *The Los Angeles Bar Bulletin*, 45 (November, 1969), 11.

[1881]Leavy, Zad. "Living with the Therapeutic Abortion Act of 1967." *Clinical Obstetrics and Gynecology*, 14 (December, 1971), 1154-64.

[1882]Leavy, Zad, and Kummer, Jerome M. "Abortion and the Population Crisis: Therapeutic Abortion and the Law: Some New Approaches." *Ohio State Law Journal*, 27 (Fall, 1966), 647-78.

[1883]Leavy, Zad, and Alan F. Charles. "California's New Therapeutic Abortion Act: An Analysis and Guide to Medical and Legal Procedure." *UCLA Law Review*, 15 (November, 1967), 1-31.

[1884]Leavy, Zad, et al. "Therapeutic Abortion Act of 1967." *Los Angeles Bar Bulletin*, 43 (January, 1968), 111.

[1885]Lebacqz, K. "Pre-Natal Diagnosis and Selective Abortion." *Linacre Quarterly*, 40 (May, 1973), 109-27. [The author raises the question of what justification is offered for pre-natal diagnosis and selective abortion. The rationale given for selective abortion is the benefits accruing to individual women and their families and as a response to societal needs. Many justifications offered for selective abortions are similar to specific arguments used to establish other categories of "indication of abortion." Arguments are examined for selective abortion in the context of "abortion on demand" and in the cases of defects.

The author then presents what are the implications of the ethical reasoning embodied in these justifications. Prenatal diagnosis establishes a distinction between the normal and defective fetus and, on this basis, allows a differential treatment of the fetus. Two problems result: 1) Determining the *categories* of fetuses considered destructible" fetuses from clear *genetic* categories of *social desirability*. The line drawing becomes difficult for categories of destructible fetuses and for the time continuum. The locus of decision-making is also discussed.]

[1886]Lebensohn, Z. M. "Legal Abortion as a Positive Mental Health Measure in Family Planning." *Comprehensive Psychiatry*, 14(2) (1973), 95-98.

[1887]Lebensohn, Z. M. "Therapeutic Abortion—The Other Side of the Coin." *Medical Annals for the District of Columbia*, 39 (May, 1970), 275-77.

[1888]Lederberg, J. "A Geneticist Looks at Contraception and Abortion." *Annals of Internal Medicine*, 67 (suppl. 7) (September, 1967), 25-27.

[1889]Lederman, J. J. "The Doctor, Abortion and the Law: A Medico-Legal Dilemma." *Canadian Bar Journal*, 6 (1963), 136.

[1890]Lederman, J. J., and Parker, G. E. "Therapeutic Abortion and the Canadian Criminal Code." *Criminal Law Quarterly*, 6 (1963), 36.

[1891]Lee, F. "Catholic Political Leaders and Abortion: A House Divided: A Look at the Record of Prominent Catholic National

Political Leaders and Their Stance on Pro-Life Legislation." *Our Sunday Visitor,* 65 (August 29, 1976), 1+.

[1892]Lee, F. "What About an Abortion Amendment?" *America,* 132 (March 8, 1975), 166-68. [Lee states that the Supreme Court's decision is not irreversible. Article Five of the Constitution provides two means of overturning the recent abortion decision.
He then goes on to discuss several proposed amendments, especially Buckley, Hogan and Whitehurst ("states' rights")].

[1893]Lee, L. T., and Paxman, J. M. "Pregnancy and Abortion in Adolescence. A Comparative Legal Survey and Proposals for Reform." *Columbia Human Rights Law Review,* 6(2) (1975), 307-56.

[1894]Lee, L. T., *et al.* "Legal Aspects of Menstrual Regulation: Some Preliminary Observations." *Journal of Family Law,* 14 (1975), 181-221.

[1895]Lee, N. H. *The Search for an Abortion* (Chicago: University of Chicago Press, 1969).

[1896]Leete, R. "Some Comments on the Demographic and Social Effects of the 1967 Abortion Act." *Journal of Biosocial Science,* 8(3) (1976), 229-52.

[1897]Leeton, J. "Population Control in Australia Today. Contraception, Sterilization and Abortion." *Medical Journal of Australia,* 2(17) (1975), 682-85.

[1898]"Legal Abortion, the South Australian Experience." *Medical Journal of Australia,* 1 (April 28, 1973), 821-23.

[1899]"Legal Abortions." *Christianity Today,* 14 (November 21, 1969), 860.

[1900]"Legal Abortion Reviewed." *Medico-Legal Journal,* 42 (Pt. 2) (1975), 25-26.

[1901]"Legalized Abortion." *Hospital Progress,* 49 (January, 1968), 16.

[1902]"Legalized Abortion in New Zealand." *British Medical Journal,* 2 (1970), 117.

[1903]"Legalized Abortion: Report by the Council of the Royal College of Obstetricians and Gynecologists." *British Medical Journal,* 2 (April 2, 1966), 1649.

[1904]"Legalized Abortions." *LINK,* 14 (September 5, 1971), 43.

[1905]"Legislation—Abortion—Michigan's 'Conscience Clause'." *Wayne Law Review,* 21 (November, 1974), 175-82.

[1906]Leiter, N. "Elective Abortion. Women in Crisis." *New York State Journal of Medicine,* 72(23) (1972), 2908-10.

[1907]Le Lirzin, R. "L'Avortement et la Nouvelle Loi: Point de Vue d'un Accoucheur." *Etudes,* 343 (August-September, 1975), 199-209.

[1908]Lenhardt, W. A. "Abortion and Pre-Natal Injury: A Legal and Philosophical Analysis." *Western Ontario Law Review,* 13 (1974), 97-123.

[1909]Lenta, C. "Abortion Calls for Public and Private Reparation Effort: Program of Reparation and Apology and Spiritual Adoption to Save the Unborn Baby." *Our Sunday Visitor,* 64 (July 20, 1975), 1+.

[1910]Leo, J. "Reaching a Consensus on Abortion." *National Catholic Reporter,* 3 (February 8, 1967), 11.

[1911]Leo, J. "Why Control Births with a Knife?" *National Catholic Reporter,* 3 (February 22, 1967), 8.

[1912]Leon, J. J., and Steinhoff, P. G. "Catholics—Use of Abortion." *Sociological Analysis,* 36(2) (1975), 125-36.

[1913]Lerner, R. C., Bruce, J., Ocks, J. R., Wassertheil-Smolle, and Arnold, C. B. "Abortion Programs in New York City Services, Policies, and Potential Health Hazards." *The Milbank Memorial Fund Quarterly,* 52(1) (1974), 15-38.

[1914]Lerner, R. C., *et al.* "New York's Obstetricians Surveyed on Abortion." *Family Planning Perspectives,* 3 (January, 1971), 56.

[1915]Le Roux, R., *et al.* "Abortion." *American Journal of Nursing,* 70 (September, 1970), 1919-25.

1916-
1938

[1916]Le Roy, Walters. "Fetal Research and the Ethical Issues (Bibliography)." *Hastings Center Report,* 5 (June, 1975), 13-18.

[1917]Lerry, C. "Doctor's Bona Fides and the Abortion Act." *Lancet,* 2 (July, 1973), 212.

[1918]Lessard, Suzannah. "Aborting a Fetus: The Legal Right, the Personal Choice." *Washington Monthly,* 4 (August, 1972), 29-37.

[1919]Lester, A. D. "Abortion Dilemma." *Review and Expositer,* 68 (Spring, 1971), 227-44.

[1920]"Let's Look at Abortion." *Social Action,* 37 (March, 1971), 3-39. [The issues are discussed from the points of view of a physician, a pastor, an ethicist and a woman who had an abortion.]

[1921]"A Letter on Approaches to the Abortion Issue, National Federation of Priests' Councils." *Catholic Mind,* 75 (March, 1977), 9-10.

[1922]"Lettre Pastorale de L'Episcopat Hollandais sur L'Avortement Direct." *La Documentation Catholique,* 68 (May 16, 1971), 486-89.

[1923]Levene, H. I., and Rigney, F. J. "Law, Preventive Psychiatry, and Therapeutic Abortion." *Journal of Nervous and Mental Disease,* 151(1) (1970), 51-59.

[1924]Levitt, Harry N. "Abortion and the Health Services—Towards Better Medical Care." *Abortion in Britain* (London: Pitman Medical Publishing Company Ltd., 1966).

[1925]Lewis, R. A. "Producing Change in Attitudes Toward Abortion." *The Journal of Sex Research,* 9(1) (1973), 52-68.

[1926]Lewis, S. C., *et al.* "Outpatient Termination of Pregnancy." *British Medical Journal,* 4 (December 4, 1971), 606-10.

[1927]Lewis, T. L. "The Abortion Act." *British Medical Journal,* 1 (January 25, 1969), 241-42.

[1928]Lewis, T. L. "Gynaecology in a Permissive Society." *Australia and New Zealand Journal of Obstetrics and Gynaecology,* 10 (November, 1970), 244-51.

[1929]Lewit, ed. *Abortion Techniques and Services: Conference Proceedings, New York, 1971* (New York: Associated Scientific Publishers, 1971).

[1930]Lewit, Sarah. "Sterliization Associated with Induced Abortion: JPSA Findings." *Family Planning Perspectives,* 5 (Summer, 1973), 177-82. [These findings are based on a joint program for the study of examination of the abortion experience of 72,988 American women who had legal abortions, 1970-1971.]

[1931]"License to Live," editorial. *Christianity Today,* 18 (July 26, 1974), 22-23.

[1932]Lidz, Theodore. "Reflections of a Psychiatrist." *Abortion in America.* Ed. Harold Rosen (Boston: Beacon Press, 1967).

[1933]"Life and the Facts of Life." *Triumph,* 9 (July, 1974), 46.

[1934]"Life in New York." *Triumph,* 7 (June, 1972), 45.

[1935]Lieberman, E. J. "Psychosocial Aspects of Selective Abortion." *Birth Defects,* 7 (April, 1971), 20-21.

[1936]Lincoln, C. E. "Why I Reversed my Stand on Laissez-Faire Abortion." *Christian Century,* 90 (April 25, 1973), 477-79. [Lincoln, who once favored abortion in difficult situations, sees the present situation after the Supreme Court's decision as a retreat from responsibility, which seems characteristic of the times. In marriage, it is the couple who contribute to procreation, so he asks if both should not decide to terminate the pregnancy, not just the woman and her doctor. Also, the state is *in loco parentis* to every child whose parents cannot take of it. If the state can assume liability for a pregnancy that runs its course, should it not be able to say something about its termination?]

[1937]Lincoln, R. "The Institute of Medicine Reports on Legalized Abortion and the Public Health." *Family Planning Perspectives,* 7(4) (1975), 185-87.

[1938]Lindsay, Anne. "On the Slippery Slope Again." *Analysis,* 35 (October, 1974), 32.

[1939]Linton, E. B., *et al.* "Abortion. Should the Physician be the Conscience of Society?" *Obstetrics and Gynecology,* 35 (March, 1970), 465-67.

[1940]Linton, Eugene G. "Medical Indications for Therapeutic Abortion and Sterilization." *Birth Control and the Christian.* Ed. W. O. Spitzer and C. L. Saylos (Wheaton, Illinois: Tyndale House, 1969).

[1941]Linton, P. H. "Psychitric Aspects of Therapeutic Abortion." *Southern Medical Journal* (Birmingham), 64 (suppl. 1) (February, 1971), 108-10.

[1942]Lio, E. "The New Morality and Abortion." *L'Osservatore Romano* (English), 409 (no. 5) (January 29, 1976), 8-9.

[1943]Lio, E. "Religious Freedom and Abortion." *L'Osservatore Romano* (English), 413 (no. 9) (February 26, 1976), 8+.

[1944]Lion, Felix Danford. "Abortion and Theology." *The Case for Legalized Abortion Now* (Berkeley: Diablo Press, 1967).

[1945]Lipper, I., Cvejic, H., Benjamin, P., and Kinch, R. A. H. "Abortion and the Pregnant Teenager." *Canadian Medical Association Journal,* 109(9) (1973), 852-56.

[1946]Lister, J. "The London Post. The Abortion Law Reviewed—Free Contraception—Angry Angels." *New England Journal of Medicine,* 291 (July 25, 1974), 192-94.

[1947]Lister, J. "Medicine, Morals and Money." *New England Journal of Medicine,* 276 (April 27, 1967), 971-72.

[1948]Lister, J. "Unwanted Pregnancy—Medicated Survival—the Metric Spoon." *New England Journal of Medicine,* 280 (June 26, 1969), 1463-65.

[1949]Little, J. C. "Abortion: Changing Attitudes of Psychiatrists." *Lancet,* 1 (January 8, 1972), 97.

[1950]Little, J. C. "Psychiatrists—Attitudes to Abortion." *British Medical Journal,* 1 (1972), 110.

[1951]Littlewood, B. "Abortion." *New Zealand Medical Journal,* 77 (June, 1973), 411-12. Also: *New Zealand Medical Journal,* 77 (February, 1973), 126-27.

[1952]Littlewood, B. "Abortion in Perspective." *New Zealand Law Journal,* 1974 (November 5, 1974), 488-93; 1975 (March 18, 1975), 103-10.

[1953]"Live Abortion to be Investigated." *National Catholic Reporter,* 7 (May 7, 1971), 7.

[1954]Lock, F. R. "Abortion—1970." *Journal of the Louisiana State Medical Society,* 123 (September, 1971), 309-16.

[1955]Lockwood, S. "Can You Change People's Minds on Abortion?" *Liguorian,* 63 (February, 1975), 13-16.

[1956]Loewy, Arnold H. "Abortive Reasons and Obscene Standards: A Comment on the Abortion and Obscenity Cases (1972 Term of the Supreme Court)." *North Carolina Law Review,* 52 (December, 1973), 223-43.

[1957]Lohner. "Therapeutic Abortion in Salt Lake City." *Obstetrics and Gynecology,* 27 (1966), 1667-75.

[1958]Loomis, David. "Abortion: Congress Can't Duck Difficulties." *National Catholic Reporter,* 11 (May 16, 1975), 1+.

[1959]Loomis, David. "Abortion: Should Constitution Be Amended,? il. *Congressional Quarterly,* 33 (May 3, 1975), 917-22.

[1960]Loomis, David. "House Avoids Abortion Issue Despite Pressure," ports. *National Catholic Reporter,* 11 (May 23, 1975), 1+.

[1961]Loos, S., *et al.* "New Laws Bring New Approaches. Method for the Evaluation of Therapeutic Abortion Candidates Meets the Requirements of California State Law and the Needs of Patients, while Conserving the Time of the Medical Staff." *Hospitals,* 46 (July 16, 1972), 76-79.

[1962]Lorensen, W. D. "Abortion and the Crime-Sin Spectrum." *West Virginia Law Review,* 70 (December, 1967), 20.

[1963]Loth, M. F., and Hellel-
tine, H. C. "Therapeutic Abortion
at the Chicago Lying-In Hospital."
*American Journal of Obstetrics and
Gynecology,* 72 (August, 1956), 304.

[1964]Louisell, David. "Abortion: The Practice of Medicine and
the Due Process of Law (Eased on
Conference Paper)." *UCLA Law Review,* 16 (February, 1969), 233-54.

[1965]Louisell, David. "A Constitutional Amendment to Restrict
Abortion." *Catholic Mind,* 74
(December, 1976), 25-31. [This
testimony was presented before the
subcommittee on Civil and Constitutional Rights in the U.S. Congress on March 22, 1976. The actual amendment is: "The Congress
within the federal territorial
jurisdiction and the several
states within their respective
territorial jurisdictions shall
have power to protect life including the unborn at every stage
of biological development irre-
spective of age, health or condition of physical dependency."
This amendment would return
the control of abortion to the
legislative domain. It would ac-
knowledge that abortion is a
matter for state regulation.]

[1966]Louisell, David, and
Carroll, C. "The Father as Non-
Parent." *Catholic World,* 210
(December, 1969), 108-10.
[Louisell examines the abortion
statute of California. He comments on the fact that the father's rights are completely ig-
nored, yet, if the child is born,
he has certain obligations.]

[1967]Louisell, David, *et al.*
"Fetal Research: Response to the
Recommendations." *Hastings Center
Report,* 5 (October, 1975), 9-16.

[1968]Louisell, David. "Ration-
ales for Feticide." *Catholic
World,* 212 (March, 1971), 318-19.

[1969]Lowe, David. *Abortion
and the Law* (New York: Pocket
Books, 1966).

[1970]Lucas, Roy. "Federal
Constitutional Limitations on the
Enforcement and Administration of
State Abortion Statutes." *The
North Carolina Law Review,* 46
(June, 1968), 730.

[1971]Lucire, Y. "Factors Influencing Conception in Women
Seeking Termination of Pregnancy.

A Pilot Study of 100 Women." *Medical Journal of Australia,* 1(26)
(June 28, 1975), 824-27.

[1972]Lueras, L. "One Man's
Love for Life," il. *Columbia,* 53
(April, 1973), 20-27.

[1973]Luker, Kristin. *Taking
Chances: Abortion and the Decision
Not to Contracept* (Berkeley: University of California Press,
1976).

[1974]Luoni, S. "Even if Legalized, Abortion is a Crime." *L'Osservatore Romano* (English), 271
(no. 23) (June 7, 1973), 4-5.

[1975]Luoni, S. "Le Saint-Siège
et L'Avortement." *La Documentation Catholique,* 70 (June 17,
1973), 574-75.

[1976]Lüpsen, F. "Abortion Law
Reform Controversy Rages in West
Germany." *Christian Century,* 90
(April 25, 1973), 487-88.

[1977]Luscutoff, S. A., and
Elms, A. C. "Advice in the Abortion Decision." *Journal of Counseling Psychology,* 22 (March,
1975), 140-46.

[1978]Lyons, B. "Abortion's
Crucial Question." *Extension,* 62
(October, 1967), 17-21.

[1979]Lynch, J. "Legalized
Abortion." *Linacre Quarterly,* 35
(February, 1968), 38-41. [This
is a report of the Third Interna-
tional Symposium of the National
Commission on Human Life, Repro-
duction and Rhythm, held in New
York, November 1-4, 1967.]

[1980]Lynch, R. "Abortion and
1976 Politics." *America,* 134
(March 6, 1976), 177-78. [This
article describes the reasons why
the candidates in the 1976 election were relatively safe from
directly dealing with the abortion
issue. Lynch presents three problems: 1) there is a total lack of
agreement on the political solution; 2) there is a "general ma-
laise and disinterest in the
Catholic community"; 3) there is
"scandalous disunity...among the
pro-life partisans."]

[1981]Lynch, R. "The National
Committee for a Human Life Amendment Inc." Its Goals and Origins."
Catholic Lawyer, 20 (Fall, 1974),
303-08.

[1982]Mabouk, M. "Development of the Right to Abortion in Tunisia." *Columbia Human Rights Law Review,* 7(1) (1975), 136-39.

[1983]Macaluso, Christine. "Viability and Abortion." *Kentucky Law Journal,* 64 (no. 1) (1975), 146-64.

[1984]Mace, David R. *Abortion: The Agonizing Decision* (Nashville: Abingdon Press, 1972.

[1985]Machol, Libby, and Wilson, Paul T. "Abortion—The Medical Facts." *Family Health,* 8 (February, 1976), 42-5+.

[1981]McCabe, H. "Crushing the Life of a Child in the Womb." *New Black Friars,* 53 (April, 1972), 146-47.

[1987]McCance, C., *et al.* "Abortion or No Abortion—What Decides?" *Journal of Biosocial Science,* 3 (January, 1971), 116-20.

[1988]McCann, J. "Doctor Blames Fathers for Abortion." *National Catholic Reporter,* 9 (March, 1973), 1-2.

[1989]McCann, J. "Study Shows More Nurses than Before Favor Abortion." *National Catholic Reporter,* 12 (March 26, 1976), 5.

[1990]McCarthy, B. W., and Brown, P. A. "Counseling College Women with Unwanted Pregnancies." *The Journal of College Student Personnel,* 15(6) (1974), 442-46.

[1991]McCarthy, Donald. "Medication to Prevent Pregnancy after Rape." *Linacre Quarterly,* 44 (August, 1977), 210-28. Comments by William Lynch.

[1992]McCarthy, John F. *In Defense of Human Life* (Houston, Texas: Lumen Christi Press, 1970.)

[1993]McCleave, P. B. "A View on Therapeutic Abortion." *Journal of the Iowa Medical Society,* 59 (March, 1969), 195-97.

[1994]McCormick, E. Patricia. *Attitudes Toward Abortion* (Lexington, Ma.: Lexington Books, 1975).

[1995]McCormick, Richard A. "Abortion." *America,* 112 (June 19, 1965), 877-81.

[1996]McCormick, Richard A. "Aspects of the Moral Question." *America,* 117 (December 9, 1967), 716. [The theological tradition which engendered the formulations of the reverence for life is presented. Also, McCormick discusses the status of the fetus, animation and the principle of double effect.]

[1997]McCormick, Richard A. "Conference Without Consensus: International Conference on Abortion, September 6-8, 1967, Washington, D.C." *America,* 117 (September 23, 1967), 320-21.

[1998]McCormack, E. "The Game-Plan ot Pro-Life and Anti-Life." *Social Justice Review,* 68 (May, 1975), 54-55.

[1999]McCormick, R. "Life/ Death Decisions: Interview by J. Castelli," ports. *St. Anthony's Messenger,* 83 (August, 1975), 32-35.

[2000]McCormick, R. "Life-Saving and Life-Taking: A Comment." *Linacre Quarterly,* 42 (May, 1975), 110-15. [McCormick responds to the question: does the moral reasoning used with regard to the fetus before viability bear any relationship to the protection of neo-natal life. He refers to the work of Paul Ramsey, who would agree that arguments that justify abortion would also justify infanticide. Joseph Fletcher does not believe that there are clear cut differences between abortion and infanticide, but would say that fetal life is sub-human and may be aborted if there is deformity. Finally, McCormick refers to John Fletcher, who attempted to show that there are morally relevant differences between abortion and euthanasia. McCormick argues that Fletcher's three differences do not distinguish the two. McCormick's intention is to underline both the moral relevance of personal factors and the limits of this relevance.]

[2001]McCormick, R. "A Moralist Reports." *America,* 123 (July 11, 1970), 22. [This is a review of Danial Callahan's book, *Abortion, Law, Choice and Morality* (New York: Macmillan Publishing Co., Inc., 1970).]

[2002]McCormick, R. "Notes on Moral Theology: The Abortion Dossier." *Theological Studies,* 35 (June, 1974), 312-59. [Critiques

2003-
2017

of the Court's decision is offered by David Goldenberg, Danial Callahan, Dr. Andre Hellegers, John Noonan, P. T. Conley and Robert J. McKenna, Blanshard and Doen, and finally Robert M. Byrn.

For the discussion of the relationship between morality and law the folowing are referred to: Gabriel Fackre, J. Claude Evans, C. Eric Lincoln, A. Jousten, Arthur J. Dyck, Albert Broderick, Paul J. Micallef, J. M. Murray, Charles E. Curran, Roger Shimm, Pope Paul and Rachel Walberg.

Contributions to the discussion of the morality of abortion are offered by Alexandre C. Renard, R. P. Corvez, Michel Schooyans, Bernard Qudquejeu, V. Fagone, S. J., Bernard Haring, Devin O'Rourke, O. P., Charles Curran, Albert Outler, Stanley Hauerioas, James Gustafson, J. Robert Nelson, Bruno Schuller, S. J., Judy Jarvis Thompson, Baruch Brody, John Finnis, Michel Tooley, Paul Ramsey, William May, Louis Dupre, Frederick Carney and R. McCormick. McCormick offers his own comments on the moral, legal and pastoral aspects.]

[2003]McCormick, R. "Past Church Teaching on Abortion." *Catholic Theological Society of America Proceedings,* 23 (1968), 131-51.

[2004]McCoy, D. R. "The Emotional Reaction of Women to Therapeutic Abortion and Sterilization." *Journal of Obstetrics and Gynaecology of the British Commonwealth,* 75 (October, 1968), 1054-57.

[2005]McCreary, B. D., *et al.* "Letter: Mental Retardation Services." *Canadian Psychiatric Association Journal,* 19 (April, 1974), 231.

[2006]McDermott, John F., Jr., and Char, Walter F. "Abortion Repeal in Hawaii: An Unexpected Crisis in Patient Care." *American Journal of Orthopsychiatry,* 41 (July, 1971), 620-26.

[2007]McDonagh, Enda. "Ethical Problems of Abortion." *Irish Theological Quarterly,* 35 (July, 1968), 268-97. [The position of the Catholic Church is presented. Such issues as the status of the fetus, indications for abortion, prohibition of homicide, are also discussed.]

[2008]MacDonald, R. R. "Complications of Abortion." *Nursing Times,* 63 (March 10, 1967), 305-07.

[2009]MacDonald, S. "The Meaning of Abortion." *American Ecclesiastical Review,* 169 (April, 1975), 219-36. [The author believes that abortion is understood contraceptively and that the Church should fashion the pastoral response in these terms. The term "contraceptive mentality" is investigated in light of voluntariness (free will) rather than (liberty). This contraceptive mentality is examined in light of natural law and *Humane Vitae.* He concludes that a pluralism has overtaken the meaning of contraception and that the Church must heed this in her pastoral ministry to the family.]

[2010]MacDougal, D., *et al.* "Abortion Decision and Evolving Limits on State Intervention." *Hawaii Bar Journal,* 11 (Fall, 1974), 51-72.

[2011]McEllhenney, John G. *Cutting the Monkey-Rope: Is the Taking of Life Ever Justified?* (Valley Forge, Pa.: Judson Press, 1973).

[2012]McEvoy, L. R. "A Question of Credibility." *Postgraduate Medicine,* 54 (October, 1973), 33.

[2013]McEwan, J. "The Abortion Act: A General Practitioner's View." *Practitioner,* 204 (March, 1970), 427-32.

[2014]MacGillivray, I. "Abortion in the North-East of Scotland." *Journal of Biosocial Science,* 3 (January, 1971), 89-92.

[2015]McGillivray, J. W. "Instant Abortion." *Canadian Medical Association Journal,* 99 (November 30, 1968), 1056.

[2016]McGraw, R. "Legal Aspects of Termination of Pregnancy on Psychiatric Grounds." *New York State Journal of Medicine,* 56 (1956), 1605.

[2017]MacGuigan, Mark. "Morality and Legality: Abortion and the Law." Paper presented to the National Canadian Conference on Abortion, Toronto, Canada, May, 1972.

[2018]McHugh, H. "The Pastoral Care of Those Confronted with Abortion." *Clergy Review,* 60 (April, 1975), 218-23.

[2019]McHugh, J. "Abortion: The Inhumanity of it All." *St. Anthony's Messenger,* 80 (February, 1973), 12-22.

[2020]McHugh, J. "Priests and the Abortion Question." *Dimension,* 5 (Winter, 1973), 164-69. [McHugh outlines the approach by which the priest can deal with the question of abortion. He offers a three-fold perspective: 1) theological teaching (he summarizes the key points that emerge from the theological tradition); 2) public policy question; 3) pastoral concern.]

[2021]McHugh, J. "Report on the International Conference on Abortion: The International Conference on Abortion, Washington, D.C., September, 1967." *American Ecclesiastical Review,* 157 (November, 1967), 328-32.

[2022]"McHugh: Valley of Death." *National Catholic Reporter,* 8 (March 24, 1972), 5; 8 (December 24, 1971), 4.

[2023]McIntyre, Robert J. "The Fertility Response to Abortion Reform in Eastern Europe: Demo-Graphic and Economic Implications (Conference Paper)," bibl., tables. *American Economist,* 16 (Fall, 1972), 45-65. Comments by J. Thomas Lindlay.

[2024]MacIntyre, S. J. "The Medical Profession and the 1967 Abortion Act in Britain." *Social Science and Medicine,* 7 (1973), 121-34.

[2025]McKelvey, J. L. "The Abortion Problem." *Minnesota Medicine,* 50 (January, 1967), 119-26.

[2026]MacKenzie, M. "Recent Changes in Legislation. A Police Officer's Observations." *Medicine, Science and the Law* (London), 9 (January, 1969), 66-67.

[2027]MacKenzie, P. "Before and After Therapeutic Abortion." *Canadian Medical Association Journal,* 111(7) (October 5, 1974), 667-69, 671.

[2028]McKernan, M., Jr. "Compelling Hospitals to Provide Abortion Services." *Catholic Lawyer,* 20 (Fall, 1974), 317-27. [McKernan speaks on four areas: 1) New Jersey case, *Doe v. Bridgeton Hospital Association*; 2) analysis of the opinions of *Roe v. Wade* and *Doe v. Bolton*, in regards to the compulsion of health care faculties to provide abortion services; 3) the concept of state action in this area; 4) he suggests a preventative measure for health care facilities which desire not to permit the performance of elective abortions. First, a statement can be made that the performance of abortion violates the tenets of the religion which sponsors the hospital. Secondly, advocating that the simple provision of surgical abortion services is not good medical practice, facilities would be needed for pre-operative and post-operative care, psychiatric care, and a contraceptive program would be needed, and since these are not available then abortion would not be a good medical practice.]

[2029]McKernan, M., Jr. "The Due Process Clause and the Unborn Child." *Dimension,* 5 (Spring, 1973), 25-34. [McKernan states that the Declaration of Independence and the Constitution, in the fifth amendment to which absolute protection for the life of the unborn can possibly be found, must be viewed as complementary documents read in *pari materia*. He goes on to say that "it would seem that the protections which the Constitution grants become animated at the time of creation since, according to the Declaration, it is at that time that the equality of our existence comes into being." McKernan explains how the inclusion of unborn child is implicit in the word "person" in the due process clause of the fifth amendment.]

[2030]McKernan, M., Jr. "Indiana Supreme Court Upholds State Abortion Law." *Social Justice Review,* 65 (October, 1972), 197-99.

[2031]McKernan, M. J. "Recent Abortion Litigation." *Catholic Lawyer,* 17 (Winter, 1971), 1-10. [The first part of the article discusses the case in California of *People v. Belous.* Other Federal Court decisions are discussed. The author points to the contradiction that the child, *en ventre sa mere*, is entitled to certain rights on one hand—inheritance, protection by criminal statutes for parental neglect etc. Simul-

2032–
2059

taneously, the fetus can be de-
prived of that right upon which
all others depend.]

[2032]McKerron, J. "Abortion
Blacklash." New Statesman, 78
(July 4, 1969), 5–6.

[2033]McKerron, J. "Abortion:
Can Doctors Cope?" New Statesman,
75 (February 9, 1968), 166.

[2034]McKie, B. "Abortion: Con-
dencension or Prevention." Medical Journal of Australia, 1 (April
18, 1970), 821.

[2035]McKie, B., et al. "Psychiatric Indications for the
Termination of Pregnancy." Medical Journal of Australia, 1 (April
3, 1971), 771–73.

[2036]McLaughlin, M. C. "Abortion Standards, New York City
Board of Health." Modern Treatment, 8 (February, 1971), 27–37.

[2037]McLaughlin, J. "Abortion
and the Law: Sweden and United
States." St. Anthony's Messenger,
76 (November, 1968), 51–55.

[2038]McLaren, H. C. "Abortion
or Modern Obstetrics?" British
Journal of Hospital Medicine, 1
(February, 1969), 607.

[2039]McLaren, H. C. "Ethics
and Abortion." British Medical
Journal, 2 (June 8, 1968), 622.

[2040]McLaren, H. C. "Indications for Termination of Pregnancy." British Medical Journal, 1
(February 10, 1968), 376.

[2041]McLaren, H. C. "Letter:
Abortion (Amendment) Bill."
British Medical Journal, 2(5971)
(June 14, 1975), 613.

[2042]McLaren, H. C. "Letter:
Select Committee Under the Abortion Law." Lancet, 2(7942) (November 15, 1975), 986.

[2043]McLaren, H. C. "Sequels
of Unwanted Pregnancy." Lancet,
2 (September 14, 1968), 632.

[2044]McLaren, H. C. "Therapeutic Abortion." Lancet, 1
(May 11, 1968), 1032.

[2045]McLaren, H. C., et al.
"Letter: Attitudes to Abortion."
British Medical Journal, 2 (May
11, 1974), 329–30.

[2046]McMunn, R. "Bishop Maher
Stands Firm Against Abortion Advo-
cates." Our Sunday Visitor, 63
(April 27, 1975), 1.

[2047]MacNaughton, M. C. "Natural Abortion." Abortion in Britain (London: Pitman Medical Publishing Co. Ltd., 1966).

[2048]MacNaughton, M. C. "Termination of Pregnancy in the Unmarried." Scottish Medical Journal
(Glasgow), 17 (n.d.), 381–82.

[2049]McNulty, J. V. "The Thera-
peutic Abortion Law: A Fight for
Life." Linacre Quarterly, 33–34
(November, 1966), 340.

[2050]McWhirter, W. W. "Legal
Rights of the Unborn." Arizona
Medicine, 29 (December, 1972),
926–29.

[2051]Maes, J. L. "The Psychological Antecendent and Consequences of Abortion." Journal of
Reproductive Medicine, 8 (1972),
341–44.

[2052]Maher, J. "House Subcommittee Hears Wide Range of Testimony on Pro-Life Amendment." Our
Sunday Visitor, 64 (February 22,
1976), 2.

[2053]Maher, J. "Not Much Hope
House Will Approve Pro-Life Amend-
ment." Our Sunday Visitor, 64
(February 22, 1976), 2.

[2054]Mahoney, M. J. "Letter:
On Abortion and Neo-Natal Morality." American Journal of Public
Health, 65(7) (July, 1975), 747–
48.

[2055]Mahoney, M. J. "Letter:
On 'the Right to Choose Abortion',
an Editorial." American Journal
of Public Health, 65(7) (July,
1975), 748.

[2056]Mahowald, J. "Marjory
Mecklenburg is For Life: Pro-Life
Movement." Catholic Digest, 37
(June, 1973), 39–44.

[2057]"Magazine Against Total
Abortion Ban." National Catholic
Reporter, 10 (June 7, 1974), 6.

[2058]Maginnis, Patricia.
"Elective Abortion as a Woman's
Right." The Case for Legalized
Abortion Now. Ed. Alan Guttmacher
(Berkeley: Diablo Press, 1967).

[2059]Maguire, M. R. "Can

Technology Solve the Abortion Dilemma?" *Christian Century,* 93 (October 27, 1976), 918-19. [The author suggests that funds are sought to research for the artificial preservation of fetal life. Then, the woman's right to terminate a pregnancy and a fetus' right to life would no longer be considered mutually exclusive.]

2060Mahajan, A. "Social Implications of Legalization of Abortion." *Indian Journal of Social Work,* 37 (April, 1976), 31-38.

2061Mair, H. J., *et al.* "Rubella Vaccination and Termination of Pregnancy." *British Medical Journal,* 4 (November 4, 1972), 271-73.

2062Majury, A. S. "Therapeutic Abortion in the Winnipeg General Hospital." *American Journal of Obstetrics and Gynecology,* 82 (July, 1961), 10.

2063Maksymiuk, J. P. "The Abortion Law: A Study of R. V. Morgentaler." *Saskatchewan Law Review,* 39 (1975), 259-84.

2064"Male Parent Versus Female Parent: Separate and Unequal Rights." *UMKC Law Review,* 43 (Spring, 1975), 392-412.

2065Mali, H. B. "Some Thoughts on Legalization of Abortions in India, with Reference to Japanese Experience," tables. *A Bunch of Current Indian Studies.* Ed. M. R. Sinha (Bombay: published for Indian Institute of Asian Studies by Asian Studies Press, 1969), pp. 88-91.

2066Malick, G. "Thoughts on the Legalization of Abortion." *Pennsylvania Medicine,* 74 (March, 1971), 39.

2067Mallory, G. B. "Factors Responsible for Delay in Obtaining Interruption of Pregnancy." *Obstetrics and Gynecology,* 40 (1972), 556-62.

2068Malmquist, A., *et al.* "Psychiatric Aspects of Spontaneous Abortion. I. A Matched Control Study of Women with Living Children." *Journal of Psychosomatic Research,* 13 (March, 1969), 45-51.

2069Malone, J. M. "Abortion." *American Journal of Ob-* stetrics and Gynecology, 114 (September 15, 1972), 280.

2070Malpas, P. "A Study of Abortion Sequences." *Journal of Obstetrics and Gynecology of the British Empire,* 45 (1938), 932.

2071Manage, Y. "Artificial Abortion at Mid-Pregnancy by Mechanical Stimulation of the Uterus." *American Journal of Obstetrics and Gynecology,* 105 (1969), 132.

2072Mandel, M. D. "Operational and Planning Staffing Model for First and Second Trimester Abortion Services." *American Journal of Public Health,* 64 (August, 1974), 753-64.

2073Mandetta, Anne, and Gustaveson, Patricia. *A Sourcebook of Sexual Facts.* Carolina Population Center, 1975.

2074Mandy, Arthur J. "Reflections of a Gynecologist." *Abortion in America.* Ed. Harold Rosen (Boston: Beacon Press, 1967).

2075Mandy, T. E., Scher, E., Tarkas, R., and Mandy, A. J. "The Natural Childbirth Illusion." *Southern Medical Journal,* 44 (1951), 527-34.

2076Mangan, Joseph T. "The Wonder of Myself: Ethical-theological Aspects of Direct Abortion." *Theological Studies,* 31 (March, 1970), 125. Also: *Linacre Quarterly,* 37 (August, 1970), 166.

2077Manier, Edward, and Li, William T., eds. *Abortion: A New Direction for Policy Studies* (University of Notre Dame Press, July, 1977, distributed by Harper and Row Publishers, Scranton, Pa.)

2078Mankekar, K. *Abortion: A Social Dilemma* (Vikas Publishing House, PUT Ltd., India, distributed by Independent Publishing Co., 1973).

2079Mannes, Marya. "A Woman Views Abortion." *The Case for Legalized Abortion Now* (Berkeley: Diablo Press, 1967).

2080Manning, T., Card. "We Ask Protection for the Unborn: Pastoral Letter." *L'Osservatore Romano* (English), 410 (no. 6) (February 5, 1976), 10.

2081Mant, A. K. "The Dangers

2082-
2103   of Legal and Illegal Abortion."
*Proceedings of the Royal Society
of Medicine*, 62 (August, 1969),
827-28.

[2082]"Marchers for Life Amass
in D.C." *National Catholic Reporter*, 12 (February 6, 1976), 6.

[2083]Marcin, M., and R. "The
Physician's Decision-Making Role
in Abortion Cases." *Jurist*, 35
(Winter, 1975), 66-76. Replies
by: Curran, C., and Montgomery,
J., 35 (Winter, 1975), 77-87.

[2084]Marder, L. "Psychiatric
Experience with a Liberalized
Therapeutic Abortion Law." *Amer-
ican Journal of Psychiatry*, 126
(March, 1970), 1230-36.

[2085]Marder, L., *et al*. "Psy-
chosocial Aspects of Therapeutic
Abortion." *Southern Medical
Journal*, 63 (June, 1970), 657-61.

[2086]Maresh, M., *et al*. "Why
Admit Abortion Patients?" *Lancet*, 2(7885) (October 12, 1974),
888-89.

[2087]Margolis, A. J. "'Come
and Go' Aspiration Abortion."
California Medicine, 113 (December, 1970), 43.

[2088]Margolis, A. J., *et al*.
"Legal Abortion Without Hospitalization." *Obstetrics and Gynecology*, 36 (September, 1970),
479-81.

[2089]Margolis, A. J. "Some
Thoughts on Medical Evaluation
and Counseling of Applicants for
Abortion." *Clinical Obstetrics
and Gynecology*, 14 (December,
1971), 1255-57.

[2090]Margolis, A. J. "Therapeutic Abortion Follow-Up Study."
*American Journal of Obstetrics
and Gynecology*, 110 (1971), 243-
49.

[2091]Margolis, A., Rindfuss,
R. R., Coghlan, P., and Rochat,
R. "Contraception After Abortion." *Family Planning Perspectives*, 6(1) (1974), 56-60.

[2092]Margolis, Joseph. "Abortion." *Ethics*, 84 (October,
1973), 51-61.

[2093]Mariyama, Yutaka, and
Hirokawa, Osamu. "The Relationship Between Artificial Termination of Pregnancy and Abortion

of Premature Birth." *Harmful Effects of Induced Abortion* (Tokyo:
Family Planning Federation of Japan, 1966).

[2094]Marmer, S. S., Pasnau, R.
O., and Cushner, I. M. "Is Psychiatric Consultation in Abortion
Obsolete." *The International Journal of Psychiatry in Medicine*, 5
(3) (1974), 201-10.

[2095]Marr, S. "Abortion a la
Suisse." *New Statesman*, 73 (April
7, 1967), 469-70.

[2096]"Married Couples Must Decide for Themselves." *Tablet*,
221 (April 22, 1967), 447.

[2097]Marshall, John. *Medicine
and Morals* (New York: Hawthorn
Books, 1960).

[2098]"Marshall's Ruling Ripped."
National Catholic Reporter, 7
(February 26, 1971), 14.

[2099]Marshall, R. "Abortion
Ruling: Catholic Facts and Consti-
tutional Truths." *Social Justice
Review*, 66 (June, 1973), 84.

[2100]Marshner, W. "The Bishops' Strange Love." *Triumph*, 7
(June, 1972), 11-14. [This article deals with the report given by
Bishop Francis J. Mugavers of
Brooklyn, Chairman of the Bishops'
Committee on the Campaign for Human Development, on April 11,
1972. Marshner takes issue with
the third norm for distribution of
the CHD's funds. It states that
campaign funds may be used for
programs which are in accord with
Catholic teaching, even if in particular instances the organization
may promote programs which are not
in accord with Catholic teaching.
The author suggests that an
amendment to the third norm be
made, so that an organization must
be in accord with Catholic teaching before funds are given.]

[2101]Martin, C. "A Baby Girl:
One Good Argument Against Abortion: Testimony, Pennsylvania
Abortion Law Commission, February
24, 1972." *Dimension*, 4 (Winter,
1972), 144-48.

[2102]Martin, C. "Psychological
Problems of Abortion for the Unwed
Teenage Girl." *Genetic Psychology
Monographs*, 88 (1973), 23-110.

[2103]Martin, M. M. "Ethical
Standards for Fetal Experimenta-

tion." *Fordham Law Review,* 43 (March, 1975), 547-70.

[2104]Marty, F., Card. "Le Conseil Permanent de L'Episcopat Francais, Paris, 19-21 Juin 1973, Introduction." *La Documentation Catholique,* 70 (July 15, 1973), 672-74.

[2105]Marty, F., Card. "A Propos de la Nouvelle Loi sur L'Interruption Volontaire de la Grossesse: Intervention du Cardinal Marty." *La Documentation Catholique,* 72 (February 2, 1975), 125.

[2106]Marx, P. "Review of R. Joyce and M. Joyce, *Let Us Be Born.*" *Catholic World,* 212 (January, 1971), 218-19.

[2107]Marx, P. "What Sisters Should Know About Abortion: Interview by D. Durken." *Sisters Today,* 43 (May, 1972), 519-31.

[2108]"Le Marxisme—L'Avortement: Declaration du Conseil Permanent de la Conference Episcopale Italienne." *La Documentation Catholique,* 73 (January 4, 1976), 37-38.

[2109]"Maryland Bishops in Abortion Fight." *National Catholic Reporter,* 4 (February 14, 1968), 5.

[2110]Mascovich, P. R., Behrstock, B., Minor, D., and Colman, A. "Attitudes of Obstetric and Gynecologic Residents Toward Abortion." *California Medicine,* 119(2) (1973), 29-34.

[2111]Masiello, R. "A Note on the Unborn Person." *Linacre Quarterly,* 43 (May, 1976), 112-14. [Masiello discusses the concept of "potential life." He refers to the U.S. Supreme Court which maintained "the unborn have never been recognized in the law as persons in the whole sense." Masiello views the person as indivisible. The Courts wished to convey that the rights of the unborn have not been treated consistently in civil and criminal suits. The author offers the position that the human intellectual principle establishes the human person. Before birth, and immediately after birth, this principle is at first only in "potency to knowledge."]

[2112]Mason, L. E. "Letter: Unwanted Pregnancies." *Canadian Medical Association Journal,* 112 (2) (January 25, 1975), 145-47.

[2113]"Massive Anti-Abortion Protest." *L'Osservatore Romano* (English), 315 (no. 15) (April 11, 1974), 5.

[2114]Mathew, J. "The Present State of the Law of Abortion." *Medicine, Science and the Law,* 4 (July, 1964), 170-75.

[2115]Mathias, R. "Storm Rages Over Abortion in Australia." *Christian Century,* 90 (August 15-22, 1973), 810-11. [This article describes the defeat of a bill intending to introduce some changes in the law relating to abortion in the Commonwealth. The middle Protestant position was not heard in the debate which raged between the "no abortion ever" vs. the "abortion on demand."]

[2116]Matz, R. "Consent to Continued Pregnancy." *New England Journal of Medicine,* 283 (December 31, 1970), 1522-23.

[2117]Maxwell, I. D. "Medical-Legal Inquiries: Therapeutic Abortion and Sterilization." *Nova Scotia Medical Bulletin,* 46 (June, 1967), 116-17.

[2118]Maxwell, J. W. "College Students, Attitudes Toward Abortion." *Family Coordinator,* 19(3) (1970), 247-52.

[2119]May, W. "The Morality of Abortion." *Linacre Quarterly,* 41 (February, 1974), 66-78. [May presents his belief that the directly intended destruction of human fetuses is an act that human beings ought not to do if they are called to be.

He discusses the concept of the *bonum humanum,* status of the fetus, ethics of intent (and content) and the principle of double effect.]

[2120]May, W. J. "Therapeutic Abortion Experience in North Carolina Under the Liberalized 1967 Law." *North Carolina Medical Journal,* 32 (May, 1971), 186-87.

[2121]May, W. J. "Therapeutic Abortion in North Carolina." *North Carolina Medical Journal,* 23 (December, 1962), 547-51.

[2122]Mayhew, L. "Abortion: Two

2123-
2144 Sides and Some Complaints." *Ecumenist*, 5 (July-August, 1967), 75-77.

[2123]Mazur, D. P. "Social and Demographic Determinants of Abortion in Poland." *Population Studies*, 29(1) (1975), 21-36.

[2124]Mead, M. "Rights to Life." *Christianity and Crisis*, 32 (January 8, 1973), 288-92.

[2125]Means, Cyril C. "The Law of New York Concerning Abortion and the Status of the Fetus, 1964-1968: A Case of Cessation of Constitutionality." *New York Law Forum*, 14 (Fall, 1968), 411.

[2126]Means, Cyril C. "Phoenix of Abortional Freedom: Is a Prenumbral or Ninth-Amendment Right About to Arise from the Nineteenth-Century Legislative Ashes of a Fourteenth-Century Common-Law Liberty?" *New York Law Forum*, 17 (1971), 335.

[2127]Medeiros, H., Card. "Abortion Legislation and Right to Life." *L'Osservatore Romano* (English), 149 (no. 5) (February 4, 1971), 7. Also: *Social Justice Review*, 64 (June, 1971), 84-86.

[2128]Medeiros, H., Card. "Magisterial Reaching on Life Issue." *L'Osservatore Romano* (English), 440 (no. 36) (September 2, 1976), 4-5.

[2129]"Medicaid and the Abortion Right." *George Washington Law Review*, 44 (March, 1976), 404-17.

[2130]"Medicaid Assistance for Elective Abortions: The Statutory and Constitutional Issues." *St. John's Law Review*, 50 (Summer, 1976), 751-70.

[2131]"Medical Responsibility for Fetal Survival Under Roe (*Roe v. Wade*, 93 Sup Ct 705) and Doe (*Doe v. Bolton*, 93 Sup Ct 739)." *Harvard Civil Rights Law Review*, 10 (Spring, 1975), 441-71.

[2132]Medical Protection Society. *The Abortion Act 1967* (London: Pitman Medical Publishing Co., 1969).

[2133]"Medical Termination of Pregnancy Bill. Views of the British Medical Association and the Royal College of Obstetricians and Gynaecologists." *British Medical Journal*, 2 (December 31, 1966), 1649-50.

[2134]"Medical Termination of Pregnancy Act, 1971 (34 of 1971)." *Indian Journal of Public Health*, 16 (April, 1972), 37-38.

[2135]"Medical Termination of Pregnancy Act, 1971 and the Registered Medical Practitioners." *Journal of the Indian Medical Association* (Calcutta), 65(11) (December 1, 1975), 320-21.

[2136]Meehan, F., and McGroarty, C. "A Pastoral Approach to the Abortion Dilemma." *Dimension*, 4 (Winter, 1972), 131-43.

[2137]Mehland, K. H. "Changing Patterns of Abortion in the Socialist Countries of Europe." Paper delivered at the International Conference on Abortion, Hot Springs, Virginia, November 17-20, 1968.

[2138]Mehland, K. H. "Combating Illegal Abortion in Socialist Countries of Europe." *World Medical Journal*, 13(3) (1966), 84-87.

[2139]Mehland, K. H. "The Effects of Legalization of Abortion." *Third Conference of the Region for Europe, Near East and Africa of the International Planned Parenthood Federation*, 1962.

[2140]Mehland, K. H. "The Effects of Legalization of Abortion on Health of Mothers in Eastern Europe." *Proceedings of the Seventh Conference of the International Planned Parenthood Federation, February 1963, Excerpta Medica*. International Congress Series, 72 (1964).

[2141]Mehland, K. H. "Legal Abortions in Rumania." *Journal of Sex Research*, 1 (March, 1965).

[2142]Mehland, K. H. "Reducing Abortion Rate and Decreasing Fertility by Social Policy in the German Democratic Republic." *World Population Conference*, Belgrade, 1965.

[2145]Meikle, S., and Gerritz, R. "A Comparison of Husband-Wife Responses to Pregnancy." *Journal of Psychology*, 83 (January, 1973), 17-23.

[2144]Meikle, S., *et al*. Therapeutic Abortion: A Prospective Study. II." *American Journal of Obstetrics and Gynecology,* 115 (February 1, 1973), 339-46.

[2145]Melamed, L. "Therapeutic Abortion in a Mid-Western City." *Psychological Reports,* 37 (3 PT 2) (December, 1975), 1143-46.

[2146]Meloy. "Pre-Implantation Fertility Control and the Abortion Law." *Chicago-Kent Law Review,* 41 (Fall, 1964), 183.

[2147]Melton, R. J., *et al.* "Therapeutic Abortion in Maryland, 1968-1970." *Obstetrics and Gynecology,* 39 (June, 1972), 923-30.

[2148]Melvin, E. "Abortion Decision: End of an Inalienable Right." *Our Sunday Visitor,* 61 (April 29, 1973), 1+.

[2149]Melvin, E. "Court's Abortion Decisions Flawed." *Our Sunday Visitor,* 65 (January 23, 1977), 1+.

[2150]"MPs Act on Abortion." *Tablet,* 221 (May 13, 1967), 541.

[2151]"Memorandum on Working of the Abortion Act." *L'Osservatore Romano* (English), 202 (no. 6) (February 10, 1972), 12.

[2152]Menninger, Karl. "Psychiatric Aspects of Contraception." *Abortion in America* (Boston: Beacon Press, 1967).

[2153]Menudier, H. "Avortement et Divorce en Allemagne Federale." *Etudes,* 343 (July, 1975), 57-76.

[2154]Menzies, D. N., *et al.* "Therapeutic Abortion Using Intra-Amniotic Hyertonic Solutions." *Journal of Obstetrics and Gynaecology of the British Commonwealth,* 75 (February, 1968), 215.

[2155]Messenger, E. C., ed. *Theology and Evolution* (London: Sands Publishing Co. Ltd., 1949).

[2156]Mester, R. "Requests for Abortions. A Psychiatrist's View." *The Israel Annals of Psychiatry,* 14(3) (1976), 294-302.

[2157]Metcalfe, J. B. "Letter: Abortion (Amendment) Bill." *British Medical Journal,* 3(5982) (August 30, 1975), 544.

[2158]"Methods and Dangers of the Termination of Pregnancy." *Proceedings of the Royal Society of Medicine,* 62 (1969), 827. 2145-2164

[2159]Mewett, A. W. "Abortion: Editorial." *Criminal Law Quarterly,* 16 (1974), 353-54.

[2160]Meyerowitz, S., Satloff, A., and Pomano, J. "Induced Abortion for Psychiatric Indication." *American Journal of Psychiatry,* 127(9) (1971), 1153-60.

[2161]Meyerowitz, S., *et al.* "Who May Not Have an Abortion?" *Journal of the American Medical Association,* 209 (July 14, 1969), 260-61.

[2162]Micallef, P. "Abortion and the Principles of Legislation." *Laval Theologique et Philosophique,* 28 (1972), 267-303. [This article deals with the relationship between law and morality. Two traditions by which society selects its criminal offenses are outlined. The Positivist approach is multifaceted but can be seen to converge on St. Augustine's premise that man is utterly corrupt and so are his institutions. Luther, Calvin, Bentham, and Mill contributed. The Wolfenden Report (1958 Report of the Committee on Homosexual Offenses and Prositution) in Britain and the resulting controversy is examined. St. Thomas directs the other tradition. In *Treatise on Law* (1269-1272) the function of law is established as part of the moral sphere. Law is placed in the realm of value. In the moral sphere, abortion is considered to be immoral, but not homicide unless ensoulment has taken place. From the ethical-legal standpoint, St. Thomas would ask how the new abortion law would promote the human common good. Is the law within the reach of virtuous and vicious, just and equitable, possible to nature as experienced, suitable to the time and place and according to the customs of the country?]

[2163]"Michigan Abortion Refusal Act." *University of Michigan Journal of Law,* ref. 8 (Spring, 1975), 659-75.

[2164]Mietus, A. C., and Mietus, N. J. "Criminal Abortion: 'A Failure of Law' or a Challenge to Society." *American Bar Association Journal,* 51 (October, 1965), 924.

2165-
2190

[2165]Mietus, Norbert J. "The Therapeutic Abortion Act—A Statement in Opposition." *Journal of Statutes,* Sacramento, 1967. [A bill introduced into the California Legislature in February, 1967.]

[2166]Mileti, D. S., *et al.* "Nine Demographic Factors and Their Relationship to Attitudes Toward Abortion Legalization." *Social Biology,* 19 (March, 1972), 43-50.

[2167]Milhaven, John G. "The Abortion Debate: An Epistemological Interpretation." *Theological Studies,* 31 (March, 1970), 106.

[2168]Miller, C. "Abortion: Good Science=Good Morals." *Homiletic and Pastoral Review,* 70 (July, 1970), 759-63.

[2169]Miller, E. "Abortion By the Order of the C.O.?" *Liguorian,* 58 (November, 1970), 2-4.

[2170]Miller, E. "Some Catholics on Abortion." *Liguorian,* 60 (October, 1972), 8.

[2171]Miller, J. M. "Therapeutic Termination of Pregnancy in Private Practice." *Medical Journal of Australia,* 1 (April 28, 1973), 831-34.

[2172]Miller Warren B. "Psychological Vulnerability to Unwanted Pregnancy." *Family Planning Perspectives,* 5 (Fall, 1973), 199-201.

[2173]Miller, W. L. "Abortion, Politics and the Bishops." *Christian Century,* 93 (October 13, 1976), 853-54.

[2174]Mills, D. H. "Abortions, Sterilizations, and Religion." *Journal of the American Medical Association,* 229 (July 15, 1974), 338.

[2175]Mills, D. H. "Medico-Legal Forum." *Journal of the American Osteopath Association,* 72 (June, 1973), 957-58.

[2176]Miltenyi, Karoly. "Demographic Significance of Induced Abortion." *Demografia,* 3-4 (1964).

[2177]Minkler, K. H. "Abortion—The Role of Private Foundations." *Clinical Obstetrics and Gynecology,* 14 (December, 1971), 1181-89.

[2178]"Minnesota Gets New Abortion Law." *National Catholic Reporter,* 10 (April 5, 1974), 15.

[2179]"The Minor's Right to Abortion and the Requirement of Parental Consent." *Virginia Law Review,* 60 (February, 1974), 305-22.

[2180]Mirande, A. M., and Hammer, E. L. "Love, Sex Permissiveness, and Abortion. A Test of Alternative Models." *Archives of Sexual Behavior,* 5(6) (1976), 553-66.

[2181]Mirande, A. M., and Hammer, E. L. "Premarital Sexual Permissiveness and Abortion. Standards of College Women." *Pacific Sociological Review,* 17(4) (1974), 485-503.

[2182]"Missouri Catholic Bishops' Statement on Abortion." *L'Osservatore Romano* (English), 173 (no. 29) (July 22, 1971), 11.

[2183]Mitchell, W. "Easy Abortion Loses in Two States." *National Catholic Reporter,* 9 (November 24, 1972), 4.

[2184]Mitchell, W. "Coalition Aims at Abortion Ban." *National Catholic Reporter,* 9 (June 22, 1973), 1+.

[2185]Moczar, D. "Why the Pro-Life Battle is a Catholic Thing." *Triumph,* 9 (May, 1974), 24-25.

[2186]Modle, W. J. "Notifying Results of Abortions." *Lancet,* 1 (May 3, 1969), 941.

[2187]Mohan, R. P. "Abortion in India." *Social Science,* 50(3) (1975), 141-43.

[2188]Moira, Fran. "Power Lines and Disembodied Women (Abortion and Sterilization in Latin America)." *Off Our Backs,* 6 (November, 1976), 10-11.

[2189]Majic, A. "Abortion as a Method of Family Planning: Experiences of the Yugoslav Health Service." *Third Conference on the Region for Europe, Near East, and Africa of the International Planned Parenthood Federation,* 1962.

[2190]Montgomery, John Warwick. "The Christian View of the Fetus." *Birth Control and the Christian.* Ed. W. O. Spitzer and C. L. Saylor

(Wheaton, Illinois: Tyndale House, 1969).

[2191]Monagle, J. "The Ethics of Abortion." *Social Justice Review*, 65 (July-August, 1972), 112-19.

[2192]Monticello, R. "*Wade* and *Bolton:* USCC Responses and Plans." *Catholic Lawyer*, 19 (Fall, 1973), 266-68.

[2193]Monsour, K. J., and Stewart, B. "Abortion and Sexual Behavior in College Women." *American Journal of Orthopsychiatry*, 43(5) (1973), 804-14.

[2194]Monti, Joseph E. "Abortion: Pastoral Counseling and Ethical Reflection (Reply to E. De Bary)." *St. Luke Journal*, 19 (March, 1976, 112-26.

[2195]Moody, Howard. "Abortion Revised." *Christianity and Crisis*, 35 (July 21, 1975), 166-68.

[2196]Moody, Howard. "Abortion: Woman's Right and Legal Problem." *Christianity and Crisis*, 31 (March 8, 1971), 27-32. Also: *Theology Today*, 28 (October, 1971), 337-46. [Moody describes how a group of ministers and rabbis came together in 1967 to create the Clergy Consultation Service on abortion (CCS), a counseling service in New York City for women with unwanted pregnancies. They supported liberalization of the abortion laws.]

[2197]Moody, Howard. "Church, State and the Rights of Conscience." *Christianity and Crisis*, 32 (n.d.), 292-94.

[2198]Moody, Howard. "Man's Vengeance on Woman: Some Reflections on Abortion Laws." *Renewal*, 7 (February, 1967), 6-8.

[2199]Moore, Allen J. "Abortion: A Human Choice." *Abortion: A Human Choice* (Washington, D.C.: Board of Christian Social Concerns of the United Methodist Church, 1971).

[2200]Moore, E. C. "Abortion and Public Policy: What are the Issues?" *New York Law Forum*, 17 (1971), 411.

[2201]Moore, E. C., *et al.* "Abortion: The New Ruling." *Hastings Center Report*, 3 (no. 2) (1973), 4-7.

[2202]Moore-Cavar, E. C. *International Inventory of Information on Induced Abortion* (New York: International Institute for the Study of Human Reproduction, 1974).

[2203]Moore, Harold F. "Abortion and the Logic of Moral Justification." *Journal of Value Inquiry*, 9 (Summer, 1975), 140-51.

[2204]Moore, J. L., Jr. "Abortion Laws." *Journal of the Medical Association of Georgia*, 56 (October, 1967), 439.

[2205]Moore, J. L., Jr. "Georgia Abortion Law Unconstitutional." *Journal of the Medical Association of Georgia*, 59 (October, 1970), 402-07.

[2206]Moore, J., and Pamperin, J. "Abortion and the Church." *Christian Century*, 87 (May 20, 1970), 629-31.

[2207]Moore, J., and Pandall, J. H. "Trends in Therapeutic Abortion: A Review of 137 Cases." *American Journal of Obstetrics and Gynecology*, 63 (January, 1952), 28.

[2208]Moore, J. L., Jr., *et al.* "Therapeutic Abortion Law—Explanation of Required Forms." *Journal of the Medical Association of Georgia*, 57 (June, 1968), 323-28.

[2209]Moore, Margaret Witte. *Abortion: Murder or Mercy?* (Greenwich, Connecticut: Fawcett Publications, 1962).

[2210]Moore-Robinson, M. "Community and Personal Factors on Fertility Control, Future Prospects." *Journal of Biosocial Science*, 1 (July, 1969), 315-320.

[2211]Morales, L. J. "Good Neighbors' Crime Legalized." *Social Justice Review*, 63 (October, 1970), 194-95.

[2212]"More on Abortion." *California Medicine*, 118 (March, 1973), 52-54.

[2213]Morgentaler, Henry. "Abortion." *Canadian Medical Association Journal*, 102 (April 25, 1970), 876.

[2214]Morgentaler, Henry. "Unwanted Pregnancy: Abortion and the Medical Profession." Available from Doctors for Abortion Law Repeal, 3625 Ridgewood Avenue, Apt.

2215-
2239

101, Montreal, 247, Quebec.

[2215]Moriarty, Claire. "Women's Rights vs. Catholic Dogma: Why the Church Fathers Oppose Abortion," il. *International Socialist Review,* 34 (March, 1973), 8-11+.

[2216]Moritz, R., and Thompson, N. "Septic Abortion." *American Journal of Obstetrics and Gynecology,* 95 (May, 1966), 46.

[2217]Mormont, M., *et al.* "Univers Mental et Strategie des Eveques; la Declaration des Eveques de Belgique sur L'Avortement." *Social Compass,* 20 (no. 3) (1973), 475-96.

[2218]Morris, H. S. "Inconsistency or Misunderstanding?" *Canadian Medical Association Journal,* 106 (April 22, 1972), 857-58.

[2219]Morris, J. S., Jr. "Alternatives to Abortion for the Unwed Mother." *Virginia Medical Monthly,* 99 (August, 1972), 844-47.

[2220]Morris, Norman. "Abortion and the Health Services—the Hospital." *Abortion in Britain* (London: Pitman Medical Publishing Company Ltd., 1966).

[2221]Morris, Norman. "The Law Relating to Abortion." *Proceedings of the Royal Society of Medicine,* 55 (1962), 375.

[2222]Morriss, Frank. "Abortion Compromise and Ecumenism." *Social Justice Review,* 60 (December, 1967), 264-65.

[2223]Mossberg, Walter. "A Key Battle: Outcome of Next Tuesday (November 7, 1972)'s Abortion Referendum in Michigan Will Likely Have National Implications." *Wall Street Journal,* 180 (November 3, 1972), 30.

[2224]"Most Abortions by Suction in 10th Week or Less. Typical Patient is Young, Unmarried, White, Never Before Pregnant." *Family Planning Perspectives,* 8 (2) (1976), 70-72.

[2225]Mowery, E. "Mildred Jefferson: Gift to Pro-Life." *Our Sunday Visitor,* 64 (November 9, 1975), 16.

[2226]Mowery, E. "Caring for All the People: Respect Life Program on a Parish Level." *Liguorian,* 64 (November, 1976), 34-39.

[2227]Moyer, C. M. "Delaware's Abortion Reforms." *Delaware Medical Journal,* 41 (June, 1969), 199.

[2228]Moyer, T. G. "Abortion Laws: A Study in Social Change." *San Diego Law Review,* 7 (May, 1970), 237.

[2229]Moynahan, C. "On the Subject of Abortion: Massachusetts." *Social Justice Review,* 65 (May, 1972), 49-53.

[2230]"Mr. Blumenthal's Abortion Bill." *America,* 118 (January 20, 1968), 64.

[2231]Muller, Carl. "Abortion: Financial Impact on the Patient." *Clinical Obstetrics and Gynecology,* 14 (December, 1971), 1302-12.

[2232]Muller, Carl. "The Dangers of Abortion." *World Medical Journal,* 13 (May-June, 1966), 76.

[2233]Muller, Carl. "Health Insurance for Abortion Costs: A Survey." *Family Planning Perspectives,* 2(4) (October, 1970), 12-20.

[2234]Muller, Carl, and Mall-Haefelic, Marianne. "A Guide to the Medical Indications for Interrupting Pregnancy." *Fifth World Congress of Gynecology and Obstetrics.* Ed. C. Wood and W. A. W. Williams (Sydney, Australia, Sept. 1967).

[2235]Mukherjee, J. B. "The Medical Termination of Pregnancy Act, 1971 and the Registered Medical Practitioners." *Journal of the Indian Medical Association,* 65(1) (July 1, 1975), 13-17.

[2236]Mumford, Robert S. "An Interdisciplinary Study of Four Wives Who Had Induced Abortions." *American Journal of Obstetrics and Gynecology,* 87 (December 1, 1963), 865.

[2237]Munday, D. "Family Planning and Abortion." *Lancet,* 2 (December 16, 1972), 1308.

[2238]Munson, H. B. "Abortion in Modern Times: Thoughts and Comment." *Renewal,* 7 (February, 1967), 9.

[2239]Muramatsu, Minpru. "Effects of Induced Abortion on Reduction of Births in Japan." *Milbank Memorial Fund Quarterly*, 38 (April, 1960), 153.

[2240]Murdock, Harry M. "Experiences in a Psychiatric Hospital." *Abortion in America* (Boston: Beacon Press, 1967).

[2241]Murray, P. T., *et al.* "Mississippi Physician's Attitudes Toward the Supreme Court Abortion Decision." *Journal of the Mississippi State Medical Association*, 15 (July, 1974), 291-94.

[2242]Murray, R. R. "Abortion in an Upstate Community Hospital." *Clinical Obstetrics and Gynecology*, 14 (March, 1971), 141-48.

[2243]Murrell, Peggy J. "Liberal Abortion Law, Effective Today, Stirs Worries in New York (N.Y.): Doctors, Hospitals Fear they Will Be Over-Whelmed." *Wall Street Journal*, 176 (July 1, 1970), 1+.

[2244]Muslin, S. "Austria's Abortion Law." *Tablet*, 228 (March 2, 1974), 199. [The author describes the reaction of the Austrian people to the legalization of abortion in the first three months. This became law on January 1, 1975.
Most noticeable is the reluctant compromise between the Catholic Church and the Socialist government.]

[2245]Muthig, J. "Church Leaders Split on Ban on Abortions." *National Catholic Reporter*, 10 (March 22, 1974), 17.

[2246]Myers, Henry J. "The Problem of Sterilization: Sociologic, Eugenic and Individual Considerations." *Abortion in America* (Boston: Beacon Press, 1967).

[2247]Myers, L. "Abortion." *Journal of the American Medical Association*, 217 (July 12, 1971), 215.

[2248]Myers, L. "Letter: ISMS Where Do You Stand on Abortion?" *Illinois Medical Journal*, 141 (April, 1973), 393.

[2249]Nachen, D. S. "The First Year of the Abortion Act." *Lancet*, 1 (May 2, 1969), 940-41.

[2250]Nadelson, C. "Abortion Counseling. Focus on Adolescent Pregnancy." *Pediatrics*, 54(6) (1974), 765-69.

[2251]Nadelson, C. "Psychologic Issues in Therapeutic Abortion." *Woman Physician*, 27 (January, 1972), 12-15.

[2252]Nagan, Winston P. "Social Perspectives: Abortion and Female Behavior." *Valparaiso University Law Review*, 6 (Spring, 1972), 286-314.

[2253]Naiman, J. "A Comparison Between Unmarried Women Seeking Therapeutic Abortion and Unmarried Mothers." *Laval Medical Journal*, (1971), 1086-88.

[2254]Napierkowski, T. "Abortion Law—Dilemma or Duty." *National Catholic Reporter*, 10 (June 7, 1974), 8.

[2255]Nathanson, B. N. "Sounding Board. Deeper Into Abortion." *New England Journal of Medicine*, 291(22) (November 28, 1974), 1188-90.

[2256]Nazer, I. R. "Abortion in the Near East." *Proceedings of the Eighth International Conference of the International Planned Parenthood Federation* (Santiago, Chile, April, 1967).

[2257]Neel, J. V. "Some Genetic Aspects of Therapeutic Abortion." *Obstetrics and Gynecology*, 30 (October, 1967), 493-97.

[2258]Nelson, Gunnard A., and Hunter, James, Jr. "Therapeutic Abortion: A Ten-Year Experience." *Obstetrics and Gynecology*, 9 (1951), 284-292.

[2259]Nelson, J. R. "What Does Theology Say About Abortion?" *Christian Century*, 90 (January 31, 1973), 124-28. [Nelson presents eight expressions of Christian faith which are widely held among Christians belonging to various perspectives. He then describes "contextual reasoning" which is concerned with all persons involved, taking into account the complexities of human experience. Then, Nelson examines the term "sanctity of life." A distinction is made between "bios" the mere sustenance for mortal existence and "zoe" the sanctity, reality and qualitative dimension.]

2283

[2260]Neubardt, Selig, and
Schulman, Harold. *Techniques of
Abortion* (Waltham, Ma.: Little,
Brown, and Co., 1972.

[2261]Neuhas, Richard John.
"The Dangerous Assumptions." *Commonweal*, 86 (June 30, 1967), 408.

[2262]Neustatter, W. L. "Homosexuality and Abortion. A Psychiatrist's Observations." *Medicine, Science and the Law*, 9
(January, 1969), 60-64.

[2263]Neustatter, W. L. "Legal
Abortion—A Change of Outlook."
Abortion in Britain (London: Pit-
man Medical Publishing Company
Ltd., 1966).

[2264]"New Abortion Method."
National Catholic Reporter, 8
(August 4, 1972), 17.

[2265]"New Case Reporting System for Therapeutic Abortions Introduced," editorial. *Canadian
Medical Association Journal*, 106
(January 22, 1972), 196.

[2266]"A New Catholic Strategy
on Abortion." *Month*, 6 (May,
1973), 163-71.

[2267]"New Jersey's Abortion
Law: An Establishment of Reli-
gion?" *Rutgers Law Review*, 25
(Spring, 1972), 452.

[2268]New Jersey Commission to
Study the New Jersey Statutes Relating to Abortion. Final Report
to the Legislature, December 31,
1969 (1970), State House, Trenton,
New Jersey 08625.

[2269]New Jersey. General Assembly. Judiciary Com. Public
Hearing on Assembly Bill no. 762
(abortion bill): Held April 9,
1970 (1970), State House, Trenton,
New Jersey 08625.

[2270]"New Law Gives Rights to
Fetus." *National Catholic Reporter*, 9 (March 23, 1973), 1.

[2271]Newlinds, J. "Abortion
Law." *Medical Journal of Australia*, 2 (Septdmber 9, 1972),
627.

[2272]Newman, Lucile. "Abortion as Folk Medicine." Paper
read at the Kroeber Anthropological Society Annual Meeting, Berkeley, California, May 8, 1965.

[2273]Newman, Lucile. "Between

the Ideal and Reality: Values in
American Society." *The Case for
Legalized Abortion Now*. Ed. Alan
Guttmacher (Berkeley: Diablo Press,
1967).

[2274]Newman, Sidney H., *et al.*,
eds. *Abortion, Obtained and Denied: Research Approaches* (Bridgeport, Ct.: Key Book Service, 1971).

[2275]"New Problems and Old Ones
Back Again." *Lancet*, 2 (October
24, 1970), 872-73.

[2276]Newton, B. W. "The Art of
Abortion. I. Curettage of the Pregnant Uterus." *Postgraduate Medicine*, 50 (August, 1971), 131-36.

[2277]Newton, J. H. "Abortion:
A Protestant Position." *Pastoral
Psychology*, 22 (January, 1971),
56. [Newton believes that the law
should allow women to obtain abortion at their request, keeping
them safe from malpractice. Women
have the right to self-determina-
tion. God has given not only life,
but the responsibility of how that
life should be lived. The author
reflects on the creation story in
Genesis, the influence of existentialism in theology, and the
experience of living. The fetus
is seen as a "potential" human
being, not an "actual" one.]

[2278]Newton, J., *et al.* "Hospital Family Planning: Termination
of Pregnancy and Contraceptive
Use." *British Medical Journal*, 4
(November 3, 1973), 280-84.

[2279]Newton, Lisa. "Humans
and Persons: A Reply to Tristram
Englehardt." *Ethics*, 85 (July,
1975), 332-36. [The author states
that the personhood of the fetus
cannot be logically tied to any
biological facts at all, but must
be decided on other grounds.]

[2280]"New York Abortion Reform
and Conflicting Municipal Regulations: A Question of Home Rule."
Buffalo Law Review, 20 (Winter,
1971), 524.

[2281]"New York Abortion Reform
Law: Considerations, Application
and Legal Consequences—More than
We Bargained For?" *Albany Law Review*, 35 (1971), 644.

[2282]"N.Y. Abortion Stirs Out-
cry." *National Catholic Reporter*,
11 (January 24, 1975), 6.

[2283]New York Academy of

Medicine: Committee on Public Health. "Therapeutic Abortion." *Bulletin of the New York Academy of Medicine,* 41 (April, 1965), 407.

2284"N.Y. Appeals Court Rules Against Fetus." *National Catholic Reporter,* 8 (March 10, 1972), 21.

2285"New York Bishops Issue Pastoral on Abortion Laws." *Catholic Mind,* 65 (April, 1967), 5.

2286New York State Supreme Court, Kings County. *A Presentment on the Suppression of Criminal Abortion by the Grand Jury for the Extraordinary Special and Trial Term* (New York: The Hamilton Press, 1941).

2287"N.Y. Times is For the Birds but Not For Unborn Babies." *Our Sunday Visitor,* 63 (March 9, 1975), 1.

2288"NFPC Says Bishops Place Too Much Emphasis on Abortion." *Our Sunday Visitor,* 65 (September 26, 1976), 1.

2289Nicolini, G. "In a Permissive Society: Defence of Life." *L'Osservatore Romano* (English), 173 (no. 29) (July 22, 1971), 3-4.

2290Nielsen, H. "Toward a Socratic View of Abortion." *American Journal of Jurisprudence,* 18 (1973), 105-13.

2291"Nigerian Bishops Condemn Abortion." *L'Osservatore Romano* (English), 216 (no. 20) (May 18, 1972), 3-4.

2292"Nigerian Bishops Condemn Abortion." *Social Justice Review,* 65 (June, 1972), 85-86.

2293Nigro, S. A. "Letter: Brain Surgery and Abortionists." *Journal of the American Medical Association,* 227 (January 14, 1974), 204.

2294Niswander, K. R. "Medical Abortion Practices in the United States." *Abortion and the Law.* Ed. David T. Smith (Cleveland: Western Reserve University Press, 1967).

2295Niswander, K. R. "Psychologic Reaction to Therapeutic Abortion. Subjective Patient Response." *Obstetrics and Gynecology,* 29 (1967), 702-06.

2296Niswander, K. R., Singer, J., and Singer, M. "Psychological Reaction to Therapeutic Abortion. II. Objective Response." *Journal of Marriage and the Family,* 30 (1968), 263-72. Also: *American Journal of Obstetrics and Gynecology,* 114 (September 1, 1972), 29-33.

2297Nixon, R. "Letter to Cardinal Cooke: President Nixon Condemns Abortion." *L'Osservatore Romano* (English), 216 (no. 20) (May 18, 1972), 3.

2298Nixon, R. "President Nixon Condemns Abortion." *Social Justice Review,* 65 (June, 1972), 88.

2299Nixon, R. "President Nixon Issues Statement." *L'Osservatore Romano* (English), 162 (no. 18) (May 6, 1971), 5.

2300Nixon Takes Stand Against Abortion." *National Catholic Reporter,* 7 (April 16, 1971), 5.

2301"Nixon Signs Hospital Law." *National Catholic Reporter,* 9 (July 6, 1973), 15.

2302"No New Abortion Laws, Checks Show." *National Catholic Reporter,* 7 (September 10, 1971), 5.

2303"Non-Consentual Destruction of the Fetus: Abortion or Homicide?" *UCLA-Alaska Law Review,* 1 (Fall, 1971), 80.

2304"Non-Residents Have Most N.Y. Abortions." *National Catholic Reporter,* 8 (March 10, 1972), 21.

2305Noonan, J., Jr. "Responding to Persons: Methods of Moral Argument Over Abortion." *Theology Digest,* 21 (Winter, 1973), 291-307. [Various models and methods used in the debate on abortion are examined to distinguish such means as fantasized situations, hard cases and linear metaphors (which according to the author do not work) from seeing and the appeal to human experience. The author moves from models and metaphors, which take the rule against abortion as a single value, to various sorts of argument that suggest the numerous values that have gone into the formulation of the rule. Many values are involved in the abortion question because person to person relations are constituent. Persons are more than single

2306-
2327

values. An act in a social context such as abortion cannot be
reduced to a single value.]

[2306]Noonan, J. T., Jr. "Abor-
tion and the Catholic Church, A
Summary History." *Natural Law
Forum* (now known as the *American
Journal of Jurisprudence)*, 12
(1967), 85-131.

[2307]Noonan, J., Jr. "An Al-
most Absolute Value in History."
The Morality of Abortion. Ed.
John Noonan (Cambridge, Mass.:
Harvard University Press, 1970).

[2308]Noonan, J., Jr. "Amendment of the Abortion Law: Relevant Data and Judicial Opinion."
Catholic Lawyer, 15 (Spring,
1969), 124-35.

[2309]Noonan, J., Jr. "The
Catholic Church and Abortion."
Dublin Review, 514 (Winter, 1967-
1968), 300.

[2310]Noonan, J. T., Jr. "Constitutionality of the Regulation
of Abortion." *Hastings Law Journal,* 21 (November, 1969), 51.

[2311]Noonan, J., Jr. *Contraception* (Cambridge, Mass.: Harvard University Press, 1965).

[2312]Noonan, J., Jr. "Deciding Who Is Human." *Natural
Law Forum,* 13 (1968), 134 (now
called *American Journal of Jurisprudence)*.

[2313]Noonan, J., Jr. "History
of Abortion and the Church."
Theology Digest, 16 (Autumn,
1968), 251.

[2314]Noonan, J., Jr. "Judicial Power and the Right to Life."
Tablet, 227 (April 7, 1973), 323-
26. [Noonan describes in detail
the U.S. Supreme Court decisions
of *Roe* and *Doe*. Two ironies are
pointed out. The author sees
two lines of attack. Expand the
Court from 9 to 15. It is suggested that the change in member-
ship in the Court is a constitutional way of correcting a bad
decision. An amendment to the
Constitution is also possible.]

[2315]Noonan, J., ed. *The Morality of Abortion: Legal and
Historical Perspectives* (Cambridge, Mass.: Harvard University
Press, 1970).

[2316]Noonan, J., Jr. "Only a

Constitutional Amendment Can Stop
the Flood of Abortions." *National
Catholic Reporter,* 9 (February 16,
1973), 9.

[2317]Noonan, J., Jr. "The Reasons Against Abortion." Statements before the Codes and Health
Committees of the New York Legislature,February 3, 8, and 10,
1967. Distributed by the New York
State Catholic Welfare Committee
(mimeographed).

[2318]Noonan, J., Jr. "USA and
Abortion." *Tablet,* 230 (May 22,
1976), 4946. [The author describes
how the abortion question became
an issue in the 1976 presidential
campaign.]

[2319]Noonan, John T., Hellegers,
A., and Richardson, H. *Abortion*
(Cambridge, Mass.: Harvard Uni-
versity Press, 1968).

[2320]Norberg, Tilda. "Female
Anguish and Abortion." *Abortion:
A Human Choice* (Washington, D. C.:
Board of Christian Social Concerns
of the United Methodist Church,
May, 1971).

[2321]North, Douglas C., and
Miller, Roger L. *Abortion, Base-
ball & Weed: Economic Issues of
Our Times* (New York:Harper and
Row, 1973).

[2322]"Not a Fetus But a Baby,
Jury Decides in Boston." *Our Sunday Visitor,* 63 (March 2, 1975),
1.

[2323]"Note Doctrinale sur
L'Avortement." *La Documentation
Catholique,* 68 (March 21, 1971),
285-90.

[2324]"Notifications of Abortions." *British Medical Journal,*
1 (1969), 531.

[2325]Notman, M. T. "Pregnancy
and Abortion. Implications for
Career Development of Professional
Women." *Annals of the New York
Academy of Sciences,* 208 (1973),
205-10.

[2326]Novak, Franc. "Abortion
in Europe." *Proceedings of the
Eighth International Conference of
the International Planned Parenthood Federation, Santiago, Chile,
April, 1967* (London: International
Planned Parenthood Federation,
1967).

[2327]Novak, Franc. "Effect of

Legal Abortion on the Health of the Mothers in Yugoslavia." *Seventh International Conference on Planned Parenthood,* 1963.

[2328]Novak, M. "Dependent but Distinct: the Fetus." *National Catholic Reporter,* 11 (May 9, 1975), 11.

[2329]Nozue, Genichi. "Abortion in the Far East." *Proceedings of the Eighth International Planned Parenthood Federation, Santiago, Chile, April, 1967* (London: International Planned Parenthood Federation, 1967).

[2330]Nugent, D. "Abortion, An Aquarian Perspective." *Critic,* 31 (January-February, 1973), 32-36.

[2331]"Numbers Go On Rising." *Economist,* 247 (May 26, 1973), 30.

[2332]"Nurses Refuse to Aid Abortion." *National Catholic Reporter,* 6 (July 3, 1970), 5.

[2333]O'Beirn, S. F. "Fetal Rights and Abortion Laws." *British Medical Journal,* 1 (March 24, 1973), 740.

[2334]Obeng, B. B. "The Lay Use of Potassium Permanganate As An Abortifacient." *British Journal of Clinical Practitioners,* 22 (November 11, 1968), 465-69.

[2335]"O'Boyle Denounces Abortion Plan." *National Catholic Reporter,* 6 (December 17, 1969), 6.

[2336]O'Boyle, P. "Abortion Kills Unborn Baby." *Social Justice Review,* 63 (February, 1971), 327-73+.

[2337]O'Boyle, P. "Abortion—Respect Life—Legality vs. Morality." *Social Justice Review,* 65 (February, 1973), 372-73.

[2338]O'Boyle, P. "Anti-Life Programs vs. Social Justice." *Social Justice Review,* 63 (April, 1970), 20-22.

[2339]O'Boyle, P. "Death by Abortion Absolutely Unacceptable." *Social Justice Review,* 65 (November, 1972), 234-37.

[2340]O'Boyle, P. "In Defense of Human Life." *Columbia,* 50 (December, 1970), 5.

[2341]O'Boyle, P. "On Abortion." *L'Osservatore Romano* (English), 236 (no. 40) (October 5, 1972), 9-10.

[2342]O'Boyle, P. "The Priceless Value of Every Person." *Social Justice Review,* 65 (December, 1972), 269-73.

[2343]O'Boyle, P., and Shehan, L. "Cardinals Condemn Abortion: Pastoral Letters." *L'Osservatore Romano* (English), 148 (no. 4) (January 28, 1971), 4.

[2344]O'Boyle, P., and Shehan, L. "Two Pastorals on Abortion; October, 1970." *Catholic Mind,* 69 (March, 1971), 5-11. [The text of the two cardinal archbishops of Washington and Baltimore presents the moral aspects of abortion. They stress the right to life for the fetus and make the distinction between contraception and birth control.]

[2345]O'Brien, Michael. "The Morality of Abortion." *Furrow,* 21 (December, 1970), 762-69. [O'Brien discusses the views of Joseph Donceel, Father Patrick J. O'Mahony, Malcolm Potts and Father Edna McDonagh.
He concludes that abortion is morally unjustifiable even in the early stages of pregnancy or when there may be serious reasons for it. He offers three reasons for his conclusion: 1) the teaching of the Second Vatican Council is clear on this matter; 2) once the female ovum is fertilized by the male sperm, then human life is present; 3) there is sufficient probability that this life is already the life of a human being.]

[2346]O'Brien, R. "Abortion: Conscience and the Law." *Tablet,* 222 (April 27, 1968), 411-12.

[2347]O'Connell, T. "For American Catholics: End of an Illusion." *America,* 128 (June 2, 1972), 514-17. [O'Connell presents a discussion of natural law and positive law. The natural law is served by positive law, but it is difficult to apply this theory. Many Americans never thought that the government would do anything opposed to the common good, the natural law. The Supreme Court decision went a long way in striking down the myth of American life—of their belief in government, and the political order. O'Connell speaks of the death of this old

2348-
2373

naivete and sees its extinction as growth.]

[2348]O'Connor, J. "On Humanity and Abortion." *Natural Law Forum*, 13 (1968), 127-33. [John Noonan's article, "Abortion and the Catholic Church: A Summary History," in *Natural Law Forum*, 12 (1967), 85-131, is discussed. O'Connor does not view the fetus as a human person. He contends that adults decide the criterion for humanity, they do not discover it.]

[2349]O'Connell, W. "The Silent Life: An Embryological Review." *Linacre Quarterly*, 35 (August, 1968), 179-89.

[2350]O'Donnell, T. "The Question of Abortion." *Linacre Quarterly*, 34 (November, 1967), 364-66. [The development of the delayed animation theory is described.]

[2351]O'Donnell, T. "Abortion, II (Moral Aspect)." *New Catholic Encyclopedia* (New York: McGraw-Hill, 1967).

[2352]"Offers Pro-Life Amendment." *National Catholic Reporter*, 9 (February 9, 1973), 18.

[2353]Oggioni, G., Bp. "Abortion and Law on Abortion." *L'Osservatore Romano* (English), 367 (no. 15) (April 10, 1975), 5+.

[2354]O'Hare, J. "(Abortion Debate)." *America*, 132 (March 1, 1975), (inside front cover). [O'Hare discusses the conviction of Kenneth C. Edelin. This case provided the stage whereby the residual ambiguities of the 1973 decisions of the Supreme Court could be resolved.]

[2355]"Oh My God. I'm Pregnant." *Ohio Northern University Law Review*, 1 (1973), 119-29.

[2356]Olley, P. C. "Personality Factors and Referral for Therapeutic Abortion." *Journal of Biosocial Science*, 3 (1971), 106-15.

[2357]Oliver. "Abortion and Huntington's Chorea." *British Medical Journal*, 1 (March 2, 1968), 576-77.

[2358]O'Mahony, P., and Potts, M. "Abortion and the Soul." *Month*, 38 (July-August, 1967), 45-50.

[2359]O'Meara, J. "Abortion: The Court Decides a Non-Case." *Supreme Court Review*, 1974 (1974), 337-60.

[2360]Omran, Abdel R., ed. *Liberalization of Abortion Laws: Implications* (Chapel Hill: Carolina Population Center Publishers Office, 1976).

[2361]"100 College Students Form Group to Oppose Abortion." *National Catholic Reporter*, 8 (December 10, 1971), 5.

[2362]"100,000 Sign OSV Pro-Life Petition." *Our Sunday Visitor*, 62 (May 20, 1973), 1+.

[2363]"1,000 Mourn Innocents Slain by Abortion." *National Catholic Reporter*, 7 (January 15, 1971), 12.

[2364]O'Neil, Daniel J. *Church Lobbying in a Western State: A Case Study on Abortion Legislation* (Tucson, Arizona: University of Arizona Press, 1970).

[2365]O'Neill, P. T., et al. "Father and the Unborn Child." *Modern Law Review*, 38 (March, 1975), 174-85.

[2366]"On Imposing Catholic Views on Others." *America*, 116 (February 25, 1967), 273-74.

[2367]"Only Amendment will Save the Unborn, Professor Says." *Our Sunday Visitor*, 65 (October 31, 1976), 3.

[2368]"Ontario Bishops Blast Government on Abortion." *Our Sunday Visitor*, 64 (May 25, 1975), 2.

[2369]"On Responsibility for Children Not Yet Born." *L'Osservatore Romano* (English), 208 (no. 12) (March 23, 1972, 8.

[2370]Ooi, O. S. "The Demand for Abortion in an Urban Malaysian Population." *Medical Journal of Malaya*, 25 (March, 1971), 175-81.

[2371]"Open Letter to American Doctors." *America*, 122 (May 9, 1970), 490-91.

[2372]"Operations for Abortion." *British Medical Journal*, 3 (1969), 751.

[2373]Oppel, W., Athanasiou, R., Cushner, I., Sasaki, T., Unger, T., and Wolf, S. "Contraceptive Antecedents to Early and Late Therapeutic Abortions." *Journal of Public Health,* 62(5) (1972), 824-27.

[2374]Oppel, W., *et al.* "Liberalized Abortion and Birth Rates Changes in Baltimore." *American Journal of Public Health,* 63 (May, 1973), 405-08.

[2375]"Opposing Sides Mobilizes for War on Abortion." *St. Anthony's Messenger,* 73 (April, 1967), 10-11.

[2376]"Options in the Abortion Debate." *Christian Century,* 93 (February 18, 1976), 139-40. [This article deals with the abortion question as a political issue in the 1976 presidential election. Three options are presented as choices of the various candidates.]

[2377]Orloski, R. "Abortion: A Deeper Look at the Legal Aspects." *U. S. Catholic,* 38 (September, 1973), 39-40. [Orloski points out the difficulty of imposing moral codes into criminal laws. The mother can easily conceal the effects of abortion of the three month fetus, more so than the newly born infant. When there is universal agreement within a society then the moral precept can be written into the criminal statute, such as monagamous marriage. But, the opinion of abortion is divided.
Orloski believes that moral theology involves a commitment of the hearts of men not necessarily of their laws.]

[2378]Orloski, R. "Abortion: Legal Questions and Legislative Alternatives." *America,* 131 (August 10, 1974), 50-51. [The author suggests state legislation as a more immediate and effective way of resisting the Supreme Court's decision rather than a constitutional amendment.
He sees two major concessions by the Supreme Court to the "right to life" movement. The state legislature can pass statutes preventing abortions in the third trimester, with the implied recognition of the humanness of such fetal life. Also, legislation regulating abortions during the second trimester is constitutionally sound when the purpose is the protection of the

mother's life.
Legislative reform is needed to define the rights of fathers of fetal life and the matter of abortions for minors.]

[2379]"Or Manslaughter?" *Economist,* 254 (February 22, 1975), 61.

[2380]O'Rourke, K. "Because the Lord Loved You." *Hospital Progress,* 54 (August, 1973), 73-77.

[2381]O'Rourke, K. "The Right of Privacy: What Next?" *Hospital Progress,* 56 (April, 1975), 58-63.

[2382]"O'Rourke, Teacher Uphold Abortion." *National Catholic Reporter,* 10 (September 27, 1974), 17.

[2383]"Orthodox Church Condemns Abortion and Euthanasia." *Our Sunday Visitor,* 64 (December 7, 1975), 3.

[2384]Osofsky, Howard J., and Osofsky, Joy D. *The Abortion Experience* (New York: Harper and Row, 1973).

[2385]Osofsky, J. D. "Psychologic Effects of Legal Abortion." *Clinical Obstetrics and Gynecology,* 14 (1971), 215-34. Also: *Modern Treatment,* 8 (February, 1971), 139-58.

[2386]Osofsky, J. D., and Osofsky, H. J. "The Psychological Reaction of Patients to Legalized Abortion." *American Journal of Orthopsychiatry,* 42(1) (1972), 48-50.

[2387]Ostfeld. "ISMS Symposium of Medical Implications Current Abortion Law in Illinois." *Illinois Medical Journal,* 131 (May, 1967), 686-87.

[2388]Ostro, E. "East Europe Nations Tighten Abortion Laws." *National Catholic Reporter,* 10 (February 1, 1974), 14.

[2389]Ostro, M. "Liberal Abortion Laws are Worldwide Trend." *National Catholic Reporter,* 10 (November 9, 1973), 3-4.

[2390]O'Sullivan, J. "The Effects of Legalized Abortion in England," tabs. *Hospital Progress,* 52 (June, 1971), 75-78.

[2391]Oteri, J. S., *et al.* "Abortion and the Religious Liberty Caluses." *Harvard Civil Right Law Review,* 7 (May, 1972), 559.

[2392]Otten, Alan L. "Highly Combustible (Anti-Abortion as a Campaign Issue)." *Wall Street Journal,* 184 (October 17, 1974), 22.

[2393]Ottosson, Jan-Otto. "Experience Under Law in Sweden." Harvard Divinity School—Kennedy Foundation International Conference on Abortion, Washington, D.C., September, 1967.

[2394]Ottosson, Jan-Otto. "Legal Abortion in Sweden: Thirty Years' Experience." *Journal of Biosocial Science,* 3 (April, 1971), 173-92.

[2395]Ough, R. N. "Letter: Therapeutic Abortion." *Canadian Medical Association Journal,* 113 (9) (November 8, 1975), 818-21.

[2396]"Our Decision, Say Women." *Economist,* 257 (Dec. 13, 1975), 49.

[2397]"Outside the Law." *Lancet,* 2 (July 19, 1969), 148.

[2398]"Override of Fund Bill Veto Leaves Abortion Ban Intact." *National Catholic Reporter,* 12 (October 8, 1976), 14.

[2399]Overstreet, E. W., ed. *Clinical Obstetrics and Gynecology,* 7 (New York: Harper and Row —Hoener Inc., March, 1964).

[2400]Overstreet, E. W. "Forward Symposium on Therapeutic Abortion and Sterilization." *Clinical Obstetrics and Gynecology,* 7 (March, 1964), 11.

[2401]Overstreet, E. W. "Logistic Problems of Legal Abortion." *American Journal of Public Health,* 61 (March, 1971), 496-99.

[2402]Overstreet, E. W. "The Role of the University Hospital in Solving the Logistic Problems of Legal Abortion." *Clinical Obstetrics and Gynecology,* 14 (December, 1971), 1243-47.

[2403]Overstreet, E. W. "The World-Wide Problem of Abortion— North America." Paper presented to the *International Planned Parenthood Federation World Congress, Santiago, Chile, April, 1967* (London: International Planned Parenthood Federation, 1967).

[2404]Pable, M. "Pastoral Counseling and Abortion." *Priest,* 31 (October, 1975), 15-16+.

[2405]Packer, H. L., and Campbell, R. J. "Therapeutic Abortion: A Problem in Law and Medicine." *Stanford Law Review,* 11 (May, 1959). Also: *The Case for Legalized Abortion Now.* Ed. Alan F. Guttmacher (Berkeley: The Diablo Press, 1967).

[2406]Packwood, B., and Rarick, J. R. "Should the United States Legalize Abortions? 'Yes'. by Bob Packwood; 'No'. by John R. Rarick." *American Legion of Mary,* 88 (June, 1970), 22-23.

[2407]Paganelli, Vitale H. "A Review of the March, 1970, *Theological Studies:* Abortion Issue." *Linacre Quarterly,* 37 (August, 1970), 206.

[2408]Pakter, J., *et al.* "Effects of a Liberalized Abortion Law in New York City." *Mount Sinai Journal of Medicine* (New York), 39 (November-December, 1972), 535-43.

[2409]Pakter, J., *et al.* "Impact of the Liberalized Abortion Law in New York City on Deaths Associated with Pregnancy: A Two-Year Experience." *Bulletin of the New York Academy of Medicine,* 49 (September, 1973), 804-18.

[2410]Pakter, J., *et al.* "Legal Abortion: A Half-Decade of Experience (New York, N.Y.; 1970-1975)," il., tables, charts. *Family Planning Perspectives,* 7(6) (November-December, 1975), 248-55.

[2411]Pakter, J., *et al.* "Surveillance of the Abortion Program in New York City: Preliminary Report." *Clinical Obstetrics and Gynecology,* 14 (March, 1971), 267-99. Also: *Modern Treatment,* 8 (February, 1971), 169-201.

[2412]Pakter, J., *et al.* "Two Years Experience in New York City With the Liberalized Abortion Law— Progress and Problems." *American Journal of Public Health,* 63 (June, 1973), 524-35.

[2413]Pannell, C. "Three Years' Experience of the Working of the Abortion Act in Britain." *New Zealand Medical Journal,* 76 (n.d.), 117-19.

[2414]Paoletti, Robert A. "Developmental-Genetic and Psycho-

Social Positions Regarding the Ontological Status of the Fetus." *Linacre Quarterly,* 44 (August, 1977), 243-61.

2415Papola, G. "Abortion Today." *L'Osservatore Romano* (English), 208 (no. 12) (March 23, 1972), 9-10.

2416Pare, C. M. B., and Raven, Hermione. "Follow-Up of Patients Referred for Termination of Pregnancy." *Lancet,* 1 (March 28, 1970), 635.

2417"Parent and Child: Minor's Right to Consent to an Abortion." *Santa Clara Lawyer,* 11 (Spring, 1971), 469.

2418"Parent and Child— Right of Unwed Minor to Obtain Abortion Without Parental Consent." *Journal of Family Law,* 14 (1975-1976), 637-43.

2419Parenteau, R. "Church Abortion Stand Called Sexist." *National Catholic Reporter,* 10 (November 2, 1973), 3+.

2420Paris, Charles B. "Abortion: A Question of Heart and Mind." *CRUX,* 12 (no. 4) (1974-1975), 7-8.

2421Parker, G. E. "Bill C-150; Abortion Reform." *Criminal Law Quarterly,* 11 (1969), 267.

2422Parry, L. A. *Criminal Abortion* (London: John Bale, 1932).

2423Parsons, E. S. "Abortion: A Private and Public Concern." *Critic,* 10 (Winter, 1971), 13-16.

2424"Particulars Filed in Boston Abortion—Manslaughter Suit." *National Catholic Reporter,* 10 (August 16, 1974), 15.

2425Partridge, J. R. "Therapeutic Abortion. A Study of Psychiatric Applicants at North Carolina Memorial Hospital." *North Carolina State Medical Journal,* 32 (1971), 131-36.

2426Parvey, C. F. "Abortion." *Dialog,* 11 (Autumn, 1976), 304-07.

2427Pasnau, R. O. "Contemporary Psychiatric Consultation: Evaluation of Rehabilitation?" *Clinical Obstetrics and Gyne-*

cology, 14 (December, 1971), 1258-62,

2428Pasnau, R. O. "Psychiatric Complications of Therapeutic Abortion." *Obstetrics and Gynecology,* 40 (1972), 252-56.

2429"Past and Present." *L'Osservatore Romano* (English), 204 (no. 8) (February 24, 1972), 3.

2430"Pastoral Guidelines for the Catholic Hospitals and Health Care Personnel in the United States." *L'Osservatore Romano* (English), 273 (no. 25) (June 21, 1973), 11-12.

2431"Pastoral Letter for All Bishops Calls Abortion Laws Unjust and Immoral: Asks for Action." *Our Sunday Visitor,* 64 (January 18, 1976), 1.

2432"Pastoral Message on Abortion." *Catholic Mind,* 71 (September, 1973), 7-9. [Prompted by the U.S. Supreme Court decision in *Roe v. Wade,* January 22, 1973, the Administrative Committee of the National Conference of Catholic Bishops issued a statement on February 13, 1973. The article contains the text.]

2433"A Pastoral Plan for Pro-Life Activities." *Catholic Mind,* 74 (March, 1976, 55-64. [The American Catholic bishops approved of a plan for pro-life activities, at their general meeting in Washington, D.C., November 17-20, 1975.

It contained four parts: 1) Public Information/Education Program; 2) Pastoral Care; 3) Legislative/Public Policy Effort; 4) Means of Implementation of Program.

2434Patel, H. N. "Knowledge and Attitudes of Married Women Towards Medical Termination of Pregnancy." *The Journal of Family Welfare,* 22(4) (1976), 66-75.

2435Paton, T. "Unwanted Pregnancy in Japan." *Japan Christian Quarterly,* 40 (Spring, 1974), 93-101.

2436Patrinos, D. "AMA Eases Abortion Rule." *National Catholic Reporter,* 6 (July 3, 1970), 5.

2437Patt, S. L., Rappaport, R. G., and Barglow, P. "Follow-Up of Therapeutic Abortion." *Archives of General Psychiatry,* 20(4) (1969), 408-14.

2438-
2461

[2438]Patterson, Janet, and
Patterson, Robert C. *Abortion:
The Trojan Horse* (Chicago: Nel-
son-Hall Company, 1974).

[2439]Paul, E. W. "Legal
Rights of Minors to Sex-Related
Medical Care." *Columbia Human
Rights Law Revew,* 6 (Fall-Win-
ter, 1974-1974), 357-77.

[2440]Paul VI, Pope. Address
to participants in the 23rd National Congress of the Union of
Italian Catholic Jurists, December 9, 1972.

[2441]Pawlick, T. "The Reality of Abortion." *National
Catholic Reporter,* 6 (April 10,
1970), 4.

[2442]"Pax Romana, Catholic
Jurists Against Abortion."
L'Osservatore Romano (English),
447 (no. 43) (October 21, 1976),
10.

[2443]Payne, E. C., Kravitz,
A. R., Notman, M. T., and Ander-
son, J. V. "Outcome Following
Therapeutic Abortion." *Archives of General Psychiatry,*
33(6) (1976), 725-33.

[2444]Pearch, J. D. W. "The
Psychiatric Indications for the
Termination of Pregnancy."
*Proceedings of the Royal Socie-
ty of Medicine,* 50 (May, 1957),
321.

[2445]Pearlmutter, F. A.
"Letter: Tay-Sachs Disease."
*Journal of the American Medical
Association,* 230(1) (October 7,
1974), 38.

[2446]Pearson, J. F. "Pilot
Study of Single Women Requesting a Legal Abortion." *Journal
of Biosocial Science,* 3(4)
(1971), 417-48.

[2447]Pearson, J. F. "Social
and Psychological Aspects of
Extra-Marital First Conceptions."
Journal of Biosocial Science,
5(4) (1973), 453-96.

[2448]Peck, A. "Psychiatric
Sequelae of Therapeutic Interruption of Pregnancy." *Journal
of Nervous and Mental Disease,*
143 (1966), 417-25.

[2449]Peck, A. "Therapeutic
Abortion: Patients, Doctors,
and Society." *American Journal
of Psychiatry,* 125 (December,

968), 797-804.

[2450]Peck, Margery H. "More on
Abortion." *Christian Century,* 88
(December 1, 1971), 1424. [This is
a reply to R. H. Hamill's conclu-
sion in his article, "Abortion: A
Campus Chaplain's Reply to His Col-
leagues," *Christian Century,* 28
(August 11, 1971).

[2451]Peel, John. "Attitudes to
Abortion—Attitudes in Britain."
Abortion in Britain (London: Pitman
Medical Publishing Company Ltd.,
1966).

[2452]Pellegrino, M., Card.
"Pellegrino Condemns Abortion."
L'Osservatore Romano (English), 338
(no. 38) (September 19, 1974), 6.

[2453]Pells, J. "Prolonging
Life. 3. The Hope in Experiment."
Nursing Times, 70 (March 7, 1974),
352-53.

[2454]Pelrine, Eleanor Wright.
Abortion in Canada (Don Mills,
Ont.: New Press, 1971).

[2455]Peratis, Kathleen, and
Rindskopf, Elisabeth. "Pregnancy
Discrimination as a Sex Discrimina-
tion Issue." *Women's Rights Law
Reporter,* 2 (June, 1975), 26-34.

[2456]Perez-Reyes, M. G., and
Falk, R. "Follow-Up After Therapeutic Abortion in Early Adolescence." *Archives of General Psychiatry,* 28(1) (1973), 120-26.

[2457]Perkins, Robert L. *Abortion: Pro & Con* (Cambridge, Mass.:
Schenkman Publishing Company Inc.,
1974).

[2458]Perlmutter, I. K. "Analysis of Therapeutic Abortions, Bell-
vue Hospital, 1935-1945." *American
Journal of Obstetrics and Gynecology,* 53 (1947), 1008.

[2459]Perr, I. N., *et al.* "Position Stand of the Ohio Psychiatric
Association on Suggested Changes in
the Abortion Laws of Ohio." *Ohio
Medical Journal,* 64 (December,
1968), 1343-44.

[2460]Perry, M. J. "Abortion,
the Public Morals, and the Police
Power. The Ethical Function of
Substantive Due Process." *UCLA Law
Review,* 23(4) (1976), 689-736.

[2461]"Personal Experience at a
Legal Abortion Center." *American
Journal of Nursing,* 72 (January,

1972), 110-12.

[2462]Peters, D. "N.Y. Nurses Quit Over Abortions." *National Catholic Reporter,* 7 (November 6, 1970), 20.

[2463]Petersen, L. R., and Mauss, A. L. "Religion and the Right to Life. Correlates of Opposition to Abortion." *Sociological Analysis,* 37(3) (1976), 243-54.

[2464]Peterson, M. L. "Control of Fertility." *New England Journal of Medicine,* 282 (June 18, 1970), 1432-33.

[2465]Peterson, W. F. "Contraceptive Therapy Following Therapeutic Abortion: An Analysis." *Obstetrics and Gynecology,* 44(6) (December, 1974), 853-57.

[2466]"Petition for Withdrawal of Abortion Bill." *Tablet,* 221 (March 11, 1967), 277.

[2467]Peyton, R. W., *et al.* "Woman's Attitudes Concerning Abortion." *Obstetrics and Gynecology,* 34 (August, 1969), 82-88.

[2468]Pfanner, D., *et al.* "Termination of Pregnancy, Sydney, 1972." *Medical Journal of Australia,* 1 (April 7, 1973), 710-11.

[2469]Pfanner, D., *et al.* "Therapeutic Abortion at a Sydney Teaching Hospital." *Medical Journal of Australia,* 1 (June 21, 1969), 1315-16.

[2470]Pfeiffer, E. "Psychiatric Indications or Psychiatric Justification of Therapeutic Abortion?" *Archives of General Psychiatry,* 23 (November, 1970), 402-07.

[2471]Phillips, D. F. "Abortion, the Hospital and the Law." *Hospitals,* 44 (August 16, 1970), 59-62.

[2472]Phillipson, D. "Morgentaler Case Divides Supreme Court in Interpretation of Criminal Code." *Canadian Medical Association Journal,* 112(8) (April 19, 1975), 1003-04.

[2473]Phillipson, D. "Supreme Court Considers Morgentaler Abortion Case." *Canadian Medical Association Journal,* 111(8) (October 19, 1974), 872-73.

[2474]Picher, P. C. "The Invalidity of Canada's Abortion Law: Section 251 of the Criminal Code." *Criminal Reports* (New Series), 24 (1974), 1-31.

[2475]Piguet, L. "Easy Abortion: Who's to Blame?" *U.S. Catholic,* 36 (February, 1971), 39-40. [The author suggests that those very people who abhor abortions can contribute to the social climate that welcomes abortions. Public acceptance may be fostered by their own attitudes toward illegitimacy, justifiable homicide, and human freedom.]

[2476]Pike, C. C. "Therapeutic Abortion and Mental Health." *California Medicine,* 111 (October, 1969), 318-20.

[2477]Pilpel, Harriet F. "The Abortion Crisis." *The Case for Legalized Abortion Now.* Ed. Alan F. Guttmacher (Berkelye: Diablo Press, 1967).

[2478]Pilpel, Harriet F. "Abortion. USA Style." *The Journal of Sex Research,* 11(2) (1975), 113-18.

[2479]Pilpel, Harriet F. "The Fetus as Person: Possible Legal Consequences of the Hogan-Helms Amendment." *Family Planning Perspectives,* 6 (Winter, 1974), 6-7.

[2480]Pilpel, Harriet F., and Norwick, Kenneth P. "When Should Abortion be Legal?" Public Affairs Commission, pam no. 429, 1969.

[2481]Pilpel, Harriet F., and Patton, D. E. "Abortion, Conscience, and the Constitution." *Columbia Human Rights Law Review,* 6 (2) (1975), 279-306.

[2482]Pilpel, Harriet F., *et al.* "Abortion: Public Issue, Private Decision." Public Affairs Commission, pam no. 527, 1975.

[2483]"Pinning Down the Politicians." *Economist,* 258 (February 14, 1976), 40+.

[2484]Piper, G. W. "Letter: Unwanted Pregnancies." *Canadian Medical Association Journal,* 112(2) (January 25, 1975), 145.

[2485]Pion, R. J. "Abortion

Request and Post-Operative Response. A Washington Community Survey." *Northwest Medicine,* 69 (1970), 693-98.

[2486]Pius, Fr. "Moral Theology Forum: Conscience and the Abortion Law." *Clergy Review,* 55 (April, 1970), 288-93. Replies by C. Flood, M. Dawkins, F. Lydon, 55 (April, 1970), 293-97.

[2487]Plagenz, L. "States Legislate Abortion Reform, But Hospitals are Reluctant to Comply." *Modern Hospital,* 113 (July, 1969), 82-85.

[2488]Planned Parenthood of New York City, Inc. *Abortion: A Woman's Guide* (Abelard-Schuman Ltd., 1973, c/o Harper and Row, Scranton, Pa.).

[2489]Planned Parenthood of New York City, Inc. *Abortion: A Woman's Guide, 1975* (New York: Pocket Book, Inc., 1975).

[2490]Ple, A. "Alerte au Traducianisme." *Le Supplément* 96 (February, 1971), 59-71.

[2491]Pleasants, Julian. "A Morality of Consequences." *Commonweal,* 86 (1967), 413.

[2492]Plummer, S. A. "Problem Pregnancy. A Perspective on Abortion and the Quality of Human Life." *Rocky Mountain Medical Journal,* 69 (November, 1972), 64-66.

[2493]Pohlman, E. W. "'Wanted' and 'Unwanted'. Toward Less Ambiguous Definitions." *Eugenics Quarterly,* 12 (1965), 19-27.

[2494]"Poland." *Situation Report* (London: International Planned Parenthood Federation, August, 1968).

[2495]Poland, B. J., *et al.* "The Use of Spontaneous Abortuses and Stillbirths in Genetic Counseling." *American Journal of Obstetrics and Gynecology,* 118 (February 1, 1974), 322-26.

[2496]Pole, Nelson. "To Respect Human Life." *Philosophy in Context,* 2 (1973), 16-22. [The author sees the dignity of human life being promoted by having a general right to abort. The adult is recognized as being naturally good. It is not responsible to prevent the abortion since the mother is left with a twenty year obligation to raise the child. She alone must make the decision to have an abortion. In order to meet our responsibility but not to aid in the abortion, the woman must be aided in some other way.

[2497]Poletti, U., Card. "No Bargaining About Abortion; Exhortation of Bishops of Lazio." *L'Osservatore Romano* (English), 449 (no. 45) (November 4, 1976), 11.

[2498]Polgar, S., and Fried, E. S. "The Bad Old Days. Clandestine Abortions Among the Poor in New York City Before Liberalization of the Abortion Law." *Family Planning Perspectives,* 8(3) (1976), 125-27.

[2499]"Policy Bans Foreign Aid for Abortions." *National Catholic Reporter,* 10 (July 19, 1974), 27.

[2500]"Politics and Abortion." *Commonweal,* 103 (February 27, 1976), 131-32. [This editorial states that abortion has become an issue in the 1976 presidential campaign. This issue, instead of helping to solidify the Christian community, will distract both Catholics and Candidates from the broader social-justice crisis and isolate the Church.]

[2501]"Politics of Abortion." *New Statesman,* 91 (March 5, 1976), 275.

[2502]"Political Responsibility and Abortion." *America,* 134 (March 6, 1976), 173. [This article discusses the statement from the Administrative Board of the U.S. Catholic Conference, entitled "Political Responsibility: Reflections on an Election Year."

The statement calls for citizen participation in the electoral process. Three disclaimers are issued by the bishops. They do not want to form a "religious voting block" to endorse particular candidates or single out one decisive issue.

They go on to say that a candidate's stand on abortion must be weighed on the same scale as the other issues supported by the bishops.]

[2503]Polityka, T. "From *Poe* to

Roe (Roe v. Wade 93 Sup Ct 705): A Bickelain View of the Abortion Decision—Its Timing and Principle." *Nebraska Law Review*, 53 (1974), 31-57.

2504 "Poll Says Catholics Back Abortion." *National Catholic Reporter*, 8 (September 15, 1972), 6.

2505 Pommerenke, W. T. "Abortion in Japan." *Obstetrical and Gynecological Survey*, 10 (April, 1955), 145.

2506 Pond, D. A. "No Questions Asked...?" *Lancet*, 1 (March 18, 1967), 611-13.

2507 Pond, M. A. "Politics of Social Change: Abortion Reform. The Role of Health Professionals in the Legislative Process." *American Journal of Public Health*, 61 (May, 1971), 904-09.

2508 "Pope, Cardinal, Medics All Condemn Abortion." *National Catholic Reporter*, 6 (October 23, 1970), 2.

2509 Popenoe, P. "Abortion in Japan." *Catholic Digest*, 35 (September, 1971), 27-29.

2510 "Population, Contraception and Abortion." *Journal of the Royal College of General Practitioners*, 21 (July, 1971), 377-78.

2511 "Population Problems Past and Present." *Public Health Report*, 82 (May, 1967), 377-85.

2512 "Position Statement on Abortion." *American Journal of Psychiatry*, 124 (1967), 450.

2513 "A Positive Alternative to Abortion in England." *L'Osservatore Romano* (English), no. 20 (May 18, 1972), 3.

2514 Potter, Ralph B. "The Abortion Debate." *Updating Life and Death*. Ed. Donald Cutler (Boston: Beacon Press, 1968).

2515 Potter, Robert G. "Additional Births Averted When Abortion is Added Contraception." *Studies in Family Planning*, 3 (April, 1972), 53-59.

2516 Potter, Robert G. "Competition Between Spontaneous and Induced Abortion." *Demography*, 12(1) (February, 1975), 129-41.

2517 Potter, Robert G., and Kathleen Ford. "Repeat Abortion." *Demography*, 13 (February, 1976), 65-82. [The authors examine the repeat abortion experience of New York City residents during July 1, 1970 to June 30, 1972. It was done on the basis of a probability model that generates repeat abortion ratios as a function of assumptions about fecundity, contraceptive efficiency and exposure lengths.]

2518 Potts, D. M. "Patterns of Abortion and Contraceptive Usage." *Royal Society of Health Journal*, 91 (November-December, 1971), 294-96.

2519 Potts, D. M. "Termination of Pregnancy." *British Medical Bulletin*, 26 (January, 1970), 65-71 (60 ref.).

2520 Potts, D. M., ed. *A Guide to the Abortion Act, 1967* (London: Abortion Law Reform Association, 1967).

2521 Potts, M. "Bibliography (With Review) On Out Patient Abortion." *Bibliography of Reproduction*, 79 (1972), 753-54.

2522 Potts, M. "Induced Abortion in the United Kingdom." Unpublished paper, University of Chicago Conference on Abortion, Spring, 1968.

2523 Potts, M. "Legal Abortion in Eastern Europe (Legal, Medical, Demographic Aspects)," tables, charts. *Eugenics Review*, 59 (December, 1967), 232-50.

2524 Potts, M. "Letter: Legal Abortion." *Medical Journal of Australia*, 2 (November 10, 1973), 909-10.

2525 Potts, M., et al. *Abortion* (Cambridge: Cambridge University Press, August, 1977).

2526 Potts, M., et al. "Legal Abortion in the U.S.A. A Preliminary Assessment." *Lancet*, 2 (September 18, 1971), 651-53.

2527 "Power to Start and End a Life." *Economist*, 245 (December 2, 1972), 45.

2528 Powledge, T. M., and Sollitto, S. "Pre-Natal Diagnosis: The Past and the Future." *Hastings*

2529-
2550

Center Report, 4 (no. 5) (1974), 11-13.

[2529]Pratt, G. L., *et al.* "Connecticut Physicians' Attitudes Toward Abortion." *American Journal of Public Health*, 66 (March, 1976), 288-90. Reply with Rejoinder: K. Solomon, 66 (September, 1976), 905-06.

[2530]Preece, J. D. "An Obstetrician's View of Abortion." *Journal of the Medical Society of New Jersey*, 64 (December, 1967), 648-50.

[2531]"Pre-Natal Diagnosis and Selective Abortion." *Lancet*, 2 (July 12, 1969), 89-90.

[2532]"Preparing for Abortion Procedures." *Hospitals*, 33 (August 16, 1970), 69.

[2533]Prescott, James W. "Abortion or the Unwanted Child: A Choice for a Humanistic Society." *Humanist*, 35 (March-April, 1975), 11-15. [An examination of the social and behavioral characteristics of human cultures, individuals who deny or permit abortion, and an evaluation of the social and moral consequences of these practices reveal that pro-abortion cultures and individuals are significantly more humanitarian in their social behaviors than anti-abortion cultures and individuals.]

[2534]"The Present Status of Abortion Laws: A Statement by the New York Academy of Medicine Prepared by the Committee on Public Health." *Bulletin of the New York Academy of Medicine*, 46 (April, 1970), 281-85.

[2535]Price-Bonham, S., Santee, B., and Bonham, J. M. "An Analysis of Clergymen's Attitude Toward Abortion." *Review of Religious Research*, 17(1) (1975), 15-27.

[2536]"Priest Asks Study of Fetuses' Rights." *National Catholic Reporter*, 7 (April 23, 1971), 3.

[2537]Priest, R. G. "The British Candidate for Termination of Pregnancy: A Quantified Survey of Psychiatric Referrals." *British Journal of Psychiatry*, 118 (May, 1971), 579-80.

[2338]Priest, R. G. "The Impact of the Abortion Act: A Psychiatrist's Observations." *British Journal of Psychiatry*, 121 (September, 1972), 293-99.

[2539]Priest, R. G. "New Trends in Therapeutic Abortion." *Lancet*, 2 (November 18, 1972), 1085.

[2540]"Priest Suggests Abortion Dialogue." *National Catholic Reporter*, 10 (May 17, 1974), 5.

[2541]"Priests Urged to Pro-Life Leadership in New Booklet: Abortion, Attitudes and the Law, by NCCB and Our Sunday Visitor." *Our Sunday Visitor*, 64 (August 31, 1975), 1.

[2542]"Le Probleme de L'Avortment: Lettre Pastorale des Eveques Allemands." *La Documentation Catholique*, 70 (July 1, 1973), 626-29.

[2543]"Procedural Due Process Limitations on State Abortion Statutes." *Marquette Law Review*, 55 (Winter, 1972), 137.

[2544]Proceedings of a Conference of the National Committee on Maternal Health. *The Abortion Problem* (Baltimore: Wilkins and Wilkins Company, 1944).

[2445]"Procuring Abortion." *British Medical Journal*, (suppl. 2) (1969), 168.

[2546]"Pro-Life Activities Committee Set Up." *National Catholic Reporter*, 9 (November 24, 1972), 15.

[2547]"Pro-Life Leaders Think Edelin Reversal Could Accelerate an Amendment." *Our Sunday Visitor*, 65 (January 2, 1977), 2.

[2548]"Proposed Statute for Implementing the Abortion Decisions (*Roe v. Wade*, 93 Sup Ct 705) (*Doe v. Bolton*, 93 Sup Ct 739)." *Journal of Family Law*, 13 (1973-1974), 332-65.

[2549]"A Propos de la Nouvelle Legislation sur L'Avortement: Declaration des Eveques d'Allemagne Federale." *La Documentation Catholique*, 73 (October 17, 1976), 868-71.

[2550]"Prostaglandin Analogue Device Used for Inducing Abortions." *Journal of the American Medical*

Association, 235 (May 17, 1976), 2179-80.

2551"Prostaglandin May Be 'Too Safe' for Abortions." *Journal of the American Medical Association,* 236 (July 19, 1976), 247-49.

2552"Protestant Anti-Abortion Leader Scores Prejudice." *Our Sunday Visitor,* 65 (October 24, 1976), 2.

2553"Protestant Leaders Back Catholic Pro-Life Stand." *Our Sunday Visitor,* 64 (December 14, 1975), 2.

2554"Protestant Pro-Life Women Launch National Task Force." *Our Sunday Visitor,* 64 (May 2, 1976), 2.

2555"Protestant Women Mobilize Forces Against Abortion." *Our Sunday Visitor,* 64 (September 7, 1975), 2.

2556"Protestants Back Catholic Efforts Against Abortion." *Our Sunday Visitor,* 64 (March 7, 1976), 1.

2557"Protestants Organize to Speak Out on Abortion: the Christian Action Council." *Our Sunday Visitor,* 64 (July 20, 1975), 1.

2558"Provisional Estimates of Abortion Need and Services in the Year Following the 1973 Supreme Court Decisions: U.S., Each State, and Metropolitan Area." Alan Guttmacher Institute, 1975. (88 p.)

2559"Psychiatric Indications for the Termination of Pregnancy." *Medical Journal of Australia,* 2 (December 19, 1970), 1212-13.

2560"Psychiatric Indications for the Termination of Pregnancy." *Medical Journal of Australia,* 1 (January 16, 1971), 171.

2561Psychological Factors in Contraceptive Failure and Abortion Request." *Medical Journal of Australia,* 1(26) (June 28, 1975), 800.

2562"Psychological Sequelae of Therapeutic Abortion." *British Medical Journal,* 1(6020) (May 22, 1976), 1239.

2563"Public Policy and Abortion Laws." *America,* 120 (March 1, 1969), 239-40.

2564Pulley, H. C. "Abortions —First Annual Report." *California Medicine,* 108 (May, 1968), 403.

2565Pulliam, Edward Hyde. "North Carolina Abortion Laws." (Health Law Bul. No. 16) Free— Institute of Government, University of North Carolina, PO Box 990, Chapel Hill, N.C. 27514 (October, 1968). (5 p.)

2566Purdy, L. M. "Abortion and the Husband's Rights. A Reply to Wesley Teo." *Ethics,* 86(3) (1976), 247-51.

2567"Puritans in Retreat." *Economist,* 223 (May 13, 1967), 682.

2568"Putative Father's Rights After *Roe v. Wade* (93 Sup Ct 705)." *St. Mary's Journal,* 6 (Summer, 1974), 407-20.

2569Puxon, M. "Abortion, 1967 Style." *Solicitor's Journal,* 111 (December 8, 1967), 934.

2570Quay, Eugene. "Justifiable Abortion—Medical and Legal Foundations." *Georgetown Law Journal,* 49 (Winter, 1960), 179; (Spring, 1961), 395.

2571"Question Fetus Experiments." *National Catholic Reporter,* 8 (March 17, 1972), 23.

2572"A Question of Conscience." *British Medical Journal,* 2 (July, 1976), 43.

2573"Q: What, Doctor is the Difference Between You and Adolph Hitler..." *Triumph,* 7 (February, 1972), 18-20+. [Two doctors are interviewed over the telephone concerning abortion. Both doctors performed abortions regularly.]

2574"Questions to Ask." *Economist,* 239 (May 1, 1971), 24+.

2575Quinn, J. R. "The Right to Live." *America,* 123 (August 8, 1970), 56. [A brief statement regarding abortion as an attack on human rights.]

2576Rahmeier, Paul W. "Abortion and the Reverence for Life." *Christian Century,* 88 (May 5, 1971),

2577-
2595

556-60. [The author supports abortion in situations where an abortion would enhance the lives of those already born. He views life as beginning at birth.]

[2577]"Rallies Back, Oppose Abortion." *National Catholic Reporter,* 8 (December 3, 1971), 3-4.

[2578]Ramsey, Paul. "Abortion: A Review Article." *Thomist,* 37 (January, 1973), 174-226. [Daniel Callahan's book, *Law, Choice and Morality* (MacMillan, 1970), is discussed at great length. Other authors considered are: Robert S. Morison, Joseph T. Mangan, S. J., Andre Hellegers, Germain Grisez, Joseph F. Donceel, John Fletcher, Mary Douglas, Judith Jarvis Thompson, and Ramsey himself.]

[2579]Ramsey, Paul. "The Ethics of a Cottage Industry in an Age of Community and Research Medicine." *New England Journal of Medicine,* 284 (April 1, 1971), 700-06.

[2580]Ramsey, Paul. "Feticide/ Infanticide Upon Request." *Religion in Life,* 39 (Summer, 1970), 170-86.

[2581]Ramsey, Paul. "The Morality of Abortion." *Moral Problems: Collection of Philosophical Essays.* Ed. James Rachels (New York: Harper and Row, 1971). [Animation, the sanctity of life, the principle of double effect are discussed.]

[2582]Ramsey, Paul. "Protecting the Unborn." *Commonweal,* 100 (May 31, 1974), 308-14. [The contents of this article is based on the written testimony presented to the subcommittee of the Senate Judiciary Committee holding hearings on the various abortion amendments.]

[2583]Ramsey, Paul. "Reference Points in Deciding About Abortion." *The Morality of Abortion.* Ed. John Noonan (Cambridge, Mass.: Harvard University Press, 1970). [The author expands on the allegation that religious belief of any kind should be excluded from any bearing on public policy. He goes on to discuss the nature of ethical commitments, the difference between sin and crime, the scientific possibilities for de-

termining when life begins, the distinction between feticide and infantifide, birth, viability and the practice of fetal medicine.]

[2584]Ramsey, Paul. "The Sanctity of Life." *Dublin Review,* 241 (Spring, 1967), 3-23.

[2585]Ramsey, Paul. "Some Terms of Reference for the Abortion Debate." Unpublished paper, Harvard Divinity School—Kennedy Foundation International Conference on Abortion, September, 1967.

[2586]Ranck, L., and McConnell, N. F. "To Pass or Block an Amendment to the Constitution (On Abortion)." *Engage/Social Action,* 2 (February, 1974), 51-62.

[2587]Ransil, Bernard. *Abortion.* Ed. P. Ramsey (New Jersey: Paulist Press, 1969).

[2588]Rao, B. Krishna. "The Impact of Legislation of Induced Abortion: International Experience." *Journal of the Indian Medical Association,* 45 (July 16, 1965), 97.

[2589]Rao, I. B. "The New Abortion Law—Some Salient Features." *Journal of the Indian Medical Association* (Calcutta), 59 (October 16, 1972), 332-36.

[2590]Rao, K. N. "Abortion and Family Planning." *Journal of the Indian Medical Association* (Calcutta), 59 (October 16, 1972), 337-41.

[2591]Rao, S. L. N., and Bouvier, L. F. "Socioeconomic Correlates of Attitudes Toward Abortion in Rhode Island. 1971." *American Journal of Public Health,* 64(8) (1974), 765-74.

[2592]Rao, V. N., and Panse, G. A. "Analysis of Acceptors of Medical Termination of Pregnancies in Maharashtra." *Journal of Family Welfare,* 22(1) (1975), 64-71.

[2593]Raphael, B. "Psychosocial Aspects of Induced Abortion. Its Implications for the Woman, Her Family and Her Doctor." *Medical Journal of Australia,* 2 (1972), 35-40.

[2594]Rapp, M. S. "Letter: Contraception and Abortion." *Canadian Medical Association Journal,* 112(6) (March 22, 1975), 682.

[2595]Rashke, R. "Abortion: Key Issue in '76?" ports. *National*

Catholic Reporter, 11 (May 30, 1975), 1+.

[2596]Rashke, R. "Reaction Split to Kennedy Abortion View: Federal Funds for Abortion." *National Catholic Reporter,* 11 (May 2, 1975), 1+.

[2597]Rashke, R. "Senate Unit Kills Pro-Life Amendments." *National Catholic Reporter,* 11 (September 26, 1975), 1+.

[3598]Ratner, Herbert. "Abortion." *Journal of the South Carolina Medical Association,* 69 (February, 1973), 69-70.

[2599]Ratner, Herbert. "A Doctor Talks About Abortion." *Catholic Mind,* 64 (May, 1966), 45. [This is an interview of the author by Gordon Gerbec. He speaks on the movement to legalize abortion and the position of the Planned Parenthood League.]

[2600]Ratner, Herbert. "ISMS Symposium on Medical Implications of Current Abortion Law in Illinois." *Illinois Medical Journal,* 131 (n.d.) 687-93.

[2601]Ratner, Herbert. "A Public Health Physician Views Abortion." *Child and Family,* 7 (Winter, 1968).

[2602]Rauramo, L. "Outpatient Abortions." *Annales Chirurgiae et Gynaecologiae Fenniae* (Helsinki), 61 (1972), 45-46.

[2603]Raven, C. "Testimony in Favor of Abortion Reform Hearings Before the Michigan State House Committee on Social Services." *Woman Physician,* 26 (November, 1971), 584-86.

[2604]Rawls, W. E., *et al.* "Serologic Diagnosis and Fetal Involvement in Maternal Rubella." *Journal of the American Medical Association,* 203 (February 26, 1968), 627.

[2605]Rawls, W. E., *et al.* "World Health Organization Collaborative Study on the Sero-Epidemiology of Rubella." *Bulletin of the World Health Organization,* 37 (1967), 79-88.

[2606]"Reactions Against the Bill for the Liberalization of Abortion: in Germany." *L'Osservatore Romano* (English), 270 (no. 22) (May 31, 1973), 10.

[2607]"Reasons for Abortion." *British Medical Journal,* 3 (August 15, 1970), 362.

[2608]Reback, Gary L. "Fetal Experimentation: Moral, Legal, and Medical Implications (of Experimentation on Aborted Fetuses)." *Stanford Law Review,* 26 (May, 1974), 1191-207.

[2609]"Recommendation of the Ad Hoc Committee to Study the Abortion Law." *Maryland Medical Journal,* 16 (December, 1967), 12.

[2610]Redman, L. J., and Lieberman, E. J. "Abortion, Contraception and Child Mental Health." *Family Planning Perspectives,* 5(2) (1973), 71-72.

[2611]Redford, Myron H., and Marcuse, Edgar K. "Legal Abortion in Washington State: An Analysis of the First Year's Experience." (1973). Battelle Population Study Center, 4000 NE 41st St., Seattle, Wash. 98105. Published jointly with the School of Public Health and Community Medicine, University of Washington.

[2612]Reed, Evelyn, and Moriarity, Claire. *Abortion and the Catholic Church: Two Feminists Defend Women's Rights* (New York: Pathfinder Press Inc. Publishers, 1973).

[2613]Reed, R. E. "Therapeutic Abortion." *North Carolina Medical Journal,* 32 (July, 1971), 287-88.

[2614]Rees, W. M., *et al.* "Abortion and Class: A Comment on the Lane Report." *Modern Law Review,* 37 (November, 1974), 663-70.

[2615]Rehnquist, W. "Rehnquist: Ruling Confuses Privacy." *National Catholic Reporter,* 9 (February 2, 1973), 14.

[2616]Reichelt, Paul A., and Werley, Harriet H. "Contraception, Abortion and Venereal Disease: Teenagers' Knowledge and the Effect of Education (Based on Conference Papers)," il., tables, charts. *Family Planning Perspectives,* 7 (March/April, 1975), 83-88.

[2617]Reinsdorf, W. "On Human Life." *Homiletic and Pastoral Re-*

2618-
2637

view, 75 (January, 1975), 65-
68. [This is a homily describing the evils of abortion.]

[2618]"Reforming the Abortion
Law." *Tablet,* 226 (February 5,
1972), 119-22. [This is a copy
of the memorandum submitted by
the Catholic committee formed
by the Bishops' Conference of
England and Wales to consider
the operation of the Abortion
Act. The Chairman was Rev. P.
J. Casey, Bishop of Brentwood.
This report was presented to the
Lane Committee. It contained
their conclusions and recommendations. These include: 1) abortion on demand should be prevented; 2) two doctors should
authorize abortion under the
act; one should hold office
with the National Health Service; 3) obstetrical and gynaecological appointments are *not*
determined by reference to the
doctor's views on abortion; 4)
more counseling and care services should be provided for women with unwanted pregnancies;
5) abortions should not be performed after the 12th week of
pregnancy.]

[2619]"Reforms Accepted."
Economist, 257 (October 25.

[2620]Regan, L. J. "The Law
of Abortion." *Annals of Western
Medicine and Surgery,* 6 (January,
1952), 26-44.

[2621]Reid, D. E. "Assessment
and Management of the Seriously
Ill Patient Following Abortion."
*Journal of the American Medical
Association,* 199 (March 13,
1967), 141.

[2622]Reilly, Christopher, T.
"Threatened Health of Mother as
an Indication for Therapeutic
Abortion." *Birth Control and
the Christian.* Ed. W. O. Spitzer and C. L. Saylor (Wheaton,
Illinois: Tyndale House, 1969).

[2623]*The Religious Situation
1969.* Ed. Harold Rosen (Boston:
Beacon press, 1969).

[2624]Renard, A. "Divorce et
Avortement: Interview." *La Documentation Catholique,* 67 (December 6, 1970), 1088-89.

[2625]Renzi, M. "Ideal Family
Size as an Intervening Variable
Between Religion and Attitudes

Towards Abortion." *Journal for the
Scientific Study of Religion,* 14(1)
(1975), 23-27.

[2626]"Report of the Ad Hoc Committee on Abortion Guidelines."
Journal of the Kentucky Medical Association, 72 (January, 1974), 35-
36.

[2627]Requena, Mariano B. "Induced Abortion in Latin America."
Unpublished paper delivered at the
International Conference on Abortion,
Hot Springs, Virginia, November 17-
20, 1968.

[2628]Requena, Mariano B. "Social
and Economic Correlates of Induced
Abortion in Santiago, Chile." *Demography,* 2 (1965), 539.

[2629]Resnik, H. L., *et al.* "Abortion and Suicidal Behaviors: Observations on the Concept of 'Endangering the Mental Health of the Mother'." *Mental Hygiene,* 55 (January,
1971), 10-20.

[2630]"The Responsibilities of Research." *Tablet,* 224 (June 6,
1970), 537-38.

[2631]"Respect Life Week in U.S.A."
L'Osservatore Romano (English), 233
(no. 37) (September 14, 1972), 4.

[2632]"Restrictions in Missouri
Abortion Statute Upheld." *Journal
of the Mississippi State Medical
Association,* 16(12) (December, 1975),
382.

[2633]Reuter, C. "30 Ways to
Fight Abortion." *Our Sunday Visitor,*
63 (August 25, 1974), 1+.

[2634]"Reversal of Abortion Decisions Urgent Issue U.S. Bishops
Say After Series of Meetings." *Our
Sunday Visitor,* 64 (August 24, 1975),
1.

[2635]Rheingold, Joseph. "Some
Psychiatric Aspects of Induced Abortion." Unpublished manuscript from
the Harvard Divinity School—Kennedy Foundation International Conference on Abortion, 1967.

[2636]Rhodes, Philip. "Illegal
Abortion—A Gynaecologist's View."
Abortion in Britain (London: Pitman
Medical Publishing Company Ltd.,
1966).

[2637]Ribs, B. "Les Chretiens
Face a L'Avortement. *Etudes,* 339
(October, 1973), 405-23; (November,

1973), 571-83. Reply by F. Marty. 339, 579-70; rejoinder (November, 1973), 570.

[2638]Ribes, B. "Dossier sur L'Avortement, L'Apport de nos Lecteurs." *Etudes,* 338 (April, 1973), 511-34.

[2639]Rice, C. "Government and the Copulation Explosion." *Triumph,* 4 (March, 1969), 16-19.

[2640]Rice, C. "Overruling *Roe v. Wade* (93 Sup Ct 705): An Analysis of the Proposed Constitutional Amendments." *Boston College Industrial and Commercial Law Review,* 15 (December, 1973), 307-41.

[2641]Rice, E. "Dred Scott Case of the Twentieth Century." *Houston Law Review,* 10 (July, 1973), 1059-86.

[2642]Richard, E. F. "Abortion Act in Practice." *British Medical Journal,* 1 (March 22, 1969), 778.

[2643]Richardson, Herbert. "Abortion in Technological Perspective." Paper presented at the National Canadian Conference on Abortion, Toronto, Canada, May, 1972.

[2644]Richardson, Herbert. "What is the Value of Life?" *Updating Life and Death.* Ed. D. P. Cutler (Boston: Beacon Press, 1968).

[2645]Richardson, J. A., and Dixon, G. "Effects of Legal Termination on Subsequent Pregnancy." *British Medical Journal,* 1(6021) (1976), 1303-04.

[2646]Richardson, J. T., and Fox, S. W. "A Longitudinal Study of the Influence of Selected Variables on Legislator's Voting Behavior on Abortion Reform Legislation." *Journal for the Scientific Study of Religion,* 14(2) (1975), 159-64.

[2647]Richardson, J. T., and Fox, S. W. "Religious Affiliation as a Predictor of Voting Behavior in Abortion Reform Legislation." *Journal for the Scientific Study of Relition,* 11(4) (1972), 347-59.

[2648]Richardson, J.T., and Fox, S. W. "Religion and Voting on Abortion Reform: A Follow-Up Study." *Journal for the Scientific Study of Religion,* 14 (June, 1975), 159-64.

[2649]Richardson, P. A., *et al.* "Abortion and the Hospital." *New York Journal of Medicine,* 70 (August 15, 1970), 2144-45.

[2650]Riga, P. "Abortion." *Priest,* 27 (January, 1971), 24-31. Reply by P. Driscoll, 27 (May, 1971), 73-76.

[2651]Riga, P. "Let's Break the Law to Stop Abortions." *U.S. Catholic,* 40 (September, 1975), 13-14. [The author suggests that those who believe abortion on demand is wrong should stop paying their taxes.]

[2652]Riga, P. "*Roe vs. Wade*: the New Class Warfare." *Priest,* 29 (September, 1973), 13-16+.

[2653]Rigali, N. "Catholics and Liberalized Abortion Laws." *Catholic World,* 213 (September, 1971), 283-85. [The author contends that the problem of liberalized abortion laws cannot be dismissed by regarding Catholics as distinct from society. Catholics must be viewed in light of the insights that they as members of the society can bring to the question.]

[2654]Rigali, N. "Theologians and Abortion." *Priest,* 30 (June, 1974), 22-25.

[2655]"Right to Abortion: Expansion of the Right to Privacy Through the Fourteenth Amendment." *Catholic Lawyer,* 19 (Winter, 1973), 36-57.

[2656]"The Right of Equal Access to Abortions (United States)." *Iowa Law Review,* 56 (April, 1971), 1015-27.

[2657]"Right of a Husband or a Minor's Parent to Participate in the Abortion Decision." *University of Miami Law Review,* 28 (Fall, 1973), 251-56.

[2658]"The Right to Life." *Tablet,* 228 (April 13-20, 1974), 364.

[2659]"Right to Life: New Strategy Needed." *Triumph,* 7 (April, 1972), 46. [This article points out, to the anti-abortionists, the faulty assumption that once the unborn's humanity is shown then the American constitutional system's guarantee of the right to life will be invoked.

2660- The author states the case of
2680 Robert M. Byrn who managed to
get the New York State Court to
appoint him special guardian at
law of all unborn children whose
mothers were awaiting abortions
at New York City hospitals.
Byrn won an injunction against
the abortions on the grounds of
violating the Fourteenth Amendment. But the injunction was
appealed in higher court. The
court said there was no question
about the facts "the child begins a separate life from the
moment of conception." The argument of the court is over
"values", whether the state may
constitutionally allow the killing of that separate life.]

2660"Right to Privacy: Does
it Allow a Woman the Right to
Determine Whether to Bear Children?" *American University Law
Review,* 20 (August, 1970), 136.

2661"Rights of the Retarded."
Inquiry, 6(4) (August, 1976),
4, 30-33.

2662Ringrose, C. A. "Letter:
Therapeutic Abortion." *Canadian
Medical Association Journal,*
112(1) (January 11, 1975), 22,
25.

2663"The Risks of Abortion,"
editorial. *Canadian Medical Association Journal,* 106 (February
19, 1972), 295.

2664Rivet, M. "Le Dr. Morgentaler (*Sa Majeste la Reine
v. Henry Morgentaler.* Court
d'Appel. Dist. de Montreal, no.
10-000289 -73 [1973]) Devant la
Court d'Appeal." *Les Cahiers de
Droit,* 15 (1974), 889-96.

2665Rivet, M. "Quelques Reflexions sur le Droit a L'Avortement Dans le Monde Anglo-Saxon."
Les Cahiers de Droit, 13 (1972),
591-97.

2666Robb, D. F. "The Abortion Act 1967." *Practitioner,*
201 (1968), 694.

2667Robb, D. F. "Everyday
Problems in General Practice. X.
The Abortion Act, 1967." *Practitioner,* 201 (October, 1968),
694-700.

2668Roberts, B., *et al.* "Abortion and the Courts." *Environ-
mental Law,* 1 (Spring, 1971),
225-37.

2669Roberts, E., Jr. "Thoughts
After Viewing an Abortion." *Catholic Digest,* 36 (April, 1972), 6-8.
Cond. from: *National Observer* (December 18, 1971), 36.

2670Robertson, J. A. "Medical
Ethics in the Courtroom: the Role
of Law vs. Professional Self-Disci-
pline." *Hastings Center Report,* 4
(no. 4) (1974), 1-3.

2671Robinson, E. "Letter: Viability and Abortion." *American Journal of Obstetrics and Gynecology,*
118 (March 15, 1974), 882-84.

2672Robinson, H. A. "Implementing the Abortion Act." *British Medical Journal,* 2 (April 20, 1968), 173-
74.

2673Robinson, John Arthur Thomas.
"Abortion Beyond Law Reform." Lec-
ture delivered by the Bishop of
Woolwich on October 22, 1966 to a
meeting of the Abortion Law Reform
Association (London: Abortion Law
Reform Association, 1966).

2674Robinson, K. "The Law Relating to Abortion." *Proceedings of
the Royal Society of Medicine,* 55
(1962), 376.

2675Robinson, Martha, *et al.*
"Medical Coverage of Abortions in
New York City: Costs and Benefits
(Based on Conference Paper)," tables.
Family Planning Perspectives, 6
(Fall, 1974), 202-08.

2676Robinson, William J. *The
Law Against Abortion* (New York: Eugenics Publishing Company Inc.,
1933).

2677Rochat, R. W., *et al.* "An
Epidemiological Analysis of Abortion
in Georgia." *American Journal of
Public Health,* 61 (March, 1971),
543-52.

2678Roche, Anne. "On Killing In-
convenient People: If We Allow Abortion Now, Do We Allow Murder of
Living Persons Tomorrow? Before You
Decide, Listen to the Argument."
Saturday Night, 88 (September, 1973),
29-31.

2679Rock, John and Maillot,
Armand. "Abortion." *Gynecology and
Obstetrics,* 1 (Hagerstown, Maryland:
W. P. Prior Company, 1963).

2680"Rockefeller Vetoes Abortion

Repeal." *National Catholic Reporter,* 8 (May 26, 1972), 21.

[2681]Rodgers, T. F. "Attitudes Toward Abortion." *American Journal of Psychiatry,* 125 (1968), 804-08. [The author speculates about the future possibility of a deformed adult suing the state, or his doctor, because he has been allowed to be born with serious defects. The assumption is that the right to life means the right of the unborn without deformity.]

[2682]"*Roe v. Wade* (93 Sup Ct 705)—The Abortion Decision—An Analysis and its Implications." *San Diego Law Review,* 10 (June, 1973), 844-56.

[2683]"*Roe v. Wade* (93 Sup Ct 705) and *Doe v. Bolton* (93 Sup Ct 739): Compelling State Interest Test in Substantive Due Process." *Washington and Lee Law Review,* 30 (Fall, 1973), 628-46.

[2684]"*Roe v. Wade* (93 Sup Ct 705) and the Traditional Legal Standards Concerning Pregnancy." *Temple Law Quarterly,* 47 (Summer, 1974), 715-38.

[2685]"*Roe v. Wade* (93 Sup Ct 705): What Rights the Biological Father?" *Hastings Constitutional Law Quarterly,* 1 (Spring, 1974), 251-72.

[2686]Roemer, R. "Abortion Law: The Approaches of Different Nations." *American Journal of Public Health,* 57 (November, 1967), 1906-22 (71 ref.).

[2687]Roemer, R. "Abortion Law Reform and Repeal: Legislative and Judicial Developments." *American Journal of Public Health,* 61 (March, 1971), 500-09. Also: *Clinical Obstetrics and Gynecology,* 14 (December, 1971), 1165-80.

[2688]Roemer, R. "Editorial: The Right to Choose Abortion." *American Journal of Public Health,* 64 (August, 1974), 751 passim.

[2689]Rogers, A. F. C., and Lenthall, J. F. "Characteristics of New Zealand Women Seeking Abortion in Melbourne, Australia." *New Zealand Medical Journal,* 81 (536) (1975), 282-86.

[2690]Roghmann, K. J. "The Impact of the New York State Abortion Law on Black and White Fertility in Upstate New York." *International Journal of Epidemiology,* 4(1) (March, 1975), 45-49.

[2691]Roht, L. H., *et al.* "The Impact of Legal Abortion: Redefining the Maternal Mortality Rate." *Health Service Report,* 89 (May-June, 1974), 267-73.

[2692]"The Role of the Law of Homicide in Fetal Destruction." *Iowa Law Review,* 56 (February, 1971), 658-74.

[2693]"Roman Catholic Fertility and Family Planning: A Comparative Review of the Research Literature." *Studies in Family Planning,* 34 (October, 1968), 1-27.

[2694]Romanowski, R. "Abortion: A Fetal Viewpoint." *Linacre Quarterly,* 34 (August, 1967), 276-81. [The author examines some justifications for having abortions, which are considered false, on the grounds of the fetus' right to life.]

[2695]Romm, May E. "Psychoanalytic Considerations." Ed. Harold Rosen (Boston: Beacon Press, 1967).

[2696]Rongy, A. J. *Abortion: Legal and Illegal* (New York: Vanguard Press, 1933).

[2697]Rose, Barbara. "Behavior: The New York Abortion." *New York* (May 29, 1972), 72-73.

[2698]Roseborough, J. F. "Letter: Therapeutic Abortion." *Canadian Medical Association Journal,* 111(7) (October 5, 1974), 645.

[2699]Rosen, H. "Abortion." *Encyclopedia of Mental Health,* 1 (1963).

[2700]Rosen, H. "Abortion." *Today's Health* (Chicago: American Medical Association, April, 1965).

[2701]Rosen, H. "Abortion Anno Domini 1967: The Year of the State Abortion Bill." *Abortion in America.* Ed. Harold Rosen (Boston: Beacon Press, 1967).

[2702]Rosen, H. "Abortion in America." *American Journal of Psychiatry,* 126 (March, 1970), 1299-301.

[2703]Rosen, H. "Abortion: The Increasing Involvement of Psychiatry."

2704-
2722
*Frontiers of Clinical Psychia-
try,* 2 (December, 1965).

[2704]Rosen, H. "A Case
Study in Social Hypocrisy."
Abortion in America. Ed. Harold
Rosen (Boston: Beacon Press,
1967).

[2705]Rosen, H. "The Emotionally Sick Pregnant Patient: Psychiatric Indications and Contra-
Indications to the Interruption
of Pregnancy." *Abortion in
America* (Boston: Beacon Press,
1967).

[2707]Rosen, H. "Psychiatric
Implications of Abortion: A
Case Study of Social Hypocrisy."
Abortion and the Law. Ed.
David T. Smith (Cleveland: Western Reserve University Press,
1967). [The author attempts to
clarify the complexities sur-
rounding the actual fact of
abortion. He discusses the
medical, psychiatric and socioeconomic indications for abortion. He goes on to speak about
the situation of criminal abortion and discusses the merits of
four proposed alternatives to
remedy it (forced marriage,
adoption, foster home and orphan-
age care; liberalization of the
interpretation of existing statutes, the passage of more liberal laws—he favors the latter).
He ends with a comment on the
recommendations that certain
authoritative bodies have put
forth who have studied the problem.]

[2708]Rosen, Harold. *Therapeutic Abortion* (New York:
Julian Press Inc., 1954). (Now
known as *Abortion in America*
(Boston: Beacon Press, 1967).

[2709]Rosen, R. A. H. and
Martindale, Lois J. "Abortion
as 'Deviance': Traditional Female Roles vs. the Feminist Perspective." *ERIC* (1975), 21 p.

[2710]Rosen, R. A. H., Werley,
H. H., Ager, J. W., and Shea,
F. P. "Health Professionals.
Attitudes Toward Abortion."
Public Opinion Quarterly, 38(2)
(1974), 159-73.

[2711]Rosen, R. A. H., Werley,
H. H., Ager, J. W., and Shea,
F. P. "Some Organizational Cor-
relates of Nursing Students—
Attitudes Toward Abortion."
Nursing Research, 23(3) (1974),
253-59.

[2712]Rosenwaike, I., and Melton,
R. J. "Legal Abortion and Fertil-
ity in Maryland, 1960-1971."
Demography, 11(3) (1974), 377-96.

[2713]Rosner, F. "Abortion Law
Reform." *Journal of the American
Medical Association,* 216 (April 15,
1971), 147.

[2714]Rosoff, J. I. "Is Support
of Abortion Political Suicide?
(United States)," il., tables.
Family Planning Perspectives, 7
(January/February, 1975), 13-22.

[2715]Rosoff, J. I. "Pregnancy
Counseling and Abortion Referral
for Patients in Federally Funded
Family Planning Programs." *Family
Planning Perspectives,* 8(1)
(January-February, 1976), 43-46.

[2716]Rossi, Alice. "Abortion
Laws and Their Victims." *Transac-
tion,* 3 (September-October, 1966),
7-12. [Ms. Rossi discusses public
attitudes toward abortion and sex,
legal barriers, opposition to
change, legal and illegal abortions,
the right to be born, and alternatives for the unwed mother.]

[2717]Rossi, Alice. "Public
Views on Abortion." *The Case for
Legalized Abortion Now* (Berkeley:
The Diablo Press, 1967).

[2718]Rothstein, Atden. "Abortion: A Dyadic Perspective." *American Journal of Orthopsychiatry,* 47
(January, 1977), 1.

[2719]Routledge, J. H., Sparling,
D. W., and MacFarlane, K. T. "The
Present Status of Therapeutic
Abortion." *Obstetrics and Gynecol-
ogy,* 17 (February, 1971), 168-174.

[2720]Rovijsky, J. J. "Abortion
in New York City. Preliminary Experience with a Permissive Abortion
Statute." *Obstetrics and Gynecology,*
38 (September, 1971), 334-42.

[2721]Rovinsky, J. J. "Impact of
a Permissive Abortion Statute on
Community Health Care." *Obstetrics
and Gynecology,* 41 (May, 1973),
781-88.

[2722]Rovinsky, J. J., and Gubberg,
S. B. "Current Trends in Therapeu-
tic Termination of Pregnancy."
*American Journal of Obstetrics and
Gynecology,* 90 (1967), 11-17.

[2723]Roy, W. R. "Abortion: A Physician's View." *Washburn Law Journal,* 9 (Spring, 1970), 391.

[2724]"The Royal College of Psychiatrist's Memorandum on the Abortion Act in Practice." *British Journal of Psychiatry,* 120 (April, 1972), 449-51.

[2725]Royal Medico-Psychological Association. "Memorandum on Therapeutic Abortion, June, 1966." *Archives of General Psychiatry* (Chicago), 16 (January, 1967), 127-29.

[2726]"The Royal Medico-Psychological Association's Memorandum on Therapeutic Abortion." *British Journal of Psychiatry,* 112 (October, 1966), 1071-73.

[2727]Rozovsky, L. E. "Legal Abortions in Canada." *Canadian Hospitals,* 48 (February, 1971), 39-41.

[2728]Rozovsky, L. E. "Morgentaler vs. The Queen." *Dimensions Health Service,* 52(6) (June, 1975), 8-9.

[2729]"Rubella Vaccination and the Termination of Pregnancy." *British Medical Journal,* 4 (December 16, 1972), 666.

[2730]Rubin, E. R. "Abortion Cases: A Study in Law and Social Change." *North Carolina Central Law Journal,* 5 (Spring, 1974), 215-53.

[2731]Rudel, Harry W., *et al. Birth Control: Contraception & Abortion* (New York: MacMillan Publishing Company Inc., 1973).

[2732]Rudinow, Joel. "Further in the Modest Defence." *Analysis,* 35 (January, 1975), 91-92.

[2733]Rudinow, Joel. "On 'The Slippery Slope'." *Analysis,* 34 (April, 1974), 173-76. [The author criticizes an argument based on the continuity of the gestation process, which purports to show that the fetus is a bearer of rights from the moment of conception. The criticism is then located within a strategy for the defense of abortion.]

[2734]"Running Scared on Abortion." *New Statesman,* 90 (October 24, 1975), 489.

[2735]Rushton, D. I. "Effects of Legalising Abortions." *Lancet,* 1 (March 30, 1968), 692-93.

[2736]Rushton, D. I. "Effects of Legalising Abortions." *Lancet,* 1 (May 11, 1968), 1033-34.

[2737]Rusinow, Dennison. "Population Review 1970: Yugoslavia." Fieldstaff Reports: Southeast Europe Series v.17, no. 1. [There is a dependence on abortion as the principle means of family planning. In some areas, notable the Kosovo, there is an unsatisfactory high rate of natural increase of population.]

[2738]Russel, D. "Abortion Laws and the Physician. I." *New England Journal of Medicine,* 276 (May 4, 1967), 1027-28.

[2739]Russel, D. "Abortion Laws and the Physician. II." *New England Journal of Medicine,* 276 (June 1, 1967), 1250-51.

[2740]Russell, Keith. "Changing Indications for Therapeutic Abortion." *Journal of the American Medical Association,* 151 (January 10, 1953), 108.

[2741]Russell, Keith. "Current Comment—Therapeutic Abortions." *Western Journal of Surgical Obstetrics and Gynecology,* 60 (1950), 497.

[2742]Russell, Keith. "Therapeutic Abortions in California in 1950." *Western Journal of Surgery,* 60 (October, 1952), 497.

[2743]Russell, Keith. "Therapeutic Abortion in a General Hospital." *American Journal of Obstetrics and Gynecology,* 62 (August, 1951), 434.

[2744]Russell, Keith. "Therapeutic Abortions in California: First Year's Experience Under New Legislation." *American Journal of Obstetrics and Gynecology,* 105 (1969), 757-65.

[2745]Russell, Keith, and Moore, George F. "Maternal Medical Indications for Therapeutic Abortion." *Clinical Obstetrics and Gynecology,* 7 (March, 1964), 43.

[2746]Russell, C., and Russell, W. M. S. "Community and Personal Factors in Fertility Control: Socio-

2747-
2765

logical Factors." *Journal of Biosocial Science,* 1 (July, 1969), 289-296.

[2747]"Russell Shaw Criticizes New Media." *Our Sunday Visitor,* 63 (March 2, 1975), 1.

[2748]Rutledge, Al. "Is Abortion Black Genocide?" *Essence,* 4 (September, 1973), 36-37+.

[2749]Ruzicka, L. T. "Induced Abortions. Experience of South Australia 1970-1973." *The Australian Quarterly,* 47(3) (1975), 17-25.

[2750]Ryan, D., Abp. "Moral Ethics Seminar: Opening Address of Medical Ethics Seminar in Dublin." *L'Osservatore Romano* (English), 401 (no. 49) (December 4, 1975), 9.

[2751]Ryan, J. "Human Abortion Laws and the Health Needs of Society." *Abortion and the Law.* Ed. David T. Smith (Cleveland: Western Reserve University Press, 1967).

[2752]Ryan, K. J. "The Legitimacy of a Diverse Society." *Journal of the American Medical Association,* 233(7) (August 18, 1975), 781.

[2753]Ryberg, A. "Destroying the Foundations of Democracy." *Our Sunday Visitor,* 63 (November 10, 1974), 1+.

[2754]Ryberg, A. "A Victim's Testimony on Abortion." *Our Sunday Visitor,* 63 (September 1, 1974), 10.

[2755]Ryberg, A. "A Victim's Testimony on Abortion." *Our Sunday Visitor,* 63 (August 18, 1974), 16.

[2756]Ryder, J. "Give Me Your Tired, Your Poor, the Wretched Refuse of Your Teaming Shore." *Social Justice Review,* 67 (June, 1974), 82-83.

[2757]Ryder, J. "Suffer the Little Children..." *Social Justice Review,* 64 (July-August, 1971), 123-26.

[2758]Sabol, Blair. "Menstrual Extraction: The At Home Abortion." *Village Voice,* 17 (August 3, 1972), 11-12.

[2759]Sadoff, R. L., *et al.* "The Psychiatrist as Consultant for Therapeutic Abortion." *Pennsylvania Medicine,* 74 (May, 1971), 63-64.

[2760]St. John-Stevas, N. "Abortion, Catholics and the Law." *Catholic World,* 296 (January, 1968) 149-52.

[2761]St. John-Stevas, N. "Abortion: The Case for Supervision." *Tablet,* 223 (July 5, 1969), 662-64. [The author comments on the situation thirteen months after the British Abortion Act was passed. Even though St. John-Stevas is against most abortions, he understands that laws employing moral precepts are only enforceable if they are supported by a moral consensus in the community, and that consensus is closer to the middle of the road. Legal abortions increased since the Act; the demand for abortion is not from the married women but single women, and the Act has given rise to legalized abortion rackets within the law.
St. John-Stevas plans to introduce an amending Bill which would stop the racketeering, making it necessary to consult with a gynecologist from the National Health Service.]

[2762]St. John-Stevas, N. "Abortion and the Law: The English Experience." *Dublin Review,* 514 (Winter, 1967-1968), 274. [The legal development of abortion law in England from Lord Ellenborough's Act of 1803 to the Abortion Bill of 1966 is traced. He concludes that most people felt change in the law was desirable. Theology can still be an effective moderating force in society. Abortion on demand is dehumanizing.]

[2763]St. John-Stevas, N. "Abortion Laws." *Commonweal,* 85 (1966), 163.

[2764]St. John-Stevas, N. "A Challenge to Abortionists: The Liverpool Rally." *Tablet,* 226 (April 29, 1972), 394. [The author comments on the purpose of a rally held by the Mersey-side section of the Society for the Protection of Unborn Children. The purpose is an act of prophetic witness to remind people of the values which society is missing—such as the value of nascent life.]

[2765]St. John-Stevas, N. "The English Experience." *America,* 117

(December 9, 1967), 707.

2766 St. John-Stevas, N. "Experiments and the Unborn Child." *Tablet*, 226 (June 3, 1972), 514. [The author comments on the report by Sir John Peel, "The Use of Fetuses and Fetal Material for Research," H.M.S.O. 18½ p). The conflict of interest in this case is between the rights of the fetus and the demands of medical research.

The experiments are categorized into 4 areas: 1) experiments carried out in utero on the living fetus; 2) on fetuses that can survive independently of the mother; 3) fetuses who are pre-viable, that is, by the report's definition not yet 20 weeks old; 4) on dead fetuses.

St. John-Stevas makes an appeal for an amendment to the law and for the medical profession to accept a binding code of practice following the report's principal recommendations.]

2767 St. John-Stevas, N. "Law and the Sanctity of Life." *Dublin Review*, 508 (Summer, 1966), 99. Also in *Life or Death: Ethics and Options* (Seattle: University of Washington Press, 1968). [The author is convinced that law in the common law tradition is inseparable from morals. St. John-Stevas questions the concept of a right to life as expounded by the present moral consensus. The focus is on various questions; when does human life begin; how does the law view this life; also the question of illegal abortion, and the related questions of euthanasia and capital punishment.]

2768 St. John-Stevas, N. "Little Enlightenment from Lane; Lane Committee on the Working of the Abortion Act, Report 1974." *Tablet*, 228 (April 13-20, 1974), 362. [Three commendations are given: 1) abortion on demand is rejected and maintains the position on which the 1967 act is based; 2) a distinction is maintained between contraception and abortion; 3) stress is given to the need for adequate counseling for mothers faced with an abortion choice. But certain aspects of the abortion problem were neglected: 1) the suggestions were dismissed that a special panel of doctors and others should be appointed to authorize abortions; 2) an assertion is made that abortion is now a duty under the national health service.

St. John-Stevas urges that witness against abortion must be carried out and that a Catholic commission offer a critique of the Lane Report.

2769 St. John-Stevas, N. "The Muddled Issue of Abortion: Interview by H. Cargas." *National Catholic Reporter*, 9 (November 3, 1972), 7.

2770 St. John-Stevas, N. "Progress Against Abortion." *Tablet*, 225 (October 23, 1971), 1022. [The author describes the meeting of the Commission for Justice and Peace and the Laity Commission. The purpose was to seek means of countering the international campaign for easier abortion.

The first conclusion was that abortion should not be considered in the sphere of sexuality and family life but as a matter of human rights. Secondly, a need was expressed to have some central office to act as a clearing for information and to provide advice for those engaged in the abortion struggle.]

2771 St. John-Stevas, N. "Right to Life—The Abortion Dilemma." *Gonzaga Law Review*, 4 (Fall, 1968), 1.

2772 St. John-Stevas, N. *The Right to Life* (New York: Holt, Rinehart and Winston, 1964).

2773 St. John-Stevas, N. "The Rising Tide of Abortion." *Tablet*, 226 (February 5, 1972), 98. [This article is in response to the Lane Committee investigating the working of the British Abortion Act. The number of abortions increased drastically.

N. St. John-Stevas poses the question, "how, as Catholics opposed to abortion, does one bring influence to bear in a society which does not reject the practice as totally immoral?" He sees the solution in separating the prophetic and law-making functions. The work of Bishop Casey's Committee in responding to the Lane Committee is mentioned.]

2774 St. John-Stevas, N. "The Tragic Results of Abortion in England." *Linacre Quarterly*, 39 (February, 1972), 30-38. [The author views women's rights, population growth and contraception as invalid

2766-2774

arguments for legalized abortion. He articulates the principles of love and care.

[2775]Sainz, Santiago Gaslonde. "Abortion Research in Latin America," bibl., tables. *Studies in Family Planning,* 7 (August, 1976), 211-17.

[2776]Sala, S. L., and Salerno, E. "Psychological Factors in Obstetrics and Gynecology: Spontaneous Emotional Abortion." *Bol. Soc. Obstetrics and Gynecology of Buenos Aires,* 24 (July, 1945), 243-254.

[2777]Salman, D. H. "The Natural History of Abortion." National Canadian Conference on Abortion, Toronto, Canada, May, 1972.

[2778]Salmans, Sandra. "Abortion: The Campaign Issue No One Wants." *MS,* 4 (May, 1976), 76-77.

[2779]Saltman, Jules, and Zimering, Stanley. *Abortion Today* (Springfield, Ill.: Charles C. Thomas, Publishers, 1973).

[2780]Saltz, A. "Implementation of Therapeutic Abortion in the Kaiser Hospital-Southern California Permanente Medical Group." *Clinical Obstetrics and Gynecology,* 14 (December, 1971), 1230-36.

[2781]Samuels, A. "The Abortion Act 1967: The Legal Aspects." *Medicine, Science and the Law* (London), 9 (January, 1969), 3-10.

[2782]"The Sanctity of Human Life." *Tablet,* 224 (May 30, 1970), 514.

[2783]"The Sanctity of Life." *Central Africa Journal of Medicine,* 14 (August, 1968), 177.

[2724]Sanders, R. S., *et al.* "Counseling for Elective Abortion." *Journal of the American College of Health Association,* 21 (June, 1973), 446-50.

[2785]Sandosham, A. A. "Legal Abortion." *Medical Journal of Malaya,* 22 (March, 1968), 167-71.

[2786]Sandu, H. S., and Allen, D. E. "Family Planning in Rural India. Personal and Community

Factors." *Journal of Marriage and the Family,* 36(4) (1974), 805-13.

[2787]"Sane Lane." *Economist,* 251 (April 6, 1974), 24.

[2788]Sarvis, Betty, and Rodman, Hyman. *The Abortion Controversy.* 2nd edition (Irvington-on-Hudson, N.Y.: Columbia University Press, 1974).

[2789]Sauer, R. "Attitudes to Abortion in America, 1800-1973." *Population Studies,* 28(1) (1974), 53-67.

[2790]Save, Lewis E. "Adjudication of Therapeutic Abortion and Sterilization." *Clinical Obstetrics and Gynecology,* 7 (1964), 14.

[2791]Sawazaki, Chiaki, and Shinobu, Tanaka. "The Relationship Between Artificial Abortion and Extra-Uterine Pregnancy." *Harmful Effects of Induced Abortion* (Tokyo: Family Planning Federation of Japan, 1966).

[2792]Sayers, W. "Unwanted by Whom." *Family Digest,* 27 (August, 1972), 2-5.

[2793]"Says Support for Abortion Cuts Catholic From Church: A New Publication with Comments on the Document by the Congregation for the Doctrine of the Faith, November 18, 1974." *Our Sunday Visitor,* 64 (August 31, 1975), 2.

[2794]Scanzoni, John. "A Sociological Perspective on Abortion and Sterilization." *Birth Control and the Christian.* Ed. W. O. Spitzer and C. L. Saylor (Wheaton, Illinois: Tyndale House, 1969).

[2795]Scanlan, A. "Recent Developments in the Abortion Area." *Catholic Lawyer,* 21 (Fall, 1975), 315-21. [His remarks are divided into four parts: 1) recent abortion cases in the wake of *Roe v. Doe;* 2) the conscience clause as it affects religious related hospitals; 3) the contraction of the state or governmental action theory; 4) comments on pending proposals for a human life amendment to the Constitution.]

[2796]Schaffer, C., and Pine, F. "Pregnancy, Abortion and the Developmental Tasks of Adolescence." *Journal of the American Academy of Child Psychiatry,* 11(3) (1972), 511-36.

[2797]Schaffer, G. "Statistics on

Abortion in New York State from Questionnaire." *Clinical Obstetrics and Gynecology,* 14 (1971), 258-65.

[2798]Schaffer, Helen B. "Abortion in Law and Medicine." *Editorial Research Reports,* 11 Washington, D.C., October 6, 1965).

[2799]Schall, J. "The 'Conditional' Right to Life." *Furrow,* 26 (August, 1975), 455-61. [Schall asserts that life in all its human forms is sacred. If the worth of this human life becomes conditioned, then a new philosophy and practice is espoused which puts the right to life in human power. He gives various examples of how human life has already become relativized and conditioned.]

[2800]Schall, J. "The French Abortion Dossier." Commentary on, "Les Chretiens Face a L'Avortement," by B. Ribes, *Etudes* (October, 1973); *Furrow,* 24 (November, 1973), 647-53. [Schall discusses the dossier on the nature and practice of abortion. He notes that it is one of the first times that a favorable argument for abortion on a theoretical level was presented under private Catholic auspices.
The argument in the dossier is offered at two levels: 1) what should government do about the large scale practice of abortion?; 2) what is the reason why abortion can now be accepted by Catholics? The authors of the dossier say that abortion can be justified if the definition of human life be sufficiently restricted so that a living fetus does not have an irreducible claim to be born.]

[2801]Schaller, W. "Slavery and Abortion." *Catholic Digest,* 37 (December, 1972), 24-26. Cond. from a press release distributed by Minnesota Citizens Concerned for Life, August 18, 1972.

[2802]Scheiber, R. "Now I Understand Abortion." *Our Sunday Visitor,* 61 (July 16, 1972), 5.

[2803]Scheiber, R. "Why They Didn't Kill My Son." *Our Sunday Visitor,* 61 (February 11,

1973), 7.

[2804]Scheidler, J. "Wecular Press Snubs Abortion Death Report." *Our Sunday Visitor,* 64 (March 14, 1976), 1+.

[2805]Schenk, R. "Let's Think About Abortion." *Catholic World,* 207 (April, 1968), 15-17.

[2806]Schick, T. "A Matter of Life and Death." *St. Anthony Press,* 77 (August, 1969), 36-37.

[2807]Schlesinger, Benjamin. *Family Planning in Canada: A Source Book* (Toronto: University of Toronto Press, 1974).

[2808]Schmidt, Mary Saxon. *Abortion: A Selective Bibliography.* General Library Bureau, State ibrary of Pennsylvania, August, 1971.

[2809]Schmitz, J. G. "Abortionism: The Growing Cult of Baby Murder," il. *American Opinion,* 17 (March, 1974), 1-8.

[2810]Schneider, G. "Letter: Therapeutic Abortion." *Canadian Medical Association Journal,* 112 (9) (May 3, 1975), 1045.

[2811]Schneider, Ilene. "Abortion and Jewish Law." *Reconstructionist,* 40 (June, 1974), 26-30.

[2812]Schneider, S. M., *et al.* "Repeat Aborters." *American Journal of Obstetrics and Gynecology,* 126(3) (October 1, 1976), 316-20.

[2813]Schneiderman, L. F., Prichard, L., Fuller, S., and Atkinson, L. "Birth Control, Sterilization and Abortion. Attitudes of Catholic and Protestant Clergymen in San Diego Toward Use in Families with Genetic Illness." *Western Journal of Medicine,* 120 (2) (1974), 174-79.

[2814]Schulder, Diane, and Kennedy, Florynce. *Abortion Rap* (New York: McGraw-Hill Book Company, 1971).

[2815]Schulman, H. "A Critical Analysis of Induced Abortion." *Bulletin of the New York Academy of Medicine,* 49(8) (1973), 694-707.

[2816]Schulte, E. "Tax-Supported Abortions: The Legal Issues." *Catholic Lawyer,* 21 (Winter, 1975), 1-7.

[2817]Schur, Edwin M. "Abortion (Present Status: Trend Toward Liberalization of Abortion Laws: United States)." *Annals of the American Academy,* 376 (March, 1968), 136-47.

[2818]Schur, Edwin M. "Abortion and the Social System." *Social Problems,* 3 (1955), 94-99.

[2819]Schur, Edwin M. "Abortion and the Social System." *The Family and the Sexual Revolution.* Ed. Edwin M. Schur (Bloomington: Indiana University Press, 1964).

[2820]Schur, Edwin M. *Crimes Without Victims. Deviant Behavior and Public Policy: Abortion, Homosexuality, Drug Addiction* (Scarborough, Ont.: Prentice-Hall, Inc., 1965).

[2821]Schwartz, H. "The Parent or the Fetus? A Survey of Abortion Law Reform (United States)." *Humanist,* 27 (July/August, 1967), 123-26.

[2822]Schwartz, H. *Septic Abortion* (Philadelphia: J. B. Pippencott Company, 1968).

[2823]Schwartz, H. "Will Medicine be Strangled in Law?" *Journal of Family Practitioners,* 2(3) (June, 1975), 232.

[2824]Schwartz, R. A. "The Abortion Laws. A Severe Case of Resistance to Change." *Ohio State Medical Journal,* 67 (January, 1971), 33-38.

[2825]Schwartz, R. A. "Psychiatry and the Abortion Laws: An Overview." *Comparative Psychiatry,* 9 (March, 1968), 99-117. (66 ref.)

[2826]Schwartz, R. A. "The Social Effects of Legal Abortion." *American Journal of Public Health,* 2(10) (1972), 1331-35.

[2827]Sclare, A. B., *et al.* "Therapeutic Abortion: A Follow-Up Study." *Scottish Medical Journal,* 16 (October, 1971), 438-42.

[2828]Scott, Anne Frior. "Discussion Paper on Abortion." Paper presented to the National Conference on Abortion, Toronto, Canada, May, 1972.

[2829]Scott, G. A. D. "Abortion and the Incarnation." *Journal of the Evangelical and Theological Society,* 17 (Winter, 1974), 29-44.

[2830]Scott, J. S. "Implications of Abortion Law Reform." *Nursing Times,* 62 (November 11, 1966), 1478-80.

[2831]Scott, J. S. "Interpreting the Abortion Act." *Lancet,* 2 (September 27, 1969), 694.

[2832]Scott, L. "Possible Guidelines for Problem Pregnancy Counseling." *Pastoral Psychology,* 23 (May, 1972), 41-49. [Scott discusses the counseling aspects of the consultation process. Two goals are expected of a Problem Pregnancy Interview. First, the stage of decision-making process current at the time of the interview is assessed. Secondly, to facilitate further movement in the decision-making process through reflection and clarification of concerns of the counselee and provide information relevant to those concerns. Five typical stages in the decision-making process are presented.]

[2833]Scott, Michael J. *Abortion: The Facts* (London: Darton, Longman and Todd Limited, 1973).

[2834]"Scottish Abortion Statistics—1971." *Health Bulletin* (Edinborough), 31 (January, 1973), 39-50.

[2835]"Scottish Abortion Statistics 1974." *Health Bulletin* (Edinborough), 33(4) (July, 1975), 167-81.

[2836]"Scores Abortion Code." *National Catholic Reporter* 8 (August 18, 1972), 13.

[2837]Seager, C. P., *et al.* "Requests for Termination of Pregnancy in the East Midland Area—Sheffield Region." *Journal of the Royal College of General Practitioners,* 24 (142) (May, 1974), 320-28.

[2838]Sebai, Z. A. "Knowledge, Attitudes and Practice of Family Planning. Profile of a Bedouin Community in Saudi Arabia." *Journal of Biosocial Science,* 6(4) (1974), 453-62.

[2839]Secretaria Status (Papal). "Letter of Cardinal Jean Villot, Secretary of State, to the International Federation of Catholic

Medical Associations Concerning Abortion." December 22, 1970.

Secretaria Status Papal). "Pontifical Letter to the Congress of the International Federation of Catholic Medical Associations on Abortion and Euthanasia." October 3, 1970.

[2841]Seegar, J. K., Jr. "Report on Therapeutic Abortions for Fiscal 1971." *Maryland State Medical Journal,* 21 (February, 1972), 32-35.

[2842]Segers, M. "Abortion: The Last Resort." *America,* 133 (December 27, 1975), 456-58. Replies: 134 (February 21, 1976), 140-42; rejoinder (February 21, 1976), 143. [Mary Segers presents a personal position paper in which she tries to make sense of some of her conflicting intuitions and experiences of first, having her child, and then, visiting an abortion clinic.

Her writing is rather contradictory at various points especially as to the rights of the fetus but she discusses the rights of the father, the government, and the Catholic Church. Overall the article is inconsistent, nevertheless, Mary Segers has articulated the responses to pregnancy and abortion that many women feel.]

[2843]Seki, Sachiko. "How Japan's Housing Conditions Spawn Abortion." Unpublished paper presented at a meeting of the Catholic Population Research Association, Tokyo, April 25, 1964.

[2844]Select Committee on Abortion." *Lancet,* 2(7980) (August, 1976), 306, 7.

[2845]Selstad, G. M., Evans, J. R., and Welcher, W. H. "Predicting Contraceptive Use in Post-Abortion Patients." *American Journal of Public Health,* 65(7) (1975), 708-13.

[2846]Seltzer, A. L., et al. "Therapeutic Abortion: The Role of State Government. II." *Clinical Obstetrics and Gynecology,* 14 (December, 1971), 1208-11.

[2847]Selzer, R. "What I Saw at the Abortion." *Catholic Digest,* 40 (July, 1976), 47-50.

Cond. from: *Esquire,* 85 (January, 1976), 66.

[2848]"Semantics Can't Justify Abortion, Lutheran Says." *Our Sunday Visitor,* 64 (August 10, 1975), 2.

[2849]Sem-Jacobsen, C. W., et al. "The Ethics of Abortion." *American Journal of Psychiatry,* 127 (October, 1970), 536-38.

[2850]"Senate OKs Fetal Experiments Ban." *National Catholic Reporter,* 9 (September 28, 1973), 20.

[2851]"Senate Votes Against Even Considering Pro-Life Bills." *Our Sunday Visitor,* 65 (May 16, 1976), 2.

[2852]"Senator Kennedy Explains his Position on Abortion in Letter to Boston Paper." *Our Sunday Visitor,* 64 (August 31, 1975), 2.

[2853]Senay, E. C. "Therapeutic Abortion. Clinical Aspects." *Archives of General Psychiatry,* 23 (November, 1970), 408-15.

[2854]Sendor, Benjamin B. "Medical Responsibility for Fetal Survival Under *Roe* and *Doe* (Applies the Balance of Various Interests Struck by the Supreme Court to the Potential Criminal Liability of a Physician Performing an Abortion)." *Harvard Civil Rights—Civil Liberties Law Review,* 10 (Spring, 1975), 444-71.

[2855]Serb, A. "The Anti-Life Movement Cover-Up: Reformers Using Words as Weapons." *Our Sunday Visitor,* 64 (August 31, 1975), 1+.

[2856]Sereda, M. M. "Abortion: Where Is It At?" *Canadian Bar Journal,* 3 (1972), 12.

[2857]Sesboue, B. "Les Chretiens Devant L'Avortement: D'Apres le Temoignage des Peres de L'Eglise." *Etudes,* 339 (August-September, 1973), 263-82.

[2858]Shachtman, R. M., and Hogue, C. J. "Markov Chain, Model for Events Following Induced Abortion." *Operations Research,* 24(5) (1976), 916-32.

[2859]Snafer, R. "New Abortion Laws Won't Change Old Attitudes." *Modern Hospital,* 118 (February, 1972), 96-98.

[2860]Shaffer, T. L. "Abortion,

2861-
2885   the Law and Human Life." *Valparaiso University Law Review,*
2 (Fall, 1967), 94.

[2861]Shainess, N. "Abortion:
Inalienable Right." *New York
State Journal of Medicine,* 72
(July 1, 1972), 1772-75.

[2862]Shainess, N. "Abortion.
Social, Psychiatric and Psychoanalytic Aspects." *New York
Journal of Medicine,* 68 (1968),
3070-73.

[2863]Shainess, N. "Abortion
is No Man's Business." *Psychology Today,* 3 (1970), 18. [Vari-
ous problems created by the unwanted pregnancy are presented.
It is concluded that the unwanted child should not be born,
for it is the child who is the
real victim.]

[2864]Shanholtz, M. I. "The-
rapeutic Abortions in Virginia."
Virginia Medical Monthly, 99
(August, 1972), 876-78.

[2865]Shanklin, D. R. "Editorial: It is Time to Take a
Stand." *Journal of Reproductive
Medicine,* 14(2) (February, 1975),
41-42.

[2866]Shapiro, S. "Regulating
Abortions." *New England Journal
of Medicine,* 288 (May 10, 1973),
1027-28.

[2867]Sharkey, N. "Birth-
right New York." *Catholic Digest,* 36 (February, 1972), 100-
03.

[2868]Sharkey, N. "A New
Yorker Looks At Abortion," il.
St. Anthony's Messenger, 79
(February, 1972), 10-14.

[2869]Sharp, K. J. "Abor-
tion's Psychological Price."
Christian Times, 15 (June 4,
1971), 4-6.

[2870]Shaw, R. "Abortion and
the Courts." *Marriage and
Family Living,* 52 (April, 1970),
22-25.

[2871]Shaw, R. *Abortion and
Public Policy* (Washington, D.C.:
Family Life Bureau, National
Catholic Welfare Conference,
1966).

[2872]Shaw, R. *Abortion on
Trial* (Dayton, Ohio: Pflaum
Press, 1968).

[2873]Shaw, R. "Annual Battle
Over Abortion Laws Reaches Peak in
State Legislature." *National Catholic Reporter,* 5 (March 19, 1969),
1+.

[2874]Shaw, R. "Abortion Reform:
Good or Bad Genie?" *Columbia,* 48
(November, 1968), 20-22.

[2875]Shaw, R. "4 States Pass
Easier Abortion Laws. 20 Don't."
National Catholic Reporter, 5
(July 16, 1969), 3.

[2876]Shaw, R. "Will Congress
be Allowed to Dodge the Abortion
Issue?" *Columbia,* 55 (July, 1975),
38.

[2887]Shaw, R. "What Chance do
Pro-Life Amendments Have?" *Columbia,* 53 (October, 1973), 10.

[2888]Shea, P. E. "Letter: Inquiry into British Law on Abortion."
*Canadian Medical Association Jour-
nal,* 111(5) (September 7, 1974),
388.

[2879]Shea, P. E. "Letter: Abortion and the Pregnant Teenager."
*Canadian Medical Association Jour-
nal,* 110 (January 19, 1974), 143.

[2880]Sheerin, John B. "The
Abortion Controversy a Jolt to
Ecumenism." *Catholic World,* 205
(May, 1967), 68.

[2881]Shehan, L., O'Boyle, P.,
and Taggart, P. "Relaxation of
Maryland's Abortion Law Opposed by
Bishops." *Catholic Mind,* 66 (March,
1968), 1-3.

[2882]Shelton, J. D., Brann, E.
A., and Schultz, K. F. "Abortion
Utilization. Does Travel Distance
Matter?" *Family Planning Perspec-
tives,* 8(6) (1976), 260-62.

[2883]Sherain, Howard. "Beyond
Roe and *Doe:* The Rights of the
Father (Extent of the Biological
Father's Rights with Regard to the
Abortion Decision)." *Notre Dame
Lawyer,* 50 (February, 1975), 483-
95.

[2884]Sherman, F. "Supreme Court
Speaks on Abortion," editorial.
Dialog, 12 (Spring, 1973), 87-88.

[2885]Sherwin, L., *et al.* "Therapeutic Abortion. Attitudes and
Practices of California Physicians."
California Medicine, 105 (November,
1966), 337-39.

2886Shoemaker, Donald P. *Abortion, The Christian and the Bible* (Cincinnati, Ohio: Hiltz & Hayes, 1976).

2887Shoemaker, S. "Pro-Lifers Bring High Hopes, Food, to Washington March." *National Catholic Reporter*, 11 (January 31, 1975), 1-2.

2888Shopper, M. "Psychiatric and Legal Aspects of Statutory Rape, Pregnancy, and Abortion in Juveniles." *Journal of Psychiatry and the Law*, 1(3) (1973), 275-95.

2889Short, J. "The Pro-Life Agenda." *Triumph*, 9 (January, 1974), 17-19.

2890Shriver, E. "The Right to Be Born." *Marriage and Family Life*, 54 (June, 1972), 8-12.

2891Shriver, E. "Life: the Other Choice." *Our Sunday Visitor*, 61 (July 16, 1972), 6.

2892Shulman, J. J., *et al.* "Postpartum Contraception: Subsequent Pregnancy, Delivery, and Abortion Rates." *Fertility and Sterlity*, 27(1) (January, 1976), 97-103.

2893Siegel, I., and Kanter, A. E. "Therapeutic Abortion: A Five-Year Survey at Mt. Sinai Hospital." *Chicago Medical School Quarterly*, 21 (March, 1960).

2894Siegel, Seymour. "A Bias For Life." *Hastings Center Report*, 5 (June, 1975), 23-25. [The ethics of fetal research is dealt with, especially those fetuses which are previable both *in utero* and *ex utero*. The author opposes any procedure that is not directly beneficial to the fetus itself.

Informed consent is impossible for research of this sort, because the fetus cannot give it and the parents do not have the right to give consent for a life they are planning to terminate.]

2895Siener, C. H., *et al.* "Coordination of Outpatient Services for Patients Seeking Elective Abortion." *Clinical Obstetrics and Gynecology*, 14 (March, 1971), 48-59.

2896Sigworth, H. "Abortion Laws in the Federal Courts—the Supreme Court as Supreme Platonic Guardian." *Indiana Legal Forum*, 5 (Fall, 1971), 130.

2897Silverstein, E. "From Comstockery Through Population Control: The Inevitability of Balancing." *North Carolina Central Law Journal*, 6 (Fall, 1974), 8-47.

2898Sim, Myre. "Abortion and the Psychiatrist." *British Medical Journal*, 2 (July 20, 1963), 145.

2899Sim, Myre. "Advice on Abortion." *Lancet*, 2 (November, 1968), 1138.

2900Sim, Myre. "G.M.C. and Abortion Act, 1967." *British Medical Journal*, 2 (May 4, 1968), 298.

2901Sim, Myre. "Psychiatric Sequelae of Termination of Pregnancy." *British Medical Journal*, 1 (1967), 563-64.

2902Simanski, R. "Dr. Andre Hellegers: in the Year 2000 Abortion will be Considered Backward." *National Catholic Reporter*, 8 (October 5, 1972), 5-6.

2903Simon, N. M., *et al.* "Psychological Factors Related to Spontaneous and Therapeutic Abortion." *American Journal of Obstetrics and Gynecology*, 104 (July 15, 1969), 799-808.

2904Simon, N. M., and Senturia, A. G. "Psychiatric Sequelae of Abortion. Review of the Literature." *Archives of General Psychiatry*, 15 (1966), 378-89.

2905Simmons, N. A. "Letter: Termination of Pregnancy." *Lancet*, 2(7928) (August 9, 1975), 281.

2906Simms, M. "Abortion." *Twentieth Century Magazine*, 175 (no. 1032) (1967), 4-8.

2907Simms, M. "The Abortion Act—One Year Later." *British Journal of Criminology*, 9 (July, 1969), 282.

2908Simms, M. "The Abortion Act After Three Years." *Political Quarterly*, 42 (July/September, 1971), 269-81.

2909Simms, M. "Abortion Act: What Has Changed? J. M. Finnis,

2910-
2936

A Reply." *Criminal Law Review,* 1971 (January-February, 1971), 3.

[2910]Simms, M. "Abortion and the Facts." *World Medicine,* 6 (January 27, 1971), 51.

[2911]Simms, M. "Abortion Law and Medical Freedom." *The British Journal of Criminology.* 14 (2) (1974), 118-31.

[2912]Simms, M. "Abortion Law Reform: How the Controversy Changed." *Criminal Law Review,* 1970 (October, 1970), 567.

[2913]Simms, M. "Abortion—A Note on Some Recent Developments in Britain." *The British Journal of Criminology,* 4 (July, 1964), 491.

[2914]Simms, M. "Abortion Since 1967." *New Humanist,* 91 (February, 1976), 269-71.

[2915]Simms, M. "The Ethical Foundations of Psychiatric Opinion in Abortion." *Medical Gynaecology and Sociology,* 2(6) (1967), 10.

[2916]Simms, M. "Family Planning and Abortion." *Lancet,* 2 (November 18, 1972), 1085.

[2917]Simms, M. "How Do We Judge The Abortion Act? Reflections on the Lane Committee and the 1967 Abortion Act." *Public Health,* 87(5) (July, 1973), 155-64.

[2918]Simms, M. "Letter: More Abortions?" *British Medical Journal,* 1 (5949) (January 11, 1975), 95.

[2919]Simms, M. "Letter: The White Bill on Abortion." *Lancet,* 1(7905) (March 1, 1975), 523-24.

[2920]Simms, M. "U.S. Supreme Court on Abortion." *Lancet,* 1 (March 10, 1973), 544.

[2921]Simms, M. "U.S. Supreme Court on Abortion." *Lancet,* 1 (March 31, 1973), 721.

[2922]Simms, M. and Hindell, K. *Abortion Law Reformed* (London: Peter Owen Press, 1971.

[2923]Simms, M. and Hindell, K. "How the Abortion Lobby Worked." *Political Quarterly,* 39 (July-September, 1968), 269-82.

[2924]Simon, Alexander. "Psychiatric Indications for Therapeutic Abortion and Sterilization." *Clinical Obstetrics and Gynecology,* 7 (March, 1964), 67.

[2925]Simon, N. M. "Psychiatric Illness Following Therapeutic Abortion." *American Journal of Psychiatry,* 124 (1967), 59-65.

[2926]Simon, N., *et al.* "Psychiatric Sequelae of Abortion." *Archives of General Psychiatry,* 15 (October, 1966), 378.

[2927]Simons, J. H. "Statistical Analysis, 1,000 Abortions." *American Journal of Obstetrics and Gynecology,* 37 (1939), 840.

[2928]Simonsz, C. G. "Psychiatric Indications for the Termination of Pregnancy." *South African Medical Journal,* 42 (1968), 710-14.

[2929]Simpson, J. "Psychiatric Indications for the Termination of Pregnancy." *Medical Journal of Australia,* 1 (February 20, 1971), 449-50.

[2930]Simpson, Keith. "Abortion Risks." *Abortion in Britain.* (London: Pitman Medical Publishing Company, Ltd., 1966).

[2931]Singer, A., *et al.* "Letter: Induction of Labour and Perinatal Mortality." *British Medical Journal,* 2(5961) (April 5, 1975), 35.

[2932]Singer, K. "Psychiatric Aspects of Abortion in Hong Kong." *The International Journal of Social Psychiatry,* 21(4) (1975), 303-06.

[2933]Sipes, Lynda M. "Abortions: Report for Calendar Year 1975." Washington (State) Department of Social and Health Services, Special Services Sect., P.O. Box 709, Public Health Building, Olympia, WA 98507 (May, 1976).

[2934]Sisler, G. C. "The Psychiatrist and Therapeutic Abortion." *Canadian Psychiatric Association Journal,* 16 (June, 1971), 275-77.

[2935]Skalts, Vera and Norgaard, Magna. "Abortion Legislation in Denmark." *Abortion in Britain* (London: Pitman Medical Publishing Company, Ltd., 1966).

[2936]Sklar, J. "Abortion, Illegitimacy, and the American Birth Rate." *Science,* 185(4155) (1974), 909-15.

2937Sklar, J. and Berkov, B. "The Effects of Legal Abortion on Legitimate and Illegitimate Birth Rates: The California Experience." *Studies in Family Planning,* 4 (November, 1973), 281-92.

2938Skowronski, Marjory. *Abortion and Alternatives* (Millbrae, California: Les Femmes Pub., 1977).

2939Slesinski, R. "Created in the Image of God: Man and Abortion." *Linacre Quarterly,* 43 (February, 1976), 36-48. [The author explores the biblical doctrine of man as created in the image (imageo Dei) and likeness of God (similitudo Dei) as a point of departure for evaluating and synthesizing various moral positions regarding abortion.]

2940Sloane, R. Bruce, ed. *Abortion: Changing Views and Practice* (New York: Grune and Stratton, 1971).

2941Sloane, R. Bruce. "The Unwanted Pregnancy." *New England Journal of Medicine,* 280 (May 29, 1969), 1206-13. (40 ref.)

2942Sloane, R. Bruce and Harvitz, Diana F. *A General Guide to Abortion* (Chicago, Ill.: Nelson-Hall, 1973).

2943Sloane Hospital for Women, Transactions of Annual Meeting of Alumni. "Symposium on 'The Social Problem of Abortion'." *Bulletin of the Sloane Hospital for Women,* 11 (Fall, 1965).

2944Sluglett, J. "Abortion, A General Practitioner's Point of View." *Journal of College General Practitioners,* 13 (n.d.) 263.

2945Author unknown."A Smell of Burning." *Lancet,* 1(7911) (April 12, 1975), 844-45.

2946Smibert, J. "Abortion in Victoria After Menhennit." *Medical Journal of Australia,* 1 (May 19, 1973), 1016-17.

2947Smiley, C. W. "Sterilization and Therapeutic Abortion Counseling for the Mentally Retarded." *Current Therapeutic*

Research (N.Y.), 15 (February, 1973), 78-81. Also: *International Journal of Nursing Studies,* 10(2) (1973), 137-41; *Canadian Psychiatric Association Journal,* 19(1) (1974), 65-68; *Illinois Medical Journal,* 147(3) (1975), 291-92.

2948Smith, D. F. "Therapeutic Abortion—Should the Law be Changed?" *Nova Scotia Medical Bulletin,* 46 (June, 1967), 118-20.

2949Smith, E. "The Abortion Controversy." *Journal of the National Medical Association,* 62 (September, 1970), 379.

2950Smith, E., *et al.* "Social Aspects of Abortion Counseling for Patients Undergoing Elective Abortion." *Clinical Obstetrics and Gynecology,* 14 (March, 1971), 204-14.

2951Smith, E. "Counseling for Women who Need Abortion." *Social Work,* 17(2) (1972), 62-68.

2952Smith, E. "A Follow-Up Study of Women who Request Abortion." *American Journal of Orthopsychiatry,* 43(4) (1973), 574-85.

2953Smith, H. L. "Abortion and the Right to Life." *Ethics and the New Medicine* (Nashville, New York: Abingdon Press, 1970), 17-54.

2954Smith, J. C. "The Complexity of Compiling Abortion Statistics." *Public Health Reports,* 90 (6) (1975), 502-03.

2955Smith, K. A. and Johnson, R. L. "Medical Opinion on Abortion in Jamaica. A National Delphi Survey of Physicians, Nurses, and Midwives." *Studies in Family Planning,* 7 (12) (1976), 334-39.

2956Smith, K. D. and Wineberg, H. S. "A Survey of Therapeutic Abortion Committees." *Criminal Law Quarterly,* 12 (1970), 279.

2957Smith, Lorenne M. G. "Material for Abortion Conference." Paper presented to the National Canadian Conference on Abortion, Toronto, Canada, May, 1972.

2958Smith, R. G., *et al.* "Abortion in Hawaii: The First 124 Days." *American Journal of Public Health,* 61 (March, 1971), 530-42.

2959Smith, R. G., *et al.* "Physicians' Attitudes on the Abortion

2960-
2984

Law. Report of Survey, 1969."
Hawaii Medical Journal, 29
(January-February, 1970), 209-
11.

2960 Smith, R. N. "A Time
to Speak Out." *Journal of the
Oklahoma Medical Association,*
61 (April, 1968), 139-40.

2961 Smithurst, B. A. "The
Abortion Act, 1967, of the
United Kingdom——An Unsatisfac-
tory Law." *Medical Journal of
Australia,* 2 (October 25, 1969),
863-65.

2962 Snegroff, S. "The Development of Instruments to
Measure Attitudes Toward Abortion and Knowledge of Abortion."
The Journal of School Health,
46(5) (1976), 273-77.

2963 Snortland, Neil. "Abortion Laws: A Commentary." *Your
Government* (Kan), 25 (March 15,
1970), 3-4.

2964 Snyder, E. L. "Letter:
Incidence of Unwanted Pregnancy
in Australia." *Medical Journal
of Australia,* 2(6) (August 9,
1975), 233-34.

2965 Snyder, R. "Roselia:
Alternative to Abortion." *Catholic Forum,* 55 (April, 1971),
20-22.

2966 Sobrera, A. J. and
Lewit, S. *Advances in Planned
Parenthood* (Cambridge: Schenk-
mann, 1965).

2967 Social Effects of Abortion." *New England Journal of
Medicine,* 292(9) (February 27,
1975), 484-86.

2968 "Some Abortions May Lead
to Murder Charges." *National
Catholic Reporter,* 9 (April 3,
1973), 3.

2969 "Some Genetic Aspects of
Therapeutic Abortion." *Perspectives in Biology and Medicine,*
11 (Autumn, 1967), 129-35.

2970 Somers, R. L. and Gam-
meltoft, M. "The Impact of
Liberalized Abortion Legislation
on Contraceptive Practice in
Denmark." *Studies in Family
Planning,* 7(8) (1976), 218-23.

2971 Solomon, K. "Letter:
Random Thoughts on Abortion Attitudes." *American Journal of*

Public Health, 66(9) (September,
1976), 905-06.

2972 Soltau, D. H., *et al.*
"Abortions and Gynaecological Prac-
tice." *British Medical Journal,* 1
(February 22, 1969), 506-07.

2973 Soni, K., Velandkar, S.,
Kapoor, I., and Arvindakshan, S. T.
K. "Characteristics of Women Seeking Medical Termination of Pregnancy." *Journal of Family Welfare,*
22(3) (1976), 51-61.

2974 Sonsmith, M. "Rape and
Abortion: Is the Argument Valid?"
Liguorian, 64 (June, 1976), 45-47.

2975 Sorrell, W. E. "Abortion.
Its Psychodynamic Effects." *Psychosomatics,* 8 (1967), 146-49.

2976 South Africa Commission of
Inquiry into the Abortion and
Sterilization Bill. Report 1974.
South Africa, Government Printer,
Bosman St., Pretoria, South Africa.

2977 Southard, Helen F. "Abortion——Current Concern and Action."
Y.W.C.A. Monthly, 63 (May, 1969),
24-26.

2978 South Carolina——Act to Provide for Legal Abortions Under Certain Conditions. (No. 1215, Acts,
1974).

2979 "South Dakota's Abortion
Experience: Constitutional Right or
Unfulfilled Promise?" *South Dakota
Law Review,* 20 (Winter, 1975), 205-
26.

2980 Southgate, M. T. "Troubled
Waters." *Journal of the American
Medical Association,* 213 (August
17, 1970), 1182-83.

2981 Southwick, Thomas P. "Compromise Reached on Use of Federal
Funds for Abortions." *Congress
Quarterly Weekly Report,* 34 (September 18, 1976), 2541.

2982 Speaker, F. "Legal Counsel
Analyzes Abortion Ruling." *Pennsylvania Medicine,* 76 (April, 1973),
21-22.

2983 Spencer, Hope. "Abortion
Clinics: An Evaluation." *New York*
(July 24, 1972), 31-36.

2984 Spencer, Hope. "The City
Politic: The Case of the Missing
Abortion Lobbyists." *New York*
(May 29, 1972), 8-9.

²⁹⁸⁵Spiazzi, R. "The Problem of Abortion," il. *L'Osservatore Romano* (English), 391 (no. 39) (September 25, 1975), 9-10.

²⁹⁸⁶Spitzer, W. O. and Saylor, C. L., eds. *Birth Control and the Christian* (Wheaton, Illinois: Tyndale House, 1969).

²⁹⁸⁷Spivak, M. "Therapeutic Abortion. A 12 Year Review at the Toronto General Hospital, 1954-1965." *American Journal of Obstetrics and Gynecology,* 97(3) (1967), 316-23.

²⁹⁸⁸"Spontaneous and Induced Abortion. Report of a WHO Scientific Group." *World Health Organization Technical Report Series,* 461 (1970), 3-51.

²⁹⁸⁹*Spontaneous Abortion.* Ed. David N. Danforth (New York: P. B. Hoeber Publishing Co., Ltd., 1959).

²⁹⁹⁰Springer, R. H. "Notes on Moral Theology; July-December, 1966: Abortion and the Law (Bibliog. essay)." *Theological Studies,* 28 (June, 1967), 330-35.

²⁹⁹¹Springer, R. H. "Notes on Moral Theology; July, 1969-March, 1970." *Theological Studies,* 31 (September, 1970), 476-511.

²⁹⁹²Springer, R. H. "Notes on Moral Theology; September, 1970-March, 1971: Abortion." *Theological Studies,* 32 (September, 1971), 483-87.

²⁹⁹³Spry, William B. "Abortion and the Psychiatrist." *British Medical Journal,* 2 (August 10, 1963).

²⁹⁹⁴Stack, J. M. "Abortion Law Reform Progress in Michigan." *Michigan Medicine,* 69 (January, 1970), 23-27.

²⁹⁵⁵"Stage of Pregnancy is Key to Public Approval of Abortion," tables. *Gallup Opinion Index* (July, 1975), 11-13.

²⁹⁹⁶Stallworthy, J. "The Right to Live." *Journal of the Royal College of General Practitioners,* 19 (April, 1970), 187-90.

²⁹⁹⁷Stallworthy, J. "Therapeutic Abortion." *Practitioner,* 204 (March, 1970), 393-400.

²⁹⁹⁸Stampar, Dubravka. "Croatia: Outcome of Pregnancy in Women Whose Requests for Legal Abortion Have Been Denied." *Studies in Family Planning,* 4 (October, 1973), 267-69.

²⁹⁹⁹Stanfield, C. "Colorado's Abortion Law. A Psychiatrist's View of its Operation." *Nebraska Medical Journal,* 54 (November, 1969), 745-47.

³⁰⁰⁰"State Limitations Upon the Availability and Accessibility of Abortions After *Wade* and *Bolton.*" *Kansas Law Review,* 25 (Fall, 1976), 87-107.

³⁰⁰¹"A Statement on Abortion." *Catholic Lawyer,* 15 (Summer, 1969), 259-64.

³⁰⁰²"A Statement on Abortion by One Hundred Professors of Obstetrics." *American Journal of Obstetrics and Gynecology,* 112 (April 1, 1972), 992-98.

³⁰⁰³"A Statement on Abortion in Victoria." *Medical Journal of Australia,* 1 (February 26, 1972), 443.

³⁰⁰⁴"Statement on Abortion: Plenary Assembly." *L'Osservatore Romano* (English), 135 (no. 44) (October 29, 1970), 5.

³⁰⁰⁵"Statement from the Bishops of the Netherlands on Abortion." *L'Osservatore Romano* (English), 346 (no. 46) (November 14, 1974), 14-15.

³⁰⁰⁶"Statement of the Catholic Bishops of Canada on Abortion." *Nova Scotia Medical Bulletin,* 47 (October, 1968), 185-87.

³⁰⁰⁷"Statement on Implementation of the New York State Abortion Law by the Committee on Public Health of the New York Academy of Medicine." *Bulletin of the New York Academy of Medicine,* 46 (September, 1970), 674-75.

³⁰⁰⁸"Statement of National Conference on Catholic Bishops: Pastoral Message." *Catholic Lawyer,* 19 (Winter, 1973), 29-35.

³⁰⁰⁹"Statement of the Roman Catholic Bishops of Illinois About Abortion." Illinois Catholic Conference, March 20, 1969.

[3010]"State Protection of the Viable Unborn Child After *Roe v. Wade:* How Little, How Late?" *Iowa Law Review,* 37 (Fall, 1976), 270-82.

[3011]Stapleton, J. G. "Therapeutic Abortion in a Canadian City." *Canadian Medical Association Journal,* 104 (January 9, 1971), 70.

[3012]Steel, David. "The Act 4 Years After (Operation of the Abortion Act, 1967; Great Britain," il. *Mental Health* (Summer, 1971), 6-9.

[3013]Steel, S. "Family Planning Advice After Abortion." *Lancet,* 2(7466) (1966), 742-43.

[3014]Steele, Joanne. "Pickles, Dentists, Old-Timers and the Right-to-Life (Stamford, CT Right-to-Life Day)." *Majority Report,* 5 (February 7-21, 1976), 1.

[3015]Steinfels, P. "The Unclear Voice Against Abortion." *National Catholic Reporter,* 7 (May 14, 1971), 12.

[3016]Steinhoff, Patricia G. and Diamond, Milton G. *Abortion Politics: The Hawaii Experience* (Honolulu: University Press of Hawaii, June, 1977).

[3017]Steinman, T. I. "Abortion: Pro and Con." *New England Journal of Medicine,* 284 (April 1, 1971), 728-29.

[3018]Stencel, Sandra. "Abortion Politics," bibl., map. *Editorial Research Reports* (October 22, 1976), 767-84.

[3019]Stenchever, M. A. "An Abuse of Pre-Natal Diagnosis." *Journal of the American Medical Association,* 221 (July 24, 1972), 408.

[3020]Stephens, R. D. "Abortion: Some Considerations." *CRUX,* vol. 4 (no. 4) (1974-1975), 2-6.

[3021]Stephenson, B. "Abortion: An Open Letter." *Canadian Medical Association Journal,* 112(4) (February 22, 1975), 492, 494, 497.

[3022]Stern, S. "Abortion: Reform and the Law." *Journal of Criminal Law, Criminology, and Police Science,* 59 (March, 1968), 84.

[3023]Stern, S. G. "The Issue of Legalized Abortion." *Canadian Medical Association Journal,* 88 (1963), 899.

[3024]Stevenson, L. B. "Maternal Death and Abortion. Michigan, 1955-1964." *Michigan Medicine,* 66 (March, 1967), 287-91.

[3025]Stewart, A. B. "Abortion and the Health Services—The Local Authority." *Abortion in Britain* (London: Pitman Medical Publishing Company, Ltd., 1966).

[3026]Stewart, G. K., *et al.* "Therapeutic Abortion in California. Effects of Septic Abortion and Maternal Mortality." *Obstetrics and Gynecology,* 37 (April, 1971), 510-14.

[3027]Still, J. W. "The Three Levels of Human Life and Death, the Presumed Location of the Soul, and Some of the Implications for the Social Problems of Abortion, Birth Control and Euthanasia." *Medical Annals of the District of Columbia,* 37 (June, 1968), 316-18.

[3028]Stith, R. "A Secular Case Against Abortion on Demand." *Commonweal,* (November 12, 1971), 151-54. Reply: Ducore, J. 95 (February 18, 1972) 468-69; rejoinder 95 (February 18, 1972), 469-70. [Richard Stith believes that the issue of "abortion on demand" is still worth debating. In the issue, what is publicly at stake is respect for human life and for their fellow citizens. The fetus is considered as a public value, primarily as organized and growing human life, and to destroy it would require public justification. He points to an underlying assumption of those who support "abortion on demand": dependency entails control. We have assumed that we have the right to control those who are dependent upon us. Stith urges not control, but care. The issue is not abortion, but pregnancy—that which has promise.]

[3029]Stith, R. "The World As Reality, As Resource, and As Pretense." *American Journal of Jurisprudence,* 20 (1975), 141-53.

[3030]"Stoking Hell's Fire." *Economist,* 257 (December 20, 1975), 40.

[3031]Stone, M. L., *et al.* "3. The Impact of a Liberalized Abortion Law on the Medical Schools."

American Journal of Obstetrics and Gynecology, 111 (November 1, 1971), 728-35. [The authors examine cost, facilities, and complications after eight months of operation. They conclude that it is safer and less costly to the women, hospital, and community to attempt to prevent pregnancy.]

[3032]Storer, Horatio R. Criminal Abortion in America (Philadelphia: J. B. Lippincott and Co., 1966).

[3033]Storer, Horatio R. and Heard, Franklin F. Criminal Abortion (Sex, Marriage and Society) (New York: Arno Press, 1974).

[3034]Stott, D. H. "Physical and Mental Handicaps Following A Disturbed Pregnancy." Lancet, 1 (May 18, 1957), 1006.

[3035]Stout, Alan Ker. Abortion Law Reform (Melbourne: Victorian Council for Civil Liberties, 1968).

[3036]Stratton, R. "State Legislation Can Lessen Impact of Court's Abortion Decision." Hospital Progress, 54 (October, 1973), 8-9+.

[3037]Strauss, S. A. "Therapeutic Abortion and South African Law." South African Medical Journal, 42 (July 20, 1968), 710-14.

[3038]Strauss, S. A. "Therapeutic Abortion: Two Important Judicial Pronouncements." South African Medical Journal, 46 (March 11, 1972), 275-79.

[3039]Streeter, G. L. "Embryological Defects and Their Relation to Spontaneous Abortion." The Abortion Problem. National Committee on Maternal Health, Inc. Ed. H. C. Taylor (New York: The Silliams and Wilkins Co., 1944).

[3040]Stubblefield, P. G. "Abortion vs. Manslaughter." Archives of Surgery, 110(7) (July, 1975), 790-91.

[3041]Studdiford, William C. "Common Medical Indications for Therapeutic Abortion." Bulletin of the New York Academy of Medicine, 26 (November, 1950), 721.

[3042]"Study Calls D & E Best Midtrimester Abortion." Medical World News, 18 (January 10, 1977), 71.

[3043]"Struggle Renewed." Economist, 223 (May 27, 1967), 892.

[3044]Sturgis, S. H. "Editorial: Allan Guttmacher, M.D.—A Life Fulfilled." New England Journal of Medicine, 290 (May 9, 1974), 1085.

[3045]Su, I. H. and Chow, L. P. "Induced Abortion and Contraceptive Practice. An Experience in Taiwan." Studies in Family Planning, 7(8) (1976), 224-30.

[3046]Such-Baer, M. "Professional Staff Reaction to Abortion Work." Social Casework, 55(7) (1974), 435-41.

[3047]Sullivan, D. "The Abortion: England." Tablet, 230 (July 24, 1976), 710-11. [The author presents two reasons why the moral arguments supporting the traditional teaching have been undermined. First, at times the Church seems to be speaking at the level of abstraction and not at the lived reality of the situation. Secondly, the Church did not set up an effective system to help people socially and morally, which would help remove the need for abortion. Sullivan points to a distinction made by some priests between moral theology and pastoral theology. In pastoral teaching, the Church must elaborate a hierarchy of values (for example, contraception or abortion as a means of birth control).]

[3048]Sullivan, J. M., Su, K. H., and Lio, T. H. "The Influence of Induced Abortion on Taiwanese Fertility." Studies in Family Planning, 7(8) (1975), 231.

[3049]Sullivan, P. R. "The Role of Human Conscience in Therapeutic Abortion." American Journal of Psychiatry, 127 (August, 1970), 250.

[3050]Sumner, L. W. "The Mortality of Abortion." Paper presented to the National Canadian Conference on Abortion, Toronto, Canada, May, 1972.

[3051]Sumner, L. W. "Toward a Credible View of Abortion." Canadian Journal of Philosophy, 4 (September, 1974), 163-81. [The author describes two views (privacy and homicide arguments) which he sees as dominating the debate on the morality of abortion. He offers reasons for rejecting both views.

3052-
3076

In their place another position is offered. This is a developmental account of the moral status of abortion, which allows a reasonable compromise between a woman's need for an abortion and the protection of fetal life.]

[3052]"Supreme Court to Consider Woman's Right to Abortion." *Hospital Progress,* 53 (March, 1972), 10-11+.

[3053]"Supreme Court to Hear Abortion Cases in 1977." *Our Sunday Visitor,* 65 (July 25, 1976), 2.

[3054]"Supreme Court: Right of Privacy Includes Abortion: Excerpts from Abortion Decision." *National Catholic Reporter,* 9 (February 2, 1973), 8+.

[3055]"Supreme Court Takes Up Abortion." *National Catholic Reporter,* 6 (May 8, 1970), 10.

[3056]Surawicz, F. G. "Therapeutic Abortion: Middle-Class Privileges or Curse?" *Journal of the American Medical Women's Association,* 27 (November, 1972), 590-97.

[3057]"Survey of Abortion Reform Legislation." *Washington Law Review,* 43 (March, 1968), 644.

[3058]"Survey on the Mortality of Abortion." Unpublished. Nogoya: Koseki Eugenics Protection Consultation Center, 1964.

[3059]"Survey of the Present Statutory and Case Law on Abortion: The Contradictions and the Problems." *University of Illinois Law Forum,* 1972 (1972), 177.

[3060]"Survey Shows New York is Abortion Capital of Nation." *Our Sunday Visitor,* 64 (February 8, 1976), 2.

[3061]Sussman, W., *et al.* "General Practitioners' Views on Pregnancy Termination." *Medical Journal of Australia,* 2 (July 25, 1970), 169-73.

[3062]Suter, H. H. "Population Crisis and Extremism." *Science,* 168 (May 15, 1970), 777.

[3063]Sutin, Jonathan B. "New Mexico's 1969 Criminal Abortion Law," table. *Natural Resources Journal,* 10 (July, 1970), 591-614.

[3064]Suzumura, M., *et al.* "Induced Abortion in Japan—Review of Literature." *Journal of the Japanese Obstetrics and Gynecology Society* (English), 13 (July, 1966), 179-97. (71 ref.)

[3065]Swan, G. S. "Abortion on Maternal Demand: Paternal Support Liability Implications." *Valparaiso University Law Review,* 9 (Winter, 1975), 243-72.

[3066]Swan, G. S. "Compulsory Abortion: Next Challenge to Liberated Women?" *Ohio North Law Review,* 3 (1975), 152-75.

[3067]Swartz, D. P. "The Impact of Voluntary Abortion on American Obstetrics and Gynecology." *Mount Sinai Journal of Medicine* (New York), 42(5) (September-October, 1975), 468-78.

[3068]Swidler, A. "A Time for Dialogue on Abortion." *National Catholic Reporter,* 9 (December 1, 1972), 7.

[3069]Swigar, M. E., *et al.* "Grieving and Unplanned Pregnancy," bibl. *Psychiatry,* 39 (February, 1976), 72-80.

[3070]Swigar, M. E., Breslin, R., Pouzzner, M. G., Quinlan, D., and Blum, M. "Interview Follow-Up of Abortion Applicant Dropouts." *Social Psychiatry,* 11(3) (1976), 135-44.

[3071]Szablya, H. "European Communist States Turn Away from Abortion." *Our Sunday Visitor,* 64 (January 25, 1976), 3.

[3072]Szablya, H. "What Liberal Abortion Has Done to Hungary." *Our Sunday Visitor,* 61 (September 23, 1973), 1+.

[3073]Szabody, Egon. "The Legalizing of Contraceptives and Abortions." *Impact of Science on Society,* 21 (July-September, 1971), 265-70.

[3074]Szasz, Thomas S. "The Ethics of Abortion." *Humanist,* 26 (September/October, 1966), 147-48.

[3075]Szekely, P., *et al.* "Indications for Termination of Pregnancy." *British Medical Journal,* 2 (June 1, 1968), 556.

[3076]Talan, K. H. and Kimball,

C. P. "Characterization of 100 Women Psychiatrically Evaluated for Therapeutic Abortion." *Archives of General Psychiatry*, 26(6) (1972), 571-76.

[3077]"Talked Out." *Economist*, 256 (August 9, 1975), 18.

[3078]Tannenbaum, Jeffrey A. "A New Cause: Many Americans Join Move to Ban Abortion; Legislators Take Note." *Wall Street Journal*, 182 (August 2, 1973), 1+.

[3079]Taubenfeld, H. J. "Beginnings of Personhood: Legal Considerations." *Perkins Journal*, 27 (Fall, 1973), 16-19.

[3080]Taylor, H. C., Jr. and Lapham, R. J. "A Program for Family Planning Based on Maternal Child Health Services." *Studies in Family Planning*, 5(3) (1974), 71-82.

[3081]Taylor, R. "The Politics of Abortion." *Tablet*, 225 (June 12, 1971), 568-69.

[3082]Taymor, M. L. "Abortion Law in Massachusetts." *New England Journal of Medicine*, 283 (September 10, 1970), 602.

[3083]Taymor, M. L. "A Medical Case for Abortion Liberalization." *Archives of Surgery*, 102 (March, 1971), 235.

[3084]Teeter, R. R. "Psychiatric Indications for Abortion." *Minnesota Medicine*, 50 (January, 1967), 49-51.

[3085]Teitelbaum, Michael S. "Fertility Effects of the Abolition of Legal Abortion in Romania. 1956-1970." *Population Studies*, 26 (November, 1972), 405-17. [The focus is on the period 1966-1967 when the government reversed its policy on abortion.]

[3086]Temkin, J. "Lane Committee Report on the Abortion Act." *Modern Law Review*, 37 (November, 1974), 657-63.

[3087]Teo, W. K. H. "Abortion. The Husband's Constitutional Rights." *Ethics*, 85(4) (1975), 337-42.

[3088]Teper, S. "Recent Trends in Teenage Pregnancy in England and Wales." *Journal of Biosocial Science*, 7(2) (1975), 141-52.

[3089]"Texas Abortion Law Unconstitutional." *National Catholic Reporter*, 6 (July 3, 1970), 9.

[3090]"Texas Abortion Statutes: Constitutional Issues and the Need for Reform." *Baylor Law Review*, 23 (Fall, 1971), 605.

[3091]"Text on Abortion." *National Catholic Reporter*, 7 (April 16, 1971), 5.

[3092]"Therapeutic Abortion." *Canadian Medical Association Journal*, 98 (March 9, 1968), 512-13.

[3093]"Therapeutic Abortion." *Canadian Medical Association Journal*, 111(12) (December 21, 1974), 1299-1301.

[3094]"Therapautic Abortion." *Lancet*, 1 (n.d.), 678-79.

[3095]"Therapeutic Abortion." *Medical Journal of Australia*, 2 (n.d.), 146-47; 1 (n.d.), 1068-69; 1 (n.d.), 273-74.

[3096]"Therapeutic Abortion and South African Law." *African Medical Journal*, 42 (July 20, 1968), 710-14.

[3097]"Therapeutic Abortion in a Canadian City." *Canadian Medical Association Journal*, 103 (November 1, 1970), 1085 passim.

[3098]*Therapeutic Abortion: Medical, Psychiatric, Legal, Anthropological and Religious Considerations.* Ed. Harold Rosen (New York: The Julian Press, 1954). Now called: *Abortion in America* (Boston: Beacon Press, 1967).

[3099]"Therapeutic Abortion—The Psychiatric Indication—A Double-Edged Sword?" *Dickinson Law Review*, 72 (Winter, 1968), 270.

[3100]Thielicke, Helmut. *The Ethics of Sex.* Translated by John W. Doberstein (New York: Harper and Row, 1964).

[3101]"3rd Aborted Baby Died, Paper Says." *National Catholic Reporter*, 10 (May 10, 1974), 3.

[3102]"30 Bishops Attack Abortionist Profits." *National Catholic Reporter*, 7 (December 11, 1970), 5.

[3103]Thompson, D. "Thomas Sees Birth Control Policy Change." *National Catholic Reporter*, 4 (July 24, 1968), 3.

[3104]Thompson, H., *et al.*
"Therapeutic Abortion. A Two-
Year Experience in One Hospital."
*Journal of the American Medical
Association,* 213 (August 10,
1970), 991-95.

[3105]Thomson, Judith Jarvis.
"A Defense of Abortion." *Philosophy and Public Affairs,* 1 (Fall,
1971), 47-66. [Even though the
author rejects the premise that
the fetus is a person from conception, she grants the premise
to show that arguments for the
impermissibility of abortion
based on it are invalid. A detailed analysis of "the right to
life" is given. She shows that:
1) it does not guarantee the
right to use another person's
body; 2) it is not the right not
to be killed, but the right not
to be killed unjustly; 3) there
is a difference that is not de-
ducible between the moral decency
of the mother and just claim of
just fetus.]

[3106]Thomson, J. M. "Requests
for Abortion." *British Medical
Journal,* 1 (February 3, 1968),
311.

[3107]Thompson, Margaret W.
"Why Abortions are Done." Paper
presented to the National Canadian
Conference on Abortion, Toronto,
Canada, May, 1972.

[3108]Thompson, Pauline A. "To
Abort or Not to Abort: Whose Decision is It?" *CRUX,* vol. 12
(no. 4) (1974-1975), 22-24.

[3109]Thompson, P. Paul. A
Study in the Morality of Abortion."
CRUX, vol. 12 (no. 4) (1974-1975),
9-21.

[3110]Thorman, D. "Strategy
Questioned." *National Catholic
Reporter,* 12 (December 12, 1975),
8.

[3111]Thornton, W. N., Jr.
"Therapeutic Abortion: Responsibility of the Obstetrician." *Obstetrics and Gynecology,* 2 (November, 1953), 470-475.

[3112]"Three Abortion Amendments in Congress." *National
Catholic Reporter,* 9 (June 22,
1973), 16.

[3113]"Three Protestant Theo-
logians Join in Opposing Abortion."
National Catholic Reporter, 7
(February 26, 1971), 18.

[3114]Thurstone, P. B. "Therapeutic Abortion. The Experience of
San Mateo County General Hospital
and the State of California." *Journal of the American Medical Association,* 209 (July 14, 1969), 229-31.

[3115]Thurtle, Dorothy. *Abortion:
Right or Wrong?* (London: T. Werner
Laurie, Ltd., 1940).

[3116]Tichauer, R. W., *et al.* "Increasing Consumer Participation in
Professional Goal Setting: Contraception and Therapeutic Abortion."
*Journal of the American Medical Wo-
men's Association,* 27 (July, 1972),
365 passim.

[3117]Tiefel, Hans O. "The Cost
of Fetal Research: Ethical Considerations." *New England Journal of
Medicine,* 294 (January 8, 1976), 85-
90.

[3118]Tietze, C. "Abortion in
Europe." *American Journal of Public
Health,* 57 (November, 1967), 1923-32.
Also: *The Case for Legalized Abor-
tion Now.* Ed. Alan Guttmacher
(Berkeley: The Diablo Press, 1967).

[3119]Tietze, C. "Abortion as a
Cause of Death." *American Journal
of Public Health,* 38 (October, 1948),
1434.

[3120]Tietze, C. "Contraceptive
Practice in the Context of a Non-
Restrictive Abortion Law. Age
Specific Pregnancy Rates in New York
City, 1971-1973." *Family Planning
Perspectives,* 7(5) (1975), 197-202.

[3121]Tietze, C. "Abortion on Request: Its Consequences for Population Trends and Public Health."
Seminars in Psychiatry (in press).

[3122]Tietze, C. "The Demographic
Significance of Legal Abortion in
Eastern Europe." *Demography,* 1
(1964).

[3123]Tietze, C. "The Effect of
Legalization of Abortion on Population Growth and Public Health."
Family Planning Perspectives, 7(3)
(1975), 123-27.

[3124]Tietze, C. "Induced Abortion and Sterilization as Methods of
Fertility Control." *Journal of
Chronic Disease,* 18 (1965), 1147-
1161.

[3125]Tietze, C. "Introduction to
the Statistics of Abortion." *Pregnancy Wastage* (Springfield, Illinois:
Charles C. Thomas, 1953).

[3126]Tietze, C. "Legal Abortion in Industrialized Countries." *Family Planning and Population Programs*. Paper given at the International Family Planning Conference, Decca, Pakistan, January 28-February 4, 1969.

[3127]Tietze, C. *Maternal Mortality Associated With Legal Abortion* (London: The International Planned Parenthood Federation, 1955).

[3128]Tietze, C. "The 'Problem' of Repeat Abortions." *Family Planning Perspectives*, 6 (3) (1974), 148-50.

[3129]Tietze, C. "Report of the Swedish Abortion Committee." *Studies in Family Planning*, 3 (February, 1972), 28.

[3130]Tietze, C. "Therapeutic Abortion in New York City, 1943-1947." *American Journal of Obstetrics and Gynecology*, 60 (1950), 146.

[3131]Tietze, C. "Therapeutic Abortions in the United States." *American Journal of Obstetrics and Gynecology*, 101 (July 15, 1968), 784-87.

[3132]Tietze, C. "Two Years Experience with a Liberal Abortion Law. Its Impact on Fertility Trends in New York City." *Family Planning Perspectives*, 5 (1) (1973), 36-41.

[3133]Tietze, C. "Some Facts About Legal Abortion." *Human Fertility and Population Problems*. Ed. Roy O. Greep (Cambridge, Mass.: Schenkman, 1963).

[3134]Tietze, C. "United States: Therapeutic Abortions, 1963 to 1968." *Studies in Family Planning*, 59 (November, 1970), 5-7.

[3135]Tietze, C. and Bongaarts, J. "Fertility Rates and Abortion Rates. Simulations of Family Limitation." *Studies in Family Planning*, 6(5) (1975), 114-20.

[3136]Tietze, C. and Dawson, D. *Induced Abortion: A Factbook* (Bridgeport, Conn.: Population Council, Inc., Key Book Service, 1973). [This contains an overview of current data, primarily from the demographic and public health points of view.]

[3137]Tietze, C. and Lehfeldt, H. "Legal Abortion in Eastern Europe." *Journal of the American Medical Association*, 175 (April, 1961), 1149.

[3138]Tietze, C. and Lewit, S. "Early Medical Complications of Abortion by Saline: Joint Program for the Study of Abortion." *Studies in Family Planning*, 4 (June, 1973), 133-38.

[3139]Tietze, C. and Lewitt, S. "Joint Program for the Study of Abortion (JPSA): Early Medical Complications of Legal Abortion." *Studies in Family Planning*, 3 (June, 1972), 97-122.

[3140]Tietze, C. and Lewitt, S. "Abortion." *Scientific American*, 220 (January, 1969), 21.

[3141]Tietze, Christopher and Murstein, M. C. *Induced Abortion: 1975 Factbook*, 2nd edition. (Bridgeport, Conn.: Population Council, Key Book Service, 1975).

[3142]Tietze, C., *et al.* *Birth Control and Abortion* (New York: MSS Information Corp., Arno Press, 1970).

[3143]Tietze, C., *et al.* "Interim Report on the Joint Program for the Study of Abortion." *Clinical Obstetrics and Gynecology*, 14 (December, 1971), 1317-35. Also: *Journal of Sex Research*, 8(3) (1972), 170-88.

[3144]Tietze, C., *et al.* "Legal Abortions: Early Medical Complications. An Interim Report of the Joint Program for the Study of Abortion." *Journal of Reproductive Medicine*, 8 (April, 1972), 193-204.

[3145]Tindall, V. "Advances in Obstetrics and Gynecology." *Practitioner*, 209 (October, 1972), 437-43. (15 ref.)

[3146]"To Be or Not To Be: The Constitutional Question of the California Abortion Law." *University of Pennsylvania Law Review*, 118 (February, 1970), 643.

[3147]Tobin, W. "Ethical and Moral Considerations Concerning Abortion." *Homiletic and Pastoral Review*, 67 (September, 1967), 1023-31; 68 (October, 1967), 48-58.

[3148]Todd, N. A. "Follow-Up of Patients Recommended for Therapeutic Abortion." *British Journal of Psychiatry*, 120 (1972), 645-46.

[3149]Todd, N. A. "Psychiatric

3150-
3172   Experience of the Abortion Act,
         1967." *British Journal of Psychiatry,* 119(552) (1971), 489-96.

[3150]Tooley, Michael. "Abortion and Infanticide." *Philosophy and Public Affairs,* 2 (Fall, 1972), 37-65. [The focus of this paper centers on the question of what properties an organism must possess in order to have a right to life. The author suggests that an organism must be capable of regarding itself as a continuing subject of experiences and other mental states in order to have a serious claim for a right to life. The author contends that there is a connection between the possession of a given right and the capacity of having the corresponding desire. Because newborns and fetuses do not satisfy this condition, they do not have a serious right to life. Thus, abortion and infanticide are morally acceptable. He also discusses the "potentiality principle".]

[3151]Toongsuwan, S., et al. "Therapeutic Abortions in Siriraj Hospital." *Journal of the Medical Association of Thailand,* 56 (April, 1973), 237-40.

[3152]"Toronto Archbishop Appeals for Anti-Abortion Campaign." *L'Osservatore Romano* (English), 218 (no. 22) (June 1, 1972), 4.

[3153]"Torts—Dignity as a Legally Protectable Interest." *North Carolina Law Review,* 46 (December, 1967), 205.

[3154]"Torts—the Illinois Wrongful Death Act Held Inapplicable to a Viable Fetus." *Loyola University Law Journal* (Chicago), 3 (Summer, 1972), 402.

[3155]"To Study Anti-Abortion Brief." *National Catholic Reporter,* 8 (December 10, 1971), 1-2.

[3156]"Toward a Judicial Reform of Abortion Laws." *University of Florida Law Review,* 22 (Summer, 1969), 59.

[3157]Towers, B. "Foetus Experiments: A Scientist's View." *Tablet,* 224 (June 6, 1970), 540-41.

[3158]Tracy, Phil. "Right-to-Lifers/'Never Say We Acted Like Good Germans'." *Village Voice,* 17 (no. 19) (May 11, 1972), 1+.

[3159]Traina, Frank J. "Catholic Clergy on Abortion, Preliminary Findings of a New York State Survey." *Family Planning Perspectives,* 6(3) (1974), 151-56.

[3160]Treadwell, M. "Is Abortion Black Genocide?" *Family Planning Perspectives,* 4 (January, 1972), 4-5.

[3161]Tredgold, Roger. "Legal Abortion—The Psychiatrist's View." *Abortion in Britain* (London: Pitman Medical Publishing Company, Ltd., 1966).

[3162]Tredgold, Roger. "Psychiatric Indications for Termination of Pregnancy." *Lancet,* 2 (December 12, 1964), 1251.

[3163]Treffers, P. "Abortion in Amsterdam." *Population Studies,* 20(3) (1967), 295-309.

[3164]"Trends in Abortion Legislation." *St. Louis University Law Journal,* 12 (Winter, 1967), 260.

[3165]Trlin, A. D. "Abortion in New Zealand. A Review." *The Australian Journal of Social Issues,* 10(3) (1975), 179-96.

[3166]Trout, Monroe. "Therapeutic Abortions Need Therapy." *Temple Law Quarterly,* 37 (Winter, 1964), 172.

[3167]Truskett, I. D., and Pfanner, D. W. "Abortion. Community Trends." *Medical Journal of Australia,* 2(8) (1974), 288-91.

[3168]Tunkel, V. "Modern Anti-Pregnancy Techniques and the Criminal Law." *Criminal Law Review,* 1974 (August, 1974), 461-71.

[3169]Turner, J. "Whose Interests?" *Nursing Times,* 71(45) (November 6, 1975), 1763.

[3170]Turney, B. "Abortion: Where It's At, Where It's Going?" *Journal of the Canadian Bar Association,* 3 (April, 1972), 26.

[3171]"Two Bishops Protest Easing Abortion Laws." *National Catholic Reporter,* 3 (February 8, 1967), 3.

[3172]"Two Condemnations of Abortion." *Catholic Mind,* 69 (November, 1971), 9-11. [The bishops of

Illinois on February 3, 1971, and the bishops of Maryland on January 27, 1971, each issued jointed statements expressing their opposition to the passage of a liberalized abortion bill. The article contains the texts of the statements.]

[3173]"2,000 Catholic Abortions." *National Catholic Reporter,* 8 (August 18, 1972), 13.

[3174]Tyler, C. W. "Editorial: Legal Abortion and Public Health." *American Journal of Public Health,* 64 (August, 1974), 823-24.

[3175]Tyler, C. W., Jr., *et al.* "The Logistics of Abortion Services in the Absence of Restrictive Criminal Legislation in the United States." *American Journal of Public Health,* 61 (March, 1971), 489-95.

[3176]Udry, J. R. and Bauman, K. E. "Effect on Unwanted Fertility of Extending Physician Administered Birth Control in the United States." *Demography,* 11 (2) (1974), 189-94.

[3177]Udry, J. R. and Poolf, W. K. "Estimating the Effect on Unwanted Fertility of a Post-Partum Recruitment Strategy." *American Journal of Public Health,* 64 (1974), 696-99.

[3178]Ullman, A. "Social Work Service to Abortion Patients." *Social Casework,* 53(8) (1972), 481-87.

[3179]"Unborn Child: Consistency in the Law." *Suffolk University Law Review,* 2 (Spring, 1968), 228.

[3180]"The Unborn Child and the Constitutional Conception of Life (United States)." *Iowa Law Review,* 56 (April, 1971), 994-1014.

[3181]"Unborn Child in Georgia Law: Abortion Reconsidered." *Georgia Law Review,* 6 (Fall, 1971), 168.

[3182]"Unexpected Results of the Change in Britain's Abortion Law." *Journal of the Iowa Medical Society,* 59 (June, 1969), 509-10.

[3183]"Unexpectedly Cautious." *Economist,* 260 (July 31, 1976), 29-30.

[3184]"UN Study Group Reports, Msgr. McHugh Dissents: Study Paper on Abortion." *Our Sunday Visitor,* 64 (March 7, 1976), 2.

[3185]"U.S. Bishops Oppose Supreme Court Decision." *L'Osservatore Romano* (English), 255 (no. 7) (February 15, 1973), 6-7.

[3186]"U.S. Bishops' Pastoral On Abortion." *Our Sunday Visitor,* 61 (March 11, 1973), 4.

[3187]"U.S. Bishops Resolutions." *Priest,* 25 (June, 1969), 364-68.

[3188]"United States' Cardinals Protest Court's Decisions: Abortion." *L'Osservatore Romano* (English), 253 (no. 5) (February 1, 1973), 5.

[3189]United States. House. Com. on the Judiciary. Subcom. on Civil and Constitutional Rights. Proposes Constitutional Amendments on Abortion: Hearings: Pts. 1-2, February 4-March 26, 1976. '76 2Pts (1089 p) tables (94th Cong., 2d sess.) (Serial no. 46) pa Pt 1.

[3190]"U.S. Supreme Court Lets Lower Court Decision Stand on Right of Hospital to Refuse Abortion." *Our Sunday Visitor,* 64 (December 14, 1975), 1.

[3191]"U.S. Supreme Court on Abortion." *Social Justice Review,* 65 (February, 1973), 359+.

[3192]"U.S. Supreme Court on Abortion. *Roe v. Wade,* 41 U.S.L.W. 4213 (1973)." *Connecticut Medicine,* 37 (June, 1973), 279-89.

[3193]"The Unmet Need for Legal Abortion Services in the U.S," tables, chart, maps. *Family Planning Perspectives,* 7(1) (September/October, 1975). Adapted from a report prepared by the Alan Guttmacher Institute, by A. Weinstock, *et al.,* 23-31.

[3194]"Unwanted Pregnancy and Mental Health." *Nursing Times,* 70 (April 11, 1974), 554.

[3195]*Updating Life and Death.* Ed. by D. P. Cutler (Boston: Beacon Press, 1968).

[3196]"Urges Link with Foes to Defeat Abortion." *National Catholic Reporter,* 4 (July 24, 1968), 3.

[3197]de Valk, Alphonse. *Morality*

3198-
3216 and Law in Canadian Politics: The Abortion Controversy (Dorval, Que.: Palm Publishers, 1974).

[3198]Van der Marck, W. "Objections Aim at Wrong Target." National Catholic Reporter, 9 (March 16, 1973), 11.

[3199]Van der Marck, W. Toward A Christian Ethic (Westminster: Newman Press, 1967).

[3200]Van der Poll, Cornelius J. "The Principle of Double Effect." Absolutes in Moral Theology. Ed. Charles E. Curran (Washington: Corpus Books, 1968).

[3201]Van der Pool, J. P., et al. "Psychiatry and the Abortion Problem." Texas Medicine, 64 (January, 1968), 48-51.

[3202]Van der Tak. Abortion, Fertility and Changing Legislation (Lexington, Ma.: Lexington Books, 1974).

[3203]Vann, D. "Psychiatric Indications for the Termination of Pregnancy." Medical Journal of Australia, 1 (February 13, 1971), 404.

[3204]"Vatican Reaffirms Opposition to Abortion." National Catholic Reporter, 11 (December 6, 1974), 1+.

[3205]Vaughn, Richard P. "Psychotherapeutic Abortion." America, 113 (October 16, 1965), 436-8. [The author concludes that having an abortion may be even more harmful psychologically than not having one.]

[3206]Vaupel, James W. "Structuring An Ethical Decision Dilemma." Soundings, 55 (Winter, 1975), 506-24.

[3207]Vaux, Kenneth. "After Edelin: The Abortion Debate Goes On." Christian Century, 92 (March 5, 1975), 213-14. [Vaux discusses the inconsistencies of the guilty verdict in the "Edelin" case and the Roe v. Wade decision.

He asks if we have not been asking the wrong questions. We appeal to two different sources to establish value in the person —biological, sociological criteria and in an affirmation of a transcendent root of value. Perhaps both traditions require each other?]

[3208]Vaux, Kenneth. "Giving and Taking of Life: New Power at Life's Thresholds." Christian Century, 92 (April 16, 1975), 384-87. [Vaux distinguishes two definitions of personhood in our culture. One locates personhood in the biological, neurological and sociological criteria imposed by our society. The other tradition which is rooted in Judeo-Christian practice transmitted through Roman, medieval and common law to the American Constitution, stress what E. J. Corwin has called the "higher law background of our legal tradition."

Vaux hopes that our scientific knowledge will be coordinated with our moral wisdom so that there will be a transformation which will bring a new "faithfulness to God and a derivative humanism."

[3209]Veitch, Edward and Tracey, R. R. S. "Abortion in the Common Law World." American Journal of Comparative Law, 22 (Fall, 1974), 652-96. [They examine the existing legislation, opposing views on abortion law and proposals for reform in Great Britain, Canada, Australia and the United States.]

[3210]Vankatacharya, K. "Reductions in Fertility Due to Induced Abortions. A Simulation Model." Demography, 9(3) (1972), 339-52.

[3211]Vere, Duncan W. "Therapeutic Abortion and Sterilization as Ethical Problems." Birth Control and the Christian. Ed. Alan Guttmacher (Berkeley: Diablo Press, 1967).

[3212]Vernaschi, A. "The Defense of the True and Complete Values of Life." L'Osservatore Romano (English), 421 (no. 17) (April 22, 1976), 8-9.

[3213]"Viability and Abortion." Kentucky Law Journal, 64 (1975-1976), 146-64.

[3214]"Victory for Liberalism." Economist, 225 (October 28, 1967), 372.

[3215]Vieira, N. "Roe (Roe v. Wade, 93 Sup Ct 705) and Doe (Doe v. Bolton, 93 Sup Ct 739): Substantive Due Process and the Right of Abortion." Hastings Law Journal, 25 (March, 1974), 867-79.

[3216]Villiers, J. N. "The Indications for Therapeutic Abortion,

Obstetrician's Point of View." *South Africa Medical Journal,* 42 (July 20, 1968), 718-21.

[3217]Villot, J. "Abortion: An Unspeakable Crime." *L'Osservatore Romano* (English), 134 (no. 43) (October 22, 1970), 4.

[3218]Vincent, M. L. and Barton, D. "Attitudes of Unmarried College Women Toward Abortion." *Journal of School Health,* 43(1) (1973), 55-59.

[3219]Vincent, M. O. "Psychiatric Indications for Therapeutic Abortion and Sterilization." *Birth Control and the Christian.* Ed. Alan Guttmacher (Berkeley: Diablo Press, 1967).

[3220]Visentin, Charles. *A Message to an Aborted Baby Killed by the Cowardice of His Mother and the Venal Complicity of the Attending Physician* (Albuquerque, N.M.: American Classical College Press, 1976).

[3221]"A Voice was Heard in Rama, Weeping and Loud Lamentation." *St. Anthony's Messenger,* 74 (June, 1967), 8-9.

[3222]Volk, H., Card. "German Bishops Urge Defence at All Cost of the Lives of the Unborn." *L'Osservatore Romano* (English), 354 (no. 2) (January 9, 1975), 8.

[3223]Vorherr, H. "Contraception After Abortion and Post Partum. An Evaluation of Risks and Benefits of Oral Contraceptives with Emphasis on the Relation of Female Sex Harmones to Thromboembolism and Genital and Breast Cancer." *American Journal of Obstetrics and Gynecology,* 117 (December 1, 1973), 1002-25. (118 ref.)

[3224]Waite, M. "Consultant Psychiatrists and Abortion." *Psychological Medicine,* 4(1) (1974), 74-88.

[3225]Wahlberg, R. C. "Abortion: Decisions to Live With (Conference on Abortion at Southern Methodist University." *Christian Century,* 90 (June 27, 1973), 691-93. [This conference dealt with: 1) plight of indigent women who want abortions and cannot get them; 2) counseling for women with unwanted pregnancies; 3) the involvement of the father in decision-making;

4) the influence of the counselor whose bias can influence a client's decision.] [3217-3235]

[3226]Wahlberg, R. C. "The Woman and the Fetus: One Flesh?" *New Theology no. 10.* Ed. M. E. Marty and D. G. Peerman (New York: Macmillan Company, 1973), p. 130-9. Also: *Christian Century,* 88 (September 8, 1971). [Wahlberg discusses how the pregnant woman feels about her situation. She states that if women are to be free, they must have power over their reproductive systems.]

[3227]Wahlberg, R. C. "Woman, Anger and Abortion." *Christian Century* (July 7, 1976), 622-23. (Wahlberg discusses the anger many women feel over restrictive abortion laws. There is specific mention of Italy.]

[3228]Walbert, David F. and Butler, J. Douglas, eds. *Abortion, Society and the Law* (Cleveland: Press of Case Western Reserve University, 1973).

[3229]Walker, W. B., *et al.* "Attitudes and Practices of North Carolina Obstetricians: The Impact of the North Carolina Abortion Act of 1967." *Southern Medical Journal,* 64 (April, 1971), 441-45.

[3230]Wallace, D. C. "Abortion and Immigration." *Medical Journal of Australia,* 1 (March 20, 1971), 659-60.

[3231]Wallace, J. D. "Uneasy Lies the Head that Wears a Crown." *Canadian Medical Association Journal,* 112(3) (February 8, 1975), 344.

[3232]Wallace, V. H. "Abortion and Immigration." *Medical Journal of Australia,* 1 (February 13, 1971), 404-05.

[3233]Wallerstein, J., *et al.* "Seesaw Response of a Young Unmarried Couple to Therapeutic Abortion." *Archives of General Psychiatry,* 27 (August, 1972), 251-54.

[3234]Wallerstein, J. S., Kurtz, P., and Bar-Din, M. "Psychosocial Sequelae of Therapeutic Abortion in Young Unmarried Women." *Archives of General Psychiatry,* 27 (1972), 828-32.

[3235]Walley, R. L. "Conscientious Objection to Abortion." *British Medical Journal,* 4 (October 28, 1972), 234.

3236-
3256

[3236]Walsh, D. "Medical and Social Characteristics of Irish Residents Whose Pregnancies were Terminated Under the 1967 Abortion Act in 1971 and 1972." *Irish Medical Journal*, 68(6) (1975), 143-49.

[3237]Walsh, D. "Pregnancies of Irish Residents Terminated in England and Wales in 1973." *Irish Medical Journal*, 69(1) (1976), 16-18, 17.

[3238]Walsh, M. "What the Bishops Say." *Month*, 6 (May, 1973), 172-75.

[3239]Walsh, Noel. "In Defence of the Unborn," bibl. *Studies* (Ireland), 61 (Winter, 1972), 303-14.

[3240]Watson, C. "Population Policy in France." *Population Studies*, 7 (1952), 263-286.

[3241]Walter, G. S. "Psychologic and Emotional Consequences of Elective Abortion." *Obstetrics and Gynecology*, 36 (1970), 482-91.

[3242]Waltke, Bruce K. "Reflections From the Old Testament on Abortion." *Journal of the Evangelical Theological Society*, 19 (Winter, 1976), 3-13.

[3243]Walton, L. A. "The Kings County Abortion Story." *Modern Treatment*, 8 (February, 1971), 97-100. Also: *Clinical Obstetrics and Gynecology*, 14 (March, 1971), 149-52.

[3244]Walton, L. A., *et al.* "Development of an Abortion Service in Large Municipal Hospital." *American Journal of Public Health*, 64 (January, 1974), 77-81.

[3245]Walvekar, V., Mallapur, A. M., and Palekar, B. S. "An Attitude Study of 500 Persons to Abortion." *Journal of Family Welfare*, 19(3) (1973), 30-34.

[3246]Warren, Mary Anne. "On the Moral and Legal Status of Abortion." *Monist*, 57 (January, 1973), 43-61.

[3247]"Washington Abortion Reform." *Gonzaga Law Review*, 5 (Spring, 1970), 270.

[3248]"Washington (State)—Act Relating to Abortion." (Ch. 3. Session Laws, 1970).

[3249]Wasmuth, C. E. "Abortion Laws: The Perplexing Problem." *Cleveland State Law Review*, 18 (September, 1969), 503.

[3250]Wasserman, Richard. "Implications of the Abortion Decision: Post *Roe* and *Doe* Litigation and Legislation." *Columbia Law Review*, 74 (March, 1974), 237-68. [Various questions left unresolved by the *Roe* and *Doe* decisions are discussed. These issues are considered: 1) constitutionality of spousal or parental consent statutes; 2) the validity of limiting Medicaid payments, 3) the woman's right to privacy and the method that abortions are reported; 4) state control in advertising abortion services; 5) requirements that hospitals provide abortion facilities; 6) the retroactivity of the *Roe* decision as to non-physician and physician abortionists.]

[3251]Wassertheil-Smolle, Lerner R. C., Arnold, C. R., and Heimrath, S. L. "New York State Physicians and the Social Context of Abortion." *American Journal of Public Health*, 63(2) (1973), 144-49. Also: *American Journal of Obstetrics and Gynecology*, 113 (August 1, 1972), 979-86.

[3252]Wassmer, Thomas. "Contemporary Attitudes of the Roman Catholic Church Toward Abortion." *Journal of Religion and Health*, 7 (October, 1968), 324-332. [The author discusses the Catholic position in light of the mediate and immediate animation theory. He examines the principle of probabilism in cases of doubt of fact and doubt of law.]

[3253]Wassmer, Thomas. "The Crucial Question About Abortion." *Catholic World*, 206 (November, 1967), 57-61. [Wassmer sees the crucial question as, when does life begin. He reviews two views: those of mediate and immediate animation, and two principles: doubt of fact and doubt of law.]

[3254]Wassmer, Thomas. "Questions About Questions." *Commonweal*, 86 (1967), 416.

[3255]Waterson, N. "After the Lane Report." *New Law Journal*, 124 (August 15, 1974), 761-63.

[3256]Watkins, R. E. "A Five Year Study of Abortion." *American Journal of Obstetrics and Gynecology*,

26 (1933), 161.

[3257]Watson, T. "Why Therapeutic Abortion?" *Minnesota Medicine,* 50 (January, 1967), 55-59.

[3258]Watt, Robert L. "A New Constitutional Right to an Abortion (Commenting on the 1973 U.S. Supreme Court Decisions in *Roe v. Wade* and a Companion Case)." *North Carolina Law Review,* 51 (October, 1973), 1573-84.

[3259]Watters, W. W. "Letter: Therapeutic Abortion." *Canadian Medical Association,* 112(5) (March 8, 1975), 558.

[3260]Watters, W. W. *Compulsory Parenthood: The Truth About Abortion* (Tornoto: McClelland, 1976).

[3261]Way, R. C. "Cardiovascular Defects and the Rubella Syndrome." *Canadian Medical Association Journal,* 97 (November 25, 1967), 1329.

[3262]"We Are Lovers of Life, Archbishop Sheen Says." *Our Sunday Visitor,* 65 (July 11, 1976), 2.

[3263]Weber, P. "Perverse Observations on Abortion." *Catholic World,* 212 (November, 1970), 74-77.

[3264]Weddington, S. R. "Woman's Right of Privacy (To Bear Children or Not)." *Perkins Journal,* 27 (Fall, 1973), 35-41.

[3265]Weiler, K. M., *et al.* "Unborn Child in Canadian Law." *Osgoode Hall Law Journal,* 14 (December, 1976), 643-59.

[3266]Weinberg, J. "ISMS Symposium on Medical Implications of the Current Abortion Law in Illinois." *Illinois Medical Journal,* 131 (May, 1967), 680-83.

[3267]Weinberg, Roy D. *Laws Governing Family Planning* (Dobbs Ferry, N.Y.: Oceana Publishers, 1968). Also: *Family Planning and the Law,* 2nd ed. (Legal Almanac Series: No. 18) (Dobbs Ferry, N.Y.: Oceana Publishers, 1978).

[3268]Weiner, M. and Friedlander, Robert L. "Abnormal Progesterone Synthesis on Placental Tissue from a Spontaneous Abortion." *American Journal of Obstetrics and Gynecology,* 111, 924 (December 1, 1971).

[3267]Weinstock, E., Tietze, C., Jaffe, F. S., and Dryfoos, J. G. "Abortion Need and Services in the United States, 1974-1975." *Family Planning Perspectives,* 8(2) (1976), 58-69.

[3268]Weinstock, E., Tietze, C., Jaffe, F. S., and Dryfoos, J. G. "Legal Abortions in the United States Since the 1973 Supreme Court Decisions." *Family Planning Perspectives,* 7(1) (1975), 23-31.

[3271]Weir, J. G. "Illegal Abortion—Lay Abortionists." *Abortion in Britain* (London: Pitman Medical Publishing Company, 1966).

[3272]Weisheit, Eldon. *Should I Have an Abortion?* (St. Louis, Mo.: Condordia Publishing House, 1976).

[3273]Weisheit, Eldon. *Abortion? Resources for Pastoral Counseling* (St. Louis, Mo.: Concordia Publishing House, 1976.)

[3274]Weisman, A. I. "Open Legal Àbortion 'On Request' is Working in New York City, But is it the Answer?" *American Journal of Obstetrics and Gynecology,* 112 (January 1, 1972), 138-43. [The author investigates the cost, conditions, and the various facilities available for abortion in New York City. He laments the fact that stress is not laid on better sex education to avoid unwanted pregnancies.]

[3275]Welborn, Ricky L. "Abortion Laws (in Various States): A Constitutional Right to Abortion." *North Carolina Law Review,* 49 (April, 1971), 487-502.

[3276]Welch, Delpfine. "Defending the Right to Abortion in New York (Based on Conference Paper)," il. *International Socialist Review,* 34 (January, 1973), 10-13.

[3277]Wenkart, A. "Abortion." *American Journal of Psychoanalysis,* 34(2) (Spring, 1974), 161.

[3278]Wentz, Fredderick K. and Weitmer, Robert H. *The Problem of Abortion* (New York: Board of Social Ministry, Lutheran Church in America, 1967).

[3279]Werman, D. S. "Abortion

3280-
3293

and Guffaws for Chastity." *New England Journal of Medicine,* 281 (July 31, 1969), 276.

3280Werman, D. S., *et al.* "Some Problems in the Evaluation of Women for Therapeutic Abortion." *Canadian Psychiatric Association Journal,* 17 (June, 1972), 249-51.

3281Werman, D. S., *et al.* "Some Psychiatric Problems Related to Therapeutic Abortion." *North Carolina Medical Journal,* 34 (April, 1973), 274-75.

3282Werner, R. "Abortion: The Moral Status of the Unborn." *Social Theory and Practice,* 3 (Fall, 1974), 201-22. Reply: Narveson, J. 3 (Fall, 1975), 461-85. [The author attempts to show that we are committed to the view that one is a human being from conception by our ordinary common sense. Abortion in most cases is immoral in light of our prima facie obligation against taking human life. We cannot reconcile our beliefs concerning future generations and the dead with the belief that persons not biological humans have full moral rights. Accordingly, rights cannot be refused to biological humans while granting them to persons.]

3283Wert, D. S. "Allegations, Actions, and Ad Interim." *Pennsylvania Medicine,* 74 (May, 1971), 59-62.

3284Wertheimer, Roger. "Understanding the Abortion Argument." *Philosophy and Public Affairs,* 1 (Fall, 1971), 67-95. [The author asks at what stage of fetal development is abortion ever justified. The question centers around the humanity of the fetus. He explores the Catholic position, that the fetus is a human, and the liberal position, that the fetus is not a person. Logic does not settle the question because of the "factual indeterminateness" of the fetus. Because the state cannot show that the fetus is a person, anti-abortion laws are illegitimate. However, this does not prove that abortions are morally right.]

3285"West German High Court Denies Right of Abortion." *Our Sunday Visitor,* 63 (March 9, 1975), 2.

3286West, N. D., *et al.* "The Need for Pre-Abortion Counseling—Now More than Ever." *Nebraska Medical Journal,* 59 (February, 1974), 34-36.

3287Westenhaver, E. "New York's Abortion Fighters." *National Catholic Reporter,* 8 (February 25, 1972), 1+.

3288Westley, R. "Abortion Debate: Finding a True Pro-Life Stance." *America,* 134 (June 5, 1976), 489-92. [Westley's article goes to the heart of the abortion issue. In his discussion of the ambiguity of life he explains the source of the two sides of the abortion question.

He sees the strategy of the Pro-Life stance as following the ministry of the Lord. This demands that we become gracious as the Lord, we believe that each man can throw off ambiguity and transform his life.

He continues his article saying that a person who views ministry in this way will help the pro-life attitude as much as, and alongside social activism.]

3289Westley, R. "The Right to Life Debate: Excerpt from 'What a Modern Catholic Believes About the Right to Life'." *Critic,* 31 (July-August, 1973), 50-59.

3290Westoff, C. F., *et al.* "The Structure of Attitudes Toward Abortion." *Milbank Memorial Fund Quarterly,* 47 (January, 1969), 11-37.

3291Westoff, Leslie Aldridge and Charles, F. *From Now to Zero: Fertility, Contraception and Abortion in America* (Boston: Little Brown and Company, 1971). [This book includes a general account of the reasons that women seek abortion, the techniques of abortion, medical views, the legal state of the question and the results of four major surveys of women's attitudes described from the point of view of education, race and religion. The problems involved in procuring an abortion at this time are also presented.]

3292Weston, F. "Psychiatric Sequelae to Legal Abortion in South Australia." *Medical Journal of Australia,* 1(7) (1973), 350-54.

3293Wetrich, D. W. "Therapeutic Abortions and University Hospitals 1951-1969 with Emphasis on Current Trends." *Journal of the Iowa Medical Society,* 60 (1970), 691-96.

[3294]"What For?" *Economist,* 258 (February 14, 1976), 34.

[3295]"What is Distress?" *Economist,* 257 (October 18, 1975), 42+.

[3296]Wheeler, L. A. *"Roe v. Wade* (93 Sup Ct 705): The Right of Privacy Revisited." *Kansas Law Review,* 21 (Summer, 1973), 527-48.

[3297]Whelan, C. "(Abortion on Demand)." *America,* 128 (February 10, 1973), (inside front cover). [Whelan offers three items on a legal agenda in response to the U.S. Supreme Court's decision on abortion: 1) effective "conscience clauses" must be secured; 2) a determined effort should be made to "contain" the present law within the limits set down by the Supreme Court.]

[3298]Whelan, C. "Evolution in the Law." *America,* 122 (January 10, 1970), 11-12.

[3299]Whelpton, B. S. "Frequency of Abortion. Its Effect on the Birth Rates and Future Population of America." *The Abortion Problem.* Ed. H. C. Taylor (New York: The Williams and Wilkins Co., 1944).

[3300]"When Abortion is Made Easier: More and More States are Discovering What Happens when Abortion Laws are Relaxed: Demand is Rising to Make Such Operations, by Licensed Physicians, More Available; Even a National Law is Proposed," il. *United States News,* 68 (June 8, 1970), 83.

[3301]"When a Bug is Good For You." *Economist,* 249 (December 22, 1973), 39.

[3302]"Where is the Abuse?" *Economist,* 232 (July 12, 1969), 24.

[3303]"Where We Stand on the Question of Therapeutic Abortion." *California Medicine,* 106 (April, 1967), 318-19.

[3304]Whieldon, David. "New Abortion System: 'It's Working Beautifully': Despite Some Dire Predictions Made When its Law was Being Framed, Colorado Hasn't Become an Abortion Mecca Under the Nation's First Liberalized Legislation." *Medical Economist,* 45 (October 28, 1968), 238-43.

[3305]White, B. *"Roe v. Wade*—The Abortion Case." *Catholic Mind,* 71 (April, 1973), 11-12. [This article contains the text of the statements of the Bishops of Illinois on February 3, 1971 and the Bishops of Maryland on January 27, 1971, expressing their opposition to the passage of a liberalized abortion bill in the Maryland legislature.]

[3306]White, B. "White: Beyond the Constitution." *National Catholic Reporter,* 9 (February 2, 1973), 14.

[3307]White, M. G. "The Michigan Abortion Refusal Act (Considers Whether the 1973 Act Extending to all Hospitals the Right to Refuse Admission of Abortion Patients is Legally Necessary and Constitutional)." *University of Michigan Journal of Law Reform,* 8 (Spring, 1975), 659-75.

[3308]White, M. S. "Letter: Attitudes to Abortion." *British Medical Journal,* 2 (June 29, 1974), 725.

[3309]White, R. B. "Induced Abortions. A Survey of Their Psychiatric Implications, Complications and Indications." *Texas Reports on Biology and Medicine,* 24 (1966), 531-58.

[3310]Whitehead, K. "From Abortion to Sex Education." *Homiletic and Pastoral Review,* 74 (November, 1973), 60-69.

[3311]Whittington, H. G. "Evaluation of Therapeutic Abortion as an Element of Preventive Psychiatry." *American Journal of Psychiatry,* 126 (9) (1970), 1224-29.

[3312]"Who May Not Have an Abortion?" *Journal of the American Medical Association,* 209 (1969), 1080.

[3313]"Whose Right to Life? Implications of *Roe v. Wade* (93 Sup Ct 705)." *Family Law Quarterly,* 7 (Winter, 1973), 413-32.

[3314]"Why New Uproar Over Abortions: Pushing to the Foreground of '76 Politics is an Issue Candidates Would Like to Avoid; the Reason: It's Trouble—No Matter What They Say," il., chart. *U.S. News,* 80 (March 1, 1976), 14-15.

[3315]Wicker, B. "Two Enemies of Life: Pax Christi Annual Conference,

3316-
3336

1973." *Tablet*, 227 (November 10, 1973), 1061-62.

[3316]Widholm, O., Kantero, R. L., and Rautenen, E. "Medical and Social Aspects of Adolescent Pregnancies. I. Adolescents Applying for Termination of an Illegitimate Pregnancy." *Acta Obstetricia et Gynecologica Scandinavica*, 53(4) (1975), 347-53.

[3317]Wilhelmsen, F. "Empty Womb, Empty Altar." *Triumph*, 5 (June, 1970), 18-21.

[3318]Wilkins, R. G. "Letter: Abortion and Promiscuity." *British Medical Journal*, 3(5977) (July 26, 1975), 233.

[3319]Williams, B. "The March of Dimes and Abortion." *Homiletic and Pastoral Review*, 74 (October, 1973), 48-58.

[3320]Williams, E. A. "Thrapeutic Abortion." *Lancet*, 1 (May 31, 1969), 1093-94.

[3321]Williams, G. H. "The Legalization of Medical Abortion." *Eugenics Review*, 56 (April, 1964), 19-25.

[3322]Williams, G. H. "The No. 2 Moral Issue of Today." *America*, 116 (March 25, 1967), 452.

[3323]Williams, G. H. "Prof. Williams on Abortion." *America*, 120 (March 22, 1969), 320.

[3324]Williams, G. H. "Religious Residues and Presuppositions in the American Debate on Abortions." *Theological Studies*, 31 (March, 1970), 10. [The author traces the sources of current religious thought on abortion through the patristic period of Christian thought, the Protestant influence on Catholic thinking and their interaction, the potential support for the official Catholic position in sectors of liberal Protestant and Jewish opinion, the notion of procreation as the prime goal of marriage and the politics and casuistry of abortion.]

[3325]Williams, G. H. "The Sacred Condomonium." *The Morality of Abortion*. Ed. John Noonan (Cambridge, Mass.: Harvard University Press, 1970). [The author offers a theoretical construct wherein the progenitor and the state are co-sovereigns in the domain of preserving life. In crucial cases he has the state withdraw after sufficient investigation and leaves the decision in the hands of the mother. He outlines the roles of the lawyers, psychiatrists and clergy in the service of the two sovereignties. He observes the operation of the sacred condomonium in such cases as saving the mother's life, felonious intercourse and eugenic problems.]

[3326]Williams, G. H. "Attitude to Abortion-Moral Issues." *Abortion in Britain* (London: Pitman Medical Publishing Co., Ltd., 1966).

[3327]Williams, G. H. "Euthanasia and Abortion." *University of Colorado Law Review*, 38 (Winter, 1966), 178.

[3328]Williams, G. H. "Legal and Illegal Abortion." *British Journal of Criminology*, 4 (October, 1964), 557.

[3329]Williams, G. H. *The Sanctity of Life and the Criminal Law* (London: Faber and Faber, 1958). (See especially Chapts. 5 and 6.)

[3330]Williams, G. L. "The Law Relating to Abortion." *Proceedings of the Royal Society of Medicine*, 55 (1962), 374.

[3331]Williams, H. "Tennessee's New Abortion Law." *Journal of the Tennessee Medical Association*, 66 (June, 1973), 651-52.

[3332]Williams, Jean Morton and Hindell, Keith. *Abortion and Contraception: A Study of Patients' Attitudes* (London: Political and Economic Planning), 1972.

[3333]Williams, S. J. "A Methodology for the Palnning of Therapeutic Abortion Services." *Health Service Report*, 87 (December, 1972), 983-91.

[3334]Williams, S. J. and Pullman, T. W. "Effectiveness of Abortion as Birth Control." *Social Biology*, 22 (1) (1975), 23-33.

[3335]Williams, S. J., *et al.* "Therapeutic Abortion." *Lancet*, 2 (November 27, 1971), 1197.

[3336]Williams, S. J. and McIntosh, E. N. "Requirements for Abortion Services." *American Journal of*

Public Health, 64 (July, 1974), 716-17.

[3337]Williamson, J. "The Problem of Abortion." *Royal Society of Health Journal,* 92 (April, 1972), 85-87.

[3338]Williamson, J. D. "Legal Abortion." *British Medical Journal,* 3 (August 5, 1972), 349-50.

[3339]Willaimson, N. W. "Abortion: A Legal View." *New Zealand Medical Journal,* 72 (October, 1970), 257-61.

[3340]Willke, J. and Willke, J. *Handbook on Abortion,* revised edition (Cincinnati, Ohio: Hiltz & Hayes, 1975).

[3341]Willke, J. and Mrs. J. "Abortion is Killing." *Columbia,* 53 (April, 1973), 10-19.

[3342]Wilson, David C. "The Abortion Problem in the General Hospital." *Abortion in America* (Boston: Beacon Press, 1967).

[3343]Wilson, David C. "Psychiatric Implications in Abortion." *Virginia Medical Monthly,* 79 (August, 1952), 448-451.

[3344]Wilson, David C. and Caine, B. L. "The Psychiatric Implications of Therapeutic Abortions." *Neuropsychiatry,* 1 (1951), 6-21.

[3345]Wilson, E. "The Organization and Function of Therapeutic Abortion Committees." *Canadian Hospital,* 48 (December, 1971), 38-40.

[3346]Wilson, E. R. "Letter to the Editor." *Canadian Bar Journal* (N.S.), 4 (1972), 11.

[3347]Wilson, J. R. "Abortion—A Medical Responsibility?" *Obstetrics and Gynecology,* 30 (August, 1967), 94-303.

[3348]Wilson, Paul. *The Sexual Dilemma: Abortion, Homosexuality, Prostitution, and the Criminal Threshold* (Brisband: University of Queensland Press, 1971).

[3349]Wilson, P. and Chappell, D. "Australian Attitudes Towards Abortion, Prostitution and Homosexuality (Based on Interviews with a Statistical Sampling of 1045 Informants)." *Australian Quarterly,* 40 (June, 1968), 7-17.

[3350]Wilson-Davis, K. "The Contraceptive Situation in the Irish Republic." *Journal of Biosocial Science,* 6(4) (1974), 483-92.

[3351]Wisconsin. Legis. ref. bur. "The Issue of Abortion in Wisconsin." (Fall, 1971), 11p tables. (Informational bul. 71-72). State Capitol, Madison, Wisconsin 53702.

[3352]"Wise Axiom: Cui Bono?" *America,* 117 (September 23, 1967), 292.

[3353]Witherspoon, J. "Impact of the Abortion Decisions Upon the Father's Role." *Jurist,* 35 (Winter, 1975), 32-65.

[3354]Wojcichowsky, Stephen. *Ethical-Social-Legal Annotated Bibliography of English Language Studies on Abortion.* T.I.P.C., 1967-1972. (Toronto: University of St. Michael's College, 1973).

[3355]Wolf, S. R., *et al.* "Assumption of Attitudes Toward Abortion During Physician Education." *Obstetrics and Gynecology,* 37 (January, 1971), 141-47.

[3356]Wolfe, R. "The Abortion Question and the Evangelical Tradition." *Dimension,* 5 (Summer, 1973), 84-89. [The author approaches the question first, with scriptural insight. He notes that the passages he chose do not provide in prescriptive language the answer to the abortion question, but they do provide some insight into the value of life as God views it. Then Wolfe presents the view of Carl F. H. Henry. Finally, Dietrich Bonhoeffer's book, *Ethics,* is commented upon. Wolfe sees that some of Bonhoeffer's principles in the area of euthanasia can be applied to the area of abortion.]

[3357]Wolff, J. R., *et al.* "Therapeutic Abortion: Attitudes of Medical Personnel Leading to Complications in Patient Care." *American Journal of Obstetrics and Gynecology,* 110 (July 1, 1971), 730-33.

[3358]Wolfish, M. G. "Adolescent Sexuality." *Practitioner,* 210 (February, 1973), 226-31.

[3359]Wolleat, P. L. "Abortion Information. A Guidance Viewpoint." *The School Counselor,* 22(5) (1975),

3359-
3384

[3359]Wolleat, P. L. "Abortion Information. A Guidance Viewpoint." *The School Counselor,* 22(5) (1975), 338-41.

[3360]"Woman's Choice." *Economist,* 260 (July 10, 1976), 35-36.

[3361]"Women Claim Abortion, Feminism Contradictory." *National Catholic Reporter,* 9 (March 2, 1973), 5.

[3362]Wood, C. "Abortion: Community Trends. Comment 1." *Medical Journal of Australia,* 2(8) (August 24, 1974), 291-93.

[3363]Wood, C. and Williams, W. A. W., eds. *Fifth World Congress of Gynecology and Obstetrics* (Sydney, Australia, September 1967. World Congress of Gynaecology and Obstetrics, 5th, Sydney, 1967).

[3364]Wood, Susanne. "The Abortion Report (Great Britain: Commenting on the Report of the Committee on the Working of the Abortion Act, the Hon. Mrs. Justice Lane, Chairman)." *Political Quarterly,* 45 (July/ September, 1974), 356-60.

[3365]Woodruff, C. Roy. "Pastoral Considerations on Abortion and Sterilization." *Pastoral Psychology,* 24 (Fall, 1975), 40-51.

[3366]Woodside, Moya. "Attitudes of Women Abortionists." *The Howard Journal of Penology and Crime Prevention,* 11 (1963), 93-112.

[3367]Woodside, Moya. "Illegal Abortion—The Woman Abortionist." *Abortion in Britain* (London: Pitman Medical Publishing Company, Ltd., 1966).

[3368]Woolf, L. A. "Letter: Legal Abortion." *Medical Journal of Australia,* 2 (December 15, 1973), 1102.

[3369]Woolf, L. A. "Letter: Legal Abortion." *Medical Journal of Australia,* 2 (December 15, 1973), 1102.

[3369]Woolf, L. A. "Letter: Unwanted Pregnancies and Abortion." *Medical Journal of Australia,* 2(9) (August 30, 1975),

[3370]Woolf, Rowena. "Attitudes to Abortion-Changes." *Abortion in Britain* (London: Pitman Medical Publishing Company, Ltd., 1966).

[3371]Woolnough, J. "Abortion Law." *Medical Journal of Australia,* 2 (August 5, 1972), 338-39.

[3372]"Working of Abortion Act." *British Medical Journal,* 2 (1969), 631.

[3373]Working of the Abortion Act." *British Medical Journal,* 02 (5966) (May 10, 1975), 337.

[3374]Works, M. "Abortionist Lures Legal Reprisal." *National Catholic Reporter,* 6 (December 10, 1969), 5.

[3375]WHO Meeting Geneva, 1974. *Pregnancy and Abortion in Adolescence: Report* (Albany, N.Y.: World Health Organization, 1975).

[3376]WHO Scientific Group, Geneva, 1970. *Spontaneous and Induced Abortion: A Report* (Albany, N.Y.: World Health Organization, 1970).

[3377]Worsnop, Richard L. "Abortion Law Reform," tables. *Editorial Research Reports,* (July 24, 1970), 545-62.

[3378]Wright, N.P. and David, H. P. "Abortion Legislation: The Romanian Experience." *Studies in Family Planning,* 2 (October, 1971), 205-10.

[3379]Wright, N. H. "Restricting Legal Abortion. Some Maternal and Child Health Effects in Romania." *American Journal of Obstetrics and Gynecology,* 121(2) (1975), 246-56.

[3380]"Wrongful Birth in the Abortion Context—Critique of Existing Case Law and Proposal for Future Actions." *Denver Law Journal,* 53 (1976), 501-20.

[3381]Wuerl, D. "Civil Rights in the United States and Abortion." *L'Osservatore Romano* (English), 146, (no. 2) (January 14, 1971), 9-10.

[3382]Wurm, R. S. "Abortion. Condescension or Prevention." *Medical Journal of Australia,* 1 (March 14, 1970), 557-62.

[3383]"Year's Experience." *Economist,* 231 (April 26, 1969), 22.

[3384]Yellen, Barnet. "Abortion,

the Family, and Systems Theory."
Paper presented to the National
Canadian Conference on Abortion,
Toronto, May, 1972.

[3385]Young, A. T., Berkman,
B., and Behr, H. "Women Who
Seek Abortions. A Study."
Social Work, 18(3) (1973), 60-
65.

[3386]Zachary, R. B. "Abortion: Yes or No?" *Manchester
Medical Gazette,* 50 (October,
1970), 4-5.

[3387]Zahn, G. "A Religious
Pacifist Looks at Abortion."
Commonweal, 94 (May 28, 1971),
279-82. [Gordon Zahn believes
that the concern of the pacifist for the victims of war
should be the same for the fetus. The value of human life
in the womb is affirmed. He
discusses the notion of a woman's body as her own property,
the rights of the fetus who is
human, and society's obligation
to the child, healthy or with
defects.]

[3388]Zahourek, R. "Therapeutic Abortion and Cultural Shock."
Nursing Forum, 10 (1971), 8-17.

[3389]Zahourek, R., *et al.*
"Therapeutic Abortion: The Psychiatric Nurse as Therapist,
Liaison, and Consultant." *Perspectives in Psychiatric Care,*
9 (1971), 64-71.

[3390]Zalba, M. "The Catholic
Church's Viewpoint on Abortion."
World Medical Journal, 13 (1966),
88.

[3391]Zarfas, D. C. "Psychiatric Indications for the
Termination of Pregnancy." *Canadian Medical Association
Journal,* 79 (August 15, 1958),
230.

[3392]Zelnik, M. and Kantner,
J. F. "Attitudes of American
Teenagers Toward Abortion."
Family Planning Perspectives,
7(2) (1975), 89-91.

[3393]Zelnik, M. and Kantner,
J. F. "The Resolution of Teenage First Pregnancies." *Family
Planning Perspectives,* 6(2)
(1974), 74-80.

[3394]Ziff, H. L. "Recent
Abortion Law Reforms (or Much
Ado About Nothing)." *Journal of
Criminal Law,* 60 (March, 1969), 3. 3385-
3397

[3395]Zimmerman, Anthony. "An
Abortion Explosion in Japan."
U.S. Catholic , 31 (May, 1965),
34-6.

[3396]Zimmerman, S. M. "Semantics of Abortion." *New England
Journal of Medicine,* 284 (April 1,
1971), 728.

[3397]Zimring, F. E. "Of Doctors,
Deterrence, and the Dark Figure of
Crime—A Note on Abortion in
Hawaii." *University of Chicago Law
Review,* 39 (Summer, 1972), 699.